STUDIES
IN BIOPOLITICS

Studies in Biopolitics
edited by Judit Sándor

© Judit Sándor and the authors

ISBN 978-963-88538-9-9

Copyediting: Miklós Vörös
Design and typesetting: Zsolt Sándor
Printed in Hungary by FOM kft.

Center for Ethics and Law in Biomedicine
Central European University
Budapest

STUDIES
IN BIOPOLITICS
edited by JUDIT SÁNDOR

Center for Ethics and Law in Biomedicine

CONTENTS

FOREWORD

This book is a collection of multidisciplinary case studies on biopolitical practices and discourses that have been contributed by political scientists and public policy experts, anthropologists and philosophers, biologists and bioethicists, legal scholars and human rights activists, as well as advanced graduate students at the Central European University (CEU). The majority of the authors have participated in graduate courses in political science, gender studies, and legal studies at CEU, focusing on the human rights aspects of biopolitics and the various forms of commercializing the human body. Some of the case studies have emerged from these courses and thus the chapters of this book are not only thematically interrelated but also share similar analytical perspectives. This is the result of long hours of discussion during the classes, following film screenings or emerging after public lectures on biopolitics organized by the Central for Ethics and Law in Biomedicine (CELAB).

The cultural diversity and the multilingual academic environment that characterize CEU have made it possible to develop a pool of unique cases on biopolitics from Armenia, Georgia, Germany, Egypt, Hungary, India, Israel, Poland, Romania, Russia, Serbia, Tunisia, and Turkey. For several contributors to this volume, this is their first publication: a first step in their academic carrier—while for others it is a new case explored within the multidisciplinary scholarly network developing around CELAB. We hope that this collection of essays will not only reflect the lively discussions we had during the CEU courses or CELAB events, but also provide interesting cases for further comparative studies on biopolitics.

The chapters in this book are therefore written by established scholars, young experts, and graduate students on biopolitical cases selected mostly from their own countries. Some of the essays focus on deeply ingrained cultural norms related to reproduction, others on the developing regulation of newly emerging technologies of assisted reproduction. There are chapters that discuss new, innovative forms of old population control policies, while others explore the consequences of emerging biotechnologies, including stem cell research. Some of the texts in this book analyze the biopolitical discourses of the state, while others seek to understand the 'biopractice' of traditional communities.

The book is intended to contribute to the already existing comparative studies in various fields of biopolitics and generate further research on the traditional norms, legal policies, and state practices related to biomedicine. Thus, the chapters discuss the regulation of assisted reproductive technologies in the Arab states (Orio Ikebe), Israel (April Hovav), Romania (Enikő Demény), and Serbia (Slavica Karajičić, *et al.*); the biopolitics of abortion in Poland (Joanna Różyńska and Weronika Chańska) and Hungary (Sára Vitrai); abortion used as a method of sex selection in Georgia (Mariam Gagoshashvili), Armenia and India (Shushan Harutyunyan), and sex selection used to avoid abortion in the Arab states (Ikebe) and in Germany (Anna Borbála Bodolai).

Other chapters explore local cases in a global biopolitical context: virginity tests conducted in order to humiliate women in Egypt, Tunisia, and Turkey (Anna Mondekova); transnational surrogacy commercializing the bodies of women in India (Attila Seprődy, Debjyoti Ghosh); stem cell research abused in the lack of regulation in Russia (Yuliya Pleshakova); and the representation of Roma as research subjects in human genetic research in Hungary (Barna Szamosi). Some of the essays discuss novel and unique reproductive policies, such as the pronatalist measures of a local municipality in Serbia (Ljiljana Pantović), or the utilization of pronatalist policies by originally not targeted groups, such as gay and lesbian couples in Israel (Hovav). There is also a set of case studies in the book that focus on reproductive tourism and procreative exile and analyze the practices of escaping the restrictive reproductive policies in one country and utilizing reproductive services in another (Ioana Petre, Różyńska and Chańska, Vitrai).

Acknowledgments:

I thank my colleagues and the graduate students at CEU for the long discussions and exciting presentations that we had on contemporary cases of biopolitics, either in the classroom, or at workshop meetings, or following public events of the Center for Ethics and Law in Biomedicine. Furthermore, I am grateful for the help offered by John Harbord and Eszter Timár to consult with the authors and for their contribution to the polishing of some of the chapters in this volume. And, as usual, I thank Miklós Vörös for his invaluable work of editing this book without which the publication of *Studies in Biopolitics* would not have been possible.

Judit Sándor
Director
Center for Ethics and Law in Biomedicine

INTRODUCTION: ENGENDERING BIOPOLITICS

Judit Sándor

Biopolitics, Population Control, and Reproduction

This book is an unusual collection of case studies on biopolitics that provides a wide range of geographically specific examples of policymaking in the fields of population management, human reproduction, and stem cell research. These policies, along with certain long-standing cultural traditions on which they are based, should be viewed critically as there is a widespread tendency in the world to regulate the most private sphere of our individual lives: reproduction. Thus, there are many states where population control is exercised through regulatory means—often diminishing the respect for bodily integrity, the intimacy of reproduction, and the confidential nature of personal genetic information. The concept of privacy does not simply refer to the right to be let alone but it also encompasses the individual's need to have an influence on what information is kept on his or her life, body, health, and thoughts.

Friendship and marriage, parent–child relationships, and even the experience of maternity carry certain elements of privacy that deserve protection. It is quite striking that even though the meaning of 'private sphere' has been expanded from the archaic concept of the inviolability of material things (such as private home and personal correspondence) to include the protection of personal decisions (such as those on reproduction), the law still prefers to cover the tangible aspects of privacy. This is why professional reputation, the secrecy of correspondence, or the sanctity of home enjoys well-established recognition, and data protection is (fortunately) flourishing—but much less legal respect is granted for privacy in the field of reproduction.

Still, human reproduction is perhaps the most intimate, most personal niche of the private sphere. Yet, we could quote a number of cases in the history of law in which emperors, kings, or states have attempted to bring this aspect of life under their own control. According to Michel Foucault, the French historian and social theorist who was the first to explain the institutional development of modernity in terms of the emergence of 'biopower', or the systematic control of the modern state over life, sexuality, and reproduction, "the ancient right to *take* life or *let* live was replaced by a power to *foster* life or *disallow* it to the point of death."[1] In other words, "the old power of death that symbolized sovereign power was now carefully supplanted by the administration of bodies and the calculated management of life."[2] This modern power over life emerged in two distinct, although strongly related forms. The first focused on the body as a machine and its integration into systems of efficient control: the aim was to create disciplined and docile bodies useful for expanding production. The second considered the body as an embodiment of biological processes and this perspective gave rise to the regulatory controls of births, sexuality, longevity, and mortality institutionalized in the disciplines of medicine, demography, and pedagogy.[3]

This book focuses mainly on the latter form of power over life: the biopolitics of population control targeting the 'Malthusian couple', as Foucault put it.[4] As discussed below, controlling the size and composition of the population by legal means is not only problematic due to the fact that since the 1960s there has been a general understanding that reproduction and birth control belong to the private sphere but also because there has never been a population control measure without discriminating certain groups to the advantage of others—and in most cases it is women who have been discriminated against. From this it follows that—even if we accept that there are cases in which it may be in the interest of society to increase or decrease the population—the tools available for the state are rather limited due to the general respect for privacy, and enforcement methods must pay very close attention to the issues of human dignity. As a result of the legal developments over the past 20–30 years in Europe, it is not only the respect for privacy but also the prohibition of discrimination that constitute legal obstacles to the state's desire for population control. Women and couples choose to have children for the sake of their individual happiness and do not consider the state's need to ensure the optimum number of subjects or citizens when producing or raising their children. All this is now evident, yet it seems that population control attempts somehow consider the individual's happiness, choice, and her or his own vision of human life as issues of secondary importance. The same is true for the principle of equal treatment and the hard-earned right of women to self-determination over their bodies, which seems to be forgotten whenever the state decides to deploy population control measures.

---

1   Michel Foucault, *The History of Sexuality, Volume I: An Introduction* (New York: Vintage Books, 1990), 138.
2   *Ibid.*, 139–140.
3   *Ibid.*, 139.
4   *Ibid.*, 104–105.

Pronatalist Reproduction Control

Population increase is, without doubt, the most popular form of population control. Policies to accelerate economic growth have, on a number of occasions, been supported by an appropriate legal framework to reverse unwelcome demographic trends. Applying measures to increase birth rates has been an equally favored method to intervene into the private sphere by both absolutist monarchies and totalitarian dictatorships. These measures, however, indirectly led to a high rate of maternal deaths due to frequent childbirths and banned abortion. The repressive form of this pronatalist politics carries a strict punishment for abortion, while the motivating version honors childbirth. The gentlest method is a welfare system of social benefits and allowances that may only be non-discriminative against women if the maternity allowances are coupled with labor protection and it is up to the individual to select the preferred path. This is the only way that women do not suffer from legal prejudice and are considered as valuable members of society even if they decide not to have any children or if they are infertile.

In addition to the contemporary examples of pronatalist policies, it is worth taking a look at a French royal decree from the 17th century, designed to motivate male reproduction. In the age of Louis XIV, le Roi-Soleil, it was generally accepted that the greatness of the king increased in direct proportion with the growing number of the population. The subjects of the French pronatalist reproduction control in 1666 were primarily men. If a man married before the age of 20, he received a tax discount up to the age of 25. Single males, however, had to pay a tax as soon as they turned 21. Those who fathered 10 legitimate children received a number of benefits including a special pension for the members of the nobility. The profession of the grown child also determined who was taken into account when deciding the father's eligibility for such benefits: soldier sons killed in action were eligible while those becoming priests were not.[5]

Since the second half of the 20th century, pronatalism has been often mixed with nationalism: after wars or in times of other crises (e.g. the Cold War), the state used both the 'carrot' and the 'stick' to encourage citizens to have more children. Ceaușescu's Romania emphasized its pronatalist policy by firmly prohibiting abortion and implementing a strict system of physical examinations for women of reproducing age.[6] During the Stalinist period of state-socialism in Hungary the so-called Ratkó era (between 1953 and 1956, named after the minister of health of that time) introduced anti-abortion policies, only to be followed by a sharp decline in birth rates due to the increase of abortions beginning in the late 1950s—so much so that researchers talked about a virtual "abortion

---

5   Leslie Tuttle, *Conceiving the Old Regime, Pronatalism and the Politics of Reproduction in Early Modern France* (Oxford: Oxford University Press, 2010), 8.
6   For a detailed discussion of the Romanian state policy on reproduction, see Gail Kligman, *The Politics of Duplicity: Controlling Reproduction in Ceausescu's Romania* (Berkeley: University of California Press, 1998).

epidemic" in the late 1960s and early 1970s.[7] The price was paid by women in the case of both the anti-abortion policies and the one-child family model of the Kádár era (regardless of the resulting slightly increasing living standards): women's reproductive and mental health deteriorated in both periods. Whether we consider illegal abortion or the series of abortions used as a means of conscious family planning, women were left alone in coping with the consequences.

Nowadays, pronatalist politics often involves funding for artificial reproduction procedures. A good example is Israel where childbirth is supported by social benefits and a multitude of laws.[8] Apparently, the desire to make up for the heavy losses of the Holocaust also plays a significant role, in addition to religious and nationalist arguments. Israel is a unique mix of traditionalism and the acceptance of and funding for the latest reproductive technologies.[9] The most well-known example of pronatalist discourse in Israel is the case of *Nahmani v. Nahmani and others*[10], in which the court authorized the implantation of embryos even after the couple had separated, because the mother was determined to raise the children and thereby increase the population. In this particular case, pronatalism is expressed by allowing the implantation of the embryo in the surrogate mother. In similar European or US legal cases the court did not authorize such continuation of the reproduction process, even at the cost of destroying the embryo. In the European case of *Evans vs. the United Kingdom*[11], for instance, 'the genetic mother' asked in vain for being allowed to have her embryos carried to term, because the 'genetic father', even though initially in support of the mutual reproduction process, later changed his mind. The court decided to rather favor the father's rights to privacy, and thereby approved the destruction of the embryos due to the parents' lack of agreement.

Anti-Natalist Biopolitics and Birth Restriction

State measures designed to limit population increase intervene in couples' lives even more drastically and may severely affect the intimacy and even the health and integrity of the female body when the woman is obliged to

---

7   In 1970 the number of abortions performed reached 192,000 compared to half of that figure in 1956. See Tiborné Pongrácz and Edit S. Molnár, Terhességmegszakítások a statisztikai adatok és a közvélemény tükrében [Abortions as Reflected by Statistical Data and in Public Opinion], in Andorka Rudolf, Kolosi Tamás, and Vukovich György (eds.), *Társadalmi riport 1992* [Social Report 1992] (Budapest: TÁRKI, 1992), 289–317.

8   This topic has an extensive literature; see, for instance, Nitza Berkovitch, Motherhood as a National Mission: the Construction of Womanhood in the Legal Discourse in Israel, *Womens' Studies International Forum*, September–December 1997, 20(5–6): 605–619; and Jacqueline Portuguese, *Fertility Policy in Israel: The Politics of Religion, Gender, and Nation* (Westport, CT and London: Praeger, 1998).

9   Daphna Birenbaum-Carmeli, Contested Surrogacy and the Gender Order in Israel, Daphna Birenbaum-Carmeli and Marcia C. Inhorn (eds.) *Assisting Reproduction, Testing Genes: Global Encounters with New Biotechnologies* (New York: Berghahn, 2009), 201.

10 *Ruth Nahmani v. Daniel Nahmani and Others*; F. H. c 2401/95, Civil Appeal 5587/93.

11 *Evans v. the United Kingdom*; ECtHR, application no. 6339/05, judgment of March 7, 2006.

use abortion or contraception, despite her will, not to mention the even more drastic and inhumane measure of forced sterilization.

Perhaps the most well-known example for state intervention designed to limit childbirth is found in China. The need for birth control first emerged in China in the 1950s to slow down the population influx to the cities from the starving countryside. This anti-natalist policy reached its peak during the rule of Deng Xiaoping.[12] The official campaign slogan was "later, farther and fewer" and, if the authorities saw it fit, it was enforced fully. Only few exceptions from the one-child family model were granted — for example, to peasant families living in the countryside. Moreover, since Chinese society did not consider girls equal to boys in value, the measures led to selective abortions and, in extreme cases, even to the murder or neglect of the female child.

As a result of this birth control policy, the number of induced abortion cases in the 1980s was four times higher than 10 years before, and in 1983 reached as high as 14 million.[13] The number of female infants killed especially increased during the aggressive population policy campaigns from the early 1980s to the early 1990s. Girls constituted the overwhelming majority of abandoned children. Millions of women were sterilized between 1970 and 2001.[14] All this upset the sex ratio in China, and the disparity continued to grow up to the point that for each 100 girls under the age of four there were 128 boys in Guangdong in 1999.[15] This policy, together with the culturally ingrained prejudice against women, resulted in a significant gender disproportion in China with lots of women missing from society.

In addition to abortion, several new technological solutions may be at the service of sex selection today, such as ultrasound examinations, prenatal and even pre-implantational genetic tests. Although the Chinese sex selection is the most well-known example because the one child policy made it more visible, there is a strong preference for baby boys in many other regions of the world, including South Caucasia, as the contributions to this volume show.

Biopolitics and Eugenic Birth Control

In addition to the general practice of increasing or decreasing birth rates, a number of countries have attempted to limit or encourage the reproduction of specific social groups. These regulatory efforts are primarily eugenic, often complemented by other cases of discrimination, such as racial and gender discrimination. Under the veil of science, the eugenic approach was

---

12 Susan Greenhalgh and Edwin A. Winckler, *Governing China's Population* (Stanford, Stanford University Press, 2005).
13 *Ibid.*, 260.
14 See the 1971–1983, 1982–1998, 1999–2001 editions of *China Health Yearbook* (Beijing: People's Health Press House, Ministry of Health).
15 Greenhalgh and Winckler, *op. cit.*, 266.

widely accepted and, contrary to common belief, was not limited to Nazi Germany. The earliest known American legal case was *Buck v. Bell*[16] in 1927, which authorized forced sterilization of a young woman declared mentally handicapped. As Judge Oliver Wendell Holmes phrased it notoriously, "three generations of imbeciles are enough." According to the prevalent eugenic approach of the time, the *right to life* must be distinguished from the *right to reproduction*, which may be limited even to the extent that forced sterilization is ordered if it does not cause any health damage to the individual. The court actually used the term 'sexual sterilization', implying that the intervention had sexual-moral content. Amidst the increasing spread of eugenic thinking, certain concrete cases of degeneration played a decisive role. What constituted 'degeneration' at the time was affected not only by mental disability and assumed or actual genetic traits but, for instance, also by gender-related social norms: thus, the 'liberal sexual behavior' of a woman or an extramarital child could easily be taken as such a characteristic.[17] In other words, eugenic categories were based not only on science but, either explicitly or implicitly, on moral content.

With regards to disabilities, the forms of reproduction regulation changed after World War II, and the decision of the expectant mothers was increasingly more recognized, without discounting the influence of society and the family. Mandatory diagnostic tests of the fetus, the genetic and medical control over maternity and, in certain cases, mandatory pre-marital genetic counseling still can be quoted as a mild form of eugenic type regulations. As a result of the mandatory testing, significant drop in β-thalassemia cases in Cyprus can be documented.[18]

Biopolitics and the Medicalization of Childbirth

Prior to World War II, very few infants were born in hospitals, and the majority of childbirths were not conducted by medical doctors but by midwives. Later, hospital childbirths were not only encouraged by the improving conditions and technologies of the medical profession but also promoted by health insurance. The primary appeal for women in delivering their children in hospitals was safety, as well as the availability of analgesic. But this led to the medicalization of childbirth, so much so that in Hungary, for instance, those still preferring home birth have had to start a nationwide movement to secure legal protec-

---

16 *Buck v. Bell*, 274 U. S. 200 (1927).
17 Alexandra Minna Stern, *Eugenic Nation: Faults and Frontiers of Better Breeding in Modern America* (Berkeley: University of California Press, 2005), 13.
18 Cyprus: How One Nation's Culture Influences Its Genes, *Gene Letter*, January 26, 2010; available at www.geneletter.com/cyprus-how-one-nations-culture-influences-its-genes-16/, last accessed on June 10, 2013.

tion for their decision. Medicalization[19] of childbirth, however, has become an unparalleled success story not only in Hungary but also in the majority of European countries. In Germany, for example, half of the children were born at home in 1954, whereas in 1970, 99 percent of all women delivered their children in hospitals. Up until the 1960s, midwives in Germany worked as independent freelancers with a special relationship to the women in childbirth as friends, fellow women or attendants at birth.[20] As the use of analgesic was the physicians' monopoly, midwives tried to ease the pain of labor with massage, bottles of hot water, joint housework projects, knitting or even playing cards. Grantly Dick-Read's book on natural birth was very popular among women in England as well as in Germany.[21]

The rules for the medical procedures of childbirth have by now become so prevalent that powerful civic movements have been started to fight for women's rights to home birth. This conflict has become especially sharp in Hungary, most probably because of the conditions of the patriarchal health sector and the almost exclusive male dominance in the obstetrician profession. A number of court cases were heard in Hungary in the course of the fight for home birth. In *Ternovszky v. Hungary*, for instance, the Strasbourg Court ruled that privacy rights had been violated in Hungary because there were no laws ensuring the right to home birth.[22]

Even though there is still a hot debate on this issue, there may be many reasons why someone would intentionally opt for home birth or unintentionally deliver the baby outside hospital premises. Women sometimes oppose medicalized childbirth exactly because of their previous bad experience with the health care system. In addition to the special nature of medical training, the dominance of male doctors in the obstetrician–gynecologist profession may significantly influence or even amplify the possible conflicts during childbirth. In many countries, while midwives and pediatricians are mainly female, the overwhelming majority of obstetricians and gynecologists are male doctors. Obstetricians are primarily surgeons and are not trained to monitor natural childbirth closely. As a result, gender based power inequalities are expressed in the relationship between the obstetrician and the patient. The reproductive power of women is unquestionably huge, and the only 'antidote' is regulated childbirth assisted by male doctors using surgical methods or even artificial removal of the fetus.

---

19 Emily Martin, *The Woman in the Body A Cultural Analysis of Reproduction* (Boston: Beacon Press, 1987), 156–165.
20 Marion Schumann, From Social Care to Planning Childbirth, in Kathrin Braun (ed.), *Between Self-Determination and Social Technology* (Bielefeld: Transcript Verlag, 2011), 31.
21 Grantly Dick-Read, *Revelation of Childbirth: The Principles and Practice of Natural Childbirth* (London: Heinemann, 1942).
22 *Ternovszky v. Hungary*; ECtHR, application no. 67545/09, judgment of December 14, 2010.

Delay or Restriction of Medical Services as a Means of Regulation

In addition to legal restrictions, delaying or preventing the use of medical service may also act as means of reproduction control.

In 2011 in the case of *R.R. v. Poland*, the European Court of Human Rights (ECtHR) dealt with the complaint of a young Polish mother of several children[23] who, for a month, had to travel from one medical institution to the next between Łódź and Kraków to confirm or dismiss the possibility of a severe fetal disorder, suspected at a previous ultrasound exam, and consequently allow her to request an abortion. In a number of cases her request was denied because genetic exams required a special doctor's referral. After long delays, the genetic test that finally took place in April 2002 confirmed that the fetus did in fact suffer from Turner syndrome and, in accordance with a 1993 Polish law, the request for abortion could be granted. But then fulfillment of her request was denied on the grounds that her pregnancy was way too far ahead. Thus, on July 11, 2002, the plaintiff gave birth to a girl diagnosed with Turner syndrome. The young woman went to several Polish courts and in her claim she wanted recognition that her doctors prevented her from the timely completion of the genetic test and an application for abortion based on Polish laws. The peculiarity of the case is that the Strasbourg Court not only found the violation of privacy rights based on information restraint, involuntary pregnancy, and living in fear but also ruled that the inhuman and degrading treatment shown towards the complainant violated Article 3 of the European Convention on Human Rights (ECHR).[24]

With regards to the specific case, as the Court has pointed out, it is irrelevant how certain the doctors were in their diagnosis based on the ultrasound test. As already stressed in the case of *Glass v. United Kingdom*,[25] the Court was not to review the doctors' decision. However, it was also stated that abortion is a decision where time is a key factor. Therefore, the medical doctor or a family protection agency, granted with the power to provide medical opinion, is capable of obstructing a right by a simple delay if they do not want to respect a right (of privacy or dignity) granted by law. Even if the doctor or the agency is unwilling to openly oppose the law, their omission or slow response may still infringe women's rights. Freedom of conscience could be used as grounds for refusal only in the case of performing an abortion. However, the refusal to perform a prenatal examination based on the request by another doctor and the patient cannot be judged by the same standard as abortion.

---

23 *R.R. v. Poland*; ECtHR, application no. 27617/04, judgment of May 26, 2011.

24 "No one shall be subjected to torture or to inhuman or degrading treatment or punishment." Official English title of the Convention: *European Convention of Human Rights*; full text available at www.echr.coe.int/NR/rdonlyres/D5CC24A7-DC13-4318-B457-5C9014916D7A/0/Convention_ENG.pdf, last accessed on June 10, 2013.

25 *Glass v. United Kingdom*; ECtHR, application no. 61827/00, judgment of March 9, 2004.

A similar Polish case was *Tysiąc v. Poland*[26], in which the applicant claimed of not having received a supporting medical opinion on the likelihood of deterioration of her eyesight, if she continues her pregnancy. The medical opinion is a requirement under Polish law to initiate the abortion procedure. The Court held that it was a violation of privacy rights. The applicant's repeated requests for medical certificate were denied and thus the abortion was not authorized, and the mother suffered permanent and severe deterioration of her sight after childbirth. In the other Polish case[27] mentioned above the applicant did not get access to the necessary genetic tests and she gave birth to a baby with Turner syndrome. A special aspect of the *R.R v. Poland* case is that while ultrasound was available, the latest technology (genetic testing) that could have confirmed the suspect raised by the ultrasounds was not available, only when it was too late to request for abortion.

Regulations on Infertility Treatment and on the Selection of the Embryo

Although reproduction should belong to the individual's most private and intimate sphere that cannot and should not regulated in details, the legislator seems to be overcome sometimes by some missionary zeal when approaching this issue and tries to solve many social, demographic, and other problems all at once. A number of ethical and legal questions of the new procedures, commonly referred to only as the "test tube baby" technology, have drawn into the realm of regulation such essential elements of private life, like issues of fatherhood and motherhood, human relationships and ancestry. Legislators finding themselves in this field have only a few months to find somewhat acceptable solutions to debates dating back thousands of years and probing basic moral, ethical and philosophical issues. What, for instance, should enjoy more legal recognition: inherited or learnt characteristics? What is to be considered a family? Where is exactly the borderline between medical therapy and eugenic enhancement?[28]

Contrary to the often voiced opinion that law always lags behind science and scientific advances, in certain cases law has actually started to regulate new reproductive technologies *before* those are subjected to public debate. Even though the options offered by liberal eugenics—for example, improving the child's characteristics prior to birth or even before the embryo is implanted— are utilized by future parents not under pressure from the state, the decision to chose them may be influenced by social expectations. From the perspective of bodily integrity and health these methods cannot be considered neutral as they subject the female body to intense medicalization and a long series of medi-

---

26 *Tysiąc v. Poland*; ECtHR, application no. 5410/03, judgment of March 21, 2007.
27 *R.R. v. Poland, op. cit.*
28 Jürgen Habermas, *The Future of Human Nature* (Cambridge: Polity Press, 2003).

cal, genetic, and infertility treatments. There are, of course, cases when these procedures save the woman from a lot of suffering by finding the genetic reasons for years of unsuccessful pregnancies and ultimately selecting the healthy embryo.[29]

Among the European countries, a number of completely different and mutually inconsistent rules have reacted to the available artificial reproduction procedures. In some countries egg donation is forbidden; in some others the ban applies only to embryo donation. National laws also differ as to whether such procedures are open only to infertile couples—or also to others, even single individuals. There is a lot of inconsistency in the legislation procedures even within specific countries; some of these have also been addressed by the European Court of Human Rights. In the case *S.H. and Others v. Austria*[30], for instance, the Court highlighted the contradictions in the laws of Austria regulating reproduction.[31] In line with the traditionalist approach, Austrian law distinguishes between egg and sperm donation, confirming the Roman law principle: *mater semper certa est, pater est, quem nuptiae demonstrant* ("the mother is always certain, while the father is to whom marriage points"). The rules require that the donor and the surrogate mother are the same person. However, the biological origin of fatherhood was considered less important. Austrian law also restricted infertility treatment for married couples if a third-party sperm donor was needed, even though this rule meant the violation of privacy and the prohibition of discrimination.

Population increase and birth control in one part of the world and fight against infertility on the other not only authorized new medical treatments and implanted them in the public mind but also introduced new methods for influencing birth control. Since Aldous Huxley, literary representations contribute to the strengthening of the belief that intervention in human reproduction may result in different types of social control ranging from determining the quality of embryos, through the selection of parents, to the creation of human copies or clones, and to the enhancement of human capacities. In reality, of course, there is a sharp difference between these apocalyptic visions and the everyday struggles of infertile couples. These men and women simply want healthy children and consider the series of procedures as a medical treatment rather than evil experiments in Frankenstein's style.

Assisted reproduction technologies (ARTs) are seen today not simply as technical solutions for infertility problems. ARTs give control to people over

---

29 Ruth Schwarz Cowan, *Heredity and Hope: The Case for Genetic Screening* (Cambridge, MA: Harvard University Press, 2008).

30 *S.H. and Others v. Austria*; ECHtR, application no. 57813/00, judgment of November 3, 2011.

31 Fortpflanzungsmedizingesetz (FMedG) [Act of June 4, 1992 on Reproductive Medicine]; available at www.ris.bka.gv.at/Dokumente/BgblPdf/1992_275_0/1992_275_0.pdf; amended by Fortpflanzungsmedizingesetz-Novelle (FMedGNov) on December 30, 2004, available at www.ris.bka.gv.at/Dokumente/BgblAuth/BGBLA_2004_I_163/BGBLA_2004_I_163.pdf, last accessed on June 10, 2013.

their reproductive choices and allows for enhancing the health of the offspring: it is a means for those who want to postpone childbirth, it creates new bonds that was not possible before the emergence of *in vitro* fertilization techniques, and it can be used even to cure sick children within the family. With each case of extending the use of technology it has become possible to conceive an even wider scope of applying assisted reproductive technologies.

As Lemke stated in his work on biopolitics, "The growing significance of genetic and reproductive technologies raised concerns about the regulation and control of scientific progress. If the results of biological and medical research and its practical applications demonstrated how contingent and fragile the boundary between nature and culture is, then this intensified political and legal efforts to reestablish that boundary. It was deemed necessary to regulate which processes and procedures were acceptable and under what conditions. There was also a need to clarify what kind of research would be supported with public fund and what would be prohibited."[32]

From the birth of the first test-tube baby in 1978, the technologies of assisted reproduction have been repeatedly transformed in significant ways and now serve many other purposes besides helping the infertile. Today, pre-implantational genetic testing and genetic diagnosis are often requested in conjunction with many reproductive procedures, making it possible to assess the well-being of future offspring by a variety of different and controversial criteria. Should he or she be physically healthy, as similar as possible to the parents, or endowed with the best possible genetic make-up? These conflicting yardsticks have provoked public debates and have already resulted in legal cases where embryo selection and genetic testing were rejected on basis of concerns for the protection of unborn life even while granting abortion subsequent to prenatal diagnosis at a later stage of pregnancy.

The need for pre-implantation genetic tests originates from the desire to avoid abortion following the unwanted results of prenatal genetic examinations and the physical suffering and emotional distress that comes with abortion. It provides help primarily to families where hereditary diseases may be screened before the embryo is implanted in the uterus. The technology of pre-implantation genetic tests has undergone numerous changes since 1989 when Alan Handyside and his team successfully screened for a birth defect related to the X chromosome on embryos and this could result in the birth of a healthy child in England. As far as the regulatory environment is concerned, very little consensus exists on this field. Two of the articles of the 1997 Oviedo Convention contain some reference to the topic: Article 14 prohibits the selection of sex and says "the use of techniques of medically assisted procreation shall not be allowed for the purpose of choosing a future child's sex, except where serious hereditary sex-linked disease is to be avoided." In other words, selection of the sex is permitted to screen for serious,

---

32 Thomas Lemke, *Biopolitics: An Advanced Introduction* (New York: New York University Press, 2011), 26.

sex-linked disorders, but this applies only to some of the pre-implantation genetic tests. Article 18 of the Convention, on the other hand, specifies that "where the law allows research on embryos in vitro, it shall ensure adequate protection of the embryo. The creation of human embryos for research purposes is prohibited." It was in 2012 when the human rights aspects of pre-implantation genetic tests were brought before the European Court of Human Rights in a petition submitted against Italy[33] by parents who wanted to avoid the birth for another child with disability and wanted pre-implantational embryo selection instead of a later stage abortion. As the technology develops, it can be envisaged that more and more cases will reach the courts and with more and more complex choices.

In reflecting on and regulating these developments, law has proven to be a double edge sword: on one hand, it has repeatedly made attempts to restrict the application of certain contested techniques and, on the other hand, it has provided a tool to remove existing obstacles to a wider ranging use of other technologies that had been available to a select few and thus involved some form of discrimination. As a result, new groups of individuals can claim access to assisted reproduction and to the use of pre-implantation diagnostics. So the question emerges: can the law still shape the contours of legitimate uses of these technologies? What kind of ethical principles can guide lawmakers and judges to develop grounded responses to the new demands for technology?

Biopolitics of the Cell

Biopolitics in the 21st century does not exert power only on the human body, on sexuality and human reproduction; 'biopower' has now started to influence the molecular level. Thus, human gametes, DNA cells, or stem cell lines of human origin have become subjects of various legislative policies. In *Politics of Life Itself*[34] Nikolas Rose identifies the main elements of the twenty-first century biopolitics: the shift from molar to molecular biopolitics; the development of technologies of optimization (especially because the term 'healthy' is now rather hard to define in the new age of technosciences); the emergence of new subjects (such as DNA groups) and new citizenship projects; the appearance of new expertise on life and new professions (such as those working in the fields of reprogenetics, neuroscience, molecular gerontology, or bio-informatics); and the spread of bioeconomics. Consequently, not only patients but people with certain genetic characteristics or presymptomatic diagnosis may form new social groups, and define themselves as health care consumers. The new, but already widely used notions of biovalue[35] and biocapital delimit the contours of a new field in which

---

33 *Costa and Pavan v. Italy*; ECtHR, application no. 54270/10, judgment of August 28, 2012.
34 Nikolas Rose, *The Politics of Life Itself* (Princeton: Princeton University Press, 2007).
35 Catherine Waldby, Stem Cells, Tissue Cultures, and the Production of Biovalue, July 2002, *Health*, 6(3): 305–323.

certain elements and vital properties of the human body, such as human cells and tissues, can be transformed into commodities.

One of the new promising fields of capitalizing on vitality is stem cell procurement and stem cell research. But even during the relatively short history of stem cell research the race between scientists has led to several legal disputes, and cases of fraud, such as the scandal of a prominent Korean researcher, Woo-Suk Hwang.[36] In 2006 Hwang was condemned as it became proven that in 2004 and 2005 he had fabricated the data on his alleged success on creating human embryonic stem cells. Nevertheless, in a purely scientific light, embryonic stem cell research provides hopes for various kinds of new diagnostic models and therapies for the future.

Stem cell research is now a part of a new medical paradigm called *regenerative medicine*. In the legal, ethical and political field much debate has been given to the issue of embryonic stem cell research and whether scientists should be allowed to conduct research using these specialized cells that are harvested from embryos. Current legal models differentiate between harvesting embryonic cells, producing embryonic stem cell lines, or simply using or importing already existing stem cell lines.

Ethical and legal questions are multi-layered: Where do the embryos come from? What is the legal status of the *in vitro* embryo? What are the guarantees of avoiding exploitation of women in the use of human eggs? Can embryos be 'created' for research purposes? Can hybrids be considered as alternatives? There are still many unanswered questions with regard the use of stem cells and stem cell lines: since the *Brüstle case*[37], for example, even the patentability of embryonic stem cell lines has been challenged.[38]

Closing Remarks

As seen above, the legislative drive has not slowed down in the case of regulating traditional forms of reproduction nor in relation to artificial methods of reproduction and the connected genetic tests. This regulatory reaction is not trivial if you look at the issues related to the development of biotechnology. Namely, there is a false assumption that any time a new scientific discovery is made or new technical opportunities are found, the law has to react to those with new regulations. Actually, law should not regulate science *per se* but, instead, the areas where scientific paradigms, methods, and techniques are applied and where they have controversial influences on human relationships.

---

36 Péter Kakuk, Cloning and Research Misconduct: The Woo-Suk Hwang Case, in Judit Sándor (ed.) *Perfect Copy? Law and Ethics of Reproductive Medicine* (Budapest: CELAB, 2009), 35–52.
37 *Oliver Brüstle v. Greenpeace e.V.*; ECJ, Case C-34/10, judgment of October 18, 2011.
38 Judit Sándor and Márton Varju, The Multiplicity of Norms: The Bioethics and Law of Stem Cell Patents, in Andrew Webster (ed.), *The Global Dynamics of Regenerative Medicine: A Social Science Critique* (New York: Palgrave Macmillan, 2013), 169–194.

If you take a look at the early examples of reproduction and birth control, you can see that regulation created the opportunity to knowingly interfere with the private sphere by offering advantages to certain groups of people while threatening other social groups with sanctions. In the second half of the 20th century this trend turned around and right to privacy and individual human rights have been strengthened against the instruments of population control. However, in each case when a new technology appeared in the fields of reproduction and biomedicine, it required the reinterpretation so that right to privacy, bodily integrity, and information can be reinforced. Even though these rights have gained clearer meanings through the interpretation of successive court cases, due to the increasing medicalization of many spheres of life, they still need to be constantly reexamined as new regulations are negotiated between the stakeholders. And even though the means of influencing social relations have become more refined, reproduction and population control continue to be favored subjects of regulation. If we compare them to contemporary legal principles, especially those related to equal treatment and the prohibition of discrimination, these are the last standing fortresses of the patriarchal regulatory tradition that still appear to be impossible to overcome.

DISCRIMINATORY EFFECTS OF LEGAL PROHIBITIONS IN THE FIELD OF REPRODUCTION

Ioana Petre

Introduction

Reproductive freedom is not an absolute liberty, but is rather limited by various considerations. The interests of the spouse or partner, the welfare of the child to be and the prevailing moral sentiments of the majority of the society act as constraints on individuals' procreative choices. As such, one person's conception of the good life, her autonomy and the respect that is owed to her privacy need to be weighed against the competing social and individual interests that are at stake in the field of reproduction.

Through legislation, states aim at striking the right balance between the different claims that are formulated in response to the act of conception. There is a big variation both at the global, as well as at the regional level with respect to the boundaries of procreative freedom. In this sense, while some states adopt a more permissive approach towards reproductive techniques, others are more restrictive and conservative. Even within the European Union, which is a regional construction that aims towards a harmonized legislation, there are considerable differences between its member states in terms of the freedom to access and use of procedures and technologies related to natural or artificial conception.

Prohibition in one country and liberalization in another mean that legal provisions can be circumvented by seeking medical treatment in a jurisdiction that allows it. However, crossing the border in order to receive this treatment may not be an option for certain categories of people, such as those that cannot travel due to health conditions or financial constraints. Financial problems also represent a challenge for those who might find a loophole in the legal system that does not involve traveling, but, because of a lack of resources, cannot act on it. Given all this, I argue that legal prohibitions in the field of reproduction have a discriminatory dimension, as they allow only some individuals to escape them, while others cannot.

In order to defend this argument, I will first look into the reasons for which some countries choose to heavily regulate the sphere of birth and procreation. The next section will be dedicated to an overview of the motives that might drive people towards eluding their state's reproductive policy and the manner in which they actually succeed in doing so. Finally, I will analyze the element of discrimination embedded in these legal prohibitions and conclude with a possible solution to overcome it.

Reasons for Restricting Reproductive Freedom

In the fall of 2012, Savita Halappanavar died of a blood infection after having a miscarriage at the University Hospital Galway in Ireland. This unfortunate event did not come as a surprise. Savita had been suffering from extreme back pain and, after seeing a medical specialist, had been informed about the possibility of her fetus dying in the womb. Under these circumstances, she requested to undergo an abortion, but was refused on the ground that abortion was illegal according to the Irish law.[1] Savita's death occurred against a legal background that has been previously challenged, both within and outside of the borders of Ireland. One of the most famous cases dealing with the restricted access to abortion in Ireland was brought in front of the European Court of Human Rights in 2005. The case of *A, B and C v. Ireland* was filed by three women who were denied abortion in Ireland, but traveled to the UK for that purpose. Once back in their residing country after having aborted across the border, the applicants suffered from profound and prolonged bleeding, passing of blood clots and infection, but were hesitant to seek medical advice due to the fear of legal prosecution.[2]

Restriction of abortion is one of the oldest debates that arose in relation to birth and contraception. The trend has been in recent years to depart from a state that can control this important aspect of individuals' privacy to a more liberal society whose members can freely plan the creation and enlargement of their families. However, there are still countries nowadays where discussions revolving around abortion are more relevant than ever. Ireland is one such example. The rationale behind Ireland's abortion policy resides in the country's prevailing moral attitudes that stem from a deeply embedded Catholic culture.

---

1   Laura Smith-Spark and Peter Taggart, Husband Testifies His Wife Died after Abortion Was Denied in Ireland, *CNN*, April 8, 2013; available at edition.cnn.com/2013/04/08/world/europe/ireland-abortion-controversy, last accessed on June 1, 2013.
2   See *A, B and C v. Ireland*; ECtHR, application no. 25579/05, judgment of December 16, 2010.

Ireland, however, is not the only country where culture, including the dominant morality manifested at the social level, shapes reproductive policies. There are numerous other cases. France and Italy, for instance, do not allow single women and lesbian couples to use *in vitro* fertilization (IVF) and artificial insemination techniques. Austria and Italy ban egg and sperm donation needed for IVF. In *S.H. and Others v. Austria,* which challenged Austria's Artificial Procreation Act, ova donation was perceived by the Austrian state to result in the exploitation of women, especially the economically disadvantaged ones, and in the commercialization of their bodies. *In vitro* fertilization, on the other hand, was regarded as a technique that potentially engenders unusual relationships, such as that of the division in motherhood (separating the genetic and biological mother), which would shake one of the most solid foundations on which social relations are built in the Western world.[3] Children's identity would also be at stake, as the split in motherhood would make it difficult for them to be informed about their actual genetic descent. Lastly, the Austrian government added that IVF would lead to selective reproduction, which would touch upon the well-being of children.[4] As it can be easily noticed, Austria's prohibitions related to assisted reproduction are based on several interrelated arguments: social morality, the interests of the children that would be born through these techniques, the interests of the economically disadvantaged sectors of the society. Other countries that ban the donation of eggs are Germany and Norway. Their discourse regarding birth policies is similar to a large extent to that constructed by Austria. However, the case of Germany brings even more social input with respect to its policy making, given its historical past, relation to eugenics and the mark that they have left on the German society.

The interests of the poor and the avoidance of the commercialization of their bodies is one of the strongest reasons for which surrogacy is prohibited in most European countries. However, states such as Ukraine or India do not only allow it, but have actually transformed it into a quite profitable business. Lastly, public policy considerations that target the collective wellbeing of a state's citizenry may result in diminished procreative liberty as well. China, for instance, and its one-child policy can very well illustrate this situation.

The examples that I have gathered in this section show that there is a vast array of reasons and justificatory arguments that can support a state's prohibition of a certain reproductive technique or procedure. However, although public morality or the interests of various social sectors have an important say in procreative policies, one should not disregard their impact on individual life, privacy, and autonomy.

---

3 *Mater semper certa est, pater est quem nuptiae demonstrant* [The mother is always certain, while the father is to whom marriage points], a well-known principle of Roman law.
4 See *S.H. and Others v. Austria*; ECtHR, application no. 57813/00, judgment of November 3, 2011.

Escaping Legal Prohibitions in the Field of Reproduction: Why And How?

As states have several reasons for banning some procreative techniques, individuals, at their turn, have their own motives for wanting to avoid the bans. Usually, the segment of the society that would try to find a possibility to elude restrictive legislation is part of the political and social minority, rather than of the majority. The relation between the majority and the minority/minorities, on the one hand, and legislation, on the other, can be perceived from two different angles. According to Bayertz, democracy is founded on majority rule, and not on the principle of consensus.[5] As such, the majority is justified in imposing its conception of the good life upon the minority. However, there are other scholars that argue in favor of moral pluralism, perceiving legal prohibitions that are not founded on a common basis as discriminatory against the minority or minorities.[6] Wellman, for instance, is of the opinion that:

> Legislation, at least in a democratic society, reflects, and is supposed to reflect, a compromise between the diverse preferences and interests of the members of that society . . . Hence, a legislative acceptable compromise can be attained only if some considerable degree of moral agreement can be achieved during the course of the political debate.[7]

The second position can better accommodate the structure of current political communities, characterized by multiculturalism, moral pluralism, lack of consensus, and increasing concern for individual and group rights. The first position, although based on the democratic principle of majority rule, violates other democratic values, such as minority protection or the safeguard of individual autonomy and liberty. It can be reasonably argued that those individuals that do not agree with the majoritarian moral path have the moral right to conscientiously object against legal coercion that threatens to undermine their own ethical views and conception of the good life.[8]

Legislation in the field of reproduction contains important loopholes that can be exploited by those who wish to avoid certain legal sanctions. Traveling across the border to seek medical service in a country that resonates with one's own ethical dispositions is the most frequently employed tool. In this sense,

---

5   Kurt Bayertz, The Concept of Moral Consensus: Philosophical Reflections, in Kurt Bayertz (ed.), *The Concept of Moral Consensus: The Case of Technological Interventions in Human Reproduction* (Dordrecht: Kluwer Academic Publishers, 1994), 41–58.

6   Hugo Tristam Engelhardt, *Bioethics and Secular Humanism: The Search for a Common Morality* (Philadelphia: Trinity Publisher International, 1991).

7   Carl Wellman, Moral Consenses and the Law, in Kurt Bayertz (ed.), *The Concept of Moral Consensus: The Case of Technological Interventions in Human Reproduction* (Dordrecht: Kluwer Academic Publishers, 1994), 109–122.

8   I am not making a case in favor of the conscientious objection *per se*, applied without any restriction, but rather focus exclusively on the value of the conscientious objection in the field of reproduction.

Irish women that want to perform an abortion can travel to the UK and resort to their medical services. French and Italian lesbian couples might go to Belgium for IVF treatments. Germans and Austrians may easily buy eggs from Romania. Hungarian, Serbian or English couples, whose countries do not allow surrogacy, might travel to Ukraine or India to contract a surrogate mother for their yet unborn child.[9, 10] Mainland Chinese women who wish to give birth to more than one child can go to Hong Kong, among other destinations, and deliver their second or third baby there.[11]

In 1991, Knoppers and Lebris[12] used the notion of "procreative tourism," later on transformed into "reproductive tourism," in order to describe the practice of traveling to another region for medical care related to birth and conception. However, for the scope of the present inquiry, the term of reproductive tourism is too broad for the universe of cases to which this paper refers. Reproductive tourism does not solely signify cross-border care which is forbidden by law, but also cross-border treatment that is unavailable in the residing country due to: (i) lack of expertise or equipment; (ii) lengthy waiting lists; (iii) higher costs, as compared to other regions.[13] Thus, a concept that can better accommodate the transnational search for procreative care caused by restrictive domestic legislation is that of "reproductive exile." As Matorras correctly points out, tourism is usually associated with leisure and vacation. However, those individuals that seek medical treatment that they cannot legally receive in their home country cannot justly be compared to tourists, but rather with exiles.[14]

Procreative exile is not the only means that can allow individuals to elude prohibitive pieces of legislation. There are situations—albeit rare—when a legal loophole can be identified and exploited without having to leave one's residing country. One such example can be found in China. The one-child policy imposed by the Chinese government does not allow women to have more than one child through multiple births, but it remains silent when it comes to delivering more than one baby through a single birth. Thus, twins and triplets represent the rare exception that is permissible under the Chinese population policy. Unfortunately, the probability of carrying twins or triplets, as opposed to a single fetus, is quite low in unassisted reproduction. However, due to advances in procreative

9   Jean Cohen, Procreative Tourism and Reproductive Freedom, *Reproductive BioMedicine Online*, 2006, 13 (1): 145–146.

10 Anna Pia Ferraretti, Guido Pennings, Luca Gianaroli, Francesca Natali, and M. Cristina Magli, Cross-border Reproductive Care: A Phenomenon Expressing the Controversial Aspects of Reproductive Technologies, *Reproductive BioMedicine Online*, 2010, 20: 261–266.

11 Sharon LaFraniere, Mainland Chinese Flock to Hong Kong to Have Babies, *The New York Times*, February 22, 2012; available at www.nytimes.com/2012/02/23/world/asia/mainland-chinese-flock-to-hong-kong-to-have-babies.html, last accessed on June 1, 2013.

12 Bartha M. Knoppers and Sonia LeBris, Recent Advances in Medically Assisted Conception: Legal, Ethical, and Social Issues, *American Journal of Law and Medicine*, Winter 1991, 17(4): 329–361.

13 Ferraretti, *et al.*, *op. cit.*

14 Roberto Matorras, Reproductive Exile versus Reproductive Tourism (letter), *Human Reproduction*, December 2005, 20(12): 3571.

technologies, many Chinese women resort to fertility treatments and *in vitro* fertilization procedures in order to make sure that they will legally conceive the desired amount of children.[15]

Escaping Legal Prohibitions in the Field of Reproduction: Who?

The previous section analyzed the justification and means employed by those who wish to avoid the limitation of their procreative freedom. The current section continues in the same line, but shifts the perspective from the 'why' and the 'how' to the 'who': who can escape legal prohibitions related to conception?

As traveling is a core element of reproductive exile, those who want to elude restrictive national legislation need to be able to go abroad. This requires both financial resources and the physical ability to board a plane, train or other means of transportation. Consequently, people that are economically disadvantaged are less likely to travel to foreign countries in search of private medical clinics. Similarly, individuals whose health and physical condition do not allow them to cross the border will have to conform to policies that they do not endorse.

One landmark case that manages to capture both the monetary, as well as the physical costs of aborting abroad is *A, B and C v. Ireland*. The first applicant, A, was unmarried, unemployed and was facing considerable financial hardships and an alcohol addiction. She was already the mother of four children, all of whom were placed in foster care due to her drinking problems. One year before her fifth pregnancy, *A* had taken active steps towards rehabilitation and resuming the custody of her children. She believed that a new pregnancy would interfere with her recovery and plans of reunifying the family. As such, she sought an abortion in England. *A* did not have the necessary amount of money for the procedure and, pressed by the time constraints associated to pregnancy, borrowed 650 euros from a money lender, while agreeing to pay an interest rate.[16]

The second applicant, *B*, became pregnant against her wish and, trying to avoid delivering a baby, resorted to the 'morning-after-pill'. Due to this, she was informed by two medical practitioners that she was at risk of developing an ectopic pregnancy. She decided to travel to England and perform an abortion there. She had difficulties with acquiring the necessary fee for the procedure and had to use a friend's credit card in order to book her flights.[17]

Finally, the third applicant, C, had been treated with chemotherapy for three years against a rare form of cancer. Her doctor told her that a pregnancy, in her case, might end up being dangerous for the fetus. C became pregnant unintentionally and unknowingly, while at the same time undergoing cancer tests. The

---

15 *China Daily*, Drug Bid to Beat Child Ban, *China Daily*, February 14, 2006; available at www.chinadaily.com.cn/english/doc/2006-02/14/content_520025.htm, last accessed on June 1, 2013.
16 See *A, B and C v. Ireland, op. cit.*
17 *Ibid.*

tests were harmful for the fetus, while the pregnancy itself threatened C's health and life. Under these unfavorable conditions, the applicant requested to be allowed to abort in Ireland. Her request was denied and she decided to perform the procedure in England. Being a non-resident, she could not have a medical abortion, which presupposes taking a drug that would provoke a miscarriage. Instead, she had to wait eight weeks to be scheduled for a surgical abortion. After the surgery, C experienced prolonged bleeding and infection.[18]

The case of *A, B and C v. Ireland* is very illustrative of the burdens placed on Irish women in their attempt to protect their freedom of choice in a very private aspect of human life, namely, that of procreation and family planning. The applicants argued that the Irish law on abortion discriminated, first and foremost, against women and, more specifically, against impoverished pregnant women. Although the first half of this allegation is not without significance, it does not relate to the aim of this text. The fact that only women, and not men, need to go through nine months of pregnancy followed by many other months of childcare does not directly touch upon the type of discrimination embedded in the access to the exploitation of legal loopholes in the field of reproduction. In this sense, A, B, and C's allegation related to the discrimination against economically underprivileged women is more relevant for issues such as birth or abortion tourism/exile. A and B themselves had difficulties in raising the sum that was needed in order to travel and seek medical care across the border.

The inequality of opportunity that characterizes restrictive legislations is also associated with a high degree of social injustice. This is the more stringent as not only *some* people are able to avoid law's prohibitions, but rather a quite large number of them. To continue with Ireland's abortion policy, which is one of the best documented cases in the literature, the yearly statistics released by the UK Department of Health indicate that the number of Irish women seeking the termination of their pregnancy in England is in the order of thousands. More specifically, 4,149 Irish women aborted in the UK in 2011, preceded by a figure of 4,402 in 2010 and 4,422 in 2000. There are periods of time, such as between 1999 and 2004, when the number of abortions increased to more than 6,000 per year.[19] Moreover, one should remember that these figures are from official statistics that do not take into account the cases in which Irish women introduced themselves as UK residents.

In 2010, Human Rights Watch interviewed several Irish women for a report on the access to abortion in their country. Many interviewees identified financial constraints as significant barriers to terminating their pregnancies abroad. According to Sarah B., a 24-year old student and part-time waitress: "First and foremost was the money thing . . . I was so broke, I was up to my eyeballs in

---

18 *Ibid.*
19 See Irish Family Planning Association, Abortion Statistics; available at www.ifpa.ie/Hot-Topics/ Abortion/Statistics, last accessed on June 1, 2013.

debt . . . on a waitress' salary. I was just, 'how am I going to do this?'"[20] Another student, Claire A., admitted that "there was panic over the money—there was a lot of panic. It was very stressful."[21]

According to the Human Rights Watch report, in 2008–2009 the median salary in Ireland revolved around the sum of 30,000 euros per year, while an abortion in the UK ranged from 800 to 1,000 euros. To the abortion cost one should also add traveling, accommodation and possibly postoperative expenses. As a result, the wages that are under the median line cannot adequately cover the fees of reproductive exile. Additionally, asylum seekers find themselves in even more desperate situations, as on top of everything else, they also need traveling documentation (different types of visas and documents issued by the Department of Justice), which adds to the total sum of an abortion across the border.

The situation of Ireland is not unique. Another striking example of the financial discrimination inherent in the legal prohibitions regarding procreation is illustrated by the Chinese case. Apart from the fact that well-off mainland Chinese citizens can give birth to a second or third child in Hong Kong or may pay for IVF treatments that would deliver them twins or triplets, there are situations when paying the fine associated to the breach of the birth policy is preferable than complying with its provisions. The individuals that can afford to choose this course of actions are mainly "officials, tycoons, and entertainment stars."[22]

Financial well-being is only one of the two possible grounds on which discrimination related to the possibility of surpassing prohibitive legislation can be based. The second one resides in the physical condition of the individual that is seeking the legal loophole. Pregnant women, for instance, who might experience pregnancy related problems—which was actually the case of Savita Halappanavar—could not be able to safely travel on their own from one jurisdiction that criminalizes abortion to another one that allows it. In *A, B and C v. Ireland*, C also applied this reasoning, while linking it to her cancer history. Another Irish case, which dates back to 1983, revolves around a former cancer patient as well. After having suffered a mastectomy, Sheila Hodgers became pregnant and requested an abortion on grounds of severe pain. Her request was refused and, as her health condition could not allow her to travel in order to perform the procedure abroad, she delivered the baby prematurely. Two days later, Sheila died at the age of 26.[23]

I conclude this section by emphasizing the fact that procreative prohibitions are inherently discriminatory because they allow some people to avoid them,

---

20 Human Rights Watch, *A State of Isolation. Access to Abortion for Women in Ireland* (New York: Human Rights Watch, 2010); available at www.hrw.org/sites/default/files/reports/ireland0110webwcover. pdf, last accessed on June 1, 2013.

21 *Ibid.*

22 *China Daily*, Over 1,900 Officials Breach Birth Policy in China, *China Daily*, July 8, 2007; available at www.chinadaily.com.cn/china/2007-07/08/content_912620.htm, last accessed on June 1, 2013.

23 Irish Family Planning Association, Psychological, Physical, and Financial Costs of Abortion; available at www.ifpa.ie/node/506, last accessed on June 1, 2013.

while others cannot. In several cases, a large part of the population is able to evade the effects of an undesirable policy, while a minority does not share the same availability of options. On the one hand, this might be due to the fact that those in the minority are situated in the lowest layers of economic ranking. If this is the case, then the inability to escape unwanted legal consequences may get them to sink even lower. Take, for instance, the example of a young impoverished woman, who, unable to legally perform an abortion in her country, nor to travel abroad for it, will have fewer prospects for finishing her education or for getting employed while also raising a child. On the other hand, health issues may also prevent individuals from seeking medical counsel outside of their state's borders, while their healthier fellows can freely pursue the desired treatment abroad. Unfortunately, in many of these latter cases, it is more than socio-economic status that is at stake, but, rather—as Savita Halappanavar and Sheila Hodgers' experience shows—life itself.

Conclusion

Pennings perceives reproductive exile as a safety valve that guarantees a minimal degree of tolerance for moral pluralism in a society.[24] However, taking into account the fact that the opportunity to access the safety valve is characterized by structural discrimination, this minimal degree of tolerance is morally problematic and, ultimately, unjustifiable.

A proper solution to the issue of moral pluralism in reproductive choice is the safeguard of individual autonomy and freedom, which can be achieved by harmonizing the legislation in the direction of the most permissive, non-restrictive and non-coercive system. This would not only be a safety valve for some, but a sign of respect for everyone's moral values and an opportunity to act according to one's conception of the good life.

---

24 Guido Pennings, Reproductive Tourism as Moral Pluralism in Motion, *Journal of Medical Ethics*, December 2002, 28(6): 337–341.

SHAPING WOMEN'S REPRODUCTIVE DECISIONS: THE CASE OF GEORGIA

Mariam Gagoshashvili

This chapter[1] explores how women's reproductive experiences are influenced and determined by different factors in Georgia. It is based on first-hand research into women's actual experiences of reproductive health and rights issues in the rural and urban areas of Georgia. In particular, I looked at the influence of Georgia's powerful Christian Orthodox values, and of the country's nationalistic concerns, including its concern with its low birth rates, on women's decision-making about child-bearing. The chapter demonstrates that patriarchal family structures, traditional and religious values exert powerful control over women's reproductive lives. Nevertheless, some women develop methods of resistance in order to carry out their decisions regarding their procreative capacities. The analysis is based on the research I conducted for my Master's thesis in 2006.[2]

Health and Gender in Georgia

Georgia, a country in South Caucasus, is a relatively newly established state. It was part of the Soviet Union until its break-up in 1991, after which the country became an independent republic. The collapse of the Soviet Union was accompanied by a civil war in Georgia and two ethnic conflicts, which remain unresolved. Furthermore, the country began to undergo the transitional period from socialism to a market economy.[3]

---

1   This chapter first appeared in the journal *Gender and Development*, July 2008, 16(2): 273–285.
2   Mariam Gagoshashvili, "Law and Tradition: Women's Reproductive Decisions in Urban and Rural Georgia: Case Studies of Tbilisi and Svaneti," MA Thesis (Budapest: Central European University, 2006).
3   Tamar Sabedashvili, *Gender and Democratization: The Case of Georgia 1991–2006* (Tbilisi: Heinrich Böll Foundation, 2007).

The fall of the Soviet regime was followed by a harsh decline in the economic conditions of the former member countries. Georgia was no exception from this general trend. The country started to initiate different economic reforms in order to tackle this problem. As a result, the Georgian health sector was also reformed: it was transformed from the Soviet model of a public state-funded health-care system into a relatively autonomous and privatized sector. The state took up the role of financing only those services that were included in public-health programs, which meant that the population had to pay for most health-care services.[4]

The key health-care facilities in Georgia including clinics, hospitals, and maternity hospitals have remained public in order to guarantee access in remote areas of the country. Thus, almost all the other facilities, including pharmacies, clinics, and family-planning services, have been privatized. Tbilisi, the capital of Georgia, has a relatively good provision of health-care facilities, including a wide range of public and private services.[5] As for the rural communities, access to health-care facilities, family-planning services, and contraception is highly limited. This situation is worsened because of the traditional prejudice existing mainly in the regions against hormonal contraceptives, which are considered to be threatening to women's health.[6]

Since the break-up of the Soviet Union, Georgia has ratified a number of different international conventions among them the Convention on the Elimination of All Forms of Discrimination against Women.[7] In line with these international conventions, Georgia has a liberal approach towards legislation on reproductive rights, abortion, and family planning. According to the law on family planning[8], every citizen of Georgia has the right to independently decide the number and timing of children.[9] Induced abortions based on medical and social reasons are legal.[10] After Georgia's independence in 1991, no significant changes were made to the abortion law, which remained similar to that of the Soviet Union, which had initially legalized abortion in 1920.[11]

---

4   Sara Bennett, David Gotsadze, David Gzirishvili, and Kent Ranson, Health Care-seeking Behavior and Out-of-pocket Payments in Tbilisi, Georgia, *Health Policy and Planning*, July 2005, 20(4): 232–242.

5   *Ibid.*, 233.

6   Tony Hudgins and Raja Rao, *Republic of Georgia, Contraceptive Availability Assessment: Final Report* (Boston: JSI Research and Training Institute Inc., 2004).

7   Ratified by the Parliament of Georgia with Resolution No. 561 of 22 September 1994; available at www. parliament.ge/files/1359_21958_326666_qalTadiskriminaciisyvelaformisaRmofxvrisSesaxeb.pdf, last accessed on June 3, 2013.

8   See Chapter 23 on Family Planning, Act of December 10, 1997 on Health Care; available at matsne. gov.ge/index.php?option=com_ldmssearch&view=docView&id=29980&lang=ge, last accessed on June 3, 2013.

9   *Ibid.*, Chapter 23, Article 136.

10 *Ibid.*, Chapter 23, Articles 139–140.

11 Larissa L. Remennick, The Patterns of Birth Control, in Igor Kon and James Riordan (eds.), *Sex and Russian Society* (London: Pluto Press, 1993), 45–63.

Because the Georgian government had ratified the international conventions, it was expected that the Georgian government would develop a new legal system that would assure equality and eliminate gender-based discrimination. However, despite these conventions and norms concerning gender equality and women's rights, implementation has been extremely low, and the state's concern about assuring gender equality remains formal and superficial.[12]

Currently, a significant number of NGOs work on the issue of gender equality and aim to protect women's rights. One researcher states that there are over 200 registered women's NGOs, though not more than 80 of them are active and functioning.[13] Sabedashvili argues that these women's NGOs lack co-ordination and a sense of solidarity, and that there is unhealthy competition between them, which discourages the formation of a strong women's movement. In addition, among most of the women's organizations in Georgia, the word 'feminism' is still highly stigmatized—many women's NGOs and their members try to avoid identifying with it.[14]

Georgia's population is currently declining, supposedly due to a high level of abortions and a low birth rate.[15] The demographic crisis has given rise to a national debate, and the government encourages certain pronatalist ideas to prevail in national family-planning policies. Women are believed to perform a crucial role in increasing the country's population. Some Georgian researchers see this trend as a revival of old traditions, according to which women's duty to raise children and, thus, act as the principal transmitters of a certain set of customs and values was essential for a nation which had long been facing the problem of maintaining its existence.[16]

The nationalistic concerns about population growth are taking place against a resurgence of the Christian Orthodox Church. The national identity of the post-Soviet Georgian citizen has become strongly linked to traditional Orthodox Christianity. The Orthodox Church became one of the most important symbolic aspects of the independent Georgia, and has thus gained significant power. Even though, officially, Georgia has no state religion, and proclaims freedom of belief and religion, the Orthodox Church has still got a lot of power to influence public opinion, and shape current politics.[17] This trend could be observed during the campaign for the presidential elections (January 5, 2008), when some of the presidential candidates included the objective of strengthening the Orthodox Church, and giving it more power, among their main priorities. While some

---

12 Sabedashvili, *op. cit.*

13 *Ibid.*, 30.

14 *Ibid.*, 31.

15 Florina Serbanescu, *et al.*, *Reproductive Health Survey Georgia, 2005: Final Report* (Atlanta: United Nations Population Fund, 2005).

16 Nino Dourglishvili, *Social Change and the Georgian Family* (Tbilisi: United Nations Development Programme, 1997).

17 Khatuna Tsintsadze, Legal Aspects of Church–State Relations in Post-Revolutionary Georgia, *Brigham Young University Law Review*, March 2007, 2007(3): 751–774.

members of the Church are, of course, moderate in their views, researchers have argued that there was a rise in religious extremism in Georgia in the late 1990s.[18]

Research in Svaneti and Tbilisi

In order to explore how women are experiencing and responding to the context outlined above, in terms of their reproductive decision-making, I undertook research in Tbilisi, Georgia's capital city, and in seven villages of Svaneti, a remote mountain region.[19] I used in-depth semi-structured interviews to provide insight into the everyday lives and experiences of women.[20] Topics included women's experiences of menstruation, child-birth, sex, and birth control, and economic functions in the household.[21] I interviewed 26 married women of reproductive age: 14 in Svaneti, and 12 in Tbilisi. The identity of respondents remained confidential. Most of the women interviewed in both areas had received higher education.

The rural and urban comparison enabled me to see how these experiences differ according to women's geographical and economic conditions, including the types of households they live in, and in terms of their different abilities to access information and resources. As I mentioned in the introduction, there is a significant discrepancy between the capital and the remote areas of the country in terms of health-service availability, which also leads to differences in women's access to family-planning services and contraceptive facilities. While in Tbilisi there is a wide range of health-care institutions, in Svaneti there is only one, in the regional centre of Mestia. I also kept in mind the widespread use of customary laws and religious customs in Svaneti such as, bride kidnapping, blood feud, institution of elders and mediators, etc. These are understood, and spoken about, as local or national traditions of Georgia.[22]

In the next section, I discuss some of the key findings of the research. I begin by reviewing most widespread forms of household and kinship arrangements among the interviewees in Tbilisi and Svaneti and their influence on the level of women's agency concerning the issues of family planning and control over reproductive capacities. I continue by discussing preventive birth control methods practiced by respondents as well as their attitudes, experiences and views on abortion and other methods of induced termination of pregnancy.

---

18 *Ibid.*, 756.
19 Gagoshashvili, *op. cit.*
20 Jennifer Mason, *Qualitative Researching*, 2nd Edition (London: Sage, 2002).
21 Sherna Gluck, What Is So Special About Women? Women's Oral History, in David K. Dunaway and Willa K. Baum (eds.), *Oral History: An Interdisciplinary Anthology* (Lanham, MD: Altamira Press, 1996), 215–230.
22 Mikhako Kekelia, *Qartuli chveulebiti samartali* [Georgian Customary Law] (Tbilisi: Metsniereba, 1988).

Methods of Family Planning in Tbilisi and Svaneti

Household and Kinship Arrangements

In order to understand the factors that shape the interviewed women's decisions concerning their fertility in Tbilisi and Svaneti, it is useful to have a look at their household and kinship arrangements, the division of labor in the family, and the power relations that exist between women and men.

The typical household form in Svaneti and the typical household form in Tbilisi are different. While describing a family structure in the mountain regions of Georgia, some researchers focus on the power distribution within the household. In the remote mountain regions a typical family structure is a patrilocally extended household. Several generations of people are usually united under one family, where the head of family is a senior man. However, together with him, a senior woman is also in the authoritative position and therefore, it is the oldest couple who have a significant power over the other family members.[23] Patrilocally extended families are traditional and well-preserved in Svaneti. Svan women's accounts of marriage focused on the extended family form. According to the local customary laws of Svaneti, women live in their father's house before getting married, and afterwards they move into their husbands' family homes.[24] Many women themselves relate this practice to the local Svan tradition. Often, they emphasize that they were "taken into" their husbands' families, rather than moving there due to their own decisions.

The household form in Tbilisi is much more varied and case-specific. Interviewees from Tbilisi almost never referred to the practice of being "taken in" to the husband's family. In Tbilisi, women's accounts suggested that couples made their decisions about where and with whom to live after marriage based on more pragmatic and/or personal reasons. Among the interviewees, there are families where three generations live together (including grandparents, parents, and children), in the same house or apartment. Yet on the other hand, more and more couples prefer to live independently from their parents and relatives.[25] The nuclear family is the 'new' household form in Tbilisi, and usually it is young people who initiate the idea of living this way.

The gendered division of labor remains the same both in urban and rural areas. In both Tbilisi and Svaneti, women are perceived as primary caretakers of children and the household. Paid employment hardly ever subverts this basic gendered division of labor in the family, either in extent or in type of work.

When women have paid jobs, their work is predominantly related to the areas of care and service. This is true for women interviewed both in Svaneti

---

23 Jamlet Merabishvili, Sergi makalatia da qartuli chveulebiti samartali [Sergi Makalatia and Georgian Customary Law], in Mikhako Kekelia (ed.), *Qartuli chveulebiti samartali* [Georgian Customary Law] (Tbilisi: Metsniereba, 1988), 120–143.
24 *Ibid.*, 122.
25 Dourglishvili, *op. cit.*

and Tbilisi. Most often, typical occupations both for rural and urban women are child-care, kindergarten and school teaching, baking, museum work, trading, and accountancy. Women's income from paid employment rarely constitutes a considerable contribution to the family budget, and men remain the main breadwinners in the household. However, several exceptional cases were found among women interviewed in Tbilisi, where some women held managerial positions and were getting a relatively high salary. Often these women perform the roles of breadwinners in their families. However, this does not free them from the responsibility of domestic labor.

The interviews conducted both in Tbilisi and Svaneti make it evident that most unemployed women see marriage and family life as preventing them from taking up a career. Further, in women's lives the patriarchal division of labor in the family rarely leaves room for paid labor and career advancement. Among women there are many who have fully internalized their place in the patriarchal division of labor. Taking care of family and household is perceived by them as women's primary function. Moreover, husbands and their priorities usually determine women's place and role in a family. Nata, an interviewee from Tbilisi, gives reasons for her unemployment: "I don't work . . . My husband is not a type of man to let me work. Actually, he is against of my working. He prefers if I stay with the children. Of course, if he wasn't supporting the family, I would have been forced to work, but he is. And he tells me, 'I will perform my function and you will perform yours'."

Regarding gendered power relations, it was interesting that it was often women who exerted power over the labor and lives of other women in their families, in both Tbilisi and Svaneti. In the extended families, the social networks of mothers-in-law and sisters-in-law exercise a powerful control over other women. It is evident that some women, in particular those of older age, gain power and authority at home. This is especially tangible in their relations with younger, often female, members of the family.

In both areas, especially in Svaneti, family is perceived as a site of revival and reinforcement of regional, family, or national traditions. In families, women are predominantly the ones who transmit cultural ideas and practices to children. As well as the procreative and caretaking functions, they are also responsible for maintaining family unity, and the local Georgian or Svan traditions. In this respect, women also contribute to the reproduction of conventional gender roles, in which the concept of womanhood is deeply intertwined with the practices of mothering and nurturing. Interestingly, this important role performed by women in the family is largely unacknowledged, even by women themselves. This tendency is revealed, for example, in the common devaluation of female children, in contrast to the desire for male offspring. Even when women carry out the responsibility of reproducing a new generation of family members and reinforcing traditional values intertwined with gender roles, the practical implication that female offspring are needed to ensure that this role continues is completely unrecognized. This argument is especially relevant for Svaneti, where the demand for male children is stronger than in Tbilisi. This kind of system of power relations in households is defined as "classic patriarchy" by Deniz Kandiyoti.[26]

Preventive Birth-Control Methods

Reproductive decisions whether to have children, how many to have, and when are believed to be among the most private decisions women and men make during their lives. However, at the same time, these very decisions, especially those of women, are strongly influenced by different political, social, and economic policies.[27] Moreover, women's reproductive behavior has always been shaped through the institutions of church, family, and marriage. In this context, individual decisions concerning reproduction seem no longer individual and private, but the opposite—they become influenced and shaped by number of social, demographic, economic, political, traditional, religious, and legal policies. In this way they become a key issue of public concern.[28]

The narratives of women in my research in Tbilisi and Svaneti revealed different factors that play important roles in the process of making reproductive decisions. The interviews showed that in both urban and rural areas of Georgia, local or familial customs determine the reproductive choices that women make. Besides these, religion is one of the most significant factors that influence women's decisions concerning their procreative capacities.

The birth-control methods and techniques that respondents chose varied from case to case, and also according to the regions that they live in. The most significant difference in birth-control methods between the urban and rural areas of Georgia reveals itself in the usage of condoms as a main technique for pregnancy prevention. In Tbilisi, almost every woman who was interviewed preferred to control her fertility by using condoms, rather than using hormonal contraception. One of my interviewees from Tbilisi told me: "I won't use any hormonal contraception, because it is dangerous for my health. I think condoms [are the] best alternative. I always prefer to use [them]."

Most interviewees stressed that women, rather than men, initiated the usage of condoms. Most women in Tbilisi who reported using condoms acknowledged the negative feelings that their husbands had towards them. The participation of men in the process of protecting themselves and their partners from unwanted pregnancies is usually limited to providing their wives with contraceptive devices. Furthermore, women stressed the importance of their partners' collaboration in the process of birth control, and expressed willingness for men to

---

26 Deniz Kandiyoti, Bargaining with Patriarchy, *Gender and Society*, September 1988, 2(3): 278–287.
27 Sharon L. Wolchik, Reproductive Policies in Czech and Slovak Republics, in Susan Gal and Gail Kligman (eds.), *Reproducing Gender: Politics, Publics and Everyday Life after Socialism* (Princeton, NJ: Princeton University Press, 2000), 58–91.
28 *Ibid.*, 70–86.

participate in this. Sofio, from Tbilisi, said: "We've used condoms as well. It was my initiative, of course, but my husband was not against it. There are situations [in which] both of us need to compromise . . . Usually women are the initiators of [using] condoms, but men should also agree. They can't think only about their pleasure, they have to consider woman's needs as well and thus, compromise."

In contrast to these narratives, interviews with Svan women showed that in this rural area, women's attitude towards using condoms as a method for controlling child-birth was often quite negative. Some women revealed misunderstandings about the side effects of using condoms, associating them with different health threats. Nana said: "Some people use condoms . . . I'm against it. People say that it causes cancer. It is very dangerous for a woman. I know that it can also infect you with HIV." This shows the great lack of adequate information on these topics, and how this lack conditions women's feelings and attitudes towards this subject.

Instead of condoms, interviewees in Svaneti rely more on the so-called 'calendar method', in order to prevent undesired conception. In this case, women try to predict ovulation, and determine the days when they are most likely to get pregnant, by taking into account their menstrual history. In Svaneti, this method is often seen as most reliable and safe, unlike contraceptive pills, which are considered to be dangerous for health. Even though women interviewed in Svaneti acknowledge that the calendar method is not completely effective, this method is still predominantly used by most of them. Some women interviewed in Tbilisi also use temporary abstinence from sexual relationships through the calendar method. Despite this, though, they believe it to be an unreliable method. Therefore, most of them simply do not count on it working, while others use it in combination with other methods.

Some of the interviewees in Svaneti reported that they did not try to avoid conception. One reason for choosing not to use contraception is the fear, mentioned above, of health complications caused by contraceptive devices. But interestingly, they also stressed the importance of having many children. In this respect, religion had an influence. Medea, from Svaneti, stated: "I will do as God will dictate. I know I will never have an abortion. I have never done it, and I think it's a terrible sin . . . I have never used anything to protect myself, and I'm not going to use anything." In some narratives of women from Tbilisi, religion also featured in women's statements about contraception. However, in the capital city, religious beliefs are not perceived to be a powerful barrier against birth control.

The interviews made it evident that women in Tbilisi were more informed about different contraceptive devices, including condoms and hormonal contraception, and have better access to them. Even though religious beliefs play an important role in the process of decision-making, women interviewed in Tbilisi preferred avoiding unwanted pregnancies by using contraceptives. Women in Svaneti, who usually did not use contraceptive methods, developed their own methods of birth control, including temporary abstinence from sexual relationships.

Induced Termination of Pregnancy

The interviews I conducted in both the rural and urban areas of the country support the argument that abortion is one of the most dominant forms of family planning in Georgia.[29] It is widely used as a method of controlling fertility among the interviewees in Tbilisi and Svaneti. Most of the respondents, except those who have fertility problems, have had induced abortions at least once during their lives. The exceptions are women who started their sexual lives only recently, and several women living in the rural areas.

As mentioned in the beginning of the article, Georgia's family planning legislation can be described as quite liberal according to which citizens of Georgia are granted with freedom to independently control their reproductive lives.[30] Induced abortions are legal for any reason during the first trimester of pregnancy. Abortion is also available within the first 28 weeks from conception in limited medical and social cases.[31]

Julia E. Hanigsberg discusses abortion in relation to the notion of bodily integrity.[32] She argues that women's choice whether to terminate unwanted pregnancies or not is tightly linked to their perceptions of bodily integrity. Therefore, a woman's inability to control her decisions concerning motherhood and reproduction is a threat to her sense of self and to her sense of wholeness.[33] Women, regardless of their reproductive choices and capacities, are seen by society as a single homogenous group, united under the label of 'mother'.

In this context, reproductive decisions women make are discussed in terms of their mothering behavior. The starting point is a certain ideal of motherhood that, among other qualities, implies self-sacrifice, dedication, and generosity. Women's reproductive behavior that does not meet this ideal is considered selfish and irresponsible. This is especially relevant to the issue of abortion.[34] The ideal described by Hanigsberg is internalized by many women, which leads them to consider induced abortions as selfish and sinful, to be accompanied by feelings of guilt.

Most of the interviewees linked their experience of induced termination of pregnancy to the sensation of guilt. This is due to religious considerations prevailing in Tbilisi and Svaneti, which lead women to consider induced abortion to be a sin. Even though not all interviewees consider themselves to be extremely religious, most of them nevertheless regard abortion as the murder of a human being. While describing their experiences and perceptions regarding abortion, the respondents use words like 'mistake', 'murder', 'sin', and 'unacceptable'.

Several respondents, in both Svaneti and Tbilisi, would not even have a therapeutic abortion (that is, an abortion performed due to a risk to the mother's

---

29 Serbanescu, *et al.*, *op. cit.*
30 Act of December 10, 1997 on Health Care, *op. cit.*
31 *Ibid.*, Chapter 23, Articles 139–140.
32 Julia E. Hanigsberg, Homologizing Pregnancy and Motherhood: A Consideration of Abortion, *Michigan Law Review*, November 1994, 94(2): 371–393.
33 *Ibid.*, 388.
34 *Ibid.*, 393.

health), because of religious principles. According to Nata from Tbilisi, "the doctors wanted to perform an urgent abortion and remove my uterus as well. They were telling me that I would definitely have a miscarriage. I went against abortion. From the religious point of view, it is a big sin." The experiences concerning abortion that women recall demonstrate that of all the factors shaping their reproductive decisions, religious beliefs, family opinion, and local customs are the strongest. Nana, from Svaneti, said: "I thought about abortion, but in Svaneti people say that it is better to give birth to nine children, than to have one abortion. And besides, it is a big sin. Everyone was against it—my parents, my husband." A further conversation with the same person revealed the demand for male children, labeled as a 'Svan custom', which influenced the decision-making process for many interviewees in Svaneti: "If I get pregnant again, I will find out if it is a boy or a girl, and then decide. If it is a girl, I will risk having an abortion."

Even though local customary laws are not legally recognized in Georgia, their importance for people's lives in the mountain regions of the country is still tangible.[35] The interviewees' narratives reveal that traditional customs maintain a significant influence on women's reproductive lives in Svaneti. These require women to give birth to as many children as possible, and enforce the cultural preference for male children.

The interviews revealed that many women have a somewhat limited access to legal abortion. This fact is especially relevant to rural women in Svaneti, who have difficulties with obtaining induced abortions for several reasons. Even though high abortion fees and the significant isolation of many villages from the regional centre constitute a barrier to women accessing safe abortion, the situation is more complex than this. Together with these factors, religious considerations and/or male-centered values of families and physicians force women to cope with their unwanted pregnancies. For instance, in Svaneti, the interviewed women's intention to terminate pregnancy is explicitly opposed by their families or doctors. In this case, mothers, mothers-in-law, or aunts are the main people who prevent women from acting on their decisions. One of the interviewees, Nino from Svaneti, told me that she failed to have an abortion as a result of a secret alliance between her aunt and the gynecologist, which was revealed to her only after the child's delivery. Another respondent, Nona from Svaneti, recalled a similar experience: "my gynecologist refused to give me an abortion. She told me that this was my second pregnancy and therefore, nobody could be sure if I would get pregnant again or not. But this was just an excuse, because she knew my mother-in-law very well, who certainly wanted me to give birth."

It is evident that, in Svaneti, it is not one single factor that shapes women's decisions concerning abortion. Rather, there are a number of geographical, economic, religious, and social factors. The intersection of these creates an oppressive system that is capable of determining women's reproductive decisions and

---

35 Stéphane Voell, Local Legal Conceptions in Svan Villages in the Lowlands, *Caucasus Analytical Digest*, September 2012, 42: 2–4.

lives. Importantly, this system enacts its power more easily in remote regions of Georgia, where local customs serve as a barrier to state regulation.

The analysis demonstrates that women's decisions concerning induced termination of pregnancy are influenced very much by different factors in Svaneti and Tbilisi. In spite of the powerful control that restricts women's access to abortion obtained through established medical methods and medical professionals, women both in Tbilisi and Svaneti manage to develop alternative techniques to terminate unwanted pregnancies. As one of my interviewees, Sophio from Tbilisi argued, "if a woman doesn't want to have children, she will find a way to avoid it." Even though these methods for pregnancy termination are not always safe and effective, in many cases women prefer to practice them.

Various techniques to terminate pregnancy were used by the women interviewed during the field work. Khatuna, from Tbilisi, recalled: "Instead of abortion, I would drink boiling water with milk and vodka. This helped me several times. I would also drink some hot herbal drinks." Nata, from Tbilisi, stated: "I was told that quinine tampons were extremely effective in this situation. You had to wet the tampon in quinine, and then insert it into the uterus. This was very useful for widening the pelvis. I have done it several times." One of the most common methods was described by Nino, from Svaneti: "When I realize that I'm pregnant, I put my legs in hot water. For me, it is very effective. If I take a hot bath, it is even better . . . Or maybe one can lift a heavy object. Twenty kilos will do well. It can harm a woman's organism, I guess . . . Actually, many women jump from a high place, a balcony for instance, or staircase. I have never tried it, because hot water helps me very much."

Many of the women I interviewed turn to these techniques if preventive methods fail to protect them from conception, in spite the fact that they can be unsafe and dangerous. These practices are often used in combination with other methods, such as induced abortions and contraception. Even though women's attempts to terminate pregnancy on their own are sometimes unsuccessful, or even cause health complications, the need for using these methods is very telling. The fact that women continuously test alternative techniques of pregnancy termination demonstrates that often they are not able to receive medical assistance, for which they have the legal right.

Conclusion

In both Tbilisi and Svaneti, women's ability to make and implement choices about their reproductive lives is constrained by different religious, customary, and familial values. The situation is more severe in remote rural communities, where the influence of religious and customary values is stronger, and access to health-care systems, family-planning services, and contraceptive devices is extremely limited.

The research findings demonstrate that women constitute a special targeted group within the state and are perceived both as biological and cultural reproducers of the nation. Women in Svaneti and Tbilisi are targeted by medical and religious institutions that dictate them their proper place in the society. In such context, women rarely have other alternatives than sticking to the rigid, pre-defined gender roles. This process has strong psychological, physiological, social, and especially "political implications" for women.[36] As reproductive interests and aims of individuals differ from those of families, communities, and states, it is obvious that, "reproduction is highly politicized, frequently at the expense of the concerns of individuals, especially women."[37] As shown in the research, various institutions such as law, religion, medicine, custom, and especially the family, all exercise control over women's life choices, especially those concerning their reproductive capacities. It becomes clear that women are serving nationalistic agendas rather than being agents of their lives. Nevertheless, no matter how repressive is the control, some women actively seek and often find ways for resisting through alternative methods of family planning and pregnancy termination as described in the research findings.

The implications of the research for service providers and policy makers are clear. Urgent improvements are needed to state-provided health care in Georgia's remote areas. The government has to pay more attention to the improvement of the standard of sexual and reproductive health care in the country. Family-planning services, which would inform the community about different contraceptive devices and women's reproductive rights, are almost non-existent in the remote regions, such as Svaneti. Special efforts have to be made in order to ensure that women in remote areas of Georgia, as well as in its capital Tbilisi, are able to make autonomous decisions concerning their procreative capacities, and feel in charge of their reproductive lives.

The NGO sector has to take up these issues, in a sustained, focused way. Its work is needed since the government has proved reluctant to engage with women's rights in practice, despite the international agreements to which it has signed up. NGOs need to develop systems and skills to monitor the development and implementation of policies which have an impact on women's ability to access the services they need; to monitor violations of women's rights; and to mediate between individual women and the government. In addition, advocacy is needed from women's rights' advocacy groups.

There is also important work to be done in health education. NGOs and government need to play a role here, to build women's, men's, health-care workers', and communities' awareness of women's reproductive and sexual rights, their autonomy to make decisions in this respect, contraceptive devices, safe abortion, sexually transmitted diseases, safe sex, and so on.

Finally, more research is needed in order to develop a fuller understanding of the problems that women are facing in Georgia and to debate and discuss solu-

---

36 Nira Yuval-Davis, *Gender and Nation* (London: Sage, 1997), 37.
37 Gail Kligman, *The Politics of Duplicity: Controlling Reproduction in Ceausescu's Romania* (Berkeley: University of California Press, 1998), 5.

tions. To do this, extensive academic research has to be produced, which will explore women's everyday experiences concerning reproduction, child-birth, contraception, access to resources, and so on. Research of this type would contribute to the work of breaking silence about women's reproductive experiences in Georgia, and thus contribute to their empowerment. The first step towards women gaining power to make real choices and enact these is making their current experience visible and accessible.

ABORTION IN POLAND: LAW AND PRACTICE

JOANNA RÓŻYŃSKA, WERONIKA CHAŃSKA

Poland has one of the most restrictive abortion laws in Europe, both on paper and in practice. Termination of pregnancy is legal, but only in limited circumstances, and, in practice, even women who meet all legally prescribed conditions, are often denied access to this procedure. Many different factors contribute to this situation: strong social and political position of the Roman Catholic Church, conservative morality of the majority of Poles, opportunistic or fearful attitudes of some medical professionals, badly drafted legal regulations, and their inappropriate application. It is the aim of this paper to discuss the main legal, political and socio-medical aspects of today's abortion reality in Poland.

A Short History of the Abortion Law in Poland

The main legal document regulating abortion in Poland is the Act of January 7, 1993, on Family Planning, Protection of the Human Fetus and Conditions Permitting Pregnancy Termination.[1] The adoption of the Act constituted a radical regulatory shift—Polish abortion law, from one of the most permissive in Europe, become one of the most restrictive.

The 1993 Act on Family Planning overturned the liberal 1956 legislation aimed at "protecting women from the negative consequences of abortions performed in unsanitary conditions or by individuals who are not physicians."[2]

---

1   Ustawa z dnia 3 stycznia 1993 r. o planowaniu rodziny, ochronie płodu ludzkiego i warunkach dopuszczalności przerywania ciąży [Act of January 7, 1993 on Family Planning, Protection of the Human Fetus and Conditions Permitting Pregnancy Termination], *Dziennik Ustaw* [Journal of Laws], 1993, no.17, item 78, with later amendments.
2   Ustawa z dnia 27 kwietnia 1956 r. o warunkach dopuszczalności przerywania ciąży [Act of April 27,1956, on Conditions Permitting Pregnancy Termination], *Dziennik Ustaw* [Journal of Laws], 1956, no. 12, item 61.

The 1956 law allowed abortion on medical, legal, and socioeconomic grounds. It did not define what kind of "difficult living conditions" entitled women to abort, nor did it set any time limits for the pregnancy termination. However, an ordinance of the Minister of Health, issued in the same year on the basis of the 1956 Act, allowed physicians to verify the truthfulness of a woman's statement on the hardship of her living conditions *via* consultation with social organizations indicated by the woman, or *via* direct domestic interviews.[3] In 1959, the 1956 law was further liberalized by a new ordinance of the Polish Minister of Health.[4] A pregnant woman's statement on her difficult living conditions started to be treated as a valid indication for pregnancy termination. No physician's verification was required. Although in theory, the law did not allow abortion simply upon a woman's request, in practice, abortion become an elective procedure.[5]

Between the 1960s and 1980s abortions were widely available in Poland, while modern contraceptives were not.[6] Many women treated abortion as an affordable, effective, and 'regular' method of birth control. Abortions were provided free of charge in public hospitals and on a fee basis in private clinics. According to the official statistics, during the period of 1960 to 1988 between 108,000 and 168,000 abortions were performed annually.[7] The total number of abortions is however difficult to determine, because private medical practice did not report. For example, depending on the data source, it is estimated that in 1985 there were between 400,000–620,000 abortions performed compared to the official figure of 136,600.[8]

Although abortion was legal and commonly practiced, it has never stopped being an extremely sensitive political and social issue. The 1956 legislation has been condemned by the leaders of the Roman Catholic Church from the moment of its adoption. However, it was the transition to democracy in 1989 that marked a new, exceptionally intense phase of the Church's anti-abortion campaign in Poland.[9] "With the fall of the regime in 1989, the Episcopate sought a legal ban on abortion

---

3   Rozporządzenie Ministra Zdrowia z dnia 11 maja 1956 r. w sprawie przerywania ciąży [Regulation of the Minister of Health of May 11, 1956, on Pregnancy Termination], *Dziennik Ustaw* [Journal of Laws], 1956, no. 13, item 68.

4   Rozporządzenie Ministra Zdrowia z dnia 19 grudnia 1959 r. w sprawie przerywania ciąży [Regulation of the Minister of Health of December 19,1959, on Pregnancy Termination], *Dziennik Ustaw* [Journal of Laws], 1960, no. 2, item 15.

5   Małgorzata Fuszara, Legal Regulation of Abortion in Poland, *Signs: Journal of Women in Culture and Society*, Autumn 1991, 17(1): 117–128, at 118.

6   See D. Peter Mazur, Contraception and Abortion in Poland, *Family Planning Perspectives*, July–August 1981, 13(4): 195–198; Marek Okólski, Abortion and Contraception in Poland, *Studies in Family Planning*, November 1983, 14(11): 263–274.

7   See Anna Titkow, Poland, in Henry P. David and Joanna Skilogianis (eds.) *From Abortion to Contraception. A Resource to Public Policy and Reproductive Behavior in Central and Eastern Europe from 1917 to the Present* (Westport, CT: Greenwood Press, 1999), 165–190, at 168–169.

8   *Ibid.*, 171.

9   For more information on the abortion debate in Poland in 1950s–1990s, see: Andrzej Kulczycki, *The Abortion Debate in the World Arena* (New York: Routledge, 1999), 110–145; Jacqueline Heinen, Anna Matuchniak-Krasuska, *L'avortement en Pologne: la Croix et la Banniere* [Abortion in Poland: the Cross and the Banner] (Paris: l'Harmattan, 1992), *passim*.

due to its doctrinal opposition to the procedure and as a part of a strategy to reassert its hold over its followers and strengthen its role as an institutional actor. This furthered the Pope's broader plan to recreate moral rules for postcommunist societies and to promote the Christian revival."[10] In the beginning of 1989 a draft of the Act on the Legal Protection of the Conceived Child was prepared under the auspices of the Episcopate. It did not allow abortion in any circumstances and prescribed punishment of three years of imprisonment both for a physician who performed the procedure and a woman who underwent it. The court could however refrain from imposing the punishment given the circumstances of a particular case. The draft bill was presented to the Parliament in March 1989. This ignited a four-year parliamentary and public debate on the shape of the Polish abortion law. (The debate was discontinued and subsequently renewed due to the parliamentary elections in June 1989, and the very first free elections in postcommunist Poland in October 1991.) 'Pro-life' and 'pro-choice' options clashed in the Parliament as well as in media and during street manifestations and protests.[11] Although opinion polls showed that the majority of society supported the *status quo* and objected to introducing a legal ban on abortion[12], the Church-backed proposals were strongly supported by the conservative parliamentarians coming from the Solidarity movement and the conservative right-wing parties.

In 1990 the Minister of Health and Social Welfare issued two regulations which significantly restricted access to legal abortion. The first one was an instruction no. 022/90 which introduced fees for abortion requested on social grounds provided by state hospitals.[13] The second one was a new ordinance on professional qualifications of physicians authorized to perform abortions that replaced the 1959 ordinance.[14] The new ordinance obliged a physician to

---

10 Andrzej Kulczycki, Abortion Policy in Postcommunist Europe: The Conflict in Poland, *Population and Development Review*, September1995, 21(3): 471–505, at 472.

11 See: Hanna Jankowska, Abortion, Church and Politics in Poland, *Feminist Review*, 1991, 39: 174–181; Hanna Jankowska, The Reproductive Rights Campaign in Poland, *Women's Study International Forum*, 1993, 16(3): 291–296; Wanda Nowicka, Struggles For and Against Legal Abortion in Poland, in Barbara Klugman and Debbie Budlender (eds.) *Advocating for Abortion Access: Eleven Countries Studies* (Johannesburg: Witwatersrand University Press, 2001): 223–249, at 231–247; available at www.federa. org.pl/dokumenty_pdf/english/Advocating-abortionAccess.pdf, last accessed on May 13, 2013.

12 The Chancellery of the Sejm: The Bureau of Research and Expertise, *Raport Nr 90: Wyniki sondaży opinii publicznej o prawnej dopuszczalności przerywania ciąży w latach 1989-1993* [*Report No.90: The Results of Public Opinion Polls on Legal Admissibility of Pregnancy Termination Conducted in 1989–1993*] (Warsaw: The Bureau of Research and Expertise, 1996): 1–31, at 11; available at biurose.sejm.gov. pl/teksty_pdf_96/r-90.pdf, last accessed on May 13, 2013.

13 Zarządzenie Ministra Zdrowia i Opieki Społecznej OZN nr 022/90 z dnia 16 stycznia 1990 r [Guidelines of the Ministry of Health and Social Welfare OZN no. 022/90, of January 16, 1990].

14 Rozporządzenie Ministra Zdrowia i Opieki Społecznej z dnia 30 kwietnia 1990 r. w sprawie kwalifikacji zawodowych, jakie powinni posiadać lekarze dokonujący zabiegu przerwania ciąży oraz trybu wydawania orzeczeń o dopuszczalności dokonania takiego zabiegu [Regulation of the Minister of Health and Social Welfare of April 30, 1990, on Professional Qualifications of Physicians Authorized to Carry out Termination of Pregnancy and on the Procedure of Issuing Certificates on Admissibility of Pregnancy Termination], *Dziennik Ustaw* [Journal of Laws], 1990, no. 29, item 178.

inform a woman who sought abortion on socioeconomic grounds about the dangers and health-related risks associated with the procedure. The physician was obliged to discuss with her in depth the reasons why she was considering the termination and to try to discourage her from having an abortion. Also, he was obliged to consult another specialist in gynecology and obstetrics as well as an internist, before issuing an official abortion certificate. Additionally, the woman herself was required to file a request for abortion in writing and discuss her decision with a psychologist selected from the list approved by the chief of a local government administration [wojewoda]. The 1990 ordinance entitled physicians to make a subjective evaluation whether the "difficult living conditions of the pregnant woman" were hard enough to justify abortion. The termination on social grounds was permitted up to the twelfth week of gestation.

The two above mentioned regulations heralded a forthcoming revolution in the Polish abortion law. Another signal of an approaching change came also from the medical community. In December 1991 the Second National Extraordinary Congress of Physicians adopted a new Code of Medical Ethics which forbade physicians to perform abortion, unless the pregnancy threatened the woman's life or health, or had resulted from a criminal act.[15] Although the binding 1956 law allowed a physician to carry out abortions for fetal malformation or social reasons, the new Code discouraged them from doing so under the threat of revoking their professional license. Also, the Code stressed that a physician had a right to act freely in concordance with his conscience and professional knowledge, and that—for justified reasons—he could refuse to start or to continue the patient's treatment, i.e. an abortion (unless in an emergency situation). This, so called 'conscience clause' or 'conscientious objection' was later officially introduced to the Act of December 5, 1996, on the Physician's Profession (Article 39).[16]

It took the catholic leaders and their parliamentary supporters one more year to repeal the liberal 1956 law. Despite the growing public movement for the referendum on introducing the restrictive abortion law, inspired by the Parliamentary Group of Women, left-wing activists and women organizations[17], on January 7, 1993 the Parliament passed the Act on Family Planning, Protection of the Human Fetus and Conditions Permitting Pregnancy Termination.

The 1993 Act, in its Preamble, recognized at that time that "life is a fundamental human good, and the care for life and health are basic duties of the state, society and its citizens." Article 1 of the Act read: "1. Every human being shall have an inherent right to life from the moment of conception. 2. The life

---

15 Kodeks Etyki Lekarskiej [The Code of Medical Ethics], adopted in Warsaw, December 14, 1991, Articles 37–38; available at www.oil.org.pl/xml/nil/wladze/str_zl/zjazd2/uc?rok=1991, last accessed on May 13, 2013.

16 Ustawa z dnia 5 grudnia 1996 r. o zawodzie lekarza [Act of December 5, 1996, on the Physician's Profession], Dziennik Ustaw [Journal of Laws], 1997, no. 28, item 152.

17 Wanda Nowicka, Two Steps Back: Poland's New Abortion Law, Planned Parenthood in Europe, June 1993, 22(2): 18–20.

and health of the child are protected by law from the moment of conception." The Act introduced a new Section 149(a) to the Polish Criminal Code which stated that "who causes the death of the conceived child is subject to two years imprisonment," except if she is the mother of the child. The article further prescribed that a physician who carried out an abortion in a public hospital did not commit the crime, if the pregnancy had constituted a threat to the mother's life or a serious risk to her health; or if the prenatal tests had indicated severe and irreversible fetal malformation; or if there had been strong grounds, confirmed by a prosecutor, for believing that the pregnancy had resulted from a criminal act. In the first two cases, the medical conditions justifying termination must have been confirmed by two other physicians who were not involved in performing the procedure.

The 'pro-lifers' called the new restrictive Act a "rotten consensus"; the 'pro-choicers'—the "women's greatest failure."[18] In 1996, after three years of efforts by the Parliamentary Group of Women and many nongovernmental organizations, the abortion law was liberalized by the left-wing Parliament.[19] Significant changes were introduced to the Preamble of the 1993 Act, as well as to its content. Article 1 of the Act now read: "The right to life, including in the prenatal phase, is protected as provided for in the present law." The provisions concerning the conditions of the legal termination of pregnancy were removed from the Criminal Code and added to the Act. Abortion could again be performed on social grounds—that is, in case where "the pregnant woman is in hard living conditions or in a difficult personal situation." She was, however, obliged to provide a written request for abortion, a certificate of obtaining counseling from a physician (general practitioner), who would not be performing the procedure, and to confirm her decision three days after the consultation. The amendment allowed a physician to perform termination in licensed private clinics.

The liberalized abortion law did not last long. In 1997 it was once again restricted as the Polish Constitutional Tribunal ruled that the new added provisions allowing for legal abortion on social grounds were unconstitutional.[20] The Tribunal removed that option from the Polish legal system. The decision did not

---

18 See Anna Czerwińska, Poland: 20 Years–20 Changes, in Justyna Włodarczyk (ed.), *Gender Issues 2009: Gender Equality Discourse in Time of Transformation, 1989–2009* (Warsaw: The Heinrich Böll Foundation Regional Office, 2009): 37–61, at 39–43; available at www.pl.boell.org/downloads/gender_issues_2009_www.pdf, last accessed on May 1, 2013.

19 Ustawa z dnia 30 sierpnia 1996 r. o zmianie ustawy o planowaniu rodziny, ochronie płodu ludzkiego i warunkach dopuszczalności przerywania ciąży oraz o zmianie niektórych innych ustw [Act of August 30, 1996, on Amending the Act on Family Planning, Protection of the Human Fetus and Conditions Permitting Pregnancy Termination, and Amending Other Acts], *Dziennik Ustaw* [Journal of Laws], 1996, no.139, item 646.

20 Decision of the Constitutional Tribunal of the Republic of Poland of May 28,1997 (K. 26/96); available at www.trybunal.gov.pl/eng/Judical_Decisions/1986_1999/K_ 26_96a.pdf, last accessed on May 13, 2013.

end the legal and social battles over abortion in Poland.[21] But since its issuance no significant legal changes has been introduced to the 1993 Act on Family Planning.

The Existing Abortion Law

Article 4(a)(1) of the 1993 Act of January 7, 1993, on Family Planning, Protection of the Human Fetus and Conditions Permitting Pregnancy Termination, as it stands at present, states that abortion can be performed only by a physician in the following three circumstances:
1. where pregnancy endangers the woman's life or health;
2. where prenatal tests or other medical findings indicate a high risk that the fetus will be severely and irreversibly damaged or suffering from an incurable, life-threatening disease;
3. where there are strong grounds for believing that the pregnancy is a result of a criminal act.

In all these circumstances abortion should be performed by a physician who is a specialist in gynecology and obstetrics.[22] It is free of charge. The costs are covered by the public health insurance. In the first case (often called "abortion on medical grounds"), the presence of a threat to the woman's life or health must be confirmed by a physician, other than the one who is to carry out the abortion, and who is a specialist in the field of medicine relevant to the woman's condition (unless the pregnancy constitutes a direct threat to the woman's life). There is no time limit for terminating the pregnancy. The procedure must be performed in a hospital.

In the second case (often called "abortion on teratogenic/embryo-pathological grounds"), the fetal malformation or disease must be ascertained either by a physician specializing in genetic defects and be based on the genetic tests results, or by a physician specializing in obstetrics and gynecology and based on the results of the ultrasonic images of the fetus. Termination of the pregnancy is possible until the fetus becomes able to live outside the mother's womb (viable). The law does not define viability. Neither does it provide any guidelines

---

21 For example, in 2011, the radical conservatives proposed a draft bill introducing a total ban on abortion. The draft was rejected. In 2012, the Parliament voted against a draft bill to prohibit termination in cases where there is a high probability of serious and irreversible damage to a fetus.

22 Rozporządzenie Ministra Zdrowia i Opieki Społecznej z dnia 22 stycznia 1997 r. w sprawie kwalifikacji zawodowych lekarzy, uprawniających do dokonania przerwania ciąży oraz stwierdzania, że ciąża zagraża życiu lub zdrowiu kobiety lub wskazuje na duże prawdopodobieństwo ciężkiego i nieodwracalnego upośledzenia płodu albo nieuleczalnej choroby zagrażającej jego życiu [Regulation of the Minister of Health and Social Welfare of January 22, 1997, on Professional Qualifications of Physicians Authorized to Carry out Termination of Pregnancy, or Authorized to Certify that the Pregnancy Endangers the Women's Life or Health, or that it Indicates a High Probability of Severe and Irreversible Damage to the Fetus or Incurable Illness Threatening its Life], *Dziennik Ustaw* [Journal of Laws], 1997 no. 9, item 49.

on which medical conditions constitute "severe, irreversible damage" or "an incurable, life-threatening disease." The decision is left to physicians and parents. Alike in the first case, abortion on embryo-pathological grounds must be performed in a hospital.

In the third case (often called "abortion on legal grounds"), the abortion may be performed until the end of the twelfth week of pregnancy. The suspicion that it had resulted from a criminal act (i.e. rape, incest) must be confirmed by a public prosecutor.

The Act on Family Planning required that in all cases a written consent of a woman (aged 13 or above) must be obtained. Where the woman is a minor (or where she is legally incapacitated), the written consent of her legal representative is also required. If the legal representative refuses to give consent, the court permission is needed to perform the procedure.

Termination of a pregnancy in breach of the conditions specified in the Act on Family Planning is a criminal offense and carries a penalty of up to three years of imprisonment [Section 152(1) and (2) of the Criminal Code]. If the aborted fetus was viable, the offenders are subject to penalty of up to eight years of imprisonment [Section 152(3) of the Criminal Code]. The pregnant woman herself does not incur criminal liability.

Official Statistics on Abortion

The Polish government is legally obliged to provide the Parliament with yearly reports on the realization of the 1993 Act on Family Planning[23]. The reports present only the official number of abortions performed in accordance with the law in public hospitals.[24] No estimates concerning the real scale of the phenomenon are provided or available.

According to the official statistics, as a result of the enactment of the restrictive Act on Family Planning in 1993, the number of legally induced abortions dropped dramatically from 11,620 in 1992 to 1240 in 1993. The same effect was observed in the year 1998, when the law was once again restricted by the Constitutional Tribunal. The number of legally performed abortions was reduced from 3047 in 1997 to 310 in 1998. In the first years of the 21st century the number of legal abortions remained rather stable, varying between 124 and 193. It rose again in 2005 to 225 procedures and has kept increasing to 669 in the year 2011.

---

23 Ustawa z dnia 30 marca 1995 r. o zmianie ustawy o planowaniu rodziny, ochronie płodu ludzkiego i warunkach dopuszczalności przerywania ciąży [Act of March 30, 1995, on Amending the Act on Family Planning, Protection of the Human Fetus and Conditions Permitting Pregnancy Termination, *Dziennik Ustaw* [Journal of Laws], 1995, no. 66, item 334.

24 Governmental reports on the realization of the 1993 Act on Family Planning in 2006–2011 are available online at the official website of the Ministry of Health: www.mz.gov.pl.

Table 1. *Legal Abortions during the Years 2002–2011, According to the Ground for Termination*

Year	Total	Pregnancy endangers the mother's life or health	Fetal malformations	Pregnancy being a result of a criminal act
2002	159	71	82	6
2003	174	59	112	3
2004	193	62	128	3
2005	225	54	168	3
2006	340	82	246	11
2007	326	37	287	2
2008	499	32	467	0
2009	538	27	510	1
2010	641	27	614	0
2011	669	49	620	0
2008	499	32	467	0
2009	538	27	510	1
2010	641	27	614	0
2011	669	49	620	0

Source: Governmental Report on the Realization of the Act on Family Planning in the year 2011.[25]

Until 2001 the governmental statistics had included information concerning the number of spontaneous miscarriages. It was rather high and varied from ca. 60,000 in 1990 to ca. 41,000 in 2000. Through the 1990–2000 period the annual rate of miscarriages per live births was cca. 10 percent. It was suspected that such a high level of miscarriages covered the fact that many women in difficult living conditions "obtained an abortion under pretext" of having a miscarriage, or they were admitted to a hospital after self-provoked miscarriages or illegal abortions.[26] From 2002 all data concerning miscarriages has been removed from the governmental reports.

25　Sprawozdanie Rady Ministrów z wykonania oraz o skutkach stosowania w roku 2011 ustawy z dnia 3 stycznia 1993 r. o planowaniu rodziny, ochronie płodu ludzkiego i warunkach dopuszczalności przerywania ciąży [Report of the Council of Ministers on the Realization and Effects of the Act January 7, 1993 on Family Planning, Protection of the Human Fetus and Conditions Permitting Pregnancy Termination in 2011] (Warsaw: the Council of Ministers, 2012): 1–59, at 51; available at www.mz.gov.pl/wwwfiles/ma_struktura/docs/sprawozdzust_matdziec_20121123.pdf, last accessed on May 13, 2013.

26　See Andrzej Kulczycki, Abortion Policy in Postcommunist Europe, *op. cit.,* 475–476.

The government also provides the information about the annual number of prenatal testing and consultations. The Act of Family Planning obliges the organs of governmental administration and local self-government to provide pregnant women with medical, social, and legal care. In particular, it obliges the above-mentioned subjects to provide free access "to information and prenatal tests, especially when there is an increased risk or suspicion of the occurrence of a genetic or developmental defect of the fetus or an incurable illness which threatens the life of the fetus" [Article 2(2)(a)].

In Poland, healthcare services during pregnancy, labor and the postnatal period are free of charge. They are financed from public funds or—in the case of uninsured women–by the Ministry of Health.[27] Every woman in pregnancy is entitled to a comprehensive prenatal and perinatal care, including three ultrasound examinations, which should be performed between 11th–14th, 21st–26th, and 27th–32nd week of pregnancy. The standard of the prenatal and perinatal care is set by the ordinance of the Minister of Health of September 20, 2012.[28] If a woman—due to her age, reproductive history, or health condition—belongs to a high risk group, or if the results of her ultrasound scan suggest the possibility of fetal malformation, she has a right to additional prenatal examinations, in particular genetic tests to confirm or dispel this suspicion. She may obtain the needed tests via the Healthcare Prenatal Testing Program (Program Badan Prenatalnych) regulated by an ordinance of the Minister of Health (in the attachment).[29] The ordinance establishes the following indications for prenatal consultations and tests, other than the regular ultrasound examination:
1. a pregnant woman is 35 or older;
2. a previous child or fetus was affected with a chromosomal aberration;
3. there is a known chromosomal rearrangement in one or both parents;
4. there is a considerably higher risk for giving birth to a child with a monogenic disorder or multigenetic disease; and
5. abnormal results of ultrasound scans or biochemical tests indicate an increased risk for chromosomal aberration or defect of the fetus.

---

27 Ustawa z dnia z dnia 27 sierpnia 2004 r. o świadczeniach opieki zdrowotnej finansowanych ze środków publicznych [Act of August 27, 2004, on Healthcare Services Provided from Public Funds], *Dziennik Ustaw* [Journal of Laws], 2004, no. 210, item 2135, with later amendments; Article 2.1.
28 Rozporządzenie Ministra Zdrowia z dnia 20 września 2012 r. w sprawie standardów postępowania medycznego przy udzielaniu świadczeń zdrowotnych z zakresu opieki okołoporodowej sprawowanej nad kobietą w okresie fizjologicznej ciąży, fizjologicznego porodu, połogu oraz opieki nad noworodkiem [Regulation of the Minister of Health of September 20, 2012, on Standard Operational Procedures in Medical Care over a Woman in Physiological Pregnancy and Physiological Labor, and Over a Newborn], *Dziennik Ustaw* [Journal of Laws], 2012, item. 1100.
29 Rozporządzenie Ministra Zdrowia z dnia 6 grudnia 2012 r. w sprawie świadczeń gwarantowanych z zakresu programów zdrowotnych [Regulation of the Minister of Health of 6 December 2012 on Healthcare Services Financed from Public Funds via Healthcare Programs], *Dziennik Ustaw* [Journal of Laws], 2012, item 1422.

The ordinance describes four types of prenatal diagnostic procedures:

1. counseling and biochemical testing, including: a measurement of estriol level in maternal serum; measurement of AFP (α-fetoprotein) level in maternal serum; a measurement of PAPP-A (pregnancy associated plasma protein A) level in maternal serum; a measurement of free β-HCG (β-human chorionic gonadotropin) level in maternal serum;
2. counseling and targeted ultrasound examinations;
3. genetic counseling and testing, including standard cytogenetic techniques, molecular cytogenetic techniques, molecular biology methods; and
4. invasive techniques, including: amniocentesis, cordocentesis, chorionic villus sampling.

A woman must obtain a gynecologist's referral for prenatal testing. In the referral the physician should indicate the reason (or reasons) for prenatal examinations. If no reason is indicated, then the diagnostic procedure will not be reimbursed by the healthcare insurance. In Polish healthcare system a gynecologist works as a gatekeeper. It is up to him/her to decide whether the woman needs to have prenatal testing done or not.

In official governmental reports the data concerning prenatal testing are divided into two parts: the first concerns the number of prenatal tests funded directly from the budget (as a part of regular healthcare services); the second provides the number of prenatal diagnostic procedures financed from public funds in the form of healthcare programs. The decision to divide statistical data into two separate categories with different subcategories makes the deduction of the total number of prenatal tests performed annually extremely laborious. There is also no possibility to establish the total number of women who use prenatal services annually.

According to the governmental report for 2011, in this year 28,531 genetic consultations and 4,076 invasive prenatal tests were carried out as a part of the regular healthcare services. As a result, 723 fetal pathologies were detected.[30] Additionally, the report states that, in 2011, 45,304 women were included in the Prenatal Testing Program. There were 74 healthcare providers participating in the program and offering state-funded prenatal examinations. 21,889 genetic consultations and 4,858 invasive prenatal tests were carried out by the healthcare providers affiliated with the Prenatal Testing Program.

There are significant differences among regions in the number of healthcare facilities providing prenatal consultation and testing. The lowest number of providers can be found in the provinces (voivodeships) of Lublin, Opole, Święty Krzyż, Warmia-Masuria, Western Pomerania—there is only one provider in each of the regions—while the provinces of Silesia (23), Mazovia (9), and Łódz (8) have the highest number of providers. The relatively small number of genetic

---

30   There is no information concerning the number of women taking prenatal services. It is also not clear whether some of the women included into this category were not calculated twice and included among the number of women participating in the Prenatal Testing Program.

centers and their uneven geographical distribution is responsible for the fact that in some parts of Poland access to prenatal genetic testing is very limited.

The 'Abortion Underground' and 'Abortion Tourism'

The Federation for Women and Family Planning is a nongovernmental organization established in 1992 to defend women's right to choose.[31] In 1999 it received the Special Consultative Status with the Economic and Social Council of the United Nations. The Federation has been monitoring the implementation of the 1993 Act since its inception. Studies conducted by the Federation in 1993, 1996, 1999, 2000, and 2007 lead to the conclusion that the restrictive law has only negative consequences on the individual and social levels.[32] It did not eliminate and probably did not reduce the number of abortions done on Polish women every year. Illegal terminations are still common. Some women go abroad to terminate the pregnancy. This phenomenon is known as 'abortion tourism'. Those who cannot afford it, undergo the procedure in private clinics in Poland. The scale of the so-called 'underground abortion' is hard to evaluate. However, the Federation claims that it can be estimated at between 80,000 and 190,000 abortions per year.

These estimations are based on two methods of comparing demographic data.[33] The first method is based on an assumption that there is a correlation between the size of a population of reproductive age and the number of abortions performed in a given country. The Federation counted the abortion index (the number of abortions per 1000 women of reproductive age) for Slovakia (13.9), France (14.6) and Hungary (27.9). Subsequently, having assumed the figure of 10 million women of reproductive age in Poland, the Federation made a simulation of the number of abortions in Poland, if the abortion index were at the level of each of those countries. The obtained figures differed radically (139,000; 146,000; 279,000), but all of them exceeded 100,000 abortions annually.

The second method is to refer to the number of legal abortions carried out in Polish public hospitals in 1980s—that is, before the restrictive legal regulations entered into force. At that time hospitals terminated approximately 150,000 pregnancies annually. It is worth to note, however, that the official statistics from that period are commonly believed to be highly underestimated due to the fact that many abortions were carried out in private medical facilities and not included into official statistics.

---

31 For further information, see the official website of the Federation: www.federa.org.pl.
32 See Wanda Nowicka, The Anti-Abortion Act in Poland—the Legal and Actual State, in Wanda Nowicka (ed.), *Reproductive Rights in Poland: the Effects of the Anti-abortion Law. Report: March 2008* (Warsaw: Federation for Women and Family Planning, 2008), 17–44, at 17–18; available at www.federa.org.pl/dokumenty_pdf/english/report%20Federa_eng_NET.PDF, last accessed on May 13, 2013.
33 *Ibid.*, 27.

The Federation for Women and Family Planning estimates that 10 to 15 percent of all Polish abortions are performed abroad. Wanda Nowicka, the head of the organization, believes that "the number is definitely growing."[34] In August 2010, leading Polish pro-choice activists held a civil hearing at the Polish Parliament on the rising number of Polish women who are travelling abroad to obtain access to abortion. According to the experts, Polish women seek abortions abroad because they are illegal in their home country and often performed in poor conditions. The women also fear social ostracism. An illegal abortion in Poland costs 2,000–4,000 zlotys ($640–$1,270), compared to 400–600 euros ($510–$760) in Germany, 280 euros in the Netherlands and 450–2,000 pounds ($700-$3,120) in Britain. It is observed that most women go to Poland's East and South neighboring countries, for example: Ukraine (Lvov), Lithuania (Druskienniki), Russia (Kaliningrad), Belarus (Minsk), the Czech Republic, and Slovakia. Fewer women can afford to seek abortion in Western countries, but those that can most frequently go to the Netherlands, Germany, Belgium, and Austria.

Barriers in Access to Legal Abortion

The studies conducted by the Federation for Women and Family Planning, as well as its rich experience in helping Polish women in exercising their reproductive right, show that the restrictive abortion law has resulted in serious limitations of access to safe and legal abortion.

Many women find it difficult to obtain a certificate allowing them to abort for medical reasons. Some Polish physicians simply do not believe that the life and health of a pregnant woman takes priority over the life of a fetus. A tragic history of a young pregnant woman from Piła, who suffered from ulcerative colitis and died in hospital of septic shock due to the lack of a necessary and adequate medical healthcare, is a shocking example of this attitude. The case is known as Z v. Poland. It has been recently decided by the European Court of Human Rights.[35]

Very often women are told by doctors that they should not give birth since there is a threat to their health. However, the same physicians do not have courage to express this opinion on paper in order to permit a legal termination of pregnancy. In result, pregnant women with serious health problems cannot be certain whether the doctor, they consult, will take into account their health needs and—if necessary—make a proper medical decision and give consent to the termination of pregnancy. A famous case of Alicja Tysiąc (which will be presented in the next section) shows that a pregnant woman's health is not always treated by physicians with due care.

---

34 Statement by Wanda Nowicka, September 26, 2010; available at www.federa.org.pl/index. php?option=com_content&view=article&id=346:sierpie-2010&Itemid=185, last accessed on May 13, 2013.
35 See Z v. Poland; ECtHR, application no. 46123/08, judgment of November 13, 2012.

Some physicians intentionally misinform women about their reproductive rights, in particular the right to undergo prenatal testing and to terminate the pregnancy, if the tests reveal fetal abnormalities. Some simply refuse to issue a referral for prenatal testing or a certificate of admissibility of terminating the pregnancy. The national case of Barbara Wojnarowska—a woman who was refused a referral for a prenatal diagnosis, despite the existence of a well-founded suspicion that her next child will also suffer from achondroplasia[36]—is a good illustration of such a behavior.

Often those physicians, who are not willing to issue a referral for genetic prenatal test or to carry out an abortion, require women to meet additional conditions which are not prescribed by law. For example, they demand additional documents or consultations. They refer pregnant women for supplementary examinations, which are unnecessary from medical and legal point of view, and often very time-consuming. Frequently all these 'techniques' have one aim—to prolong the issuance of a certificate on admissibility of abortion beyond the gestational age specified as a legal time limit for abortion. A famous case R.R. v. Poland, decided recently by the European Court of Human Rights, is a good example of such a strategy. The case is presented below.

Polish gynecologists often do not take into account the psychological distress experienced by women who are informed that their child is seriously malformed. One woman, whose fetus was diagnosed as having severe congenital abnormalities, was told by physicians that they would wait for a spontaneous miscarriage or fetal death instead of performing an abortion. The woman was also admonished that she should rather be grateful for such a solution. She was instructed that medical doctors are obliged to save life of every human being. Allowing for a miscarriage or fetal death was perceived by the physicians as an act of goodwill.[37]

According to the Federation for Women and Family Planning, women also face barriers in obtaining a certificate that entitles them to terminate the pregnancy resulting from a crime. The public prosecutors frequently question the fact that rape has taken place, particularly in the situation when the victim cannot provide witnesses. Others—contrary to the law—question a woman's right to abort in case where the pregnancy is an effect of a criminal act. One woman was told by the prosecutor that he was reluctant to issue the certificate, because "after all, the child can always be adopted afterwards."[38]

There are many regulatory, institutional, and social factors which contribute to the limited access of Polish women to legal abortions. Two of them seem to be of special importance: the so-called 'conscience clause', which was introduced to the Medical Code of Ethics in early 1990s, and later to Article 39 of the Act on

---

36 See Adam Bodnar, Case Law Concerning the Lack of Availability of Services for Terminating Pregnancy in Poland, in Wanda Nowicka (ed.) *Reproductive Rights in Poland, op.cit.*, 45–64, at 46–55.
37 See Wanda Nowicka, The Anti-Abortion Act in Poland, *op. cit.*, 22.
38 *Ibid.*, at 23.

the Profession of Physicians (subsequently renamed to the Act on Professions of Physicians and Dentists); and, broadly understood, anti-abortion pressure.

The 'conscience clause' allows physicians to refuse to provide medical services that violate their conscience, unless there is a case of emergency. It protects their individual moral integrity, within the limits compatible with the due respect for patients' rights, in particular the right to healthcare. However, many physicians perceive it as a tool that gives them almost unlimited freedom in deciding on the basis of their religious beliefs (or other personal worldviews) what kind of services they are willing to provide to the patients.[39] They often do not obey the law which prescribes conditions of using the clause. If the physician wants to make a use of the clause to refuse abortion, he is obliged by the law to indicate the woman an effective way of obtaining this service from another physician or in another health care facility. He is also obliged to justify and record the refusal in medical documentation.

Many physicians act in an opportunist manner and adapt their behavior to the views on morality of abortion that are presented by their professional or institutional supervisor, mass-media, the Church representatives, or politicians. They are afraid of performing abortion because they are aware that 'it may cause troubles'. They are afraid of the possibility of being accused of committing a moral or legal crime. They prefer to stand aside and not get their hands 'dirty'. For many of them abortion is at best a private matter—something a woman or a couple has to pay their dues, not something that is owed to them by medical professionals.

These observations find support in the report prepared for the Federation for Women and Family Planning in 2007.[40] Between May and July that year, a Polish sociologist, Anna Domaradzka, conducted a detailed research among Polish gynecologists and obstetricians on factual access to abortion and medical services concerning reproductive health. The report notes that in Poland there is a high inequality in women's access to gynecological-obstetrics services due to education, age, place of residence and income level. In the opinions of the interviewees the main cause of the differences concerning access and quality of gyneco-obstetrical care is the attitude and behavior of individual physicians, registrars, and directors of health service centers. The author of the report observes that the discussion on abortion and prenatal testing is dominated by emotional rather than scientific arguments and the language used is extremely ideological. In practice, the access to a legal abortion in Poland is extremely restricted. Doctors are unwilling to carry out the procedure and hospitals quite often send patients away, without providing them with information where and how they can obtain the service. Often it is a result of the policy adopted by managers of

---

39 See Joanna Z. Mishtal, Matters of "Conscience": The Politics of Reproductive Healthcare in Poland, *Medical Anthropology Quarterly*, 2009, 23(2): 161–183.

40 Anna Domaradzka, Report on the Expert Research with Gynaecologists and Midwives, in Wanda Nowicka (ed.), *Reproductive Rights in Poland, op. cit,* 65–79.

an institution. Some medical facilities declare that they do not provide abortion or prenatal testing. At least one of the public health institutions was named where prenatal genetic test were not carried out, although there were technical possibilities to do so, due to the fact that the procedure was defined as being "in conflict with conscience" (of the institution, *sic!*).

Polish Abortion Cases before the ECtHR

Every year, thousands of Polish women go through a real hell—often in vain—to receive the medical services they are legally entitled to.[41] Only few of them find the courage and strength to vindicate their rights in the national courts or before the European Court of Human Rights (ECtHR). However, in recent years several Polish women, who were unlawfully denied access to the legal abortions or prenatal testing, have won their cases against Poland before the Court. The Court found the Polish legal regulations and their applications to be against human rights expressed in the European Convention on Human Rights.

Tysiąc v. Poland[42]

In February 2000, Alicja Tysiąc, a mother of two children, discovered that she was pregnant for the third time. Since she suffered from severe myopia (shortsightedness, in the measurement of –20 diopters), she consulted three ophthalmologists to determine what impact this might have on her sight. Although all physicians concluded that due to pathological changes in her retina, pregnancy and delivery put her eyesight at risk, they refused to issue a certificate authorizing a termination of pregnancy. In April 2000, Alicja Tysiąc consulted a general practitioner (GP) who agreed to issue such a certificate. The GP wrote that the pregnancy posed a threat to the woman's health as there was a risk of rupture of the uterus, due to the fact that her two previous children were born by caesarean section, as well as the risk for her eyesight. In fact, her eyesight already worsened significantly during the first two months of the pregnancy to –24 diopters. Although Alicja Tysiąc obtained a valid referral for an abortion on medical grounds, the gynecologist—the head of the Gynecology and Obstetrics Department of the Clinic in Warsaw, in the area to which she was assigned on the basis of her residence—refused to perform the termination. Since there was no procedure by which she could appeal this decision, she had no possibility to terminate the pregnancy. In result, she gave birth to a child in November

---

41 See Federation for Women and Family Planning, ed., *Contemporary Women's Hell—Polish Women's Stories* (Warsaw: Federation for Women and Family Planning, 2005); available at www.federa.org.pl/dokumenty_pdf/english/pieklo_ang.pdf, last accessed on May 13, 2013.
42 See *Tysiąc v. Poland*; ECtHR, application no. 5410/03, judgment of March 21, 2007.

2000. After the delivery, her eyesight deteriorated even further. Currently, she can see objects only from a distance of 1.5 meters and faces a risk of becoming completely blind. In September 2001 she was declared by the disability panel to be significantly disabled and in need of constant care and assistance in her everyday life.

Alicja Tysiąc attempted to institute criminal as well as disciplinary proceedings against the gynecologist who refused to perform the abortion. Without success. In January 2003 she lodged a complaint against Poland to the European Court of Human Rights. In March 2007, the Court found Poland in violation of Article 8 (the right to respect for private life) of the European Convention on Human Rights. The Court concluded that Poland failed to comply with its positive obligations to secure to Alicja Tysiąc the effective respect for her private life, because "it has not been demonstrated that Polish law as applied to the applicant's case contained any effective mechanisms capable of determining whether the conditions for obtaining a lawful abortion had been met in her case. It created for the applicant a situation of prolonged uncertainty. As a result, the applicant suffered severe distress and anguish when contemplating the possible negative consequences of her pregnancy and upcoming delivery for her health."[43] The Court ordered Poland to pay Alicja Tysiąc a substantial sum in non-pecuniary damages.

R.R. v. Poland[44]

In late February 2002, being 18 weeks pregnant, R.R. underwent an ultrasound examination. Gynecologist who performed the scan informed her that it could not be ruled out that the fetus was affected with some malformation. R.R. replied that she wished to have an abortion if the suspicion proved true. Further tests were needed to determine the fetus' condition. It was suspected that the fetus suffered from Turner or Edward Syndrome. During the next five weeks R.R. attempted to obtain a formal referral for the genetic testing (amniocentesis). She visited three hospitals, consulted several doctors, and underwent numerous sonograms and other inconclusive tests. All physicians recommended genetic tests, but none of them wanted to issue such a document. One refused because he believed that the fetus' condition was not serious enough to qualify her for an abortion. Another who refused, additionally criticized her for contemplating a termination of pregnancy. In one of the hospitals she was told that the abortion would endanger her life and that the fact that her two previous children were born by caesarean section constituted the most important risk factor in deciding whether she should have a genetic test at all. Finally, when she was in the 23th week of pregnancy, R.R. was admitted to the hospital as an emergency patient,

---

43 Ibid., para. 124.
44 See R.R. v Poland; ECtHR, application no. 27617/04, judgment of May 26, 2011.

and underwent genetic testing. Two weeks later she received the result which confirmed the presence of Turner syndrome. However, the physicians refused to carry out the abortion, because the fetus had already become viable. In July 2002 R.R. gave birth to a baby girl suffering from Turner Syndrome.

R.R. attempted to institute criminal proceeding against the persons involved in handling her case. She also filed a civil suit against the doctors and hospitals involved, which reached the Supreme Court. However, being unable to obtain sufficient redress in Poland, she lodged a complaint to the European Court of Human Rights in 2004. The Court found Poland in violation of Article 3 of the Convention (the right to be free from inhuman and degrading treatment) and Article 8 (the right to respect for private life) of the European Convention on Human Rights. It ordered Poland to pay R.R. a substantial sum in non-pecuniary damages.

Analyzing R.R.'s complaint under the Article 3, the Court said that "the determination of whether the applicant should have access to genetic testing, recommended by doctors in light of the findings of the second ultrasound scan, was marred by procrastination, confusion and lack of proper counseling and information given to the applicant."[45] "As a result of the procrastination of the health professionals as described above, she had to endure weeks of painful uncertainty concerning the health of the fetus, her own and her family's future and the prospect of raising a child suffering from an incurable ailment. She suffered acute anguish through having to think about how she and her family would be able to ensure the child's welfare, happiness and appropriate long-term medical care. Her concerns were not properly acknowledged and addressed by the health professionals dealing with her case."[46] The Court expressed the view that R.R's has been humiliated. The Court noted, however, that her suffering reached the minimum threshold of severity under Article 3 of the Convention.

The Court ruled also that in the given case Poland breached its positive duties to secure for R.R. the effective respect for her private life (Article 8 of the Convention). The breach included the failure to ensure timely access to diagnostic services; to ensure effective access to relevant and full information on the fetus' condition; to reform criminal liability for doctors performing abortions to alleviate the 'chilling effect', and to adequately regulate conscientious objection.[47] The Court reminded that "States are obliged to organize the health services system in such a way as to ensure that an effective exercise of the freedom of conscience of health professionals in the professional context does not prevent patients from obtaining access to services to which they are entitled under the applicable legislation."[48]

---

45 *Ibid.*, para. 153.
46 *Ibid.*, para. 159.
47 See the judgment summary prepared by the Center for Reproductive Rights; available at reproductiverights.org/en/rr-v-poland-st-v-poland-z-v-poland, last accessed on May 13, 2013.
48 *R.R. v Poland, op. cit.*, para. 206.

P and S v. Poland[49]

In April 2008, a 14-year old P was raped by a boy of her own age. The rape was reported to the police. Several weeks later P discovered that she was pregnant. Together with her mother, S, P decided that abortion would be the best option. A public prosecutor issued a certificate that P's pregnancy had resulted from a criminal act (a sexual intercourse with a minor under 15 years of age). The mother started a crusade for obtaining an abortion for her daughter. She visited numerous hospitals in Lublin, their hometown. One of the physicians she contacted advised her to "get her daughter married." Another told her that she and P should talk to a Catholic priest. When she refused, the physician arranged a meeting between P and the priest, without the mother's knowledge. The priest pressured P to sign a statement written by the physician which stated that she wanted to continue with the pregnancy. Subsequently, the physician showed the statement to S, and refused to perform abortion. The mother contacted the Federation for Women and Family Planning in Warsaw and asked them for help. Meanwhile, the Lublin hospital issued a press release on the P's case. The case became national news. It was widely discussed in media and internet. P's mobile phone number was distributed by the priest among anti-abortion activists. Although Federation helped P to obtain the referral issued by the national consultant in gynecology that allowed her to be admitted to a Warsaw hospital for having an abortion, the procedure was not performed. The physician from Lublin informed the doctors from Warsaw that the girl signed the statement in which she declared the wish to continue with the pregnancy. Hospital staff started to manipulate the relationship between P and her mother. They allowed the priest from Lublin and two anti-abortion activists to visit the girl to persuade her to change her mind. Feeling manipulated and helpless, both the mother and the daughter decided to leave the hospital. Meanwhile, the Lublin Family Court restricted the mother's parental rights and ordered P to be placed in a juvenile shelter. She remained under the custody of the state for a week. She was kept in a locked room, with no access to her mobile phone, guarded as if she were a juvenile delinquent. Due to health problems, P was transferred from the shelter to a hospital, where she again faced media and anti-abortion activist harassment. Finally, the Ministry of Health intervened and P was able to terminate the pregnancy. The abortion was performed only a few days before the 12 week cut off point. Although the procedure was legal, it was carried out in a clandestine manner, in a hospital 500 kilometers away from her home.

P and her mother lodged a complaint against Poland to the European Court of Human Rights. The Court found Poland in violation of Article 3 of the Convention (the right to be free from inhuman and degrading treatment) and Article 5(1) of the Convention (the unlawful deprivation of liberty) in respect of the first

---

49 *P and S v. Poland*; ECtHR, application no. 57375/08, judgment of October 30, 2012.

applicant, as well as in violation of Article 8 (the right to respect for private life) as regards the determination of access to lawful abortion in respect of both applicants and the disclosure of the their personal data. The Court ordered Poland to pay P and S a substantial sum in non-pecuniary damages.

Conclusions

The European Court of Human Rights is not the only international body which finds the Poland's abortion legal framework and practice contrary to human rights. Criticism has been expressed by many other institutions for many years, i.e. the UN Human Rights Committee, the UN Committee on Economic, Social and Cultural Rights, the UN Special Rapporteur on the Right to Health, and the Council of Europe Commissioner for Human Rights.[50] In 2010, the Human Rights Committee[51] once again expressed concern that, in practice, many Polish women are denied access to prenatal testing and lawful pregnancy termination, and that illegal and unsafe abortion, endangering women's life and health, is still very common. The Committee urged Poland to review the effects of the restrictive antiabortion law on women; conduct research into and provide statistics on the use of illegal abortion; introduce regulations to prohibit the improper use and performance of the 'conscience clause' by the medical profession; reduce medical commissions' response deadline in cases related to abortions.[52] We hope that under such massive international pressure the Polish government and medical community will finally undertake necessary regulatory, as well as institutional and educational measures to guarantee every Polish woman and man access to legal, safe and adequate reproductive and sexual health services.

---

50 See the list of all such reports on the website of the Federation for Women and Family Planning, available at www.federa.org.pl/index.php?option=com_content&view=article&id=408:raporty-zakoczone-rekomendacjami-cia-midzynarodowych-dla-polski&catid=81:raporty&Itemid=75, last accessed on May 13, 2013.

51 Consideration of Reports Submitted by States Parties Under Article 40 of the Covenant. Concluding observations of the United Nations Human Rights Committee—Poland, adopted in Geneva. October 26, 2010, U.N. Doc. CCPR/C/POL/CO/6, para. 12, available at daccess-dds-ny.un.org/doc/UNDOC/GEN/G10/466/84/PDF/G1046684.pdf, last accessed on May 13, 2013.

52 *Ibid.*

THE ABORTION PILL IN HUNGARY: A HUMAN RIGHTS ANALYSIS

Sára Vitrai

Introduction

In this chapter I shall argue that in the case of introducing the abortion pill in Hungary in 2012 (or rather by preventing its introduction), the Hungarian state has violated the fundamental rights of women to health, to privacy and, indirectly, to life. These rights are provided for Hungarian women by the Hungarian Constitution, the European Convention of Human Rights and the Universal Declaration of Human Rights, and therefore are inviolable.

The licensing of the abortion pill in Hungary reignited the moral arguments against abortion even though a new available method for abortion logically should not call into question the legality of abortion itself. Even though the government has expressed its intensions to make regulations of abortion stricter, so far it had not done so, apart form preventing the use of the abortion pill.

In the first section of the chapter the current regulation on abortion in Hungary will be discussed, along with the previous attempt to license the abortion pill and the availability of medication abortion before 2012. The second section of the chapter will describe the licensing process of the pill in 2012, presenting the arguments brought up against it, pointing to the underlying assumptions and concepts of the debate, and how these arguments shed light on an underlying political power struggle, in which women's rights to health, to privacy, and their right to life are being violated.

Present Regulation of Abortion in Hungary

Currently abortion in Hungary in regulated by the 1992 law on the protection of the fetus[1] which states that abortion may take place up to the 12th week of pregnancy if: *a)* it endangers the health of the mother *b)* the fetus is likely to have a severe disability or other impairment *c)* the pregnancy being a result of a crime or *d)* in case the pregnant women is in a "serious crisis situation." The law defines serious crisis situation as whatever "causes physical or psychological shock or social impairment."[2]

When a woman applies for an abortion, she must hand in her request to the Family Protection Service (Családvédelmi Szolgálat, CsVSz), along with a verification of the upstanding pregnancy by an obstetrician-gynecologist, and take part in two mandatory consultations.[3] If she receives permission from the employee of CsVSz, presently only surgical abortion is available to her in Hungary.[4]

An abortion in Hungary costs 29,710 forints (from the 1st of January 2011) which is only paid for by the state if it is done due to health endangering reasons[5] or one may receive a 50 percent, 70 percent or a 100 percent discount from the state based on their social status, and financial dependence.[6] One gets a 50 percent discount (has to pay 14,855 forints) if they receive child care benefit, child care support, temporary benefit, regular social aid, health impairment annuity, pension, disability benefits, or disability pension. One gets a 70 per-

---

1   Act No. LXXIX of 1992 on the Protection of the Fetus; available in Hungarian at net.jogtar.hu/jr/ gen/hjegy_doc.cgi?docid=99200079.TV; last accessed on June 5, 2013.

2   Under certain circumstances abortion is also allowed up to the 18th or 20th week of pregnancy.

3   During the first consultation the woman receives information on her possibilities if she would decide to keep the baby (state support, adoption, suggestions to eliminate the crisis situation, information on the conception of the fetus and the risks of abortion). During the second consultation she receives information on the abortion process itself (the legal regulation and circumstances of abortion and information on contraceptives).

4   The D&E surgical method used in Hungary happens as follows: "Dilatation and evacuation (D&E) is used from about 12 completed weeks of pregnancy. It is the safest and most effective surgical technique for later abortion where skilled, experienced providers are available . . . D&E requires preparing the cervix with mifepristone, a prostaglandin such as misoprostol, or laminaria or similar hydrophilic dilator, dilating the cervix; and evacuating the uterus using electric vacuum aspiration with 14–16mm diameter cannulae and forceps. Depending on the duration of pregnancy, adequate dilatation can require anything from two hours to a full day. Many providers find the use of ultrasound helpful during D&E procedures, but it is not essential." See World Health Organization, *Safe Abortions: Technical and Policy Guidance for Health Systems*, Second edition (Geneva: WHO, 2012); available online at apps.who.int/iris/bitstream/10665/70914/1/9789241548434_eng.pdf, last accessed on June 5, 2013.

5   Patent Association Activists, Variációk egy szándékra—Nyíltan a burkolt abortuszszigorításról [Variations of an Intention—Speaking Openly on a Hidden Tightening of Abortion Regulation], *Abortusz.info*, July 13, 2011; available at abortusz.info/hirek/hirek/variaciok-egy-szandekra-nyiltan-a-burkolt-abortuszszigoritasrol, last accessed on June 5, 2013.

6   Patent Association, Jogi szabályozás [Legal Regulations], *Abortusz.info*; available at abortusz.info/ info/jogi-szabalyozas, last accessed on June 5, 2013.

cent discount (has to pay 8,913 forints) if they receive unemployment benefits, jobseeker's allowance, job-search aid, care allowance, temporary aid, annuity for minors, regular child protection benefit, emergency social aid, annuity for business, income supplement or availability support. One gets a 100 percent discount if they receive higher family benefits, disability support, annuity for blind people or regular social aid.

Recent Events That Suggest a Change in Abortion Law

Recent events in Hungary suggest that politicians plan to make stricter laws on abortion. These events include the adoption of a new Fundamental Law, replacing the old Constitution in April 2011, which states that "the life of the fetus deserves protection from its conception."[7] This gave rise to a concern among Hungarian NGOs[8] that this could force the Constitutional Court of Hungary to declare abortion unconstitutional as a whole.[9] When questioned, governmental officials made contradictory statements on whether they intend to modify the legislation on abortion.[10] Shortly after the adoption of the Fundamental Law, the government launched a nationwide anti-abortion campaign in the spring of 2011,[11] then later that year in October the Christian Democratic People's Party (Kereszténydemokrata Néppárt, KDNP) handed in

---

7   In accordance with the adoption of the new Fundamental Law, the "respect and protection" of fetal life from its conception has also been added to the 1992 Act on the Protection of the Fetus, but the essence of the regulation remains untouched. See The Fundamental Law of Hungary; available at www.kormany.hu/download/0/d9/30000/Alaptörvény.pdf, last accessed on June 5, 2013.

8   Such as the Hungarian Helsinki Committee (Magyar Helsinki Bizottság, HHC); the Association of Women for Women Together Against Violence (Nők a Nőkért Együtt az Erőszak Ellen Egyesület, NANE); the Labrisz Lesbian Association (Labrisz Leszbikus Egyesület); the Patent Association: Opponents of Patriarchal Society (Patent Egyesület: Patriarchátust Ellenzők Társasága); the Stop Male Violence Project (Stop Férfierőszak Projekt), and the Hungarian Civil Liberties Union (Társaság a Szabadságjogokért, TASZ or HCLU).

9   Ágnes Dreissiger, Abortuszszigorítást kényszerítene ki az Alaptörvény? [Could the Fundamental Law Lead to a Tightening of Abortion Regulation?], *HVG.hu*, January 21, 2012; available at hvg.hu/itthon/20120119_alkotmany_abortusz, last accessed on June 5, 2013.

10   Magyar Hírlap, Nem tervez változást a Fidesz az abortusz szabályozásában [Fidesz Does Not Plan to Modify the Abortion Regulation], *Magyarhirlap.hu*, September 27, 2012; available at www.magyarhirlap.hu/egeszsegugy/nem-tervez-valtozast-a-fidesz-az-abortusz-szabalyozasaban, last accessed on June 5, 2013.

11   According to Miklós Soltész (Secretary of State for Social Policy at the Ministry of Human Resources), the government wanted to raise consciousness about the value of human life, despite the current legality of abortion in the country. He also denied that the campaign is a first step towards the prohibition of abortion: "Hungarian society isn't ready for the prohibition of abortion, like Poland for example . . . That is not what we are seeking. We want to insist on the importance of life." See Matthew Cullinan Hoffman, Hungary Sponsors Bold Pro-Life Campaign with EU Money: Eurocrats Enraged, *LifeSiteNews.com*, June 15, 2011; available at www.lifesitenews.com/news/hungary-sponsors-bold-pro-life-campaign-with-eu-money-eurocrats-enraged, last accessed on June 5, 2013.

an amendment proposal to the state budget of 2012 to withdraw funding from abortion; which latter didn't come into effect. And, finally, the government blocked the licensing of the abortion pill in May 2012, which will be discussed in detail below.[12]

In one of its articles, the Patent Association calls attention to the ways in which the government could make abortion less accessible without actually amending any law or by modifying them in a way so that the general public would not notice; because abortion would not actually be made illegal.[13] First, it would be enough to modify the technical terms of abortion[14] in order to make the process of getting an abortion harder to carry through. The terms and conditions of having an abortion consultation are regulated only by a ministerial order that can be amended easily. Second, the institutions that take part in an abortion consultation may also be changed: if priests are present, for example, they may induce religious guilt in women to change their mind about abortion.[15] Third, access to abortion can also be denied by applying the doctors' conscience clause more often.[16] Applying the clause may become more popular if future medical doctors are encouraged not to perform abortion during their university studies by not teaching them how to perform an abortion.

Fourth, medical institutes and universities in Hungary are currently authorized to decide which health impairments and genetic mutations may be regarded as reasons for abortion even beyond the twelfth week. These professional guidelines may be modified without any amendment to the law. Fifth, the cost of abortion may also be raised without amending the law. According to current regulation the "fee is equal to the amount of the respective social security financing."[17] The question of who is entitled to a discount on abortion based on

---

12 Stefánia Kapronczay and Melinda Zsolt, Alkotmányos támogatás az abortuszturizmusnak? [Constitutional Support for Abortion Tourism?] *A TASZ jelenti Blog* [TASZ Reports], September 28, 2012; available at ataszjelenti.blog.hu/2012/09/28/alkotmanyos_tamogatas_az_ abortuszturizmusnak, last accessed on June 5, 2013.

13 Patent Association Activists, *op. cit.*

14 For example, by making it mandatory in the protocol to make the woman look at the fetus on the screen during the ultrasound examination as part of the mandatory consultation (similarly as in parts of the US), in order for the mother to form an emotional attachment to the fetus.

15 For example, by advocating that having an abortion leads to psychological problems in the future such as 'post abortion syndrome', which has been proven by scientific research not to be a definable illness (even though abortion can be emotionally devastating for some women). According to the 1992 Act on the Protection of the Fetus, the only legal restriction regarding the consultation is that it must be done "with respect to the feelings and dignity of the pregnant woman." See Act No. LXXIX of 1992 on the Protection of the Fetus, *op. cit.*

16 A doctor may refrain from performing an abortion based on his/her personal religious convictions or good conscience, provided that the pregnancy isn't life threatening for the woman. Although Hungarian law states that every maternity hospital must "provide at least one group [of medical processionals] who will perform abortion," there is no legal sanction if a hospital fails to do so. See Patent Association, Jogi szabályozás, *op. cit.*

17 See Patent Association Activists, *op. cit.*

their social status is also regulated by ordinance, and can easily be modified.[18] And last, the 1992 Act on the Protection of the Fetus may also be amended in ways that may not seem significant at first glance, but makes getting an abortion more difficult—for example, if the law ruled that a committee should decide if the woman wanting an abortion is truly in a serious crisis situation, or if the waiting period between two consultations were prolonged[19] (which could potentially result in missing the twelfth week terminus of getting an abortion).

Attitudes towards Abortion in Hungary

A poll was conducted by a market research firm[20] specialized in health research after it became public that the government plans to adopt a new Fundamental Law instead of the Constitution. The poll was conducted online, with the method of self-completion. The sample contained 422 respondents, representative on gender and age. I present the findings of this survey here in order to illustrate the scale of public opposition the government would face if it were to make abortion regulations stricter and also to show how informed the general public is on the subject of abortion.

Fifty percent of the respondents agree that the fetus has the right to life from its conception. The opinion of one fifth of Hungarians is that the fetus has the right to life from the twelfth week of pregnancy; and according to another one fifth, the fetus has the right to life only from its birth (most of whom share this last opinion are those who already had an abortion, are non-religious, single, received higher education and earn more than 150,000 forints or 510 euros per month).[21]

Three-fourths of the respondents believe that it is everyone's individual decision whether they have an abortion, either for economic or for family reasons. According to 60 percent of the respondents abortion is mainly an individual matter, only 15–16 percent believes that it should be a moral decision as well as a medical one.

Concerning the current regulation on abortion—that women can decide more or less freely to have an abortion up to the twelfth week of pregnancy—sixty percent of the respondents was on the opinion that the regulation is sufficiently

---

18 If modified it may deepen the financial gap between women who seek an abortion. Research done in foreign countries suggests that among those who have lower income, the number of unwanted pregnancies is higher. In contrast wealthier women have easier access to contraceptives, and to abortion tourism (discussed in detail below). Ibid.

19 A woman seeking an abortion is obliged to wait at least three days between the two mandatory consultations described in footnote 2.

20 Szinapszis, Lehet-e magánügy az abortusz?—Kutatás [Could Abortion Be a Private Matter?—Research Results], Webbeteg.hu, March 22, 2011; available at www.webbeteg.hu/cikkek/egeszseges/10647/lehet-e-maganugy-az-abortusz, last accessed on June 5, 2013.

21 Ibid.

strict, while 17 percent believed that the current regulation is too permissive[22] and five percent stated that it is too strict (even though it is a liberal regulation, in comparison with those in many other countries).[23]

When asked to name those who are responsible for educating children to live a responsible sexual life, to learn how to use contraceptives, and to prepare for raising children, the majority named the family (94 percent) and the state (82 percent). Informative state media campaigns (39 percent) and gynecologists (41 percent) were also mentioned as responsible for children's education on the above topics.

Eighty-six percent of the respondents blamed the state for the high rate of abortions, criticizing poor sexual education and state support of abortions, also the lack of part time jobs. As to the question of why are there so many abortions, they mentioned ignorance; existential problems; the high price of contraceptives; financial problems; or "insufficient moral disposition" (mentioned by religious respondents).

Answering the question what the reasons for having an abortion would be, the respondents mentioned health issues (76 percent), pregnancy induced by rape (64 percent), and not being in the desired age (53 percent).

Previous Attempts to License the Abortion Pill

The abortion pill method, also known as medication abortion, is applied by taking two pills to end an early pregnancy: *mifepristone* blocks the activity of progesterone (a hormone which keeps up pregnancy) and *misoprostol* induces the process of miscarriage.[24]

Under the coordination of the WHO at the beginning of the 1990s, the abortion pill was tested in several countries, including Hungary at Obstetrics and Gynecology Clinic of Szeged (Szegedi Szülészeti és Nőgyógyászati Klinika). In 2005 the Hungarian Chamber of Obstetrics and Gynecology (Magyar Szülészeti és Nőgyógyászati Szakmai Kollégium, MSzNSzK) officially supported the introduction of the pill; within hospital conditions, up to the eighth week of preg-

---

22 Most of those who share this opinion are religious; families with several children; live in Budapest; and believe abortion should be done only if necessary for medical reasons.

23 Eighteen percent of the respondents did not form an opinion.

24 These pills should be taken under medical supervision, two days apart. After taking both pills one may experience vaginal bleeding for 9 to 30 days or longer, and has to go back for check up after 14 days—if not all of the fetus was removed, a surgical follow up abortion is necessary. One of the main differences between medical and surgical abortion is in the case of medication abortion, the woman is awake during the whole process, thus can experience it fully, possibly in the company of others. Known brands of the abortion pill include Mifegyne, Mifepristone, Mifeprex, and Medabon. Sándor Joób, Közelít az abortusztabletta Magyarországra [The Abortion Pill Approaches Hungary], *Index.hu*, April 23, 2012; available at index.hu/belfold/2012/04/23/abortusztabletta_nincs_es_megis_van/, last accessed on June 5, 2013.

nancy.[25] It was anticipated that the pill would be registered, and become a part of medical practice. The support of the Chamber of Obstetrics and Gynecology gained such an attention that the question quickly became debated by politicians and NGOs; and thus the licensing process was postponed.[26]

Availability of the Abortion Pill before May 2012

Although the pill was not registered, medication abortion was still accessible for those who were well-informed and were in a financial position to be able to access the pill. They had three options to obtain the pill: a private clinic in Budapest, clinics in Austria, and the Internet.

A Private Clinic

With a specific import license, one private clinic in Budapest legally provided medication abortions after 2010, under the condition that the patients have undergone compulsory medical examinations. In the first year they had 80 medication abortions, 210 in the next.[27]

Out of personal moral convictions, doctors undertook medication abortions only up to the seventh week of pregnancy, so most of the women treated by them were in the fifth or sixth weeks of their pregnancy. In this stage no embryo is yet visible via ultrasound; there is only a one centimeter size cluster of cells. According to one of the doctors at the clinic, at such an early stage of pregnancy, the medication abortion method seems to be the better choice, since in the case of surgical abortion, often one has to wait a few more weeks until the embryo is visible, to have a greater chance of removing all that needs to be removed from the uterus. Out of the 290 medication abortions conducted over these two years, only in seven cases (0.5 percent) was it necessary to finish the abortion surgically.

Since this was the only clinic in Hungary where medication abortion was practiced, they had a more strict protocol than similar clinics in other European countries. Right after the medication abortion and then a month after they conducted two ultrasound and pregnancy test check-ups to confirm that there was a full miscarriage.

---

25 They listed the pill as an alternative abortion method to the surgical procedure, which is less demanding on the female body. See Magyar Távirati Iroda [Hungarian Cable Bureau], Még idén bevezethetik az abortusztablettát Magyarországon [The Abortion Pill Might Be Introduced in Hungary Already This Year], *Velvet.hu*, June 7, 2005; available at velvet.hu/onleany/abort0607/, last accessed on June 5, 2013.

26 Joób, *op. cit.*

27 *Ibid.*

Abortion Tourism to Austria

In Austria several clinics offer the abortion pill as a method of abortion. On the website of one of the clinics there is even detailed information available in Hungarian; medication abortion here costs 490 euros (cca. 144,000 forints).[28]

Several women from Hungary—approximately two to four women a week in the spring of 2012[29]—visit these clinics in Austria because of the availability of medication abortion and also because they find the mandatory consultations in Hungary invasive into their personal life, the whole procedure to be burdensome, and the waiting time (between consultations) unnecessary. Women also complain that Hungarian hospital staff tends to behave in a disrespectful and derogatory way, and that they have to pay gratitude money.[30]

Through the Internet

The abortion pill may also be ordered through the internet for 30 to 70 euros (approximately 8,800 to 20,500 forints) but anyone who chooses to do so in Hungary commits a crime under Hungarian law.[31] One must also be aware that ordering through the internet always leaves the consumer vulnerable to possible fraud.[32]

The Patent Association had to deal with such a case, when a woman ordered the abortion pill in Hungary 2012, and experienced heavy bleeding, so went to a hospital. The doctor treated her and immediately after alerted the police, and she was taken to a police station. In this situation she called the emergency abortion hotline of Patent Association, to ask for legal advice. They advised her not to confess to anything, and follow up with them on the case later. Unfortunately the woman did not contact them afterwards.[33]

---

28 *Ibid.*
29 According to the head of a clinic in Vienna, Joób, *op. cit.* Abortion tourism doesn't violate any regulation. Women in Austria do not have to report their intention to have an abortion to any authorities, and the same applies to women from abroad as well.
30 It is a common practice in Hungary that after a successful operation or delivery, patients are expected to pay the doctor 'gratitude money' for their work. The amount is informally negotiated between the patient and doctor.
31 Under Section 169 of the Penal Code, anyone who performs an illegal abortion may be sentenced to five years in prison, and the woman who had an illegal abortion may be sentenced to one year in prison.
32 Women on Waves—an international women's rights organization fighting for safe abortions—has encountered such cases, and in order to prevent further occurrences, they provide the pill safely through their own webpage. Joób, *op. cit.*
33 Here I would like to stress the importance of comprehensive education and widespread distribution of information on the use of the pill, in order to avoid endangering the health and life of women who seek to use the pill. Even though it is currently illegal in Hungary, providing sufficient information may make a significant difference, similarly to the needle exchange program in the case of drug use.

There is a lack of available information not only on the effects and side-effects of the abortion pill, but also on the legal conditions of performing a surgical abortion, despite the fact that the latter has been regulated since 1992. According to the poll results mentioned above, almost half of the respondents (45 percent) didn't know if there is a legal regulation on abortion in place. Only nearly half of them (56 percent) knew the time limit set on having an abortion without any medical reason; not surprisingly this 56 percent was made up of women, most of them already having had an abortion.[34] This situation only worsened over the past year because the Hungarian government has increased uncertainty with regards to the regulation of abortion.

Attempt at Licensing in 2012

The most recent attempt to introduce the abortion pill in Hungary occurred in the spring of 2012, when a European Union authority[35] officially registered the abortion pill in several European countries, including Hungary.[36] As mentioned earlier, this reignited the moral arguments against abortion, despite that fact that it is simply a new method that should not call into question the whole legal regulation of abortion itself. I will present the arguments brought up against the introduction of the abortion pill, and will point to some underlying assumptions and concepts of the debate.

The licensing of the pill came up on the parliamentary session of May 14, 2012, during which Kálmán Nagy (KDNP, Member of Parliament and Health Committee member) asked the government to block the abortion pill from entering the Hungarian market and, if necessary, to ask the Constitutional Court to deem the drug unconstitutional. Dr. Miklós Szócska, State Secretary for Health at the Ministry of Human Resources (Emberi Erőforrások Minisztériuma, EMMI) replied to the request that the registry of the drug was a legal obligation of Hungary as part of an international licensing process; however this does not mean that the pill will actually be in use. He reassured the Christian Democrats that the government does not support the introduction of the abortion pill to the Hungarian market.[37] What did this reassurance mean in practice?

According to the Hungarian health care law, Dr. Szócska's promise is not legally binding. The medical profession regards medically induced abortion

---

34 Szinapszis, *op. cit.*
35 This authority is the Heads of Medicines Agencies (HMA), "a network of the heads of the National Competent Authorities whose organizations are responsible for the regulation of medicinal products for human and veterinary use in the European Economic Area," see www.hma.eu, last accessed on June 5, 2013.
36 Under the brand name Medabon, see mri.medagencies.org/Human/Product/Details/26878, last accessed on June 5, 2013.
37 Népszabadság Online, Engedélyezték Magyarországon is az abortusz tablettát [The Abortion Pill Has Been Licensed in Hungary, As Well], *NOL*, May 19, 2012; available at nol.hu/belfold/engedelyeztek_magyarorszagon_is_az_abortusz_tablettat, last accessed on June 5, 2013.

as viable method, and so it should be accessible in Hungary after its registration by the National Institute of Pharmacy (Országos Gyógyszerészeti Intézet, OGYI) in mid-May 2012. What is in state secretary's power is that he can prevent the acceptance of the drug by the National Health Insurance Fund (Országos Egészségbiztosítási Pénztár, OEP), which would mean that the drug could only be bought by the hospitals at a full price, not supported by social security. According to a health policy expert, Gyula Kincses, if the government were to turn to the Constitutional Court—as MP Nagy suggested—the Court could not make a decision regarding the application of the pill (it is a medical and not a legal issue) but if asked to interpret the law—based on the recently adopted new Fundamental Law—it might come to the decision of banning abortion.[38]

In the following I will provide a description of the debate that took place during the course of May 2012 and the following month surrounding the licensing of the abortion pill. I have structured the emerging discourse into the following four major fields: first, the lack of professional debate on health risks; second, demographic concerns about unborn Hungarians; third, the view that if abortion is wrong, then medication abortion should also be wrong; and four, ulterior motives. Those who argued against medication abortion often used a combination of these four arguments.

The Lack of Professional Debate on Health Risks

In its public statement on the abortion pill on May 23, 2012, the Ministry of Human Resources stated that since the risks of medication abortion and its long term effects are still being debated, the pill will not be licensed and therefore it will not be accepted by OEP. Dr. Szócska also emphasized that the government is committed to continue the awareness raising campaign that it had started in 2010, to support responsible life and family planning. They listed as one of their top priorities to raise awareness and to educate, to shape attitudes and effectively help girls and women who are in a difficult situation due to their pregnancy.[39]

However, the organizations of the medical profession denied that there was any debate on the safety of the pill or its side effects, and assured the public that, under correct medical supervision, medication abortion is perfectly safe. There were medical professionals who actually said that although they do not support abortion in general they still advocate medication abortion, because if there has to be an abortion, it should be done in the easiest way possible for the doctors

---

38 Anna Danó, Szócska Miklós nem tilthat, van tabletta [Miklós Szócska Cannot Ban the Pill], *NOL*, May 23, 2012; available at nol.hu/belfold/20120523-van_tabletta, last accessed on June 5, 2013.

39 Dr. Miklós Szócska, Közlemény az abortusztabletta engedélyezéséről [Announcement on the licensing of the abortion pill] *Kormányportál* [Government Portal], May 23, 2012; available at www.kormany.hu/hu/emberi-eroforrasok-miniszteriuma/egeszsegugyert-felelos-allamtitkarsag/hirek/kozlemeny-az-abortusztabletta-engedelyezeserol, last accessed on June 5, 2013.

and the women as well.[40] The abortion pill is registered on the WHO Model List of Essential Medicines[41], and MSzNSzK also supported the use of the pill.[42] According to János Demeter, president of MSzNSzK, there is no professional debate concerning the pill, it could be legally used in Hungary, but simply nobody has marketed it yet. Even if it were available, the pill would not be distributed in pharmacies, only in hospitals, to ensure medical supervision.[43]

On the other hand, Dr. Szócska, when describing how medication abortion works, mentioned heavy bleeding and strong cramps, for which analgesics might be necessary. And even though the patient may go home after a few days of medical supervision, the bleeding might continue for days, even weeks.[44] After asking the government to stop the abortion pill from entering the Hungarian market, MP Nagy continued by saying that medication abortion actually comes with an even higher risk than surgical abortion—which they (the KDNP) are also against.[45] He also spoke of a long period of bleeding after taking the pill (which may even require blood transfusion[46]), and also referred to the pill actually not even being effective as an abortion pill.[47] He went on to say that he thinks taking the pill comes with much a bigger psychological burden than having a surgical abortion.[48] He said "I would like [them] to be emotionally sound mothers who are fit to give birth to a child. Furthermore they should not experience such a shock if they do not have to."[49] He emphasized that when a woman takes the second pill she is left alone, without a doctor or her partner, the responsibility being entirely hers.[50]

---

40 B.I.M., Vita az élet feletti döntés jogáról [Debate on the Right to Decide over Life], *Népszava Online*, May 23, 2012; available at www.nepszava.hu/articles/article.php?id=553101, last accessed on June 5, 2013.

41 World Health Organization, *WHO Model List of Essential Medicines for Adults*, Seventeenth Edition, March 2011 (Geneva: WHO, 2011); available at whqlibdoc.who.int/hq/2011/a95053_eng.pdf, last accessed on June 5, 2013.

42 In 2005 MSzNSzK gave its official support to the introduction of the pill, but within hospital conditions, up to the eighth week of pregnancy. They listed the pill as an alternative abortion method to the surgical procedure, which is less demanding of the female body.

43 Joób, *op. cit.*

44 Népszabadság Online, Engedélyezték . . . , *op. cit.*

45 Máté Nyusztay, Koszos lábú hangulatkeltők, szemét haszonlesők—így vitázott a "T." Ház [Dirty Footed Malcontents, Trashy Profiteers—Thus Clashed the "Honorable" House], *NOL*, May 21, 2012; available at nol.hu/belfold/hangulatkeltesnek_koszos_a_laba_-_a_parlamentbol_jelentjuk, last accessed on June 5, 2013

46 Judit Muhari, Férfiak hajtják el az abortusztablettát [It Is Men Who Drive Away the Abortion Pill], *Népszava Online*, May 22, 2012; available at www.nepszava.hu/articles/article.php?id=552689, last accessed on June 5, 2013.

47 Levente Bucsy, Ez a tabletta nem lesz bevezetve Magyarországon [This Pill Will Not Be Introduced in Hungary], *Magyar Nemzet Online*, May 23, 2012; available at mno.hu/belfold/ez-a-tabletta-nem-lesz-bevezetve-magyarorszagon-1078255, last accessed on June 5, 2013.

48 Dóra Matalin, Részvét nélkül [Without Compassion], *NOL*, May 22, 2012; available at nol.hu/belfold/20120522-reszvet_nelkul, last accessed on June 5, 2013.

49 Bucsy, *op. cit.*

50 Hirado.hu, Nem lesz abortusztabletta Magyarországon [There Will Not Be an Abortion Pill in Hungary], *Magyar Hírlap Online*, May 23, 2012; available at www.magyarhirlap.hu/node/323585, last accessed on June 5, 2013.

Interestingly the opposite of this argument was also made by MP Nagy himself when fear was expressed that since medication abortion is a less dramatic process, women wouldn't take abortion as seriously as if they have a surgical abortion, which will raise the number of abortions (see more on this argument in next chapter). He also noted that during the early use of the abortion pill, some of the women died.[51]

A third active member of the debate was Alfa Association (Alfa Szövetség), a pro-life organization that organized a demonstration against the licensing of the pill on May 23, 2012.[52] The leader of the association, Imre Téglásy stated that he thinks there is no evidence to medication abortion having a lower risk than surgical abortion.[53] He went on to say that the Alfa Association is interested in a "respectful and peaceful discussion," because the public has to be clearly informed about the pill, since it hasn't been clear so far that the pill isn't a drug but a "toxic compound" ("*méregvegyület*")[54] that caused eleven women's deaths up until 2005. He also used the expression that the pill is a "weapon in the history of modern warfare against the Hungarians."[55] This nationalist undertone, that abortion means an attack on the Hungarian nation was even more pronounced among the arguments listed under "demographic concerns" and "ulterior motives" below.[56] During this demonstration the association handed out flyers that said that taking the abortion pill may have "brutal consequences."[57] These flyers depicted an apple, its peeled off skin becoming a snake. Under the picture it read: "The RU486[58] is poison. It kills the 'fetuschild' [sic] when its heart is already beating. We know of 11 pregnant women's deaths so far. Who's next?"[59]

---

51 The argument that several women in different countries had died due to medication abortion in the previous years came up frequently as an argument against the pill, but the number of deaths varied according to who gave the argument. Ildikó Csuhaj, A KDNP megfúrta a tablettát? [Has KNDP Dodged the Pill?], *NOL*, May 22, 2012; available at nol.hu/lap/mo/20120522-a_kdnp_megfurta_a_tablettat, last accessed on June 5, 2013.

52 Ferenc Bakró Nagy and Péter Szabó, A magyarok abortusszal teszik boldoggá a Sátánt [Hungarians Make the Satan Happy with Abortion], *Index.hu Video*, May 23, 2012; available at index.hu/video/2012/05/23/abortuszellenes_tuntetes/, last accessed on June 5, 2013.

53 Dóra Matalin, *op. cit.*

54 B.I.M., *op. cit.*

55 Index, A magzatvédők szerint az abortusztabletta a rejtőzködő fasizmus eszköze [According to the Pro-Life Advocates, the Abortion Pill Is a Means of Clandestine Fascism], *Index*, May 23, 2012; available at index.hu/belfold/2012/05/23/a_magzatvedok_szerint_az_abortusztabletta_a_rejtozkodo_fasizmus_eszkoze/, last accessed on June 5, 2013.

56 Here I would like to refer to Ruth Miller, who argues that the shift from political to biopolitical in the nineteenth century involved the collapse of abortion, adultery and rape into one political/legal category, blurring of the line between sexual and reproductive crime. This meant that committing such crime was regarded as an act against the nation (possibly leading to 'race suicide'). See Ruth A. Miller, Women and the Political Norm, in *The Limits of Bodily Integrity: Abortion, Adultery, and Rape Legislation in Comparative Perspective* (Aldershot, Hampshire, England; Burlington, VT: Ashgate, 2007), 149–174.

57 Családháló.hu, Hogy pusztítja el a magzatot az abortusztabletta? [How Does the Abortion Pill Destroy the Fetus?], *Magyar Nemzet Online*, May 28, 2012; available at mno.hu/csaladhalo/hogy-pusztitja-el-a-magzatot-az-abortusztabletta-1079204, last accessed on June 5, 2013.

58 The medical code name of the drug.

59 Index, A magzatvédők szerint . . ., *op. cit.*

Those women choosing medication abortion at the mentioned Hungarian private clinic had two main reasons for doing so: first, they believe that this way they have a greater chance to get pregnant in the future, and second, this way they can maintain control over their body during the process, being less vulnerable to the hospital staff. Still some women rather quickly 'get over with it' via the surgical method.[60] According to a doctor working at the clinic, the women who had medication abortion complained the least about the cramps caused by the pill; it was the long lasting bleeding that they were concerned about.[61]

Ann Oakley argues that in order to achieve social control through antenatal care, the state and the medical profession would have to form an alliance in which the health sector is embedded in the state's corporate power: the state controls the social and economic organization of the medical profession, but provides its technical autonomy. In contemporary Hungary, this alliance seems to be disrupted, since the government is insisting on dictating through what abortion method may be conducted.[62]

Demographic Concerns about Unborn Hungarians

Apart from arguing that medication abortion in itself is a harmful method to one's health, those opposing the abortion pill, after describing the dangers of the pill, often continued by expressing their fear that the high percentage of abortions, which will supposedly grow if medication abortion is available, might lead to a (further) decrease in Hungary's population.

Kálmán Nagy argued that "in a country where for every one hundred live births there are 40–50 abortions, when in West-Europe there is only 8–15, there is no need to introduce any new form of abortion. Furthermore everything has to be done to lower the number of abortions to a minimum."[63] He went on to say that "a medium sized city isn't born in Hungary [each year]"[64] He further stated that WHO recommended the pill to overpopulated countries. However, according to the statistics of WHO, in countries where the pill is available the number of abortions did not increase.[65]

---

60 Being conscious during medication abortion—although having control—at the same time may prove to be traumatizing for some.
61 Joób, *op. cit.*
62 See Ann Oakley, *The Captured Womb: A History of the Medical Care of Pregnant Women* (Oxford: Basil Blackwell, 1984), 250–274.
63 Hirado.hu, *op. cit.*
64 Bucsy, *op. cit.*
65 On the WHO Model List of Essential Medicines there is no mention of recommending a medicine for overpopulated countries. And even though medication abortion has been available in several European countries over the past years, the number of abortions in these countries has been almost stagnant or actually decreased. See European Health for all Database; available at data.euro.who. int/hfadb/, last accessed on June 5, 2013.

During its demonstration, the Alfa Association stated that in the last half century about six million children couldn't be born due to abortions.[66] Dóra Dúró, a Member of Parliament representing the right-wing party Jobbik, said that the abortion pill shouldn't be introduced in Hungary because it would be "the continuation of the 'Holocaust of the Nation' (*'nemzeti vészkorszak'*) caused by the high number of abortions."[67]

Condemning Abortion Should Also Mean Condemning the Pill?

Many who argued against medication abortion, actually argued against abortion itself, although a newly available method logically shouldn't call into question the legality of abortion in general.

András Csókay neurosurgeon stated that "abortion is the biggest crime of the past century," that life begins with conception and everybody has a right to life (merging a religious and a legal argument).[68] Zsolt Semjén (chairman of KDNP, and Deputy Prime Minister) said during the demonstration of Alfa Association that "children in their fetus age" are the most disenfranchised and vulnerable minority who cannot "voice their own interests" and so they (the KDNP) have an obligation to do it for them.[69] I left such expressions as "children in their fetus age" and "fetuschild" in quotation marks to illustrate how, simply with the use of such words—which are essentially made up and inaccurate—try to argue for abortion being equal to murder. This argument can be derived from the added half sentence in the Hungarian Constitution as well, which I will discuss in detail below.

Economic and Political Motives

Many also argued that it was the economic interest of the European Union and the manufacturers of the medication that led to the licensing of the pill in Hungary, also that it was done without informing the general public. Dr. Szócska

---

66 Magyar Távirati Iroda, "Nemzeti vészkorszak" Együtt tilakozott Semjén, Dúró és Novák ["Holocaust of the Nation": Semjén, Dúró, and Novák Protest Together], *ATV.hu*, May 23, 2012; available at atv.hu/cikk/20120523_politikusok_is_tiltakoztak_az_abortusztabletta_bevezetese_ellen, last accessed on June 5, 2013.

67 Népszabadság Online, Vészharangot kongattak az abortusztabletta miatt [Ringing Alarm Bells Because of the Abortion Pill], *NOL*, May 23, 2012; available at nol.hu/belfold/veszharangot_kongattak_az_abortusztabletta_miatt, last accessed on June 5, 2013.

68 Index, A magzatvédők szerint . . ., *op. cit.*

69 Magyar Távirati Iroda, Abortusztabletta: együtt tüntet a Novák család és Semjén [Abortion Pill: The Novák Family and Semjén Protest Together], *HVG.hu*, May 23, 2012; available at hvg.hu/itthon/20120523_abortusztabletta_tuntetes, last accessed on June 5, 2013.

himself stated on a TV program that there were economic interests behind licensing the abortion pill.[70]

The abortion pill, however, is manufactured in several parts of the world, including France, India, or China.[71] According to the Hungarian news site *Index* there may have been actually economic interest involved in that the pill *wasn't* brought into Hungary *sooner.*[72] With the number of abortions decreasing in Hungary[73] and marketing of a drug being quite expensive, it wasn't in the manufacturers' interest before to introduce the drug in Hungary. Nevertheless, the *Index* article also cites the export manager of Exelgyn Laboratories, a French manufacturer of Mifegyne, who said that they had initiated the registration of the drug in Hungary in 2007, but it was interrupted due to administrative reasons. They also initiated the registration of Misoprostol in 2011. According to the National Institute of Pharmacy[74], another company, presumably different from Exelgyn, initiated a procedure simultaneously in several EU countries in the fall of 2009, including Hungary.[75] And, according to the *Index* interview, Exelgyn Laboratories is determined to license the drug as soon as possible (they have started negotiations with the Hungarian drug authorities).

As mentioned earlier, even if the registration is successful, the drug could be widely accessible only if it were accepted by the OEP as a medication supported by the health insurance system. Besides the moral grounds on which the state secretary and other politicians oppose the introduction of the pill, there are also economic interests involved on the part of the Hungarian government. It cannot be clearly concluded that medication abortion would cost less for social security than the surgical solution. Medication abortion is similar to surgical abortion in that both require a hospital environment and the readiness of medical personnel—although in favorable conditions there is no need for an anesthesiologist and an equipped operating room in the case of a medication abortion. In the private clinic mentioned earlier, a medi-

---

70 Magyar Távirati Iroda, Szócska: Hazánkban nem kerül forgalomba az abortusztabletta [Szócska: The Abortion Pill Will Not Be Marketed in Our Homeland], *Fidesz.hu*, May 22, 2012; available at www.fidesz.hu/index.php?Cikk=180909, last accessed on June 5, 2013.

71 Joób, *op. cit.*

72 *Ibid.*

73 There were 197,000 abortions in Hungary in 1970, 90,000 in 1990, it dropped under 50,000 after 2000. Finally there were 38,000 abortions done in 2011. Joób, *op. cit.*

74 As of May 2011, the National Institute of Pharmacy (Országos Gyógyszerészeti Intézet, OGYI) is a Directorate of the National Institute for Quality and Organization Development in Healthcare and Medicines (Gyógyszerészeti és Egészségügyi Minőség- és Szervezetfejlesztési Intézet, GYEMSZI).

75 The licensing procedure usually takes seven months, but that regards the time within which the authorities should make a decision, so in case the documentation isn't complete and the company is required to submit additional information, its response doesn't count against the seven months; see Joób, *op. cit.*

cation abortion, including medical service, costs 98,000 forints[76] as opposed to the approximately 30,000 forint cost of surgical abortion.

At the demonstration mentioned above, Gábor Jobbágyi, professor of law said that no one knew about the intention of licensing the abortion pill apart from the registration bodies and one member of the government[77] and so the whole process can be called "a coup."[78] He added that the allegation that Hungary was obligated to license the pill is not true, since the European Union deemed abortion regulation a 'matter of national competence', when Ireland joined. He asked, "what obligations can an Indian company impose on the EU?" referring to the pill being also manufactured in India, as already mentioned. He also questioned the validity of the claim brought up for supporting the use of the pill, namely that it is under a registration procedure in several countries. "The several countries are 37. And how many countries are in the world? More than two hundred. So in the majority of countries the pill isn't licensed." "I also ask: how can it be that a group of doctors exterminates their own people? Let's speak Hungarian! ("*beszéljünk magyarul!*" — meaning "let's talk clearly!" or "let's be clear!")."[79]

Mr. Téglásy stated that politicians must take responsibility for the fact that the licensing was done "undercover" ("*fű alatt*" or "under the grass") without having a public debate on the matter, and added that if it is true that Hungary had to automatically license the pill, then this EU regulation is a "serious violation of our national sovereignty."[80] Téglásy went on to say that politicians are only concerned with the issue because they know that "there is a great deal at stake, it is about our last national treasure" ("*itt nem babra megy a játék, utolsó nemzeti kincsünkről van szó.*"[81] However, it isn't clear from his statement what exactly "our last national treasure" is. The method of surgical abortion? He went on to note that the manufacturers of the pill changed their name because they didn't want to take responsibility for their involvement with supplying Hitler's gas chambers with nerve gas,[82] but they are still motivated by "the philosophy

---

76 The pill costs approximately 20,000 forints, the rest is the cost of the medical knowledge and readiness of the doctors, to minimize the health risks related to the medication abortion. It may happen that intervention is needed because of the heavy bleeding of the woman, so the private clinic in Hungary that provided medication abortion kept an operating room running 24 hours a day. See Joób, *op. cit.*

77 Zsófia Jobbágyi, Napi százötven magzatot ölnek meg hazánkban [Hundred and Fifty Fetuses Are Killed Each Day in Our Country], *Magyar Hírlap Online*, May 24, 2012; available at www.magyarhirlap.hu/belfold/napi_szazotven_magzatot_olnek_meg_hazankban.html, last accessed on June 5, 2013.

78 Bucsy, *op.cit.*

79 *Ibid.*

80 W.L. (László Wunderli), Tiltakoznak az abortusztabletta ellen [Demonstration against the Abortion Pill], *Magyar Nemzet Online*, May 21, 2012; available at mno.hu/magyar_nemzet_belfoldi_hirei/tiltakoznak-az-abortusztabletta-ellen-1077535, last accessed on June 5, 2013.

81 B.I.M., *op. cit.*

82 Bucsy, *op.cit.*

of destruction, death, demolition" ("*a pusztítás, halál, rombolás filozófiája*").[83] The "hidden fascism" ("*rejtőzködő fasizmus*") wants to scam the people of the country and the government.[84]

In sum, all arguments bought up against the abortion pill are more about an ongoing power struggle than an actual concern for women's health—since each of the four types of argument can be easily refuted by simple fact-finding. This power struggle is perpetuated between political parties and also between medical professionals and the state.

Political Struggles beyond the Question of Abortion Method

The eagerness of certain political parties to express their opinion on abortion may be interpreted as their attempt to prove that they are well-equipped for occupying the position of the sovereign, since in the age of biopower it is the right of the sovereign state "to make live and let die."[85] How the introduction of a new abortion method becomes an issue purportedly threatening *national sovereignty* can be explained by Agamben's theory of exceptional politics.[86] In a state of exception the distinction between legislative, executive and juridical powers is blurred and one branch of the state is invested with powers over other the branches. The sovereign decides on the outlines of exceptional politics and determines who is a public friend or a public enemy. The constant redefinition of public friend and public enemy results in a polarization: all relationships (political, economic, social, religious) are shifted towards each of these two 'extreme' categories. I argue that in the abortion debate the European Union has been characterized as a public enemy, threatening Hungary.

The Struggle between Political Parties

At the same time, the political spectrum in Hungary has also become more polarized than ever before: the two 'clusters' of left and right are clearly distinguishable in their views on abortion in general, and on the abortion pill, in particular. The center-right Fidesz–KDNP coalition, which has a two-thirds majority in parliament, frequently allies itself with the extreme-right party Jobbik and, in response, the left-wing parties have also closed their ranks on this matter.

---

83 Index, A magzatvédők szerint . . ., *op. cit.*
84 Bucsy, *op.cit.*
85 Michel Foucault, "*Society Must Be Defended*": Lectures at the Collège de France, 1975–1976, Mauro Berani and Alessandro Fontana (eds.), translated by David Macey (New York: Picador, 2003), 240, 246; see also Foucault, *The History of Sexuality, Volume I: An Introduction* (New York: Vintage Books, 1990), 138.
86 Giorgio Agamben, *State of Exception* (Chicago: The University of Chicago Press, 2005).

While the members of KDNP and Jobbik explicitly declared their intention to make abortion regulation stricter, they also acknowledged that they would encounter a too big resistance from society if they were to do so. This is reflected in the already quoted argument by Mr. Soltész that "Hungarian society isn't ready for the prohibition of abortion, like Poland, for example."[87] The opposing socialist party (Magyar Szocialista Párt, MSZP) stated, in contrast, they are "strongly committed against the violation women's right to self-determination." Kata Kormos (spokesperson of MSZP) stated that "a party has no say on a topic that is the free choice of citizens and belongs in the competence of science. The duty and responsibility of politics—in this question as well—is to provide rules, laws that ensure the freedom of the decision and deliberation for families and doctors."[88]

Between Medical Professionals and the State

It has become clear that although the introduction of the abortion pill has been postponed, the government coalition does not have a uniform opinion on how to regulate abortion. Moreover, the state's alliance with the medical profession has also been disrupted, as the government didn't ensure the professional autonomy of the field but, instead, it insisted on regulating abortion even to the extent of limiting the available methods by which abortion may be performed.

I have already established that there is no debate within the medical profession on the advantages and risks of the abortion pill, contrary to the claim of those opposing abortion of any kind. Nevertheless, the resistance of medical professionals against the banning of the abortion pill was not unified and strong because of the political pressure on them. For example, the private clinic in Budapest that had legally provided medication abortion after 2010 (with a specific import license), given that the patients underwent the compulsory medical examinations, had to terminate this health care service, due to the administrative obstacles created by the government. Furthermore, when the Hungarian daily newspaper *Népszabadság* wanted to ask MSzNSzK on whether they plan to change the procedure of abortion, they gave no comment. It turned out later that they were asked by State Secretary Szócska not to make public statements on the issue.[89]

---

87 Hoffman, *op. cit.*
88 Magyar Távirati Iroda, Az MSzP támogatja az abortusztablettát [The MSzP Supports the Abortion Pill], *HVG.hu*, March 23, 2012; available at hvg.hu/itthon/20120523_abortusztabletta_mszp, last accessed on June 5, 2013.
89 Danó, *op. cit.*

The Right to Health and Life

I further argue that by being more concerned with matters of power, the Hungarian government violates women's right to health, provided for them by the Universal Declaration of Human Rights and also stated in the Fundamental Law of Hungary itself. According to article 25 of the Universal Declaration of Human Rights "(1) Everyone has the right to a standard of living adequate for the health and well-being of himself and of his family, including food, clothing, housing and medical care and necessary social services . . .; (2) Motherhood and childhood are entitled to special care and assistance . . ."[90] Furthermore, the Hungarian Constitution states that "Everyone has the right to physical and mental health" and that that Hungary will facilitate this right by "the organization of health care."[91]

By denying access to the abortion pill the Hungarian state has violated Hungarian women's right to health, according to the two legal norms mentioned above. There is no other comparable case in which the political decision of blocking the most advanced medical procedure available, when it is proven safe, is supported by legal arguments.

The Hungarian state's refusal to introduce this pill also indirectly violates the right to life of Hungarian women,[92] by putting their life in danger by not providing the necessary legal framework and information on the abortion pill—thus making it possible that women ordering the abortion medication through the Internet receive fake pills (as in the case mentioned above).

Right to Privacy

Based on the decision made in the *Roe v. Wade* case[93]—which provides an example in abortion regulation all over the world—I also argue that the Hungarian state wrongly balances women's right to privacy[94] with its interest in protecting prenatal life. The United States Supreme Court argued in its decision that state's interest in protecting prenatal life becomes stronger over the course of a pregnancy, based on the trimesters of pregnancy: the state's interest is the lowest in the first trimester, where the woman's right to privacy has the highest priority. We have seen that medication abortion can be done earlier in the first trimester

---

90 Universal Declaration of Human Rights, adopted in New York on December 10, 1948; available at www.un.org/en/documents/udhr/index.shtml, last accessed on June 5, 2013.
91 The Fundamental Law of Hungary, *op. cit.*
92 Provided to them by Article 3 of the Universal Declaration of Human Rights and the Hungarian Constitution.
93 See *Roe v. Wade*, en.wikipedia.org/wiki/Roe_v._Wade, last accessed on June 5, 2013.
94 Provided to them by Article 8 of the European Convention of Human Rights, adopted in Rome on November 4, 1950; available at www.echr.coe.int/Documents/Convention_ENG.pdf, last accessed on June 5, 2013.

(as early as in the fifth week) when the state should have even less interest in the protection of fetus, and so it has no right to restrict the legal method of abortion in this period.

Conclusions

In this chapter I argued that the government of Hungary, by preventing the introduction of medication abortion in Hungary in 2012, has violated the fundamental rights of women to health, to privacy and indirectly their right to life, which are provided for them by the Fundamental Law of Hungary, the European Convention of Human Rights, and the Universal Declaration of Human Rights. I have shown how the arguments brought up against medication abortion are part of a domestic biopolitical debate on reproduction, and how these claims can be refuted.

These arguments can be summarized as follows. Concerning the *health risks* involved, the opponents of medication abortion argued that there are doubts among the doctors and medical experts regarding the safety of the pill's use, even though those working in the medical profession all denied the existence of such a debate. Furthermore, most doctors interviewed stated that medical abortion is a method easier for the doctors and gentler for the women. The abortion pill is registered on the WHO Model List of Essential Medicines, and the Hungarian Chamber of Obstetrics and Gynecology also supports the use of the pill.

Regarding *demographic concerns*, the second type of argument against the introduction of the abortion pill claims that it would increase the number of abortions in Hungary—because medical abortion is a less dramatic process and therefore women wouldn't take abortion as seriously as in the case when they have no choice other than surgical abortion. However, according to the statistics of the World Health Organization, in countries where the pill is legally available the number of abortions did not increase.

The third type of argument reasons that since *abortion is wrong*, any technique to induce abortion should also be considered wrong, including the abortion pill. This is problematic because the introduction of a new method should not call into question the legality of abortion itself. The fourth type of argument against the abortion pill cites *economic and political interests* and claims that the abortion pill was 'secretly' licensed in Hungary only because of the economic gains it means for its foreign manufacturers, thus, by extrapolation, it is yet another way of exploiting Hungary by the European Union. In this view, the lack of information available on the licensing and limited use of the pill in Hungary also serves foreign interests. The existence of economic interests is undeniable, but this in itself doesn't undermine the safety or the positive effects of the drug.

PERCEPTION OF HUMAN EMBRYOS AND ASSISTED REPRODUCTION TECHNOLOGY REGULATIONS IN THE ARAB STATES[1]

Orio Ikebe

Introduction

The advancement of embryology and reproductive technologies provided ways for people to overcome infertility but at the same time offered possibilities to become a parent in unconventional ways. Since the birth of the first baby conceived *in vitro* in the United Kingdom in 1978, the conception of an embryo was separated from pregnancy. This gives various choices at each stage, for example, whose sperm and ovule to use to conceive an embryo, whether to select only embryos with suitable genetic component and discard others, whether to cryopreserve for later use or to generate pregnancy immediately, and whose womb to use. These choices, which were not possible without the advanced technologies, now challenge the traditional concepts of family, parenthood, kinship, self-identity, and the concept of life. In an era of rapid globalization, new reproductive technologies and advanced infertility treatments are quickly applied all over the world and the countries that do not produce technologies often become big consumers of such technologies.

What happens when the imported technologies confront with the cultural and religious values embedded in the recipient society? How will the ethical

---

1   The ideas and opinions expressed in this article are those of the author and do not necessarily represent the view of UNESCO. The author is responsible for the choice and the presentation of the facts contained in this chapter and for the opinions expressed therein, which are not necessarily those of UNESCO and do not commit the Organization.

implications of new technologies be resolved in their new cultural context? This paper attempts to answer these questions while focusing on Arab countries where Islamic teachings have a strong influence in guiding the ethical conduct of people's everyday's life. Particular attention is paid to the examination of how ethical reasoning is found and formulated in their religious and traditional values in accepting or rejecting certain technologies.

As Inhorn points out, medical anthropologists are recently acknowledging "the importance of locality in the global dispersion of modern biotechnologies" which has much to do with "local moral system" or what Arthur Kleinman called "local moral worlds."[2] The assumption of this paper is that a society is not a passive recipient of globalized new technologies; imported technologies are carefully examined and only technologies that do not contradict or that serve to reinforce embedded values and morality in the society will be selected and applied. But at the same time, the shared values of the society are defined by the people in the society and are subject to change in a particular historical time and space. Likewise, the ethical reasoning employed to regulate certain technologies shifts along with the changing values in the society.

In the first part of this chapter, a discussion that took place at the United Nations over the issue of human cloning will be examined in order to understand the ethical and political ramifications of the moral status of human embryos in the international community and the position of the Arab states. Then the Islamic teachings on the concept of human embryos and national regulations on human embryo research in Arab countries will be surveyed to examine whether there is any discrepancy between theory and practice and if there is, why. In the following section, regulations on various assisted reproduction technologies (ART) in Arab countries and the ethical reasoning behind them will be examined to analyze how certain cultural and religious values are reaffirmed or shifted along with the introduction of new technologies in the Arab region. For that purpose, the regulations on certain issues that present unique ethical reasoning based on a cultural and religious context in Arab countries will be focused on, namely third party involvement in ART, creation of human embryos for research purposes and pre-implantation genetic diagnosis (PGD) for gender selection.

Finally, the impact of ARTs such as gamete donation and intracytoplasmic sperm injection (ICSI), the technique that overcomes male infertility by injecting a sperm into an ovule with a micropipette, will be examined comparing the situations in Sunni and Shi'a Muslim countries. Both groups of countries share to some extent the same ethical principles in the application of ART but prioritizing different values in their societies lead to contrasting gamete donation policies.

---

2   Marcia C. Inhorn, Making Muslim Babies: IVF and Gamete Donation in Sunni versus Shi'a Islam, in
    Aditya Bharadwaj (guest ed.) Special Issue on "Divine Intervention and Sacred Conceptions: Religion
    in the Global Practice of IVF," *Culture, Medicine, and Psychiatry*, December 2006, 30(4): 427–450; Arthur
    Kleinman and Joan Kleinman, Suffering and Its Professional Transformation: Toward an Ethnography
    of Interpersonal Experience, *Culture, Medicine, and Psychiatry*, September 1991, 15(3): 275–301.

The Moral Status of Human Embryos in the International Community and the Position of the Arab States

In 2001, France and Germany proposed to the United Nations to organize a convention against human reproductive cloning. Initially, the scope of the discussion was to prevent the use of the cloning technique for human reproduction (reproductive cloning) and not to touch upon the issue of research on human embryos created by using the cloning technique (so-called therapeutic cloning). At first, it was believed that there would be no objection to universally prohibiting human reproductive cloning, and therefore a convention against human reproductive cloning could be easily adopted at the United Nations. However, it turned out that the discussion among the Member States revolved around the moral status of human embryos created either by fertilization or cloning technique called somatic cell nuclear transfer (SCNT).

Due to the controversy and political ramifications among the Member States, after four years of discussion and negotiation, the final outcome was a non-binding Declaration on Human Cloning. The major disagreement on this issue among the Member States was the moral status of the human embryo created either by SCNT or fertilization, and the permissibility of the destruction of embryos for research purposes.

Some Member States did not agree to prohibit only human reproductive cloning but argued that so-called therapeutic cloning should also be prohibited since there should be no distinction between an embryo created for reproductive purposes and one created for research purposes. However, as some Member States like the Netherlands, UK and Japan had already adopted national laws or regulations permitting research on human embryos, it was impossible to reach an international consensus on this issue.

The final text of the UN Declaration on Human Cloning states that "(b) Member States are called upon to prohibit all forms of human cloning inasmuch as they are incompatible with human dignity and the protection of human life" without providing a definition of 'human life'. Thus, the question whether or not the creation and destruction of human embryos for research is against human dignity and the protection of human life was left unanswered.

The UN Declaration was adopted by a vote of 84 in favor to 34 against, with 37 abstentions. Since there is no definition or common understanding of the moral status of the human embryo, some Member States stated that this declaration would not hinder research on human embryos in their countries since, in their domestic law, human embryos were not considered as human life. Nevertheless, this text could be problematic for promoting human embryo research. Therefore those countries that were favorable towards research on human embryos voted against the adoption of the Declaration.

Interestingly, no single Arab country voted against the UN Declaration, but only eight countries (Bahrain, Iraq, Kuwait, Morocco, Qatar, Saudi Arabia, Sudan, and the United Arab Emirates) voted in favor, which shows their prohibitive position on human embryo research, while eight countries (Algeria, Egypt, Jordan, Lebanon, Oman, Syrian Arab Republic, Tunisia, and Yemen) abstained from the vote.

Creation of Man in the Qur'an

During the discussion at the United Nations on human cloning, countries under the significant influence of the Roman Catholic Church were strongly against the research on human embryos, whereas Islamic countries remained silent throughout the discussion and did not make their position clear. However, when we look into Islamic teachings, they mention rather clearly when life begins. According to the Qur'an, life is not considered to begin at the moment of conception, but gradually alongside the morphological development: a fetus goes through several stages to develop fully into an infant.

In the Qur'an, there are several passages that mention the creation of Man and in the chapter titled "Believers" (Sura XXIII, 12–14) it is mentioned as follows:

(a) We created Man of a quintessence of clay;
(b) then we placed him as semen in a firm receptacle;
(c) then we formed the semen into a blood-like clot;
(d) then we formed the clot into a lump of flesh; then we formed out of that lump bones and clothed the bones with flesh;
(e) then we made him another creation. So blessed be God the best creator.[3]

In this passage, the stages of fetal development are called *nutfa* (semen), *alaqa* (leech-like blood clot), and *mudgha* (lump of flesh). There is no mention in the Qur'an of how long each stage lasts but it is generally understood from the *hadith*[4], which mentions:

The Prophet said: Each of you is constituted in your mother's womb for forty days as a *nutfa*, then it becomes a *alaqa* for an equal period, then a *mudgha* for another equal period, then the angel is sent, and he breathes the soul into it.[5]

Therefore the majority of schools think that the ensoulment occurs after 120 days of conception. However, some other schools think it occurs after only 40 days of conception.

---

3   Basim Musallam, The Human Embryo in Arabic Scientific and Religious Thought, in Gordon R. Dunstan (ed.), *The Human Embryo: Aristotle and the Arabic and European Traditions* (Exeter, Devon: University of Exeter Press, 1990), 38.
4   *Hadith* is a collection of the sayings and acts of Muhammad which is regarded as an important source of jurisprudence next to the Qur'an.
5   Musallam, *op. cit.*, 39.

Research on Human Embryos in the Arab States

Although views on the protection of the fetus and regulations on abortion in the Arab States vary, the common understanding from Islamic teachings is that a human embryo in its very early stage does not have a soul and is considered as fluid or blood clot. This lends itself to a permissive position on research on human embryos such as embryonic stem cell research. Indeed, at many international conferences, scholars from Muslim countries have taken permissive positions on human embryo research for the advancement of scientific knowledge and the benefit of humanity.[6]

In the international community, the countries that permit research on human embryos agreed to use embryos no more than 14 days after conception. Muslim scholars also assimilated this notional time frame by defining the first stage of embryonic development as 14 days rather than 40.[7] The Muslim World League held in Mecca, Saudi Arabia, in 2003 concluded that it is acceptable to obtain embryonic stem cells, preserve them and conduct research on them provided that written consent is received from the patients. The Supreme Council of Health (SCH) in Qatar produced a policy which states that research on human embryonic stem cells is permissible if they are obtained from in vitro fertilization and are not viable or are surplus to requirements.

Nevertheless when we look into current national regulations in the Arab States, there is a clear vacuum on human embryo research: most of the countries do not have explicit laws or regulations, and the few countries that do have explicit laws prohibit such research. In Tunisia, the creation and preservation of human embryos is permitted solely for the purpose of infertility treatment, and the import and export of embryonic stem cells are prohibited by Law No. 2001-93 on reproductive medicine. In Saudi Arabia, the guidelines "Organizational System for Research Practices on Living Beings" produced by the National Committee of Biological and Medical Ethics prohibits the creation of embryos for research purposes. The import and export of ES cells are prohibited unless authorized by the national committee. In Qatar, the creation of human embryos is permitted only for the purpose of fertility treatments. Therefore, in practice, there would be no embryos available for research. Only in Egypt, according to the Egyptian Fatwa Council, is it allowed to conduct embryonic stem cell research using supernumerary human embryos.[8]

In short, from the Islamic religious point of view, human embryonic stem cell research is permissible and the scientific community supports such research

---

6   Gamal I. Serour, Religious Perspectives of Ethical Issues in ART, *Middle East Fertility Society Journal*, 2005, 10(3):185–190.

7   *Ibid.*

8   *Ethics and Law in Biomedicine and Genetics: An Overview of National Regulations in the Arab States* (Cairo: UNESCO Cairo Office, 2011), 50–55.

as well. Nevertheless embryonic stem cell research is not yet a pressing issue in the Arab States due to the lack of facilities and technology to conduct such research. Thus the development of explicit permissive regulations on embryo research has not yet been undertaken. The expert meeting on Ethical and Legal Issues in Human Embryo Research held in Cairo in 2008 by UNESCO also concluded with recommendations calling upon the Arab countries to establish appropriate regulations and monitoring systems for human embryonic stem cell research. Although not much embryonic stem cell research takes place in the Arab countries, adult stem cell research and umbilical cord blood stem cell research are becoming popular in some countries like Egypt, Jordan and the United Arab Emirates, but without proper national regulations. At this time, only Jordan has drafted a law to regulate human stem cell research including a provision for human embryonic stem cell research. However, the law has not yet passed the Parliament.

Regulations on ART in the Arab States

In the Arab region, although there are some population of Shi'a and other schools of Islamic teachings, the majority are Sunni Muslims. When we look into the regulations on assisted reproductive technologies in the region, we find they are very much reflective of Sunni Islamic teachings. Besides the religious influence, it seems that cultural factors also play a role in deciding what shall or shall not be done in the usage of ART.

Third-Party Assistance in ART

The very basic principle guiding the ART regulations in Sunni Muslim countries is the preservation of lineage through legal marriage. ART is permitted only for legally married couples using their gametes, and third-party assistance for reproduction, such as gamete donation or embryo donation, is prohibited considering it as adultery and also for fear of potential incest in the future generation. Since legal marriage is the basis of reproduction, cryopreserved gametes or embryos cannot be used for infertility treatment after the death of a husband or in case of divorce; surrogacy is also not an option.[9]

The very first religious guidance (*fatwa*) on *in vitro* fertilization (IVF) for Sunni Muslims was issued by Al Azhar in Egypt in 1980, only two years after the world's first IVF baby, Louise Brown was born in the United Kingdom. It mentions the basic principle prohibiting third-party donation for ART and since

---

9   Gamal I. Serour, Islamic Perspectives in Human Reproduction, *Reproductive BioMedicine Online*, on web since May 20, 2008, 17(3): 34–38; available at www.rbmonline.com/Article/3378, last accessed on May 29, 2013.

then this principle has been upheld in many *fatwas* and guidelines in Sunni Muslim countries.[10]

Creation of Human Embryos for Research

Early-stage human embryos, as examined in the previous section, are not considered as having human life. Therefore, research on human embryos could be permissible from the Islamic point of view. However, the way of obtaining embryos for research is another issue. While the main source of human embryos for research is leftover embryos produced for fertility treatments, some countries like the United Kingdom, the Netherlands, Belgium, and Japan permit the creation of human embryos for research purposes. During the expert meeting on Ethical and Legal Issues of Human Embryo Research held in Cairo in 2008, the possibility of creating human embryos for research purposes in an Islamic context was also discussed. Based on the Islamic teachings mentioned above, many scholars agreed that research on human embryos before 14 days of development as well as the creation of embryos for research purposes should be permitted and they felt the need to revise the national guidelines accordingly. However, with regard to the way of creating embryos for research purposes, two different opinions were presented.

One is that since assisted reproduction techniques are restricted only to legally married couples, the creation of embryos for research purposes should also be restricted to the donated sperms and ova of a married couple so that even if the embryo shall not develop into a human being, any potential mixing of the lineages of an unmarried man and woman or any potential adultery would be avoided.

Another opinion is that if the purpose of the creation of embryos is research, it may be better to use donated sperms and ova of a man and a woman with no marital relation. Although human embryos are not considered as having life, if a married couple donates gametes to create embryos for research purposes, they may be affected psychologically, questioning their decision to create for research embryos that could have been siblings of their children if transferred to the uterus of the mother. If the embryo is created for research using gametes donated by unrelated persons, there is no such risk since neither the sperm donor nor the ovule donor would claim ownership of such an illegitimate embryo or see the potential of the embryo to become a baby because this embryo has no place to be fostered. Such an argument had never emerged in bioethics discussions other than in Islamic cultural or religious contexts; it comes from the Islamic point of view that the creation of human life should be restricted within marriage and also that the embryo is not a human life.

---

10 Marcia C. Inhorn, Pasquale Patrizio, Gamar I. Serour, Third-Party Reproductive Assistance around the Mediterranean: Comparing Sunni Egypt, Catholic Italy and Multisectarian Lebanon, *Reproductive BioMedicine Online*, December 2010, 21(7): 848–853; available at www.rbmojournal. com/article/S1472-6483(10)00622-X/fulltext, last accessed on May 29, 2013.

Pre-Implantation Genetic Diagnosis for Sex Selection

Another interesting ethical argument and regulation in Sunni Muslim countries concerns sex selection of human embryos. Sex selection of a baby now can be achieved with more than 99 percent accuracy using the technique of pre-implantation genetic diagnosis (PGD), a technique to analyze the chromosome of an embryo by removing one cell in the early stage of its development. Sex selection of a baby is considered necessary in some cases in order to identify severe genetic diseases like thalassemia, cystic fibrosis, Huntington's disease, muscular dystrophy, and others. In such cases, PGD has advantages such as avoiding invasive intervention like abortion and lessening the psychological burden on the couple for terminating the pregnancy. However, application of PGD for sex selection for non-medical reasons, to cater to the preferences of the parents is not permitted in most of the countries in order not to encourage sex discrimination in the society or to prevent the imbalance of female and male populations.

In the Arab countries, there is a general tendency to prefer a boy over a girl. The reasons for preferring a boy to a girl seem different depending on the social and economic classes as well as the rural or urban life style differences. According to a study made in Egypt, for socially low class families, boys are expected to be working hands to support the core families or extended families. In a patriarchal society, being a man means having power not only economically but also as authorities in the communities. Women can achieve a certain social status by being associated with a man, as his daughter, his wife or his mother. Besides, it is a custom in rural areas that the bride's side of the family shall provide food and clothing to the married couple for each special occasion throughout the year. However, in rural areas the married couples normally live together with the family and relatives of the husband. Therefore it is quite a burden for the bride's family to provide food and clothing for the whole family where their daughter married in. In the case of economically higher class urban families, the preference for boys is much less strong, except where assuring the continuation of a family business or handing property down from generation to generation is a concern. In urban families, there is often preference for a girl over a boy based on psychological factors like expected closeness and affection towards parents with daughters. The preference for having a son in Egypt is moderate in general compared to other countries, but it is stronger in rural areas with low education and low income families having only daughters. But generally speaking, the most common reason in Egypt is a family balancing to have at least one boy and one girl followed by economic and other reasons.[11]

The preference of the sex of a baby is based on socio-economic or psychological reasons especially in Egypt and there are no religious factors. Nevertheless, the religious entity is reacting to this issue in response to the needs of people.

---

11 Abdel-Hacly El-Gilany and Ibrahim Shady, Determinants and causes of son preference among women delivering in Mansoura, Egypt, *Eastern Mediterranean Health Journal*, January 2007, 13(1): 119–128.

The *fatwa* issued by the Grand Mufti of Egypt which is influential to Sunni Muslim countries states "There is nothing in Islamic law that prevents the practice of gender selection on the individual level . . . The matter is different when dealing with the issue of gender selection on the level of the community. This is because the matter is connected to disturbing the natural balance which Allah the Almighty has created as well as disturbing the male-female ratio which is an important factor in human procreation."[12] This religious opinion is reiterated in other *fatwas* and guidelines issued in other Sunni Islamic countries.

An interesting line of reasoning for permitting the use of PGD for sex selection for social and cultural preference is that PGD interferes to the same extent as other conventional and permitted methods of choosing the sex of a baby such as special dieting, selecting the timing of intercourse or sorting sperms. The same *fatwa* mentioned above states: "It is likewise permissible for man to strive to increase the possibilities of gender selection as determined by specialists i.e. by choosing certain foods, engaging in intercourse before or during ovulation, sperm spinning and other methods known to experts. It is likewise permissible to use pre-implantation microscopic examination of chromosomes and DNA for the same purpose."[13]

As mentioned above, PGD for family balancing is prohibited in most of the countries outside the Arab region. The hesitation of those countries that permit PGD for detecting serious diseases to extend its scope to non-medical reasons is based on the fear of abusing the technologies and also on the consideration of the special moral status of human embryos. Although they do not consider a human embryo as human life, it is considered as different from gametes. It could be understood that, in the case of the Arab countries, according to Islamic teachings, gametes and embryos are regarded as almost the same fluid instance referred to as *nutfa* and, as such, sorting sperms and selecting an embryo by PGD can be regarded as being at the same level of intervention in the *fatwa*. Nevertheless, it is worth mentioning that Tunisia, Oman and Saudi Arabia prohibit in their national guidelines the usage of PGD for non-medical reasons.

Impact of Assisted Reproductive Technologies on Family Ties: Sunni vs. Shi'a

The strong emphasis on the preservation of lineage through legal marriage and the condemnation of adultery in Sunni Islamic societies lead them to reject the involvement of third parties, such as gamete or embryo donors and surrogate mothers, in fertility treatments. The adoption of orphans is likewise not accepted in Sunni society—though permanent fostering of children is permitted. In this situation, a new infertility treatment called ICSI (intracytoplasmic sperm

---

12 www.ali-gomaa.com/?page=fatwas&fatwa_details=478, last accessed on May 23, 2013.
13 *Ibid.*

injection), which gives the only hope for overcoming male infertility and for receiving one's own child, has become a popular treatment in Muslim countries despite its high cost and the ethical implications. But it is not without affecting the relationship within the family: as Inhorn points out, due to the introduction of ICSI, more and more infertile men in Egypt have chosen, ironically, to divorce their wives and remarry younger, fertile women, believing that it improves the chances of the treatment's success.[14]

Initially, third party involvement in procreation was strongly opposed not only in Sunni Muslim countries but also among Shi'a Muslim communities. However, the situation changed in the 1990s when a *fatwa* permitting gamete and embryo donation as well as surrogacy was issued in Iran.[15] There is controversy on this issue in Shi'a Muslim countries but, for the moment, egg donation, embryo donation and surrogacy (though no sperm donation) are permitted in Iran and also practiced in Lebanon. In Lebanon, the Christian community followed the lead of the Shi'ite community in permitting such practices. The reason for permitting third-party donation for infertility treatment is "to preserve the marriage of the infertile couple through the birth of donor children in order to prevent the 'marital and psychological disputes' that would inevitably arise from remaining childless indefinitely."[16] It contrasts with the situation in Egypt that prioritizes the preservation of lineage through advanced technology like ICSI, which has resulted in an increased divorce rate.

Kleinman argues that "experience may, on theoretical grounds, be thought of as the intersubjective medium of social transactions in local moral worlds. It is the outcome of cultural categories and social structures interacting with psychophysiological processes such that a mediating world is constituted."[17] And, at the same time, "in practical terms, that mediating world is defined by what is vitally at stake for groups and individuals."[18] In other words, experience or the meaning of experience of a person is defined by the values shared in the society with a particular cultural and historical background. But at the same time, the social values are defined and reshaped by the people›s experiences in their particular situations. The interaction of the society, individuality, and values applies to the ethical guidance based on Islamic teachings as well. "Local moral worlds" in Muslim countries, after all, are not solid and impenetrable, as it is also the case in other parts of the world, but are constantly being reshaped and reexamined through the encounters with new technologies and their ethical implications, social and economical changes, individuals› experiences and shifting ethical values in the globalized world.

---

14 Marcia C. Inhorn, Global Infertility and the Globalization of New Reproductive Technologies: Illustrations from Egypt, in Gwynne L. Jenkins and Marcia C. Inhorn (eds.), Special Issue on "Reproduction Gone Awry," *Social Science and Medicine*, May 2003, 56(9): 1837–1851.
15 *Ibid.*
16 *Ibid.*
17 Kleinman and Kleinman, *op. cit.*, 277.
18 *Ibid.*

MEDICALLY ASSISTED REPRODUCTION: CHALLENGES FOR REGULATION IN ROMANIA

Enikő Demény

Introduction

While medically assisted reproduction covers the same or very similar technologies regardless of the location where they are applied, the contexts in which these technologies are applied differ significantly from one country to another. The differences in legal frameworks, as well as the socio-cultural and economic context of a given country, all have an impact on how these technologies are applied and what implications they produce in that given context. The technology itself might be neutral, but its applications can be empowering and beneficial in some contexts and for some persons, while in others it may be a source of exploitation or of illegal profit. Unregulated application of these technologies increases the importance of the larger context in which they are applied, while regulation can make the impact of these technologies more predictable. This paper aims to present the development of the regulation of medically assisted reproduction in Romania and its impact on the practice of assisted reproduction. I will use the method of contextualization to highlight how the socio-cultural and economic context influences the outcomes of a technological application, and how this impacts various actors.

Romania, a former state-socialist country, has gone through a period of rapid and major change since the revolution in 1989, which marked the beginning of transition to a democratic regime.[1] The health system has been through equally radical changes. While in the early 1960s the health status of the Romanian population was comparable with that of Western European countries, the sharp increase in poverty and the corresponding decrease in living standards in the

---

1   Since January 1, 2007 Romania has been an EU member state.

transition period had a deeply negative effect on the Romanian population. For example, the average life expectancy in Romania is six years shorter than the EU average, and infant and maternal mortality are among the highest in the European Region.[2]

The legacy of restrictive abortion and contraception policies of the state-socialist period has an impact on the post state-socialist period too, making the regulation of reproductive health a very sensitive and complex issue in Romania.[3] The anti-abortion and pro-natalist policies in state-socialist Romania represented a specific model of state involvement in the reproductive sphere and the family model.[4] As reproductive rights were severely restricted, it was not a surprise that after the collapse of the state-socialist regime the second law Romania adopted concerned the legalization of abortion.[5] The regained reproductive freedom resulted in alarming abortion statistics in the first period after the liberalization.[6] The high number of abortions, the severe drop in the birth rate,[7] the rise in mortality, coupled with the phenomenon of emigration and migration after the 1990's resulted in a negative demographic trend. The legacy of the abortion and pro-natalist policies of state-socialist Romania, negative demographic trends, reproductive tourism, as well as the economic crisis are all important elements of the context in which the new technologies of reproduction are applied and have to be regulated in Romania.

Medically Assisted Reproduction in Romania: Facts and Figures

The first IVF clinics started their activities in Romania in the mid-1990s and the first child born as a result of an IVF procedure was born on February 6, 1996. Until 2006 assisted reproduction was not regulated in Romania. In

---

2   Cristian Vlădescu, Gabriela Scântee, and Victor Olsavszky, Romania: Health System Review. *WHO Health Systems in Transition*, 2008, 10(3): 1–181, at xiii and 18.

3   For more information on the reproductive policies in communist Romania, see Gail Kligman, *The Politics of Duplicity: Controlling Reproduction in Ceausescu's Romania* (Berkeley: University of California Press, 1998).

4   Wishing to increase the birth rate, in 1966, Ceauşescu promulgated the Decree No. 770 restricting abortion and contraception. Only women over the age of 45 who had at least four children were eligible for abortion. Mandatory gynecological checkups and penalizations against unmarried people and childless couples completed the natalist measures.

5   Decree No. 1 of December 26, 1989 repealing the Decrees 770/1966 and 441/1985, as well as Articles 185–188 on Abortion of the Penal Code. Later Article 185 on illegal abortions was reintroduced into the Penal Code through Law no. 140/1996.

6   There were 992,000 of abortions in Romania in 1990. Since than the number of abortion started to decrease, but still, the number of abortion in Romania is one of the highest in Europe (115,000 abortions in 2009).

7   In 2010 Romania reached the lowest number of births, since 1955; see National Institute for Statistics, Romania, *Statistical Yearbook 2011*, Chapter 2. Population.

2006 the IVF procedure was defined as a transplant and the field of assisted reproduction came under the law on transplantation.[8]

Currently there are 19 IVF centers in Romania, some of them working in public hospitals, but many of them in private IVF centers. The majority of these clinics are located in the capital Bucharest, but there are IVF centers in other cities too. As reporting on the activity of IVF centers was not compulsory before 2008, systematic data collection is not available until that year.[9] Since 2008 the National Transplant Agency (NTA) has been collecting data on the activity of IVF centers. More detailed data about assisted reproduction is available since 2009 on the NTA web-site. Since that year information has been available about the numbers of donations (sperm, egg, and embryo), successful pregnancies, and live births, transferred or destroyed embryos and babies born.[10]

Before 2011 there was no public reimbursement for the costs of IVF procedures. As a result, during this period only those infertile couples or persons could use this service who were able to cover the full cost of the treatment. Patient organizations and NGOs made efforts to change this situation—almost unique in Europe—that there was no public money at all allocated for financing the cost of IVF treatments.[11] After sustained efforts of organizations such as SOS Infertility, at the end of 2010 the Romanian Ministry of Health approved a program through which the state partially reimburses the costs of IVF for a number of selected infertile couples who otherwise could not afford the full cost by themselves.[12] The program started in mid-2011, and since then the first babies from this program have been born. This is certainly a great achievement for infertile couples in Romania, even if the program covers only the partial cost of a single cycle, which is unique in Europe. In other countries minimum three cycles are reimbursed.[13]

---

8   Law 95/2006 on Reform of Health Care, Chapter VI. on the Procurement and Transplant of Human Organs, Tissues and Cells for Therapeutic Purposes.

9   European Society for Human Reproduction (ESHR), *Comparative Analysis of Medically Assisted Reproduction in the EU: Regulation and Technologies*. Final Report (Strasbourg: Council of Europe, 2008), 14; available at ec.europa.eu/health/blood_tissues_organs/docs/study_eshre_en.pdf, last accessed on May 27, 2013.

10 Statistical data on IVF activity is available on the website of National Transplant Agency, www.transplant.ro/statistica.htm, last accessed on May 27, 2013.

11 ESHR, *op. cit.*, 32. The other two countries were there was no public reimbursement for IVF were Lithuania and Malta.

12 Order No. 1591/1110 of 2010 of the Ministry of Health and of the President of the National Health Insurance Agency for Approving the Technical Norms for the Realization of National Health Programs for 2011 and 2012, published in *Official Gazette of Romania/Monitorul Oficial al României*, No. 53 and No. 53 bis of January 21, 2011, with later modifications and amendments.

13 Even in Poland, where the Catholic Church formulated strong opposition to such program, three cycles are reimbursed.

The Evolution of the Regulatory Framework
of the Medically Assisted Reproduction

Before 2006 there was no legislation concerning medically assisted reproduction in Romania. There existed a draft Law on the Reproductive Health, which was never adopted, therefore until 2006 IVF clinics had functioned in Romania in an unregulated context.[14] The only existing regulations during this period were those self-imposed by the medical profession.[15] Apart from the general context of decentralization, liberalization and privatization in the health care sector that characterized the period after 1990, the liberal attitude toward medically assisted reproduction can possibly be explained by decision makers' reluctance to interfere in the field of reproductive health where very harmful and restrictive regulations had been applied before 1989.

One consequence of no regulation in the field was the case of Adriana Iliescu, who in January 2005 gave birth to her daughter at age 66 using IVF and donor gametes. This case was regarded as highly controversial, but not only in Romania. The three most common objections brought against the mother and/or against the team of healthcare professionals that made it happen were the mother's age, the fact that she was single, and the appropriateness of their motivation.[16] Her case was extensively covered not only in Romania, but in the international media too, since Adriana Iliescu was the oldest birth mother in the world until her record was broken in 2006. This single case, however, was not enough to prompt decision makers to regulate access to medically assisted reproduction. Once public money was dedicated for this purpose, the first specific regulations on access to medically assisted reproduction were introduced in Romania in 2011, specifying conditions related to applicants' age and citizenship as well as to their marital status. According to the selection criteria for the publicly financed IVF program, the applicant women must be between 24 and 40, at least one member of the couple must have Romanian citizenship and Romanian residence and they have to be married for at least two years. No specific conditions for the age of the male partner in the couple are formulated.

The non-regulated field of assisted reproduction came once again into focus in 2005 due to a paid egg 'donation' case involving Romanian donors. This case had an impact not only on the regulatory framework of assisted reproduction in Romania but on the international level too. The paid egg 'donation' case was carried out in the framework of a collaboration program between

---

14 See more details and analysis of this legislative attempt in Daniela Cutaş, On a Romanian Attempt to Legislate on Medically Assisted Human Reproduction, *Bioethics*, January 2008, 22(1): 56–63.

15 For example the necessary informed consent procedure was required before starting an IVF procedure.

16 For a detailed analysis see Daniela Cutaş, Postmenopausal Motherhood: Immoral, Illegal? A Case Study, *Bioethics*, October 2007, 21(8): 458–463.

Romania and the UK, the so called "Bridge International Embryo Importation Program." In this program the recipients were women from UK, to whom the cost of procuring the 'donated' eggs was reimbursed.[17] Two private IVF centers in Romania were involved in the program: the Global ART Clinic and Global Med Rom Clinic. The general public found out about this program in 2005, when two Romanian 'donors' (aged 19 and 24) had some serious health problems after performing egg donation in the framework of this program, but the private hospital involved in the donation did not cover their medical costs. In order to raise awareness about the phenomenon of paid egg donation and exploitation of donors, a Romanian lawyer George Măgureanu, made an interpellation at the European Parliament.[18] The European Parliament took position on the egg trade phenomenon by adopting a Resolution on the ban of the trade in human egg cells, adopted in 2005 with a majority vote.[19]

Meanwhile, in Bucharest the regulation of assisted reproduction was included in the Law on the Reform of Health System, Chapter VI on the procurement and transplant of human organs, tissues and *cells* for therapeutic purposes. The IVF procedure was regarded as transplantation and with this law the procurement, storage, donation and use of human reproductive cells came under strict control and supervision.[20] The law implemented the provisions of the EU Tissue and Cells Directive (2004/23/EC) and has installed a Competent Authority as well as the licensing/inspection procedures. The National Registry, run under legal obligation by the National Transplant Agency, has existed since 2008.

According to the law, the collection of human cells as a result of physical or moral pressure is forbidden and human cells must not be donated for obtaining material and other types of benefits. The donor, as well as the recipient shall sign a written declaration stating that the donation is a humanitarian act, it has an altruistic character, and is not done for obtaining material or any other benefits.[21] Paid donation is criminalized. According to the Law, donation of human cells with the purpose of obtaining material or other type of benefits is a crime and shall be punished with three to five years of detention. Forcing or influencing somebody with bad intentions to donate human cells is a crime

---

17 See, for example, Hiltrud Breyer, Egg Cells Trade Endangers the European Union as a Community of Values, *BioNews*, June 6, 2005; available at www.bionews.org.uk/page_37805.asp, last accessed on May 27, 2013.

18 George Măgureanu, J.D., Interpellation at the European Parliament, June 30, 2005, CORE Europa Seminar: Human Egg Trading and the Exploitation of Women; available at www.handsoffourovaries.com/pdfs/appendixg.pdf, last accessed on May 27, 2013.

19 The European Parliament, Resolution on the Trade of Human Egg Cells, Texts Adopted on the Sitting of Thursday, March 10, 2005; available at www.europarl.europa.eu/RegData/seance_pleniere/textes_adoptes/provisoire/2005/03-10/P6_TA-PROV(2005)03-10_EN.pdf, last accessed on May 27, 2013.

20 Law 95/2006 on Reform of the Health Care System, *op. cit.*, Article 142 (e).

21 *Ibid.*, Article 144 (d, e, f).

and shall be punished with three to ten years of detention.[22] As a general rule, persons without the capacity to consent can not be donors. Article 145(1) states that minors are not allowed to become donors, unless otherwise specified by the Law. In these cases the collection of biological materials can be done only with the consent of the minor if he or she is 14–18 years old, and the written consent of the parent or legal representative has been acquired. The collection of cells of human origin without the consent obtained under the conditions laid down in the Law constitutes a crime and shall be punished by five to seven years imprisonment. Importing or exporting human cells, without the special authorization of the National Transplant Agency is classified as a crime and is punishable with three to ten years of prison.[23]

Legislative Loopholes, Illegal Practices and Law Enforcement Mechanisms

In a context with no specific regulation on third party reproduction, such procedures, involving paid ova donation, were regularly carried out in some private IVF clinics in Bucharest: such practices happened not only before the adoption of the law on transplantation which also covered the IVF procedure, but went on even after the law was adopted.[24] In the context of economic crisis, high rates of unemployment and increasing social inequalities, many women find themselves in a situation in which an otherwise not small amount of money becomes an incentive to sell their biological material. The 'donors' in general are women aged 18–30, some of them students, but many of them of low socio-economic status, with poor education, and many of them Roma, occasionally without a place of residence. Since harvesting eggs implies hormonal treatment, they expose themselves to health risks in order to solve some everyday problems, such as buying food or a present for their child, to pay the rent or utilities, to pay for their studies or, in some cases, to pay the costs of their own IVF procedure. The 'donors' are paid 130 to 180 Euros for their egg cells, and these eggs, in turn, are sold for 3,000 to 4,000 Euros to couples who require in-vitro fertilization.[25] The profit the organizers of such 'networks of reproduction' make is clearly significant. The egg recipients, mainly women

---

22 *Ibid.*, Article 157(1).
23 *Ibid.*, Article 159.
24 Reference to such procedures is made in Daniela Cutaş, On a Romanian Attempt, *op. cit.*; Michal Nahman, Nodes of Desire: Romanian Egg Sellers, 'Dignity' and Feminist Alliances in Transnational Ova Exchanges, *European Journal of Women Studies*, May 2008, 15(2): 65–82.
25 A detailed analysis of the recent egg trade cases involving Romanian donors was presented in Enikő Demény, Networks of Reproduction in the Globalized World, Presented at the European Science Foundation Workshop, Essex, September 12, 2012 and forthcoming in Róisín Ryan-Flood and Jenny Gunnarsson Payne (eds.), *Transnationalizing Reproduction: Gamete and Embryo Donation in a Globalized World.*

from Israel, did not know the 'donors', neither the conditions under which they 'donated' their eggs.[26]

All these activities were illegal in Romania after 2006, since the law clearly prohibited paid donations. Moreover, the law states that organization and/or harvesting of organ, tissues and cells of human origin with the purpose of obtaining a material profit for the donor or the organizer is infraction of organ, tissue and cell trafficking and it is punishable with imprisonment from three to ten years.[27] However, Article 6 of the Methodological Norms for the Application of Chapter VI of Law 95/2006 made an exception from this Article, thus public and private IVF clinics could perform paid IVF procedures, and could make a profit for themselves out of this activity.[28] It was exactly this Article 6 that was repealed with a Ministry Order in September 2009[29], very soon after the competent Romanian authority, the Direction for the Investigation of Organized Crime and Terrorist Acts (DIICOT) arrested in July 2009 four medical doctors and one secretary from the Sabyc Medical Center. They were accused of establishing an organized criminal network, trafficking in human cells and illegal import of human cells.[30] At the same time two employees from the National Transplantation Agency were arrested; accusations were related to some procedural issues concerning the license of the Sabyc clinic.

The Sabyc case and the lack of proper legislation in this field resulted in a case at the European Court of Human Rights (ECtHR).[31] Daniela Knecht stored sixteen embryos created using donated gametes for her own future use after receiving IVF in 2008 at the S Medical Centre in Bucharest. In 2009 the clinic was closed and Knecht's embryos—among others—were transferred to the Mina Minovici Institute of Forensic Medicine (IFM). Daniela Knecht appealed to the ECtHR, which ruled that Knecht's application was admissible and that the issue engaged Article 8 of the European Convention on Human Rights.[32] The scope of the case was access to the embryos: "The legal and medical status

---

26 See also in Enikő Demény, Networks of Reproduction in the Globalized World (forthcoming); Susanne Lundin, "I Want a Baby; Don't Stop Me from Being a Mother": An Ethnographic Study on Fertility Tourism and Egg Trade, *Cultural Politics*, July 2012, 8(2): 327–343; Nahman, Nodes of Desire, *op. cit.*; Michal Nahman, 'Reverse Traffic': Intersecting Inequalities in Human Egg 'Donation', *Reproductive Biomedicine Online*, November 2011, 23(5): 626–623.

27 Law No. 95 of 2006, Article 158.

28 Methodological Norms for the Application of Chapter VI of Law No. 96 of 2006.

29 Order 1.156, Article I. published in Official Gazette of Romania September 29, 2009. This legislative measure was highly contested, because through it each paid IVF activity was declared illegal

30 Accusations were based on the violation of Article 7 of Law 39/2003 (establishing an organized criminal network) Article 158 (1) of Law 95/2006, Article 41 (2) of Penal Code (trafficking in human cells, trade with human cells) Article 159 of Law 95/2006, Article 26, Article 33 of Penal Code (illegal import of human cells).

31 See *Knecht v. Romania*; ECtHR, application no. 10048/10, judgment of October 2, 2012, final judgment February 11, 2013.

32 Antony Blackburn-Starza, No Violation of Human Rights in Romanian Egg Storage Case, European Court Says, *BioNews*, No. 682, November 19, 2012; available at www.bionews.org.uk/page_213876.asp, last accessed on May 27, 2013.

of the embryos is uncertain. The Court has indicated to the Romanian Government that the embryos are not to be destroyed while the case is pending . . ."[33]
In its final decision the ECtHR concluded that the Romanian Government had
acted lawfully in making the decision to move the embryos to a state institution. The court argued that an interference with Article 8 could be justified as
being "in accordance with the law" and "necessary in a democratic society." It
said the initial decision to put the embryos "in custody" was made under the
Romanian Penal Code and the relevant measure pursued a legitimate aim, to
prevent crime and uphold public safety, taking into account the context of a
clinic operating without the proper authority to do so.[34] Through its decision,
the ECtHR reinforced the Romanian authorities' procedural decisions put in
place in the Sabyc clinic case, and admitted that the clinic had not operated
under legal conditions.

It seems, however, that in spite of the fact that the Sabyc clinic case and the related criminal procedures received considerable public attention, and restrictive
legislative measures were adopted, a very similar network for paid egg donation
operated with very similar methods in another private IVF clinic. Following a
court decision, on February 20, 2013 the Bucharest Court upheld a request from
Romania's organized crime unit DIICOT to hold two suspects for 29 days. The
two representatives of Med New Life clinic were taken into custody by DIICOT
on suspicion of trafficking human egg cells for *in vitro* fertilization. Prosecutors
questioned dozens of people at hearings, including nurses and doctors.

Legislative Proposals: The Draft Law on Third Party Reproduction

The ongoing practice of third party reproduction in the Romanian IVF clinics,
as well as the illicit activities taking place in connection with these procedures
highlight the weaknesses of the existing regulatory framework and call for a
comprehensive regulation in the field of medically assisted reproduction. Romanian legislators are compelled to address the issue of third party reproduction in the New Civil Code of Romania too.[35]

The New Civil Code is the first legislative instrument to address the larger
implications of medically assisted reproduction, especially its implication on
family relationships.[36] The existing regulation applicable for assisted reproduc-

---

33 European Court of Human Rights (2012) *Research Report: Bioethics and the Case-Law of the Court*;
    available at www.coe.int/t/dg3/healthbioethic/texts_and_documents/Bioethics_and_caselaw_
    Court_EN.pdf.
34 *Knecht v. Romania, op. cit.*
35 Legea 287/2009 privind Codul Civil [Law No. 287 of 2009 on the New Civil Code]. The law entered
    in force on October 1, 2011, as Noul Cod Civil republicat 2011. Republished in *Official Gazette*, Part
    I., No. 505 of July 15, 2011.
36 *Ibid.*, Sections 441–447.

tion, Law 95/2006 does not address such aspects at all.[37] The New Civil Code first of all states that third party reproduction does not create any kind of lineage between donor and the child.[38] No responsibility in this regard can be claimed against the donor. According to the Penal Code only a woman and a man, or a single woman can be a parent.[39] Those parents who use third party reproduction must give their prior consent in a notary statement. The consent is not valid if one of the parties dies or if they start a divorce or separation prior to the start of the IVF procedure. Consent can be withdrawn at any time, even in the presence of the specialist who assists with the third party reproduction.[40]

The New Civil Code also states that nobody can dispute the lineage of the child for reasons related to third party reproduction. Neither may the child contest his/her lineage for this reason.[41] According to the provision of the Civil Code, any information related to third party reproduction is confidential. Such information can be released by the court to medical doctors or competent authorities if the lack of the information causes severe harm to the persons conceived with assisted reproduction or to their descendents.[42] The descendants can also request such information. According to Article 447, the legal regime of third party reproduction shall be set up in a special law. The provisions of the Civil Code on third party reproduction clearly set up some limits for the proposed new regulation on third party reproduction. Thus, the Civil Code limits the sphere of access to such procedures to heterosexual couples and single women, and by this implicitly prohibits the use of third party reproduction by homosexual couples.

The draft Law on Third Party Reproduction proposed by the Government[43] requires the anonymity of donors and allows only non-paid donations,[44] referring only to the possibility of sperm donation.[45] The draft Law does not address surrogacy arrangements either. The lack of any kind of regulation on surrogacy does not mean that surrogacy is not practiced in Romania. There are many women on Romanian internet sites searching for a surrogate or gestational mother, and there are many who offer such services. At present, the legislation makes possible to have a child through surrogacy only with adoption of the child after birth. First the child is declared as the child of the surrogate mother

---

37 For a detailed analysis on the impact of the medically assisted reproduction on the lineage in Romania see Sabin Guțan, *Reproducerea Umană Asistată Medical și Filiația* (București: Humangiu, 2011).
38 Noul Cod Civil, *op. cit.*, Section 441(1).
39 *Ibid.*, Section 441(2–3).
40 *Ibid.*, Section 442(1–3).
41 *Ibid.*, Section 443(1).
42 *Ibid.*, Section 445(1).
43 Lege privind reproducerea humană asistată medical cu terț donator [Draft Law on Third Party Medically Assisted Human Reproduction]; available in Romanian at www.cdep.ro/proiecte/2012/000/60/3/se99.pdf, last accessed on May 27, 2013.
44 *Ibid.*, Article 10(2).
45 *Ibid.*, Article 3(i).

and of the biological father. The birth certificate is issued with their names. The surrogate mother then surrenders the child. The genetic mother (or the intending mother) adopts his/her child from the competent authorities and a new birth certificated is issued.

There are some problems that may occur under the present legislative regime in which a surrogacy contract is not enforceable. First of all, the surrogate mother can not be obliged to give up the child if she gets attached to the child or if she wants to obtain more money from the intending parents for her service. Furthermore, there is no way to certify that the child is that of the genetic mother. An additional problem might arise if the surrogate mother and the intending parents are from different countries. Due to significant differences in the legal systems of European Union Member States and the occasional legal vacuum in relation to various legal questions arising from surrogacy, persons and especially children involved in international surrogacy arrangements may face various inconveniences. The most serious difficulties are that children born through surrogacy may not have legal parents, may be stateless, not enrolled in the birth register in the country of their residences, or have different citizenship than their genetic parents.

The initiator of the Draft Law on Third Party Medically Assisted Reproduction, the Romanian government, mentioned both the negative demographic trends and the unethical IVF procedures taking place in some clinics as a result of the absence of a specific law on third party assisted reproduction as reasons for the necessity of adopting regulations in this field.[46] According to its initiators, the proposed law does not have any societal impact.[47] However, the draft encountered strong opposition from some segments of the society, among them the Catholic Church. According to their position the draft law constitutes a serious attempt against human dignity, the integrity of the family and the equilibrium of the society.[48] Critics draw attention to the fact that it is strange to have a law only on this specific case of assisted reproduction, while there is no specific law to cover the whole field of assisted reproduction. The law was not adopted, since it did not get all the necessary approvals from the competent committees. Since then the Romanian government has changed, thus at present it is difficult to predict the future direction of the legislative process on assisted reproduction in Romania.

---

46 Expunere de motive: Lege privind reproducerea humană asistată medical cu terţ donator [Explanatory Memorandum to the Draft Law on Third Party Medically Assisted Human Reproduction]; available at www.cdep.ro/proiecte/2012/000/60/3/em99.pdf, last accessed on May 27, 2013.

47 *Ibid.*, 3.

48 Letter of the representatives of the Catholic Church to the Ministry of Health on the issue of Draft Law on Third Party Medically Assisted Reproduction, March 8, 2012; available at www. magisteriu.ro/scrisoarea-deschisa-a-cer-despre-reproducerea-umana-asistata-medical-2012/, last accessed on May 27, 2013.

Conclusions

The ongoing practice of third party reproduction in Romanian IVF clinics and the illicit activities taking place in connection with these procedures in some of the clinics highlight the inadequacies of the existing regulatory framework and call for a comprehensive regulation in the field of medically assisted reproduction. The implications for family relationships, on kinship, on citizenship of third party reproduction draw our attention to the broader societal implications of this medical technology, as well as to the transnational character of such procedures and point to the necessity of a global response to this issue.

By taking a look at the development of the Romanian regulative framework for assisted reproduction it becomes clear that in most situations legislators were reacting to specific cases or situation, rather than applying a consistent approach toward such procedures. While not denying the benefit and empowering nature of IVF technologies for many infertile couples, it has to be also noted that the lack of conclusive regulation in the context of economic crisis, reproductive tourism and trans-border reproductive care may make many women vulnerable to the IVF industry. First of all, the issue of equitable access has to be addressed. Unless there is sustained financial support from the state for this procedure, the availability of the technology raises unattainable possibilities for many infertile couples in Romania who can not afford the cost of interventions themselves. Not only do many women not have access to these procedures because they can not afford it, but they might become subjects of exploitation, providing 'raw material' for the benefit of those who can pay for it. Thus, for financial reasons some women might become paid egg donors or surrogate mothers risking their health, not to mention the possible psychological and legal consequences of such acts. Some other women might become victims of illicit practices: for example they might find out that their frozen embryos are confiscated, or they are becoming mothers in unclear circumstances. It is not only women whose interests have to be protected, but children born as a result of such procedures also need protection. Otherwise they might be born in uncertain legal situations, with no way of knowing, for example, their genetic origins.

Under the current legislative system, issues of access are not transparently addressed either. In the absence of a specific law on this topic anyone can have access to medically assisted reproduction in Romania. However, when individuals and couples seek reimbursement of the costs of IVF from the state, only married heterosexual couples' requestes are accepted. The new penal code also limits the sphere of access to third party reproduction to heterosexual couples and single women. Homosexual couples, like in many other countries, are thus implicitly excluded from access to third party medically assisted reproduction.

Taking all these into account, adopting appropriate regulations, strengthening law enforcement, increasing the lobby potential of NGOs, organizing public debates on the limits of acceptability of certain applications of medically assisted reproductive technologies are only some of the steps that could make the process of assisted reproduction a safer and more transparent service in Romania, for the benefit of all parties involved.

LEGAL POLICY ON ASSISTED REPRODUCTION IN SERBIA

Slavica Karajičić, Gordana Radović Tripinović, and Aleksandar Krstić

Background

For more than two decades, Serbian society has been exposed to difficult times (war, economic and social crisis), which had the side effect that many emerging social issues were left without regulation. For example, before 2009, Serbian legislators didn't deal with the legal questions of assisted reproduction (AR). Whenever assisted reproduction technologies were applied, it was mostly by following the guidelines of the ethical committees. In a country like Serbia with a strong pro-natalist policy, however, the importance of applications of *in vitro* fertilization (IVF) treatments was recognized long before 2009. The Socialist Federal Republic of Yugoslavia was the seventh country to start applying the new technique. In Serbia the first baby conceived by artificial insemination was born in 1985 in Belgrade, and the first baby conceived from frozen embryo was born in 1991 in Belgrade as well.[1] The importance of AR has been recognized by the state and public policy has turned its attention to AR issues since 2006. The Republic Fund of Health Insurance is financing three attempts of AR under certain medical conditions.[2] Finally, the need for legal framework has been responded by adopting the Act on Treatment of Infertility by Biomedically Assisted Fertilization Procedures in 2009.[3] This law regulates problems and questions that patients and medical staff had to deal with in practice over the years.

---

1   B. Mandić, Sve brojnije bebe 'sa leda' [More and More Babies 'from Ice'], *Vesti online*, Jun 24, 2011; available at www.vesti-online.com/Vesti/Srbija/146404/Sve-brojnije-bebe-sa-leda, last accessed on May 21, 2013.

2   Republički fond za zdravstveno osiguranje [Republic Fund of Health Insurance]; see www.eng.rfzo.rs/, last accessed on May 21, 2013.

3   Zakon o lečenju neplodnosti postupcima biomedicinski potpomognutog oplođenja, *Službeni glasnik Republike Srbije*, broj 72/2009 [Act on the Treatment of Infertility by Biomedically Assisted Fertilization Procedures or Infertility Treatment Act, in short]; available at www.zakon.co.rs/zakon-o-lecenju-neplodnosti-postupcima-biomedicinski-potpomognutog-oplodjenja.html, last accessed on May 21, 2013.

Legal Policy

Serbian law is based on many international and European documents (see Table 1 below). At the international level, the Universal Declaration on the Human Genome and Human Rights was adopted unanimously and by acclamation by the

Table 1. *Framework of International and European Legal Norms Incorporated in Serbian Law*

Date	International/European Document	Notification
April 4, 1997	Convention for the Protection of Human Rights and Dignity of the Human Being with regard to the Application of Biology and Medicine: Convention on Human Rights and Biomedicine (Oviedo Convention)	Signed 2005, entered in force 2011.
November 11, 1997	Universal Declaration on the Human Genome and Human Rights	Adopted unanimously and by acclamation by the General Conference of UNESCO.
March 31, 2004	European Parliament and Council Directive 2004/23/EC	Setting standards of quality and safety for the donation, acquisition, testing, processing, preservation, storage and distribution of human tissues and cells.
February 8, 2006	Commission Directive 2006/17/EC[4]	Implementing Directive 2004/23/EC of the European Parliament and of the Council as regards certain technical requirements for the donation, procurement and testing of human tissues and cells.
October 24, 2006	Commission Directive 2006/86/EC[5]	Implementing Directive of the European Parliament and Council Directive 2004/23/EC as regards traceability requirements, notification of serious adverse reactions and events and certain technical requirements for the coding, processing, preservation, storage and distribution of human tissues and cells.
April 7, 2006	The European Union Tissues and Cells Directives (EUTCD)	Adopted by the European Parliament on April 7, 2004 and came into effect between April 7, 2006 and April 7, 2007. Transposition has been executed in Serbia by the Act on Transplantation of Tissues and Cells.

---

4 Incorporated into Serbian law through the Act on Treatment of Infertility by Biomedically Assisted Fertilization Procedures, the Act on Organ Transplantation, and the Act on Tissue and Cell Transplantation (in Serbian: Direktiva Komisije 2006/17/EZ od 8. februara 2006. godine implementirana u srpski zakon kroz Zakon o lečenju neplodnosti postupcima biomedicinski potpomognutog oplođenja, Zakon o transplantaciji organa i Zakon o transplantaciji tkiva i ćelija).

5 Incorporated into Serbian law through the Act on Treatment of Infertility by Biomedically Assisted Fertilization Procedures, the Act on Organ Transplantation, and the Act on Tissue and Cell Transplantation (in Serbian: Direktiva Komisije 2006/86/EZ od 24. oktobra 2006. godine implementirana u srpski zakon kroz Zakon o lečenju neplodnosti postupcima biomedicinski potpomognutog oplođenja, Zakon o transplantaciji organa i Zakon o transplantaciji tkiva i ćelija).

General Conference of UNESCO in 1997 and endorsed by the General Assembly of the United Nations in 1998. Article 11 of this Declaration states: "Practices which are contrary to human dignity, such as reproductive cloning of human beings, shall not be permitted. States and competent international organizations are invited to co-operate in identifying such practices and in taking, at national or international level, the measures necessary to ensure that the principles set out in this Declaration are respected." It is the first international instrument to condemn human reproductive cloning as a practice against human dignity. In accordance with this, Serbian law prohibits cloning as a technique of assisted reproduction.

Table 1 is giving an overview of documents that influenced the national law in Serbia in order to harmonize it with legal norms and policies on the international and European levels. The Convention on Human Rights and Biomedicine[6] (or the Oviedo Convention, in short) was signed by Serbia back in 2005 but it entered in force only recently on June 1, 2011.[7] The lack of institutional organization and non-harmonized law acts can be considered as reasons for delaying the Oviedo convention application. The common set of values based on human rights throughout Europe has contributed to a deeper awareness of the necessity to reinforce these values by passing national laws that are compatible with the Oviedo Convention. In this manner, the Serbian Act on Treatment of Infertility by Biomedically Assisted Fertilization Procedures[8] was adopted on September 11, 2009, and entered into force on January 1, 2010. If we look at this act more closely, we can distinguish three scopes or fields of regulation.

First of all, the Infertility Treatment Act of 2009 regulates the scope of infertility treatment procedures on biomedically assisted fertilization by setting the terms and conditions for, and methods and procedures of treating the infertility of women and men in order to conceive a child. Assisted reproduction is a procedure based on the following principles: medical justification; protection of human life; common good; protection of the rights of children and persons involved in AR; equality, freedom of choice, and human dignity; protection of privacy; and security.[9] The procedures that are in accordance with this law are *in vivo* (inserting sperm cells inside reproductive organs of a woman and inserting oocytes along with sperm cells inside of a woman's body), and *in vitro* fertilization (merging ovum and sperm cells outside of a body and inserting

---

6   Convention for the Protection of Human Rights and Dignity of the Human Being with regard to the Application of Biology and Medicine: Convention on Human Rights and Biomedicine, Oviedo, April 4, 1997; for the official text, see conventions.coe.int/Treaty/en/Treaties/Html/164.htm, last accessed on May 21, 2013.

7   Steering Committee on Bioethics, Developments in the Field of Bioethics in Member States, Other States and International Organizations (Strasbourg: Council of Europe, 2011); available at: www. coe.int/t/dg3/healthbioethic/Source/developments 2011.doc, last accessed on May 21, 2013.

8   Infertility Treatment Act, *op. cit.*

9   *Ibid.*, Articles 4–12.

an early embryo inside the woman's body).[10] Practically, this means that it is allowed to perform intrauterine insemination (IUI), *in vitro* fertilization (IVF), intracytoplasmatic sperm injection (ICSI) with embryotransfer (ET). The right to AR and medical preconditions for the AR are regulated by a norm which stipulates that the right to participate in an assisted reproductive procedure is restricted to married couples or a cohabiting woman and man, who cannot be helped to conceive a child in any other manner or if AR is a means to avoid severe hereditary diseases.[11]

Secondly, this law sets the institutional conditions under which the procedures are performed in healthcare facilities, defines the tasks of state administration, and determines other issues important for the implementation of these procedures. The Infertility Treatment Act regulates, in general, the procedures of harvesting, donating, processing, preserving, utilizing, distributing reproductive cells and monitoring serious adverse reactions and serious adverse effects on these cells[12] based on main Tissue and Cells Directive from 2004[13] and two technical Directives from 2006 which have a purpose to harmonize legislation among the Member States of the European Union.

Before adopting the new law, the key organizations that had an influence on regulatory issues were the Ministry of Health, the Republic Fund of Health Insurance and the National Expert Commission of the Ministry of Health. With this new law the National Ethics Committee, the National Committee for Bioethics, and the ethics committees in health care institutions have been given a more important role. The National Ethics Committee is an expert body which is taking care of provision and implementation of health care in whole of Republic of Serbia, in accordance with professional principles.[14] The National Bioethics Committee is mandated to promote a view on ethical and legal contents derived from research in science and to give a stimulus to exchanging ideas and information, especially in the field of natural sciences in general, and genetics and biomedicine in particular.[15] The establishment of ethics commit-

10 *Ibid.*, Article 23.
11 *Ibid.*, Articles 26 and 27.
12 *Ibid.*, Article 2.
13 Directive 2004/23/EC of the European Parliament and of the Council of 31 March 2004 on setting standards of quality and safety for the donation, procurement, testing, processing, preservation, storage and distribution of human tissues and cells; official English text available at eur-lex.europa.eu/LexUriServ/LexUriServ.do?uri=OJ:L:2004:102:0048:0058:EN:PDF, last accessed on May 21, 2013.
14 Zakon o zdravstvenoj zaštiti, *Službeni glasnik Republike Srbije*, broj 107/2005 [Act no. 107of 2005 on Health Care], later amended by Acts no. 72/2009, 88/2010, 99/2010, 57/2011, and 119/2012, Articles 156 and 157; available at www.paragraf.rs/propisi/zakon_o_zdravstvenoj_zastiti.html, last accessed on May 21, 2013.
15 Nacionalni komitet za bioetiku Komisije za saradnju sa Uneskom R. Srbije [The National Committee for Bioethics of the UNESCO Commission of the Republic of Serbia]; see more in English at http://www.sanu.ac.rs/English/Bioethics/Bioethics.aspx, last accessed on May 21, 2013.

tees in health care institutions was provided by the Health Care Act of 2005 in Articles 143 and 147. On all levels (micro, middle, and macro) there are ethics committees assigned to deal with corresponding problems. Legal ground of ethical principles in scientific-research work as well as in medical practice has reached the widest application in the last 20 years or so, especially in times when Serbia was in deep isolation.[16] Through national and international institutions Serbia is catching up with world and European trends and practices. With the new act, administrative role is given to Directorate of Biomedicine[17] (a body within the Ministry of Health) which is expected to participate in the preparation of guidelines for good practice and standards for assisted reproduction procedures and procedures for conducting sampling, processing, distribution, and insertion of reproductive cells or embryos.[18] Launching the new organization with given tasks, lawmaker had the aim to foster the implementation of the new act and emphasize the importance of transparency and security/safety of the system.

The newly established legal framework, the medical procedures and institutions created better environment for carrying out the treatment of infertility by biomedically assisted fertilization procedures, in accordance with modern standards in medical science and practice. This medical field is developing intensively and offers a great potential for the treatment of various forms of infertility and sterility. At this moment various medical treatments are performed in Serbia which are regulated by the new law and wide clinical practice guidelines, good laboratory practice and ethical guidelines which helps health workers to act in the most appropriate way. Intrauterine insemination, IVF/ICSI, ovulation induction (OI) and assisted hatching (AH) are allowed by national law. Pre-implantation genetic screening (PGS), sex selection (except in cases where is it allowed for medical reasons) and surrogacy are prohibited by Article 56(25), while in vitro maturation is not at all mentioned in the act. There are some cases in Serbian legislation when pre-implantation genetic diagnostics (PGD) is allowed such as the risk of transmitting genetic diseases, chromosomal and genetic diagnostics disease or if they are necessary for the success of the AR procedure.[19] The possibility for research work Serbian legislator predicts only on early embryos which aren't of suitable quality to be implemented in the woman's body or for freezing, and on those embryos that would have to be let die.[20] Producing embryos only for research purposes is strictly prohibited by Article 24 of the Infertility Treatment Act.

---

16 Sandra Radenković, Karel Turza, Zoran Todorović, Vida Jeremić, Insitucionalizacija Bioetike u Srbiji, *Socialna ekologija*, Zagreb, 2012, 21(3): 311–328, at 314.

17 Uprava za biomedicinu [Directorate of Biomedicine], www.euprava.gov.rs/eusluge/institucija?service=servicesForInstitution&institutionId=130&alphabet=lat, last accessed on May 21, 2013.

18 Infertility Treatment Act, *op. cit.*, Article 67(13).

19 *Ibid.*, Article 54.

20 *Ibid.*, Article 60(3).

To perform AR it is necessary to obtain a written consent of all persons involved in AR, and this consent is required for every single attempt of insemination, and can be revoked by a written cancellation but only before sperm cells, unfertilized oocyte or early embryos are once inside of a woman's body.[21] Use of embryos or gametes in case of divorce or separation is not allowed while, according to Article 58(4) of the Infertility Treatment Act, post-mortem use of gametes or embryos is possible if there is a written consent.

At this moment there is no unified registry and the provision of a registry data has so far relied on the voluntary registries of clinics. Establishing the single register for assisted reproductive treatments on national level is obligatory under the law. The data kept in the Register will contain information on persons who donated their reproductive cells; persons received reproductive cells during AR procedure; data concerning the effectiveness of various procedures or on babies born with help of this procedure; as well as other significant data concerning AR and reproductive cell donation.[22]

Thirdly, this normative act focuses on regulating a question that is challenging for many countries—donation. Serbian law, basically, has to promote donation of reproductive cells on a national level in order to inform and educate citizens about the importance of donating reproductive cells. The act provides that donation of reproduction cells is possible in two cases: when a couple cannot have a child in any other manner (*in vitro* fertilization is already an exhausted option) or when it is in the interest of the health and safety of the child.[23] The area of infertility treatment by biomedically assisted fertilization procedures is maintained in accordance with the regulations and EU standards in this area. Before adopting the new act, regulations on IVF with donated oocyte were based on the approval by Ethical Committee of Clinics for Gynecology and Obstetrics, Clinical centre of Serbia. Directorate for Biomedicine is suppose to have the highest authority together with the Ministry of Health, by making decisions on approval for the procedure of assisted reproduction with donated reproductive cells.

Apart from allowing heterosexual, married and unmarried couples to undertake an assisted reproduction treatment, single women are also entitled to AR procedures in Serbia, in special cases and with justifiable reasons.[24] The legislator has made it clear that procreation of children by and for same-sex partners should be absolutely forbidden. Possibility of marriage of the same sex couples is not provided in the new draft Civil Code, which is consistent with the Serbian Constitution that proclaims: "marriage shall be entered in the free consent of man and woman under a public authority."[25]

---

21 *Ibid.*, Articles 37–38.
22 *Ibid.*, Article 44.
23 *Ibid.*, Article 27.
24 Infertility Treatment Act, *op. cit.*, article 26; the Minister of Health and the Minister of Family Relationships have to approve the procedure.
25 Ustav Republike Srbije, br. 98/2006 [The Constitution of the Republic of Serbia, 2006], Article 62.

Nowadays, a challenging issue, not just for Serbia, but for many developed countries, is a question whether donor identity should be disclosed or not. According to Serbian law, information (non personal data) about donors can be obtained only on doctors' or child's request (child who was conceived with AR procedure with reproductive cells of donor). A child, who is thus conceived in this type of procedure, has the right, only due to medical reasons, to obtain the data relating to gamete donors from the Directorate of Biomedicine, when he or she turns 18 years of age. Anonymity and confidentiality of personal data is highlighted by Serbian law (see Table 2).

Table 2. *Sperm, Oocyte and Embryo Donation in Serbia*

Serbia	Regulation
Sperm donation	Allowed if anonymous
Oocyte donation	Allowed if anonymous
Embryo donation	Not allowed
Imports and exports	Not allowed

In practice, sometimes it's difficult to avoid a non-anonymous donor. If a woman wants to become a single mother, she can enter into an 'unofficial' agreement with a man who wants to be a donor 'without obligation'. Agreement doesn't mean that a man is relieved from alimony obligation. In that case there is no donor anonymity and that underlines a different set of legal consequences.

Data of medical importance (but not any personal data of the donors) may be requested and obtained from the Directorate for Biomedicine. Serbian law is prohibiting non-anonymous oocyte and embryo donation in AR as well procedures with simultaneous application of donated oocytes and donated sperm cells.[26] In Serbian society, with still very patriarchal beliefs, non-anonymous or 'cousin' donation is not common. That is probably because the potential donor might have a fear of getting sued, even if it is guaranteed by Article 66(3) of the Infertility Treatment Act that if the child has been conceived by AR procedure where the donor sperm cell was used, it is forbidden to establish paternity. Thus, the Infertility Treatment Act specifies who is considered to be the mother or the father of the child, including all legal effects (i.e. inheritance, property, etc.), with explicitly prohibiting that a donor may become a legal mother or father.[27] The donor has also no legal or other obligation to the child born using donated reproductive cells.[28]

---

26 Infertility Treatment Act, *op. cit.*, Article 56(18).
27 *Ibid.*, Articles 65 and 66.
28 *Ibid.*, Article 51.

Based on the Oviedo Convention, in which it is explicitly stated that the human body and its parts shall not, as such, give rise to financial gain,[29] Serbian law defined as the act of crime giving own reproductive cells or embryos with any compensations.[30] Still, reimbursement of necessary and justified costs to donors, including the donor's loss of salary linked to the donation is guaranteed by the law.[31]

The Directorate of Biomedicine will have single register of donated reproductive cells which will take the precise note of who gave the cells and where, so one person cannot be a biological father more than once. According to Serbian law, the donor can donate sperm more than once but only till one baby is born of that sperm.[32] Register of donor gametes has to be under protection, because the data withdraws legal consequences, for the family, the donor and the child.

Having in mind that import/export of reproductive cells for making embryos in the biomedical assisted reproduction is forbidden by law in Serbia,[33] the law stipulates that Serbia might, for the first time, get a bank of donated gametes—oocyte and sperm, and provide the possibility of artificial insemination by donated cells. The first bank of sperm in Serbia, due to the lack of technical equipment is prolonged to be open in 2013 which still did not happen. Since there is still no reproductive cells bank in Serbia and import and export of cells are prohibited, this law makes AR difficult if not impossible, for patients who own frozen embryos, and want to transfer it to Serbia. The law is not precise when it comes to ownership of gametes. In practice, such patients need an approval paper from Directorate of Biomedicine, and the law does not define precise rule for export and import of embryos, nor biological ancestry of transported embryos, that can be transferred, for example, even between Serbia and Montenegro which were one country.

Conclusion

Serbian law on assisted reproduction doesn't have a long history, but with enactment of the Act on the Treatment of Infertility by Biomedically Assisted Fertilization Procedures in 2009, Serbian legislation has taken a huge step forward in regulating these important issues. While the adoption of this act already represents a progress compared to the previous years, the level of implementation can be still considered insufficient and not developed. The Infertility Treatment Act is harmonized with the EU legislation in this area while the laws that would regulate assisted reproduction issues in more specific details are still missing

---

29 The Oviedo Convention, *op. cit.*, Chapter VII, Article 21.
30 Infertility Treatment Act, *op. cit.*, Article 71(1).
31 *Ibid.*, Article 28(5), clause 1.
32 *Ibid.*, Article 41(3).
33 *Ibid.*, Article 39.

in Serbia, which is recognized as the main hurdle in practice. The drafting of additional laws and by-laws to implement this act is, however, in process.

Serbian legislation has a tendency to cover different aspects of assisted reproduction: weather patient will be included in AR process, under which conditions and who is eligible to undergo donor treatment. Serbia is considered as liberal country since *in vitro* fertilization is allowed, but less liberal comparing to other countries that allow surrogacy, IVF for homosexual couples or non-anonymous sperm and oocytes donation. National register is supposed to have important impact on quality and patient safety improvement avoiding possible adverse events on a long run. The existence of good and regulated evidence of achievements would enable Serbia to compare with other European countries.

With this new formed legal framework, analyzed in this paper, medical procedures and institutions created better surroundings for carrying out the treatment of infertility by biomedically assisted fertilization procedures in accordance with modern standards in medical science and practice. The process of regulating and specifying all issues in assisted reproduction in detail is not over, but the work done so far is a great stepping stone for further elaboration. The acts of lower legislation power are the next logical step in further development which will solve many dilemmas and bridge legal gaps that are present in practice today among medical staff as well as the patients.

ROMA AS RESEARCH SUBJECTS IN THE HUNGARIAN HUMAN GENETIC DISCOURSE

Barna Szamosi

Introduction

Numerous studies were published after the completion of the Human Genome Project on the tenability of the use of classical racial and ethnic categories in the contemporary genomic science. In this chapter I will analyze what are the foundations of racial and ethnic classification in the human genetics of Hungary.[1] The study is organized around the following themes that emerged from the interviews[2]: first, patronym based genetic identification; second, single-nucleotide-polymorphism (SNP) screenings for disease; and third, phylogenetics. I will try to show that human genetic practices—starting from the molecular and molar level, through family tree analysis and disease mapping, to genetic ancestry research—contribute to the construction of Roma biosocial identities. Biosocialities[3] are defined as the communities of active biological citizens, who organize themselves around a disease irrelevant to their ethnic belonging. The only important social category is the name of the disease which links these different people together. Roma as a social identity category was created by the Romani intelligentsia to empower and mobilize politically the diverse and marginalized gypsy ethnicities

---

1   This chapter is based on the empirical research that I conducted during my Gender Studies MA and partly based on the work that I continue in my PhD studies at the Central European University in Comparative Gender Studies. To develop the arguments presented here I benefited from the consultations with my supervisors Professor Judit Sándor and Professor Andrea Pető.

2   Since 2010 I recorded 18 interviews in Hungarian language with human geneticists interested in population genetics and clinical genetics. Because of textual limitations I will use here only a part of the interviews. All of the translations from Hungarian into English are my work.

3   Nikolas Rose, Race in the Age of Genomic Medicine, in Nikolas Rose, *The Politics of Life Itself* (Princeton and Oxford: Princeton University Press, 2007), 155–186, at 174.

across Europe.[4] The genetic practice of creating disease maps and linking it to Roma identity is in opposition to the intended use of these sociological terms. Research in the field of human genetics in Hungary began in the 1960s–1970s. Since this period publications have appeared in diverse fields but as we can see, for example, from the earlier works of Endre Czeizel, the most important directions were genetic counseling[5] and the genetic structure of Hungarians.[6] For more recent research on the genetic problems of the Hungarian populations we can read the works of Gyűrűs et al.,[7] or Fiatal and Ádány.[8] One can also find publications giving a description of the genetic difference between the Roma and other ethnic Hungarian people (see Béres,[9] Kósa and Ádány[10]). By now there is a burgeoning literature in medical genetics focusing on the genetic structure of Roma people in different locations within Hungary (for more information see the works of Melegh et al.,[11] Kósa et al.,[12] Vokó et al.,[13] Molnár et al.,[14] and Sipeky et al.[15]). These studies introduce to the wider scien-

4 Zoltan Barany, Ethnic Mobilization and the State: The Roma in Eastern Europe, Ethnic and Racial Studies, March 1998, 21(2): 308–327.

5 Endre Czeizel and Pál Magyar, A születendő gyermek védelmében [For the Protection of the Prospective Child] (Budapest: Medicina Könyvkiadó, 1974).

6 Endre Czeizel, A magyarság genetikája [Genetics of the Hungarian Population] (Budapest: Galenus Kiadó, 2003 [1990]).

7 Péter Gyűrűs, János Molnár, Béla Melegh, Gábor Tóth, Éva Morava, György Kosztolányi, and Károly Méhes, Trinucleotide Repeat Polymorphism at Five Disease Loci in Mixed Hungarian Population, American Journal of Medical Genetics, November 1999, 87(3): 245–250.

8 Szilvia Fiatal and Róza Ádány, A népegészségügyi szempontból jelentős betegségekre hajlamosító genetikai mutációk a magyar populációban (Genetic Mutations in the Hungarian Population That Cause Susceptibility in Significant Diseases from a Public Health Perspective), Népegészségügy, 2009, 87(3): 185–194.

9 Judit Béres, A magyarországi népesség genetikai rokonsága [Genetic Ancestry of the Hungarian Population], in Egon Hídvégi (ed.) A Genom [The Genome] (Budapest: Széphalom Könyvműhely 2003), 171–186.

10 Karolina Kósa and Róza Ádány, Studying Vulnerable Populations: Lessons from the Roma Minority, Epidemiology, May 2007, 18(3): 290–299.

11 Béla Melegh, Judit Bene, Gábor Mogyorósy,Viktória Havasi, Katalin Komlósi, László Pajor, Éva Oláh, Gyula Kispál, Balázs Sümegi, and Károly Méhes, Phenotypic Manifestations of the OCTN2 V295X Mutation: Sudden Infant Death and Carnitine-Responsive Cardiomyopathy in Roma Families, American Journal of Medical Genetics, December 2004, 131A(2): 121–126.

12 Zsigmond Kósa, György Széles, László Kardos, Karolina Kósa, Renáta Németh, Sándor Országh, Gabriella Fésüs, Martin McKee, Róza Ádány, and Zoltán Vokó, A Comparative Health Survey of the Inhabitants of Roma Settlements in Hungary, American Journal of Public Health, May 2007, 97(5): 853–859.

13 Zoltán Vokó, Péter Csépe, Renáta Németh, Karolina Kósa, Zsigmond Kósa, György Széles, and Róza Ádány, Does Socioeconomic Status Fully Mediate the Effect of Ethnicity on the Health of the Roma People in Hungary? Journal of Epidemiology and Public Health, June 2009, 63(6): 455–460.

14 Ágnes Molnár, Róza Ádány, Béla Ádám, Gabriel Gulis, and Karolina Kósa, Health Impact Assessment and Evaluation of a Roma Housing Project in Hungary, Health Place, November 2010, 16(6): 1240–1247.

15 Csilla Sipeky, Veronika Csöngei, Luca Járomi, Enikő Sáfrány, Anita Maász, István Takács, Judit Béres, Lajos Fodor, Melinda Szabó, and Béla Melegh, Genetic Variability and Haplotype Profile of MDR1 (ABCB1) in Roma and Hungarian Population Samples with a Review of the Literature, Drug Metabolism and Pharmacokinetics, April 2011, 26(2): 206–215.

tific community the genetic mutations that make Roma people susceptible to certain diseases.

There is a strong tendency to defend the standpoint that the genetic research that tries to map molecular biological differences between ethnic communities is apolitical.[16] It is argued by Raskó and Kalmár that the mapping of the distance of various ethnic communities from each other is an objective scientific method which can help to connect genetic traits with genetic diseases. In a similar manner, Judit Béres who is a leading population geneticist in Hungary focusing on the genetic structure of the Roma people, claims that there are genetic diseases which put primarily the Roma people of Hungary at risk.[17] The genetic screening of Roma people is justified by the human geneticists by reference to the large number of genetic diseases within the communities and their culturally-accepted endogamous practices.

In the following I will present a social constructivist critique to the application of race and ethnicity in genetics based on the studies of social scientists who are working on human genetics. Human geneticists are applying the cladistic race concept for establishing populations. The problem with this concept is that it views race as biologically objective and as a result it reifies racial power relations at the molecular and molar level. I will try to outline the contours of this problem in the practice of Hungarian genetic research.

Arguments against Racial and Ethnic Classification

Since the appearance of racial classification the dominant form of racial differentiation was based on phenotypical differences that are connected to the human habitation of continents. In this racializing discourse the main classificatory categories were the European, African, Asian, Pacific Islander, and Native American. The term 'race' referred and still refers to a subset of the human species. 'Ethnicity' is somewhat an extension of this original term: it similarly refers to the recently multiplied and classified subsets such as Hispanic, African American, Chinese American and, in Europe we could add, the Roma racial or ethnic category as an example for the racializing tendency of 'othering' the diverse Gipsy ethnic people of the European states.

After the completion of the Human Genome Project, in relation to racial categorization, the scientific field of human genetics became divided. Some human geneticists acknowledged that there is no scientific basis to use 'races' to describe human variation.[18] In this case the standpoint that human geneticists

---

16 István Raskó and Tibor Kalmár, Emberi populáció genetika: különbségek emberek között, politika nélkül [Human Population Genetics: Differences between Humans without Politics], in Egon Hídvégi (ed.), *A Genom* [The Genome] (Budapest: Széphalom Könyvműhely 2003), 105–112.
17 Judit Béres, *op. cit.*
18 István Raskó, *Honfoglaló Génjeink* [Our Settler Genes] (Budapest: Medicina, 2010).

take explicitly rejects any biological reality of race. In other words they subscribe to the constructivist approach: race is a social category which is used to describe power relations between dominant and non-dominant groups in different historical contexts. There are arguments set out by theorists who support the racial differentiation of human populations in contemporary biomedical research. Risch et al.[19] argue that the genetic differences that researchers find on the molecular level underscore the importance of racial classification from a medical point of view. They claim that it is possible to use these racial categories in an objective value neutral manner. According to their standpoint such utilization of this classification is purely scientific and serves the interest of the classified populations.

The tension which is related to the biological realist and social constructivist approaches to race is highlighted by scientists such as Troy Duster,[20] Joseph L. Graves and Michael R. Rose,[21] and Priscilla Wald[22] analyzing molecular genetics. Contemporary genetic screenings are targeting racial and ethnic groups. The health rationales of these programs are justified by the heredity statistics of the examined populations but the causal relation is erroneously biologized. The reasons that cause statistically distinct genetic diseases are not biological but social.

The cladistic race concept denotes 'breeding groups' and their genetic distance from each other in the phylogenetic tree.[23] It is invented to be compatible with various medical applications hence it is central in the criticism of theorists such as Glasgow[24] and Ganett[25] whose aim is to deconstruct race as a biological reality. Other researchers such as Kassim,[26] Azoulay[27] plainly refuse any race concept which is disconnected from the social sphere by arguing that race represents social hierarchy which is projected onto our bodies. Since the cladistic

19 Neil Risch, Esteban Burchard, Elad Ziv, and Hua Tang, Categorization of Humans in Biomedical Research: Genes, Race, and Disease, in Evelynn M. Hammonds and Rebecca M. Herzig (eds.), *The Nature of Difference: Sciences of Race in the United States from Jefferson to Genomics* (Cambridge, MA: MIT Press, 2008), 325–345.
20 Troy Duster, The Molecular Reinscription of Race: Unanticipated Issues in Biotechnology and Forensic Science, *Patterns of Prejudice*, November 2006, 40(4–5): 427–441.
21 Joseph L. Graves and Michael R. Rose, Against Racial Medicine, *Patterns of Prejudice*, November 2006, 40(4–5): 481–493.
22 Priscilla Wald, Blood and Stories: How Genomics is Changing Race, Medicine and Human History, *Patterns of Prejudice*, November 2006, 40(4–5): 303–333.
23 Robin O. Andreasen, A New Perspective On the Race Debate, *British Journal for the Philosophy of Science*, 1998, 49(2): 199–225.
24 Joshua Glasgow, On the New Biology of Race, *Journal of Philosophy*, September 2003, 100(9): 456–474.
25 Lisa Gannett, The Biological Reification of Race, *British Journal for the Philosophy of Science*, June 2004, 55(2): 323–345.
26 Hussein Kassim, 'Race', Genetics and Human Difference, in Justine Burley and John Harris (eds.) *A Companion to Genethics* (Oxford: Blackwell, 2004), 302–316.
27 Katya G. Azoulay, Reflections on Race and the Biologization of Difference, *Patterns of Prejudice*, November 2006, 40(4–5): 353–379.

race concept is what is applied in human genetics it is necessary to shortly summarize its role in the biological sciences and the reasons for its rejection by social scientists.

In her work Andreasen argued for a biological race concept that is based on 'clades'. "Andreasen's cladistic account of race conceives races as 'historical individuals'. . . . Races are constituted on the basis of genealogical relations among populations of organisms, and not similarities in the intrinsic properties of organisms."[28] Gannett claims that the problem with the cladistic race concept, from a methodological perspective, is that it falsely presents the genealogically related 'breeding populations' as formed independently from social categorization and hence these can be termed as objective races. Gannett thus claims that there is no way in which Andreasen could have defined her racial categories without drawing on sociocultural traditions.

In this new conceptual framework defended by Andreasen a *statistical* race concept replaces the earlier *typological*, essentialist type that characterized the pre-1945 discourse. The theoretical grounds for the usage of this concept can be traced back to the works of Theodosius Dobzhansky and Luigi Luca Cavalli-Sforza. In his works on the relation of human genetics to human races Dobzhansky argues that breeding relations are the defining elements in the conceptualization of race. He suggests that Mendelian breeding populations, where the gene flow takes place, can be considered to be races. Cavalli-Sforza similarly argues that language, ethnicity and other social barriers of gene flow define the population for the purposes of human genetic research.[29]

In their approaches breeding populations can be seen as equal to races. As a consequence this race concept, based on statistical data, allows infinite number of races within a geographical area, depending only on one factor: the reproductive history of the group members. This theoretical approach to biological race relies on ancestral data, family ties, and greater group membership. Here we can see that race emerges at the intersection of social categories just as it emerged in the pre-1945 discourse despite Andreasen's claim that this conceptualization of race is objective.

The difference in the contemporary context is that statistical data is collected from the molecular level, but group membership and hence the gene flow is channeled along the intersections of language, religion, ethnic belonging, citizenship, skin color, and class. Although Andreasen claims that the cladistic race concept is objective as it connects individuals through their reproductive relations the problem with this approach to race is that it reifies the socially constructed power relations on the molecular level without any reflection on the socio-culturally diverse meanings of race which depends on its geographical and temporal location.

---

28 Gannett, *op. cit.*, 327.
29 *Ibid.*

Let me start my argumentation with paraphrasing one of my interviewees thinking about the development of human race and its sub-races. The interviewee introduced the problem for me in the following manner (Personal Interview 8): humans belong to the same species, but as humans migrated across the globe, their bodies reacted differently to their environment. This is how simple phenotypical differences are explained. As a consequence of this historical process biologists differentiate between three main races: Africans, Orientals [Asians], and Europeans, to which, as the interviewee said, we could add Native Americans, and Australians, but they are not necessary. And from these main races, we can see how sub-races developed. The interviewee gave examples for the sub-races of the white European race: the Gypsies, the Jews, and the Arab people. Then this researcher lamented further that when thinking about Jewish people, it is hard to classify them either as a sub-race, an ethnicity, or a nationality. In the following pages I will try to show that human geneticists have the same problem with classifying Roma people.

Genetic Identification on the Grounds of Patronyms

One of the first steps that human geneticists do to locate Roma families in a given geographical area is to look for names which are stereotypically associated with the members of Roma communities. Family names are cultural tools to signify group membership, but as such they are subject to change, hence they are very imprecise markers for genetic research. The problem of genetic ancestry research based on family names is two-sided: (1) dynamic on the social-interactional level and (2) meaningless on the molecular level. I will try to give examples for these problems below.

With the application of molecular biological technologies it is not possible to identify who is Roma, "it is not possible to tell from the genes if somebody is Roma or non-Roma" (Personal Interview 1), but on the social interactional level it seems sometimes very simple:

In many cases it is very trivial, so for example, we know that an 'Orsós' name is 99.99% Roma name, so the Hungarian majority do not use it. There are names undoubtedly which are used by both populations: 'Horváth' there are many Roma who is Horváth, but this name is similarly used by Hungarians as well, so you cannot tell them apart all the time sharply. In some case it speaks for itself, sometimes the person identifies himself/herself as Roma. (Personal Interview 1)

From this formulation it is not entirely clear what it means that "it speaks for itself" but I assume that the interviewee means: identities are performatively projected onto individuals by the spectator based on phenotypes (physiology, skin color, hair texture). However this is also problematic because it stabilizes racial/ethnic identity on the molar level without taking into account other social factors such as geographic location, nationality, and language use.

And sometimes it is unequivocally problematic to use surnames as a starting point as it is visible from the quote below:

We asked for samples from the majority, Hungarian majority, who were sure that their ancestors, at least from the last four generations, nobody were neither this nor that. To my biggest surprise, some of my colleagues told me: 'I give you my DNA with pleasure but there is Bosnian in the great-grandparent branch.' So he told us, he did not make it a secret, although his name is completely Hungarian. (Personal Interview 1)

It is unambiguous from the above examples, that this method is deeply burdened with stereotypes and the 'othering' practices of the researchers. Despite their acknowledgement of its inaccuracies this practice is widely accepted by human population geneticists and this methodology is called patrilineal analysis of single surnames which is based on the custom that the father gives his name to his children. This genealogical method of tracing family origins and group relatedness through the descendants of a father is only of interest in males hence it is a very problematic gender aspect in human genetic research: it reinforces the patriarchal ideology that females are not as valuable as males in the history of a society.[30]

Mapping SNP Markers in Roma People for Identifying Diseases

To locate SNP mutations which are responsible for the development of genetic diseases, human geneticists collected biological data during their fieldwork with the method of snowball sampling: they primarily mapped the frequent communicable diseases. These are visible health problems and some of them are more common in the Roma communities—like the primary congenital glaucoma, which result in blindness at a very early age—therefore geneticists asked about people who have the disease in the community and they asked about other diseases in the family. Finally they inquired about other Roma families where diseases occurred (Personal Interview 3).

Population geneticists argue, it is important to know what kinds of diseases occur, and with what kind of frequency in these population cohorts. In the third personal interview the importance of genetic research is framed by the interviewee from the perspective of prevention. The interviewed researcher claimed that this genetic screening program is good for the individual and for the community as well: the ideal is that people have independent access to genetic counseling in their regions.

---

30 Catherine Nash, Genetic Kinship, *Cultural Studies*, January 2004, 18(1): 1–33, at 7.

With this method human geneticists mapped and continue to map the disease profile of a Roma community. The point of their work is to facilitate the genetic health management of individuals: to foster change in their health behavior, in their dieting, to promote lifestyle decisions, and to assist their reproductive life. Although human geneticists claim that they provide their clients with genetic information, the gained genetic knowledge is not sufficiently channeled back to the community members. It seems that the marginalized social positions of the Roma people place the voluntary application of genetic knowledge into the distant future:

> In connection to Roma people I would not say that it will be applied soon, because in many places they are very poor. They even do not know what to eat. Sometimes they eat potatoes for a week or just bread and butter. So they are struggling for survival day by day, this is not in their priorities. (Personal Interview 3)

Another interpretation for the difficulty of the application of genetic information in Roma communities is connected to the distrust towards the majority population. One of my interviewees (Personal Interview 7) explains that s/he met with many Roma individuals during examinations but they never came voluntarily, they were always sent by clinicians or officials for further examinations. The interviewee explained to me that s/he came to realize that Roma people tend to solve their problems, even the more serious cases, among each other. The researcher thinks that this is because:

> They might be afraid [of the police] and they might have their own authority, the voivode [their ethnic leader]. (Personal Interview 7)

In another interview, the role of the ethnic leader also stressed by a clinical geneticist:

> When he [the leader] is coming to the children's clinic, a colorful hat is on his head and some thirty people are coming with him. (Personal Interview 1)

This interviewee further explained that from their interactions it is clearly visible that he is the leader of the community. These examples are significant in the sense that they highlight the relationship of Roma people to the majority population. They preserved their own ethnic structures and as a result of their discrimination and social marginalization they are suspicious with any approach from the majority population. Although genetic screenings could contribute to the elevation of their health standards they treat these attempts very sensitively.

This attitude is underscored in another interview. In this case the researcher explained that Roma people in Hungary are very uncooperative (Personal Interview 5), and traced this medical issue to the problem of stigmatization.

> Roma people are unwilling to cooperate when they are not aware that the problem is a serious medical issue. When they understand the importance

of the medical problem they are the initiators of the interaction. It is clearly understandable that ethnic minorities do not want to be stigmatized, but this is more of a communication problem. It depends on the credibility of the communicators. They have to believe that they help these people, they have to turn to these people with good intentions, and they have to be able to explain to them that these studies serve the interest of these populations. If this is understood, then any kind of research is possible because fundamentally any kind of scientific result is future oriented. (Personal Interview 5)

The theme of necessary future research on Roma people as the building block of positive social change ties into another significant contribution of human genetics to contemporary healthcare practices which is related to pharmacogenomics, a field that works on developing drug therapies for genetic problems:
> The contemporary paradigm in therapeutic method is the practice, if we are sick we get medicine to cure the symptoms, so the ideal would be to get medicine for our genes. (Personal Interview 1)

In relation to this paradigm change, the first interviewee argues this contemporary attitude is starting to change, researchers realized for the first time in the US, that certain drugs had side effects for African-American patients because their gene-structure reacts differently to drugs from the White European gene-structure. Geneticists claim that these findings were exemplary for the conduct of population genetic studies in different regions of Hungary and for the inclusion of different ethnicities in these projects. The implication is that Roma people could benefit from pharmacogenomics in the future.

When I tried to inquire about the possible different drug reactions in the Hungarian population one of my interviewees emphasized the mainly homogenous character of the population of Hungary (mostly Caucasian), with the exceptions of Roma and Jewish people (Personal Interview 6). This researcher further explained the relationship of genes and drugs to racial belonging in the following manner:
> I only inquire about the patients [racial/ethnic] belonging in the cases of diseases which are more frequent in certain populations, because I cannot see always which race they belong to. (Personal Interview 6)

It seems that assigning race is a practical problem in a clinical interaction because medical geneticists think that they need this data for diagnostic purposes to find the best therapeutic response for a genetically related disease. In my reading clinical geneticists are looking for other information for which race serves as a very imprecise marker.

In a more detailed explanation another interviewee (Personal Interview 4) described the value of genetic information for drug related medical responses. This geneticist stressed the importance of medical knowledge on gene mutations because different mutations cause different bodily reactions to viruses. A well-known example from the international literature is a heterozygous mutation which developed as an environmental reaction against malaria in the Mediterranean. When two heterozygous carriers meet their offspring will have 25 percent chance to develop the ß-Thalassemia disease.[31] In my interview the emphasis was laid on the homozygous and heterozygous alleles of certain genes in the Hungarian population. My interviewee claimed that the Roma people statistically (but only hypothetically) are more resistant to certain viruses, as a result of their homozygous mutations. The biological explanation behind this phenomenon is the following: without the mutation the alleles function in a manner that they help to tie viruses in our bodies, which will cause our diseases. People having different mutations which are in reaction with different viruses respond to drug therapies differently. Hence, genetic information can be very important for doctors who need to prescribe different drugs for their patients in order to be effective in the process of overcoming their diseases. In other words, the location of SNP mutations are valuable in clinical genetics because this kind of genetic data can be used for a wide range of medical purposes, but beyond its clinical use, SNP mutations are seen as valuable sources for mapping the genetic ancestry of a population.

Ethnic Identity Based on Y Chromosome Research

Patronyms can be used to identify possible Roma individuals, and coupling this method with family anamnesis, and screening for SNP markers can result in genetic data that can be used for further research, such as genetic studies of ancestry. The discipline which focuses on the common ancestors of different contemporary populations is called phylogenetics. These studies investigate the biological phenomenon of how information is preserved on the Y chromosome and the way it is transmitted from father to son. The structure of the Y chromosome barely changes through time. On a small part of the X chromosome the mitochondrial DNA similarly preserves information. But in this case because of the limited number of interviews I can only specify the problems which arise from the Y chromosomes studies.

The reason to conduct Y chromosome analysis is the low information flow on these parts of the genes. When the joining of the X and Y chromosomes occur the father transmits the Y chromosome to his son, but the child gets his X chromosome from his mother. The problem for the research on the X chromosome is that its structure more easily changes in comparison to the Y chromosome hence there is no space for women in the genealogy of a population.

The research on Y chromosomes is justified as this is the only tool at hand, which can determine the possible starting point of migration of a given popula-

---

31 Ruth Schwartz Cowan, *Heredity and Hope: The Case for Genetic Screening* (Cambridge, MA: Harvard University Press, 2008).

tion. "We research Y chromosomes to find out for example how did a chosen Hungarian person's ancestors come to Europe" (Personal Interview 2). And the method of getting answers to these questions is the study of the changes (point mutations) on the Y chromosomes.

> We detect SNPs on the Y chromosome to trace back the history of these point mutations, and then with this method it is possible to follow the examined person's ancestors. These are unique mutation events, it happens once and these are population specific. And this is important in the case of Roma. (Personal Interview 2)

A point mutation (SNP) can be defined as a unique mutation in contrast to the other mutations which are occurring frequently. In my second personal interview, the researcher explained that mathematical programs help to determine from these two kinds of mutations, the time when these mutations happened and when their common ancestors lived. It is promising to research the Y chromosomes, because it "can be divided into ten major haplogroups, which are the genetic variants of the Y chromosome."[32] With these Y chromosome variants it is possible to trace back the place where the Y chromosome mutation occurred in a geographical area.

These mathematical programs can give descriptions to the ancestry of a Y chromosome, but this method cannot answer the questions which are related to the matrilineal ancestry and the reproduction of a population. It gives answers to comparison of populations if they belong to the same haplogroup but if the answer is positive, it still does not mean that they share the same ethnicity. Nevertheless, I think it is still useful to see the directions that phylogeneticists map in their research.

> In our opinion, the Roma groups started to migrate from India, they crossed the Middle-East, and then they went into the Balkans, and from the Balkans it [the H1 haplogroup] spread across Europe. And while they were travelling they picked up genetic characteristics from the populations they met on their way. (Personal Interview 2)

The only reason why geneticists are still able to detect these characteristics is the exclusion of these Roma communities from the European societies. The haplogroups that they picked up during their migration are detectable in the contemporary communities, because they live in socially isolated groups. Their social exclusion is part of their reason for endogamy.

> When a group is isolated it is possible to see that the H1 haplogroup predominates the other haplogroups and this is the consequence of inbreeding, there is no gene flow into the group from outside and there is no out-flow. (Personal Interview 2)

---

32   Luigi Luca Cavalli-Sforza, *Genes, Peoples, and Languages* (London: The Penguin Press, 2000), 156.

Geneticists apply the isolation-by-distance theory[33] in this case, because it argues that geographic, that is physical distance causes genetic differences in populations. In the case of the Roma people the geographical distance is very low for the majority populations, but the cultural exclusion is a kind of isolation which explains their closed communities in various geographical areas across the European continent.

With phylogenetic methods it is possible to define whether the studied groups had common ancestors or not. For example in the case of Roma, with the aid of network analysis we can analyze the genetic characteristics of Hungarian, Spanish, and other Roma populations and it is possible to state that because of a few shared mutations they had the same ancestors. (Personal Interview 2)

The negative stereotypical attitudes of the majority population towards the Roma ethnicities in Hungary are enforcing their isolation. This is why phylogenetic network analysis can be applied to point out that, if different ethnic groups share the same SNP mutation. If the analysis result in the ascertainment of shared SNP mutation it is concluded erroneously that they have the same ethnic origins, that is, they belong to the same racial/ethnic population.

This problem area emerges in another interview as well, which is also about ancestry research. In this discussion, the researcher hesitated when I asked about the possibility of linking ethnicity to genetic ancestry. The interviewee initially claimed that:

Yes, if they all [i.e. the research subjects] agree. You mean legally? (Personal Interview 7)

And when I tried to clarify in my response that I meant 'theoretically', not 'legally', the interviewee still responded that may be it is possible. But later in the interview this opinion changed as the researcher came up with empirical examples for what might be possible to indicate from the genetic material. In the previous answer it seems that the interviewee implicitly agreed that ethnicity depends on the intention or will of the individual, the way one thinks about one's social identity. But later, as I will show below, the researcher started to discuss an analytical direction in which the use of category of 'ethnicity' is irrelevant in the research.

When a client wanted to find out in a private genetic ancestry research whether s/he is the relative of an aristocratic Hungarian family, the researcher had to explain to the client that only the genetic mutations on the Y chromosome could be tested for and only chromosomal changes could be detected in the biological material (Personal Interview 7). The interviewee explained that

---

33   *Ibid.*, 196.

ethnicity had no role in the research at all. The researcher claimed that the only possibility to see links between genetics and populations is through geographical location. In other words, the interviewee drew on the isolation-by-distance model; namely that physical barriers of gene flow can result in the accumulation of genetic mutations in a group of people. Hence, linking genetic problems to ethnic belonging is the conflation of the geographical and social ancestral histories of individuals.

I think it is clear from the above empirical examples that there is a slippage between the biological use of the category of ethnicity and its social construction. We produce ethnic categories through cultural practices and their semantic fields are changing dynamically, which means it is impossible to find their equivalents at the molecular biological level in the studied Y chromosome mutations. Y chromosome research is about tracing back the changes that occurred on the Y chromosome at different geographical locations. This entails that the application of the Roma social identity category as a biological reality in genetics can lead to the stabilization of the various Roma ethnicities at the molecular level which can result in further discrimination.

Conclusion

I have tried to outline the problems that arise from the application of the cladistic race concept in the human genetic discourse of Hungary. I grounded my arguments on the works of social scientists who criticizing the biologization of race from a constructivist perspective. Throughout the analysis I tried to emphasize the importance of human genetic studies for the Roma communities, but at the meantime I wanted to show the problems that come about when using the sociological terminology interchangeably with the biological concepts. As a result of the number of interviews that I managed to record only partial conclusions can be drawn. Further research is necessary for drawing a more complete picture.

I organized my arguments around three main themes (1) patronym based genetic identification, (2) SNP screenings for diseases, and (3) ancestry research to underscore the misconceptualizations with empirical examples. I have argued that patronym based genetic research, as a result of dynamic social processes in individual identification with group membership, is meaningless on the molecular level. Patronyms can act as similarly imprecise markers as race. In the frame of genetic research patronyms mark for ethnic belonging, while race marks for possibly more frequent genetic problems. But the main point in both of these cases is that geneticists are looking for genetic traits, such as SNP markers, in individual gene structures that can be used as medical information for healing.

Detecting SNP markers for medical purposes is of high value for raising the health standards of marginalized communities. However, using SNPs to mark ethnic/racial belonging is problematic on the conceptual level. Tracing the history of mutation events on the chromosomes is not more than unfolding the genetic history of that particular mutation. This ancestry research can indicate historical time when and the geographical location where the specific mutation in question took place. Geneticists are going one step further by claiming that this method helps to identify the ancestors of an ethnic group. This way they are extending the social significance and semantic fields of these biological traits; however, social and geographical-biological ancestral histories must be treated separately.

As a result of their continuous historically marginalized situation, Roma people in Hungary are not strong enough economically and politically to organize their genetic screenings and manage their genetic health problems. The intention of human genetic research on Roma is to assist the management of their health. It seems however, that Roma people are not active users of the biological information but passive subjects of genetic research. The construction of Roma biosocialities by human geneticists can result in disadvantages for the members of the Roma communities. In the Hungarian socio-political context a strong right-wing radicalization took place since the turn of millennium. As a consequence, human genetic practices have to balance carefully the semantic fields of biological and sociological categories, to avoid discrimination, stigmatization, and any unintentional contribution to the racist ideology that Roma people are less valuable biologically than the majority non-Roma population.

VIRGINITY: POLITICAL IMPLICATIONS AND MISUSE OF THE CONCEPT IN TODAY'S MIDDLE EAST

Anna Mondekova

Introduction

As numerous media reported, in March 2011 eighteen young women were subjected to humiliating 'virginity tests' for mere presence in the public protests in Cairo, Egypt. The well-known human rights advocate organization, Amnesty International, insisted that the tests were nothing less than torture, precisely "a degrading form of abuse."[1] However, the fact that the tests were performed by state officials and approved of at the highest levels was even more alarming. Trying to understand the motives of those who ordered and conducted the tests raised a question regarding seeming naturalness and justifiability of the tests. The concern further resulted in public outcry both in and outside the Middle East. Human and women's rights advocates called for bringing the authorities responsible for ordering the tests to justice and broad public intensely supported the one of the eighteen women, Samira Ibrahim[2], who decided to take the case to court. Only two more victims were vocal about the tests, the rest of them remained silent.[3]

---

1 Amnesty International, Egypt: Admission of Forced 'Virginity Tests' Must Lead to Justice, *Amnesty International*, May 31, 2011; available at www.amnesty.org/en/news-and-updates/egypt-admission-forced-virginity-tests-must-lead-justice-2011-05-31, last accessed on May 30, 2013.

2 Samira Ibrahim, 25, one of the women who endured the 'virginity tests' after being detained in the Tahrir square, Cairo, on March 9, 2011. See Human Rights Watch, Egypt: Military Impunity for Violence Against Women, *Human Rights Watch*, April 7, 2012; available at www.hrw.org/news/2012/04/07/egypt-military-impunity-violence-against-women, last accessed on May 30, 2013.

3 Salwa el-Husseini was the first Egyptian woman to speak out against the virginity tests and Rasha Abdel Rahman who testified alongside Ibrahim. See Human Rights Watch, *op. cit.*

The cultural construction of the imperative of virginity in Middle East and North Africa (MENA) seems to play a crucial role in why the other women decided not to speak out and rather remain silent as virginity is what a woman supposed to take full responsibility for (even in the case of sexual assault). And thus, the pressure and shame seems to always be located on the woman's side. Additionally, the nature of the tests, particularly when located in the public sphere certainly causes humiliation to both female victim as well as the rest of the family regardless of the media framing of the tests as a clear violation of human rights.[4]

However, as the three women who spoke out, as well as the global community understood, the real issue here was recognition of the fact that the tests as such had no place and relevance in the context of detainment of the female protesters. The existing cultural imperative of virginity was therefore displaced and misused to appropriate actions of the state officials, which in turn resulted in atmosphere of fear, with inherent message that women should think twice before accessing public spaces, particularly when joining the protests and sit-ins, hence being vocal and visible when pursuing their agency. And thus, by shifting the virginity narrative into the public and admittedly political context, the underlying ambition of the authorities was to distract women and draw them away from the streets by constructing the public sphere as a space where the threat of humiliating inspections might be the response to any undesired presence of women in places that matter.

The aim of this article is therefore to portray the cultural concept of virginity and its persisting power over lives of young girls and women in the Middle East to understand why it was a taboo for majority of the victims of Cairo 'virginity tests' incident to speak out. It is however even more important to look at the misuse of the existing cultural construct of virginity through its displacement from the traditional context to public/political sphere where it aims to silence women's voices. To accomplish this, the article will largely rely on the current cases of the 'virginity test' in Egypt and Turkey as examples of serious human rights violations which pose a serious threat to women's future political and public representation and effectively undermine their agency.

Gospel of Hymens

In 2011, a Tunisian documentary titled *Hymen National*[5] was screened both in Middle East as well as in Europe, causing much controversy yet applauded by many in both regions. In Egypt and Tunisia, the timing was particularly important, as the screening followed the virginity test incident mentioned above.

---

4   Amnesty International, *op. cit.*
5   *Hymen National.* Directed by Jamel Mokni. Tunisia: Centre de l'Audiovisuel à Bruxelles (CBA), Centre National Cinématographique Tunisien, 2010.

In the case of both Egypt and Tunisia, which are currently in the process of transformation, the need to debate openly and publicly the issues that initially were considered unquestionable and largely taboo has been very strong since the overthrow of the former regimes. As the director Jamel Mokni argued, "society has become obsessed with virginity,"[6] and his documentary shows the harmful implications of the imperative of virginity and the pervasive double standards when it comes to the discussion of the morals of women and men. He also identifies the danger which such "obsession" brings about pointing to the inhuman reduction of women to their intact hymens eventually resulting in their exclusion as possible political agents in the public dialogue. Such framing of women, with their supposedly visceral desires, further paves the way to harmful incidents such as in the case of the Egyptian female detainees.

Apparently, Mokni is not the only one to talk about urgency and danger in terms of addressing some broader implications of the cultural concept of virginity in the Middle East. The Egyptian-American journalist and activist Mona Eltahawy[7] has been vocal about her own case when she was sexually assaulted while taking part in the protests. In response to the incident, she published a controversial article titled "Why Do They Hate Us?"[8], in which she identifies the disturbing obsession with women's hymens as the main problem and recounts the numerous ways in which women's bodies and women's rights are violated in the region, one of them being the virginity tests.[9] She also rightly claims that aside from the political message this obsession has partly served as a cover-up for plain sexual harassment of women by the state officials in the case of the Egyptian female detainees.[10]

Virginity as a truly pervasive and specifically gendered concept still operates in most places around the region, although to different degrees and with various implications. Regardless of the social class, urban/rural setting or access to education, the pressure on women and their sexual behavior largely governs their lives across the whole region as well as in diasporas.[11] Women's bodies are then often understood and legitimized as objects for further policing, control, questioning and inspecting. The public dimension of the concept—family members or even the wider community are involved in policing young girls and women—increases the pressure as the consequences are for the whole family

---

6   Awadalla Ahmed, Tunisian film on virginity stirs debate at Cairo screening, *Egypt Independent*, June 9, 2011; available at www.egyptindependent.com/news/tunisian-film-virginity-stirs-debate-cairo-screening, last accessed on May 30, 2013.

7   Mona Eltahawy is a columnist and an international public speaker on Arab and Muslim issues.

8   Mona Eltahawy, Why Do They Hate Us? *Foreign Policy*, May–June 2012; available at www.foreignpolicy.com/articles/2012/04/23/why_do_they_hate_us, last accessed on May 30, 2013.

9   *Ibid.*

10 *Ibid.*

11 Marrie H. J. Bekker, Reconstructing Hymens or Constructing Sexual Inequality? Service Provision to Islamic Young Women Coping with the Demand to Be a Virgin, *Journal of Community and Applied Social Psychology*, December 1996, 6(5): 329–334.

to bear. Therefore, questioning girls' virginity appeals to a sensitive individual and cultural taboo as it is really a woman's worth and self-worth that is being addressed here. In that regard, it is understandable that many affected women still choose silence and forgetting rather than public defense in a court which would bare their lives for public display and judging. Women's activism is then significantly shaped and reshaped in response to the very bodily threats that are said to be out there as a constant reminder of the double standard on women and men and their 'appropriate' position in the society.

Original Context and Cultural Construction of Virginity in the Middle East

While Eltahawy talks about violations within the context of regionally prac-ticed Islam[12], the concept of virginity has also been shaped and transformed historically and culturally. In addition, Middle East as such is a considerably broad term covering countries which have not necessarily undergone identical historical developments. However, Middle East and North Africa tend to be referred to and contextualized as sharing some common beliefs mainly as a result of the spread of Islam throughout the region from the seventh century. And although the emphasis on virginity and intact hymens has been in one or another form present in attitudes, beliefs, and practices of various religious teachings around the world, such as Judaism or Christianity, El Saadawi[13] and Bekker[14] insist that current Islam tends to reproduce and in certain regions in-tensify 'sanctions' on women who do not comply with the culturally-ascribed sexual norms.

"An Arab proverb says that a girl's virginity is her most precious possession."[15] El Saadawi, a famous Egyptian women's rights activist and author, argues that in fact women have been robbed of their minds and those have been replaced with the hymen.[16] And although El Saadawi's argument might resonate as somewhat too radical, she points to some positive correlation between prevail-ing focus on women's modesty and purity and the detectable lack of incentives to motivate young girls and women to opt for higher career ambitions as the main goal rather than getting married first.[17] More importantly, the public *versus* private distinction makes the concept even more problematic as it allows for the broader public (community or neighborhood) to judge and interfere.

---

12 Eltahawy, *op. cit.*
13 Nawal El Saadawi, *The Nawal El Saadawi Reader* (London: Zed Books, 1997).
14 Bekker, *op. cit.*
15 El Saadawi, *The Nawal El Saadawi Reader, op. cit.*, 222.
16 *Ibid.*
17 *Ibid.*

In her earlier book, *The Hidden Face of Eve*[18], El Saadawi also talks about the distorted concept of honor where the family's and man's honor is directly related to the virginity and sexual behavior of women in the family. Men's own (sexual) behavior is not at all in question. El Saadawi, a former physician in rural Egypt, points out that men within the family can be womanizers and still be seen as honorable, as long as the women of the family preserve their virginity and chastity. She also identifies a pervasive double standard in the fact that sexual experience is a source of pride for men whereas in the case of women it tends to be seen as a symbol of degradation and shame.[19]

Double moral standards are often obvious as the two sexes are not motivated to protect their purity equally, nor the sanctions are comparable if virginity is lost.[20] El Saadawi argues that it comes to conceptualizing women's and men's sexuality, men are even encouraged to lose their virginity. Boys, unlike girls are not explicitly disciplined to protect their virginity, in fact, there are opinions that virginity is only obligatory for women; men, on the contrary, are free, even encouraged to explore their sexuality. Virginity is a visibly gendered concept and it is constructed to reflect moral values of women (obviously inseparable from those of the family), who by complying and preserving it are seen as of good morals, pure and modest, hence marriageable. If a non-married woman is no longer a virgin (even in case of being a rape victim), this affects her honor and reduces the family's reputation.[21]

Also, some very distinct sets of strategies and practices are in operation to secure the alignment of women's sexual behavior with the existing norms in different areas across the region. In more traditional families and communities, harsh sanctions might follow the discovery that a woman is no longer virgin (for sex-related or sex-unrelated reasons). Marrying the sexual partner even against woman's will[22], stigmatization, rejection, even honor killings can be the result of a loss of virginity before the wedding night. And although the most severe of the practices have been largely reduced to the rural areas, numerous middle-class women currently undergo surgical reconstructions of the hymen every year in the MENA region and abroad[23], making virginity more of a commodity and a class issue, further deepening inequalities between social classes, as financial standing is crucial here. Economic inequalities are thus

---

18 Nawal El Saadawi, *The Hidden Face of Eve* (New York: Zed Books, 1977).
19 *Ibid.*, 48.
20 *Ibid.*
21 *Ibid.*, 47.
22 For instance, the recent case of a Moroccan rape victim Amina Filali who was forced to get married to the perpetrator and committed suicide afterward. See Elizabeth Flock, Morocco Outraged Over Suicide of Amina Filali, Who Was Forced to Marry Her Rapist, *The Washington Post*, March 15, 2012; available at www.washingtonpost.com/blogs/blogpost/post/morocco-outraged-over-suicide-of-amina-filali-who-was-forced-to-marry-her-rapist/2012/03/15/gIQApTq4DS_blog.html, last accessed on May 30, 2013.
23 Bekker, *op. cit.*

transformed into lived experiences, as the middle class and the poor cannot afford such expensive operations. Yet, the culturally assigned power of the concept, its projection on the whole family and its possible stain on family honor, make virginity a pervasive imperative applicable for any class. Therefore a possibility of being 'inspected' by officials, or even publicly identified, represents a great taboo and explains the silence of majority of the Egyptian 'virginity test' victims.

Framing Virginity Tests

As understood from the news and international responses to the case of virginity tests in Egypt, the continuing existence of the practice in rural areas across the MENA region has become very disturbing and controversial on the global level. However, virginity tests were identified as severe violations of human dignity and human rights only when this cultural practice was displaced from the original context (by itself ambiguous).[24]

In the situation of political struggle, virginity tests were re-discovered as a powerful tool to further humiliate women. The predominant cultural framing of virginity imperative allowed for conducting the tests witch in turn reaffirmed their perceived legitimacy. For understanding of the relatively strong disagreement on conceptualizing the virginity tests in public debates and discussions the original concept and purposes of the tests and their historic and regional construction will be outlined. This original context nowadays provides necessary grounds for naturalization and relative acceptance of the tests. Also, other cases of misuse of the tests were reported both in the MENA region as well as in the west where the one common trait—abuse of power by the authorities—has been relatively easy to identify.

As stated by the Stop Violence against Women (StopVAW) project[25] virginity testing refers to the examination of genitals as a way to determine sexual chastity. Another women's rights advocate, Mushahida Adhikari, explains that the virginity tests may currently refer to gynecological examination where the physician is able to confirm whether the hymen of a girl is intact or not.[26] As already discussed, virginity is a gendered concept; hence virginity tests are almost exclusively targeting women. Adhikari explains that the age suitable for such procedure starts from seven years and later can be conducted at any age in woman's life.[27] Often however, when the purposes are not medical,

---

24 Amnesty International, Hyman Rights Watch, and Egyptian Centre for Women's Rights.
25 A project of The Advocates for Human Rights which operates as a forum for information, advocacy and change in the promotion of women's human rights around the world
26 Mushahida Adhikari, *Submissions to the Ministry of Justice and Constitutional Development on Suggested Law Reforms in Respect of Virginity Testing* (Cape Town: Women's Legal Center, 2010).
27 *Ibid.*

the one to perform the virginity test could be any respected member of community or one of the elders who are skilled at practicing informal medicine,
particularly in rural areas where many people do not have sufficient access to
medical care.[28]

Currently, virginity tests have been almost exclusively identified within
Muslim societies as persisting practices perpetuating and reproducing traditional norms of sexual behavior. As Mushahida Adhikari further explains, virginity tests operated to secure acceptance of the dominant social norms which
promoted sexual abstinence for the unmarried women.[29] However, in context
where the practice appears natural and unquestioned, those who have access
and motivation might easily abuse their power and take advantage of it to
merely intimidate and sexually harass women. The centrality of the imperative
of virginity seems obvious and not to be questioned even in the 21st century in
some regions and among some groups.

The Case of Britain and Turkey

A very disturbing and controversial context for conducting virginity tests was
discovered thirty years ago in Britain and the findings were further published
by *The Guardian* in 1979.[30] It was found out that virginity tests were performed
on women entering Britain on the fiancé visa. Women arriving to the country
where they were supposed to get married were formally required to undergo
virginity tests and submit the results as a proof of their honest motives. In this
case women arriving to Britain were not seen as trustworthy, their motives were
questioned, and eventually their bodies were supposed to provide the answer.
In order to get this answer, however, women's bodies were objectified and violated. Once this practice was uncovered by the media, the policy was immediately changed in Britain.[31]

As opposed to other countries of the Middle East and North Africa, Turkey is typically seen as more progressive and granting women more rights
and freedoms than the rest of the region. Yet, when it comes to virginity and
its legal framing, within Turkish law, virginity and namely its absence, may
have numerous implications. On the individual level, absence of virginity may
serve as grounds for marriage annulment.[32] Even in the interpretation of the

---

28 El Saadawi, *The Hidden Face of Eve, op. cit.*
29 Adhikari, *op. cit.*
30 Melanie Phillips, From the Archive: Airport Virginity Tests Banned by Rees, *The Guardian*,
    February 3, 2010; available at www.guardian.co.uk/uk/2010/feb/03/airport-virginity-tests-banned,
    last accessed on May 30, 2013.
31 *Ibid.*
32 Zehra F. Arat, Turkish Women at the Republican Reconstruction of Tradition, in Fatma Muge
    Gocek and Shiva Balaghi (eds.), *Constructing Gender in the Middle East* (New York, Columbia
    University Press, 1994) 57–78, at 64.

contemporary legal authorities, such late discovery of absence of virginity implies a "substantial error in quality."[33]

Regarding the broader group level, virginity tests have recently become an issue for women's human rights groups in Turkey. Chanté Lasco[34] points out that Turkey has allowed for virginity testing to be performed on women applying for certain governmental jobs or special schools, also on female prisoners, female prisoners arrested for political reasons,[35] as well as many other women for unspecified reasons, such as dining alone, sitting on a public bench alone or with male friends in the evening, staying in a hotel room with male friends or with female friends, etc.[36] However, a decree banning forced virginity tests was introduced as a result of both pressure from local human rights groups as well as of the perceived need to comply with European Union standards as part of the accession process towards the EU membership.[37]

In this context, the public dimension of the imperative of virginity is intensified by the state's interest in knowing, and direct action in securing women's compliance with the norms imposed on them. Compulsory virginity then represents yet another obstacle in women's access to the public sphere, influencing not only their career choices but also the simple desire to enjoy public facilities that men can access. Such state's interference appears to be very disturbing and it has been already reflected in related women's rights campaigns which identified the practice to be humiliating and discriminatory against women and their basic human rights.

As far as numbers are concerned, currently there are no precise data available on the use of the practice around the globe. In several regions, the tests were banned as a result of interventions from the outside or after the global community expressed its concerns.[38] Yet, it is believed that in many regions the tests remain to be performed informally, especially in the rural areas where traditions are more prevalent and members of the community tend to be more closely observed. The original use of the concept then seems to justify any further exercise of the practice in context where women's sexual life is irrelevant. This way, the cultural norm of virginity, and the practice of virginity testing, not only continue to pose obstacles to women's choices and everyday activities but also effectively create sites for gender-based discrimination and violence.

---

33 *Ibid.*
34 Chanté Lasco, Virginity Testing in Turkey: A Violation of Women's Human Rights, *Human Rights Brief* (Washington, DC: American University Center for Human Rights and Humanitarian Law), Spring 2002, 9(3): 10–13; available at www.wcl.american.edu/hrbrief/09/3lasco.pdf, last accessed on May 30, 2013.
35 According to Turkish anti-terrorism laws.
36 Lasco, *op. cit.*
37 *Ibid.*
38 Turkey and South Africa.

Gender-Based Violence Implications

The Stop Violence against Women advocates stress that the imperative of being a virgin as well as the practice of virginity tests itself can be directly related to the increase in violence against women in particular regions. At the same time, this cultural norm naturalizes and justifies gender-based violence.[39]

Based on a survey[40] conducted in Egypt locally, fifty-three percent of the male respondents believed that women are responsible for sexual harassment: more specifically, their way of dressing was seen as immodest and provoking undesired sexual responses. This 'justification' of sexual violence in the streets contributed to the portrayal of the public sphere as unfriendly, even life-threatening for women. Most of the respondents also stressed that women should be at home by eight o'clock in the evening. The research has shown that women's actions and looks are tightly controlled by the male dominated society, especially when they enter public spaces. Constructing women who enter public spaces as not decent and therefore 'deserving' harassment and assaults only perpetuates the underlying logic that the place of women is in the private sphere.

The normalization of this practice clearly contributes to the desensitization of the public and thus creates an atmosphere and discourse in which not only virginity inspection but also larger-scale violence is approved. The fact that women's bodies are seen as available for such examination is dangerous as it in turn allows for any seemingly appropriate action by family members, larger communities, even broader public and state authorities. On the individual level, women can be forced to identify their sexual partner but in general the stigma remains on the woman who, as a result, might be called a prostitute, beaten by her relatives, or otherwise sanctioned. On a broader level, the threat of having their virginity questioned and genitals inspected might result in women giving up their agency and political activism as no effective protection currently exists to guarantee their safety in the public.

Second-Class Citizens

In her essay "Women's activism in the Middle East," Sarah Graham-Brown claims that at the beginning of the twenty-first century, Middle Eastern women as a group are framed and seen as largely passive, without a voice, political agency or opinion.[41] However, as the argument develops further, this does not

---

39 Stop Violence Against Women, www.stopvaw.org.
40 Bisan Kassab and Rana Mahmoud, The Widespread Plague of Sexual Harassment in Egypt, *Al-Akhbar*, September 20, 2012; available at english.al-akhbar.com/node/12456, last accessed on May 20, 2013.
41 Sarah Graham-Brown, Women's Activism in the Middle East, in Joseph Suad and Susan Slyomovics (eds.), *Women and Power in the Middle East* (Philadelphia: University of Pennsylvania Press, 2001), 23–33, at 23.

appear to be the whole truth as there have always been politically and publicly active women[42] in the modern history of the region who, to different degrees, aimed to address important issues concerning women's social, economic and political standing in the society. Nevertheless, for the most part, these women were made invisible and their credits often unrecognized.[43] Therefore, the striking change in the past years, particularly visible in the context of the Arab spring throughout the whole region, are multitudes of women of all ages who actively stood up against the former regimes, fought side by side with men and often made severe sacrifices to do so. And thus, it is justifiable to claim that the Arab spring has seen the rise of women in the Middle East. However, as Amnesty International[44] and other human rights groups have observed, and reported by various media, once the regimes were overthrown and political scene was to be re-shaped and power positions redistributed, women became increasingly subjected to gender-based violence. Again, 'justifications' for these actions were relatively easy to find among the culturally constructed concepts of women's sexuality, sexual norms, and appropriate behavior, one of the most powerful ones being precisely the imperative of virginity.

Women who access public spaces are automatically degraded to the image of the indecent woman who is 'asking for it', and this perpetuates a discourse in which all women who leave the private spaces should not wonder if they are assaulted. Additionally, in the Egyptian case, various narratives blaming the female victims for 'provoking' and directly inviting the harassment and therefore being largely responsible for the tests was present in media (mainly state-owned) but also among broader public.

The 'second-class citizen' narrative was used when describing the affected women after being subjected to harassment and eventually virginity tests. As a result, implications are clear for all those women whose decision is/will be to take part in the similar events. In the course of the trial, a high official justified the act by insisting that the women "were not like your daughter or mine, these were girls who had camped out in tents with the male protesters."[45]

Yet in this very recent case, the reasons why the women entered the public were clearly political as after former regime was dismantled and the Security Council of Armed Forces (SCAF) took over and held power for longer than desired by Egyptian citizens, the protests continued as various groups disapproved of the post-revolution development in the country. Women were one of the groups and they were becoming vocal addressing specific social, economic and political issues from both pre-revolution era as well as from the yet-to be shaped post-revolution era. One of the main critiques targeted the recent increase in gender-based harassment and violence, which various media identi-

---

42 Malek Hifni Nasif, Huda Shaarawi, Duriyya Shafiq, etc.
43 Graham-Brown, *op. cit.*
44 Amnesty International, *op. cit.*
45 *Ibid.*

fied as epidemics.[46] As even the global community could have witnessed, sexual harassment and violence have become an everyday reality in both pre- and post-revolution Egypt. Consequently, politically active women, women's rights and human rights activists and many other supporters (both physically present and online supporters from around the globe) were demanding space to address their own agenda without being scared of sexual assaults.

Hostility as well as verbal and physical harassment directed at women in public has been often seen as a strategy for leaving women behind once they 'did their part' in the revolutions and uprisings, and in case of Egypt in over-throwing Hosni Mubarak as during the revolution itself neither violence nor harassment were reported. Afterwards however, women's voices, equally present before, have now been continually silenced, women forced out of the public and pushed back into the private spaces. Cynthia Cockburn observed that in cases of uprisings and conflicts women never really achieve equality even though their participation and sacrifice in the fight are often equal to that of the men.[47] Joseph Suad does not believe either that women's roles necessarily change after they take part in political struggles or make activism part of their agency.[48] Moreover, different gendered connotations are attached to the political activism of women and men: while men are typically praised for their actions and participation, stereotypical views of women's roles hardly allow for another, fundamentally different role that could well fit with the traditional domestic tasks that women are expected to perform in the family. Women's activism, as such, is often linked to western feminism, which is highly unpopular. And as Suad adds, negative sexual and political labels might be assigned to those women who actively promote equal political participation for women and address other burning social, economic and political issues.[49] And thus, considering the above-mentioned implications, it is understandable why a substantial and structural change has rarely been a result of women's political involvement.

In the context of political struggle for power and space over the public, women, as opposed to men, are significantly more vulnerable because it is often their bodies through which the following political struggle is materialized. Women's bodies as historically and culturally accessible[50] and available for questioning, even physical inspection and sexual abuse, are being taken advantage of and gradually dismissed from the public and political life. Examining virginity as an

---

46　BBC, Egypt's Sexual Harassment of Women 'Epidemic', *BBC News*, September 3, 2012; available at www.bbc.co.uk/news/world-middle-east-19440656, last accessed on May 21, 2013.

47　Cynthia Cockburn, The Continuum of Violence: A Gender Perspective on War and Peace, in Wenona Giles and Heather Hyndman (eds.), *Sites of Violence: Gender and Conflict Zones* (Berkeley: University of California Press, 2004), 24–44, at 34.

48　Joseph Suad, Women and Politics in the Middle East, in Joseph Suad and Susan Slyomovics (eds.), *Women and Power in the Middle East* (Philadelphia: University of Pennsylvania Press, 2001), 34–40, at 37.

49　*Ibid.*, 40.

50　Carole Pateman, *The Sexual Contract* (Stanford, California: Stanford University Press, 1988).

intimately embodied practice has therefore turned out to be an effective tool of challenging women's presence in the public and undermining their attempts to express their agency.

Violations of International Law

As mentioned previously, Samira Ibrahim was the only one of the eighteen reported women detained by the military as a result of their presence in the protests who decided to demand justice in a trial against responsible authorities. Since then, Samira has become an emblematic figure for both human and women's right activists in the region. As Leila Fadel reported for *The Washington Post* later in December 2011, virginity tests on female detainees were eventually banned as a result of the trial Samira initiated directly after the incident.[51] However, even after banning the tests women can hardly feel safe as the general atmosphere reflected in increased violence and harassment only proves higher tolerance towards gender-based violence. A year after the incident, Amnesty International reported that harassment and assaults continue and are effectively building on the stigma attached to sexual violence. Simultaneously, gender-based violence and harassment are further used for ongoing marginalization of female protesters as well as other women of all ages who attempt to enter public areas and address relevant issues of social injustice.

Virginity tests as in the case of Egypt or Turkey—when imposed on women to collect employment- or study-related evidence or when under any circumstance ordered and forcefully conducted by the state or other authorities—represent an infringement of basic human rights. Such tests violate several international instruments: the Universal Declaration of Human Rights; the Convention on the Elimination of All Forms of Discrimination Against Women; the European Convention for the Protection of Human Rights and Fundamental Freedoms; the International Covenant on Civil and Political Rights; the Convention Against Torture and Other Cruel, Inhuman or Degrading Treatment or Punishment; and, in the case of Turkey, also the Convention concerning Discrimination in Respect of Employment and Occupation. Violation of privacy and humiliation are further pervasive outcomes of such inspections.

The tests that are unofficially allowed and required often violate even the national laws of a particular country. For instance, under Turkish law, vaginal inspections are only permitted by the state in cases of rape to collect evidence where the woman must participate willingly and a prosecutor or a judge has to confirm the request for the test; in the second case, vaginal tests are performed

---

51 Leila Fadel, Egyptian Court Bans Virginity Tests on Female Detainees, *The Washington Post*, December 27, 2011; available at www.articles.washingtonpost.com/2011-12-27/world/35285121_1_ virginity-tests-samira-ibrahim-tests-on-female-detainees, last accessed on May 30, 2013.

as part of the health check for the prostitutes.[52] No similar requirements for vaginal inspections for other governmental positions or study programs exist. Yet, despite the legal framing and official ban from 2002, there is evidence confirming that state officials continue to demand that women undergo the humiliating procedure for various illegitimate reasons.[53]

From the human rights perspective, forcefully conducted virginity tests violate women's (and young girls') rights to privacy and bodily integrity. But as the Stop Violence against Women (StopVAW) group stresses, no matter what the reason for the tests is, they represent a clear violation of the rights of the women examined and create atmosphere of fear which effectively limits women in their access to the public sphere as observed in the case of Egyptian detainees.

Conclusions

In the last two years, the world has witnessed women in the Middle East standing up for themselves and becoming vocal even though the reality in which they were trying to pursue their agenda was the one of a revolution and conflict. Yet, the danger did not come merely from the security instability in the region. It also emerged in the form of sexual harassment and violence often initiated by fellow male protesters and other male-dominated groups which sensed that these women, although initially useful, posed some serious threat on possibilities of future power re-distribution and could have had a potential to initiate substantial social on behalf of women and their participation in political processes in the region. As a result, pervasive cultural concepts, such as 'virginity', were engaged in the reshaping of public spaces into significantly more dangerous ones while emphasizing women's bodies as legitimately questionable and accessible when entering these spaces. Virginity tests, sexual harassment, and violence have become the dominant methods of "putting women back in their place."

Admittedly, women's situation and rights have improved in terms of access to education, employment (although job segregation is widespread and the wage gap is still significant), and property rights during the last decades in certain areas across the Middle East. Yet, when it comes to women's personal choices, sexual and political rights, the discourse still does not encourage much relevant debate. As Sarah Graham Brown[54] argues, those who endeavor to discuss the cultural norms of virginity at marriage, or to point out the difference between the sexual freedom available for men and the coercion of women's sexual behavior or female genital mutilation, are at the risk of being accused of betraying their culture, religion or their sex—which, in turn, poses threat to the honor of their families and their ability to have a decent life in the future. Whoever is

---

52 Lasco, *op. cit.*
53 *Ibid.*
54 Sarah Graham-Brown, *op. cit.*, 30.

even slightly critical of the prevailing norms might be labeled as pro-Western or Western feminist. And although many women in the region are active and vocal on behalf of issues that they find no longer acceptable, many of them do not want to be seen as 'disseminators' of Western feminism which is understood as largely alien, not responding to the actual needs and the specific character of the region.

Those women who are brave to raise their voice publicly thus have to be very careful in how they introduce and discuss particular issues. Interestingly enough, now that these women have become visible through their active engagement in the uprisings across the Middle East, a wave of discontent could be (and continues to be) observed in the typically male-dominated public and political sphere. As demonstrated above, certain old, but still very powerful cultural concepts, such as the imperative of virginity, were deployed to reverse the tide of women becoming more visible in the political sphere and to block their access to political power. Therefore, displacing virginity from its traditional context and locating it in the public sphere of political activities allowed the state authorities to threaten women not only as a gendered group but also as a political group and to approve gender-based violence by labeling these women as second-class citizens and making their presence in public very difficult and unsafe.

SEX SELECTIVE ABORTIONS IN ARMENIA: BETWEEN GENDER ISSUES, ECONOMIC CRISES, AND BODY POLITICS

Shushan Harutyunyan

Introduction

Sex selection in reproductive processes has recently become an alarming phenomenon even in countries with no history of the problem. In addition to the issue of missing girls in the societies in Asian countries[1], a departure from the natural sex ratio at birth has reached worrying proportions in countries of the Caucasus as well, including Armenia, where the sex ratio is almost 111 boys to 100 girls.

To address the problem, the Parliamentary Assembly of the Council of Europe (PACE) touched upon the Armenian case in 2011 when it drafted a resolution that, by referring to the prevalent practice of pre-natal sex selection and selective abortions in the Southern Caucasus, condemns "the phenomenon which finds its roots in a culture of gender inequality and reinforces a climate of violence against women, contrary to the values upheld by the Council of Europe."[2]

Number of recent studies followed PACE's alarm, attempting to analyze the practices of fertility intentions and behaviors in Armenia, Azerbaijan and Georgia.[3] So far, however, there has been little discussion about the particularities of

---

1 Irene D'Souza, Where Have the Girls Gone? Gender-Selection Technology Has Skewed the Number of Girls Born in Some Countries, *Herizons*, Fall 2012, 26(2): 30–33; available at www. herizons.ca/node/528.

2 Parliamentary Assembly of the Council of Europe (PACE), Committee on Equal Opportunities for Women and Men, Draft Resolution on Pre-Natal Sex Selection, 2011; available at www.assembly. coe.int/CommitteeDocs/2011/ASEGAselectionprenataleE.pdf, last accessed on June 20, 2013.

3 Géraldine Duthé, France Meslé, Jacques Vallin, Irina Badurashvili, and Karine Kuyumjyan, High Sex Ratios at Birth in the Caucasus: Modern Technology to Satisfy Old Desires, *Population and Development Review*, September 2012, 38(3): 487–501.

sex-selective abortions in each of three countries separately, which will help to understand and address the problem of sex-selection more effectively due to certain differences of abortions practices in each country. Moreover, studies are mostly limited to revising sex selection as a technologically mediated social and cultural phenomenon almost equally applicable in all three countries, this is not quite true for number of reasons that I will discuss further.

This chapter examines the case of sex selective abortions in Armenia — a country with a relatively high abortion rate[4] — analyzing overall abortion practices in the context of socio-economic and cultural developments, as well as fertilization policies and body politics. The objectives of the paper include studying dichotomies between individuals' reproductive choices and the extent of autonomy in those choices; common interests under social and demographical imbalances; as well as issues of women's position and subjectivity in reproductive procedures in the Armenian society. The chapter seeks to address whether sex selective abortions in Armenia reinforce gender discrimination; as well as intends to find answers to the questions of what the possible roots of the problem are and what future implications they might have.

The chapter uses a range of sociological and demographic studies to follow the dynamics of reproductive experiences and sex selective abortions in Armenia. It draws data from the preliminary report of the 2010 Demographic and Health Survey[5] and cites the research findings published in the 2012 report of the United Nations Population Fund Armenia Country Office (UNFPA), titled *Prevalence and Reasons of Sex Selective Abortions in Armenia*.[6] This research of UNFPA was carried out in collaboration with Ministry of Health, the National Statistical Service, and the Republican Institute of Reproductive Health, Perinatology, Obstetrics and Gynecology. The study was based partly on a survey among women aged 15–49, who lived in households randomly selected throughout Armenia and were pregnant and visited medical institutions during the period of research, and partly on focus group discussions conducted with the participation men and women and among obstetricians and gynecologists. Some of the focus group transcripts will be directly quoted in this chapter, but the findings of the study will be critically examined in

---

4   According to the Statistics Division of the United Nations, data collected in 2004 show that there are 13.9 abortions per 1,000 women of reproductive age (15–44 years) in Armenia in comparison with, for example, 0.0 in Poland, 5.7 in Croatia and 7.8 in Germany, but also with 53.7 in Russia and 27.3 in Latvia; see data.un.org/Data.aspx?d=GenderStat&f=inID:12, last accessed on June 20, 2013.

5   National Statistical Service and Ministry of Health of the Republic of Armenia, Armenia: Demographic and Health Survey, Preliminary Report, 2010; available at www.armstat.am/file/article/dhs_pr_2010_eng.pdf, last accessed on June 20, 2013.

6   United Nations Population Fund Armenia Country Office (UNFPA), *Prevalence and Reasons of Sex Selective Abortions in Armenia*, Report on a research conducted in cooperation with the Ministry of Health and the National Statistical Service of the Republic of Armenia, as well as the Republican Institute of Reproductive Health, Perinatology, Obstetrics and Gynecology (Yerevan: UNFPA, 2012); available online at unfpa.am/sites/default/files/Sex-selective_abortions_report_Eng.pdf, last accessed on June 20, 2013.

light of the various cultural and economic aspects that were not considered by the UNFPA research.

Sex Selective Abortions in the Context of Culturally Specific Gender Discrimination

During the last five years around 7,200 women of reproductive age had a sex selective abortion in Armenia, which means that on average each year around 1400 female fetuses are potentially lost in Armenia.[7] The UNFPA report suggests[8] that 0.8 percent of 900,000 Armenian women undergo sex-selective abortion. It is noteworthy that this type of abortion is popular among urban women with higher education and with a relatively high level of income for Armenia. What is probably even more interesting is that, according to the study, the decision to have a sex selective abortion is mainly made independently by the pregnant women (82.6 percent).

Looking beyond the statistical data, can we identify socio-cultural traditions that perpetuate gender bias and son preference to the extent that pregnant women make decisions on sex selective abortions? If sex-selection as a form of 'prenatal discrimination' or, as some scholars formulate, "missing girls phenomenon"[9] is a growing tendency throughout the world—which results from the gender discriminating cultural practices, irrational national population policies and unethical use of technology—which of these common characteristics of sex-selective abortion apply to the Armenian case and what particularities should be considered in order to understand it in depth?

Many commentators report on the existence of son preference in Armenian society, attributing it to the 'Armenian mentality'—at least this particular term is commonly used during the in-depth interviews and focus group discussions of the UNFPA research.[10] One of the participants in a focus group for men expressed the following opinion on the issue, which I believe would be interesting to consider within this chapter:

> It is not important to me whether a first child is male or female. It is your child and you should love him or her regardless. Simply, as it has already been said, sons continue the family lineage, while in other respects there are daughters each of whom is worth a thousand sons. (Men's focus group)[11]

---

7   UNFPA, Factsheet on Prevalence and Reasons of Sex Selective Abortions in Armenia, December 19, 2011; available at unfpa.org/webdav/site/eeca/shared/documents/Sex Selective Abortions-brief_factsheet-Eng.pdf, last accessed on June 20, 2013.
8   *Ibid.*
9   Farina Gul Abrejo, Babar Tasneem Shaikh and Narjis Rizvi, And They Kill Me, Only Because I Am a Girl' . . . A Review of Sex-Selective Abortions in South Asia, *The European Journal of Contraception and Reproductive Health Care*, February 2009, 14(1): 10–16.
10 UNFPA, Prevalence and Reasons . . ., *op. cit.*, 21.
11 *Ibid.*, 31.

Media reports cite similar reasoning to support the practice of sex-selective abortions in Armenia. "I have to bear a boy to inherit my husband's family name. He should have a son by his side," says a 35-year-old women, mother of two girls, who undertakes a sex-selective abortion.[12] Another article describes the following picture: "At one Yerevan [hospital] facility recently, the overjoyed father of a newborn baby boy danced to Armenian folk music, while medical staff consoled the mother of a newborn baby girl that she'd 'have a boy next time'."[13] Meanwhile, some of the participants in the UNFPA focus group argued that a differentiated attitude toward the child's gender is not justified and understood in the society—but they still confirm the existence of son preference:

> The phenomenon, as such, does exist in our society, I do not know why. I myself personally do not agree with the idea that sons are more valuable because I have noticed that in our society the 'son phenomenon' reaches fanaticism and I would go so far as to say that not infrequently the goal of starting a family is to have a child in general and a male child in particular. This, in my view, is extremely deep-rooted and stereotypical and has to be changed. (Mixed focus group: women and men)[14]

All in all, it seems that there is a widespread belief in Armenian society that son preference exists and it can be explained by traditional mentality and the patrilineal norms of inheritance within the family. However, it might be useful to pay attention to the issue of how the son preference influences the way girls are treated and valued in families was well as how the gender dichotomy is reinforced within these kinds of abortions, which is quite the case of many countries with sex-selective abortion problems.

To compare, in India, where sex-selective abortions are far too common, notions of biological difference between men and women play a key role in legitimizing gender and familial hierarchies in which, in a structural sense, girls are less valued than boys. The biological basis to gender hierarchy is set out in classical texts on the Hindu religion as well as in Ayurvedic ideas of procreation.[15] To the best of scholarly knowledge, there are no such structured hierarchies stated in Apostolic Christian writings at all (93% of Armenian Christians belong to the Armenian Apostolic Church). In India a female child is often seen a future bride, which is a 'burden' because of the rules prescribing marriage and the related dowry payments (where cash and goods are transferred as gifts by the bride's

---

12 Nanore Barsoumian, The Baby Doom: Selective Abortions in Armenia, *The Armenian Weekly*, November 23, 2011; available at www.armenianweekly.com/2011/11/23/the-baby-doom-selective-abortions-in-armenia/, last accessed on June 20, 2013.
13 Marianna Grigoryan, Armenia: Are Selective Abortions Behind Birth Ratio Imbalance? *EurasiaNet*, July 6, 2011; available at www.eurasianet.org/node/63812, last accessed on June 20, 2013.
14 UNFPA, Prevalence and Reasons . . ., *op. cit.*, 31.
15 Maya Unnithan-Kumar, Female Selective Abortion—Beyond 'Culture': Family Making and Gender Inequality in a Globalizing India, *Culture, Health & Sexuality*, 2010, 12(2): 153–166 (on web: May 12, 2009).

family to the groom's family)[16], but this is not the case in Armenia. Moreover, while in India if an unwanted female fetus is carried to term, these girls do not receive due care from the parents before and after birth[17], in Armenia, even though son preference in families is six times higher than daughter preference, 'unwanted' female children are taken care of and treated equally and respectably.[18]

To sum up, as we can observe, there are no particular cultural reasons for a differentiated approach to daughters and sons within the families. It is noteworthy that about a half of the respondents in UNFPA study (43.1 percent) stated that the child's gender did not matter during their first pregnancy at all. Still, sex-selective abortions do take place in Armenia and this contradiction needs to be explained. I suggest discussing it with analyzing the socio-economic and demographic problems prevalent in the country.

Sex Selective Abortions in the Absence of Family Planning Practices

Regarding sex-selective abortions in Armenia, it is more than important to look at social practices of family planning because, as statistics show, abortions in Armenia are predominantly used by married women to control fertility after completing their desired family size, rather than by unmarried women who are seeking to delay their first birth.[19] Additionally, sex-selective abortion is used mostly in case of the third or the fourth child. So can we think of abortion in Armenia as a burden that women undertake as a result of the absence of family planning practices? Where can we situate the problem of sex-selective abortion in this context and how much all these factors are related to the socio-economic development of the country? In some of the cases, the numbers speak for themselves.

A decline in total fertility rates has been observed from 2.5 in 1985 to 1.7 in 1994 in Armenia[20], which can be explained by a number of socioeconomic setbacks that have occurred in the country after the collapse of Soviet Union: natural disasters, including the earthquake in 1988[21], and the war between Armenia

16 *Ibid.*
17 Prashant Bharadwaj, Leah K. Lakdawala, Discrimination Begins in the Womb: Evidence of Sex-Selective Prenatal Investments, *The Journal of Human Resources*, Winter 2013, 48(1): 71–113, at 84; available as manuscript at mitsloan.mit.edu/neudc/papers/paper_146.pdf, last accessed on June 20, 2013.
18 UNFPA, Prevalence and Reasons . . ., *op. cit.*, 41.
19 Charles F. Westoff, Recent Trends in Abortion and Contraception in 12 Countries, *DHS Analytical Studies No. 8*, February 2005, available at pdf.usaid.gov/pdf_docs/pnadb984.pdf, last accessed on June 20, 2013.
20 Gayane Dolian, Frank Lüdicke, Naira Katchatrian, Aldo Campana, and Alfredo Morabia, Contraception and Induced Abortion in Armenia: A Critical Need for Family Planning Programs in Eastern Europe, *American Journal of Public Health*, May 1998, 88(5): 803–805.
21 25,000 people were killed, 19,000 injured and 500,000 became homeless after the devastating earthquake which ripped through Armenia. United States Geological Service, Historic Earthquakes, Spitak, Armenia; available at earthquake.usgs.gov/earthquakes/world/events/1988_12_07.php, last accessed on June 20, 2013.

and Azerbaijan.[22] The number of abortions started to decrease significantly in the mid-1990s: while the abortion rate was 35.4 abortions per 1000 women of reproductive age in 1996, it was 24.3 in 1997, and 17.4 in 1998. Since then there has been a gradual decrease and the figure oscillated around the average of 12–13 abortions per women.[23] What is also significant is that the total abortion rate, that is the number of abortions per woman has dropped considerably, from 2.6 in the year 2000, to 1.8 in 2005 and 0.8 in 2010.[24] However, the fertility rate in Armenia was 1.7 births per woman in 2010 (unchanged from 2000 and 2005), which is below the level of fertility necessary to replace the current population.[25]

In fact, the problematic relationship between the country's current socioeconomic situation and family size was indicated in the UNFPA Report[26] when the participants in focus groups and the respondents to the in-depth interviews identified it as a reason for undertaking an abortion. When they were asked to speak about the factors that underlie the decisions about family size, most of them expressed belief that at present families limit the number of children to one or two. They also expressed opinions similar to the presented one below, which is interesting to consider:

> I do not know about society at large but I, specifically, find that in the today's situation it is difficult to support more than two children. Families in previous generations had three or four children. Now people are avoiding that. It seems to me that they do so because of social conditions. It is the 21st century and the child's needs are more numerous. While in the past [parents] could have a child and raise him or her without sending them to private tutors because schools gave good and accessible knowledge, parents must now take children to private educational institutions or to private tutors and they need resources to be able to afford that. Today, not everyone can afford that. (First in-depth interview, 35-year-old respondent, has higher education).[27]

It is indicated that women in Armenia chose to have abortions when they were financially unable to support a child (73 percent) and did not want more children (57 percent).[28] But there is something paradoxical: if the abortions are

---

22 The Nagorno-Karabakh War was an armed conflict that took place from February 1988 to May 1994, taking lives of more than 16,000 people. See Armenian Research Center at The University of Michigan-Dearborn, Fact Sheet: Nagorno-Karabagh, 1996; available at www.umd.umich.edu/dept/armenian/facts/karabagh.html, last accessed on June 20, 2013.

23 William Robert Johnston, Historical Abortion Statistics, Armenia, compiled from UNICEF and WHO data; available at www.johnstonsarchive.net/policy/abortion/ab-armenia.html, last accessed on June 20, 2013.

24 National Statistical Service, *op. cit.*, 9–10.

25 *Ibid.*, 8.

26 UNFPA, Prevalence and Reasons . . ., *op. cit.*, 35.

27 *Ibid.*, 36.

28 Dolian, *et. al.*, *op. cit.*

mainly due to economic reasons as we can observe so far, why are contraception methods so limited in usage and still not widespread among Armenian women? Studies also pointed out that among the main barriers perceived by women in abortions is the cost of abortion (39 percent).[29] Just to compare: surgical abortions cost, on average, between 15,000 and 20,000 drams (35 to 50 US dollars) in hospitals[30], whereas pills cost 180 to 200 drams (40–50 cents). In a country where monthly incomes may be as little as 440 US dollars, the abortion costs are substantial for many, yet, they choose the abortion practice. Additionally, sex-selective abortions constitute 0.8 percent of overall abortions.[31] I suggest discussing it within the context of overall abortion practices and body politics in Armenia.

Sex Selective Abortions and Perceptions of Women's Bodies in Abortion Procedures

Abortion has been legal in Armenia since 1955, when under the membership of the Soviet Union abortion policy served as an asset for population control.[32] The current Act on Human Reproductive Health and Rights to Reproduction[33] confirms the legacy of induced abortion up to 12 weeks of pregnancy on request by the mother, and until the 22th week of pregnancy for medical and social reasons with a doctor's approval. This latter aspect, by the way, stirred debate on the doctors' role in sex-selective abortions in late phases of pregnancy.

On the other hand there is another critical issue to consider when speaking about sex selective abortions in Armenia. While the phenomenon of abortion is widespread in Armenian society: 63 percent of married women of reproductive age have had at least one abortion and six percent had 10 or more, it seems that neither the women themselves, nor the wider society discusses the issue openly. Apparently, abortion is associated with a 'womanly' task that one has to undergo. Since middle class families in Armenia limit the number of children to be able to sustain the family economically, and since contraception methods for family planning are still not common among couples in Armenia, it is women,

---

29 Erica Chong, Tamar Tsereteli, Susanna Vardanyan, Gayane Avagyan, and Beverly Winikoff, Knowledge, Attitudes, and Practice of Abortion among Women and Doctors in Armenia, *The European Journal of Contraception and Reproductive Health Care*, October 2009; 14(5): 340–348.

30 Marianna Grigoryan, Armenian Women Turn to Ulcer Medication for Do-It-Yourself Abortions, *EurasiaNet.org*, October 30, 2012; available at www.eurasianet.org/node/66124, last accessed on June 20, 2013.

31 UNFPA, Prevalence and Reasons . . . , *op. cit.*

32 Mary Allerton Kilbourne Matossian, *The Impact of Soviet Policies in Armenia* (Leiden: E. J. Brill, 1962), 70.

33 Act no. 474 of December 11, 2002 on Human Reproductive Health and Rights to Reproduction; available in Armenian at www.parliament.am/legislation.php?sel=show&ID=1339&lang=arm, last accessed on June 20, 2013.

with their bodies, who have to take the burden of controlling the family size. And since it is 'normal' to have an abortion for 'economic' reasons, it seems that it is not problematic for families to have a sex-selective abortion to avoid having a third or fourth child if the technology is available.

Obviously, future studies are needed to understand the common perceptions of women's bodies within the abortion practice in the Armenian society, which is assumedly connected to women's position in the society, and which will help understanding women's autonomy in abortion decisions. As we observed in the first section of the chapter the decision to have a sex selective abortion is made mainly by the pregnant women independently (82.6 percent), therefore, in further studies, it would be also critically important to address the issues of rational choice[34] in abortion cases, for a better understanding of the complexity of sex-selective abortion in Armenia.

Conclusion

Sex selective abortion, as a relatively new phenomenon in Armenian society, requires a complex approach to explore and understand it. There is evidence that many Armenian families prefer having sons and this is attributed to some 'Armenian mentality' — nevertheless, girls are equally expected and loved. There is also a significant connection between the economic situation in the country and the desired number of children in the family and this explains not only that there is still a relatively high abortion rate in Armenia, but also that 0.8 percent of Armenian women have sex-selective abortions[35], mainly in the case of the third or fourth child.

Moreover, neither men, nor women seem to realize that the burden of family planning is placed on the shoulders of women, it is their body that is used to control the number of children in the family and it is them who have to endure the physical and emotional difficulties that come with any induced abortion. In this context, therefore, sex selective abortion in Armenia becomes just another abortion procedure that women have to deal with.

Lastly, sex-selective abortions in Armenia are about gender bias; however, not so much in the sense of selecting the desired sex of the fetus, but in the problematic ways women's bodies are perceived and misperceived in the abortion procedures and in the vulnerable social position that women have in the prevalent discourse of family planning that makes the practice of abortion a commonplace.

---

34 Which is not the same as autonomous choice; see Wendy Anne Rogers, Heather Draper, Angela Jean Ballantyne, Is Sex-Selective Abortion Morally Justified and Should It Be Prohibited? *Bioethics*, November 2007, 21(9): 520–524.

35 UNFPA, Factsheet . . . , *op. cit.*

ON MEN AND GIRAFFES: POPULATION POLICY AT THE MUNICIPAL LEVEL IN SERBIA[1]

Ljiljana Pantović

In most modern countries policies are designed to encompass every aspect of the citizens' life. "From the cradle to the grave people are classified, shaped and ordered according to various policies."[2] This is why social scientists are now getting involved in the study of the social impact of these policies that govern life. The policy examined in this paper is related to questions of reproduction, and the control of the quantity and quality of the population. Population policies are "deliberately constructed or modified institutional arrangements and/or specific programs through which governments influence, directly or indirectly, demographic change."[3] Policies can be understood as guidelines or instruments of the administration of human life thus they can be seen as a form of biopower.[4] In this paper will address the process of biopower on a smaller scale, on a local level. The aim of this paper is to understand how this form of power works as a disciplining and self-regulating conduct of citizens themselves who are not forced to comply with a population policy but still choose to do so.

The case study which will be presented is a pronatalist population policy of the municipality of Jagodina, in the Republic of Serbia. This policy was implemented in 2011 and provided one-time financial aid to married couples from this municipality. What is interesting about this policy is that it was not directly addressing issues of procreation—child birth and/or child care—but the presumed

---

1 All translations from Serbian to English are made by the author, who takes full responsibility for their accuracy.
2 Susan Wright and Chris Shore, *Anthropology of Policy: Critical Perspectives on Governance and Power* (New York and London: Routlegde, 1997), 4.
3 Paul Demeny, *Population Policy: A Concise Summary* (New York: Buch, 2003), 45.
4 Michel Foucault, *History of Sexuality. Volume I: An Introduction* (New York: Vintage Books, 1990).

social prerequisite for procreation heterosexual marriage. This particular policy was subsequently abandoned after one year of implementation. The reason for its termination was the complaint filed against it to the Serbian Commissioner for Equality by the Lawyers Committee for Human Rights, in Serbia because it was proven to be was discriminatory.[5]

The main goal of this study is to understand, from a Foucauldian perspective, what kind of subjects are desired and produced through such a policy. I will show that the population policy of Jagodina municipality can understood as a form of biopower that had as its ultimate goal to prescribe a particular kind of family model as the norm—a patrifocal and patriachical, heterosexual family that, even though it presents itself as gender neutral, is targeting male citizens of Jagodina as the key recipients of the financial aid.

Theoretical Framework: Population Policies from a Foucauldian Perspective

In the earlier sovereign state, as Foucault[6] shows, power functioned through repression and prohibition. In the modern state, which emerged in the 18th century, we can trace a rupture from this mode of power. The modern state is more invested in the health and welfare of each individual citizen and the need to monitor them. This power was targeted at the human life. Under the pretense of 'care' for the population a new, more fluid form of power emerges—biopower.[7] As Greenhalgh and Winckler explains, biopower is aimed at the administration of the vital characteristics of the human population and "exercised in the name of optimizing individual or collective life, health and welfare."[8] This new form of power, arisen in the modern era, is interested in the intimate relations of social subjects towards their own body and towards the body of the entire population. Even the term itself 'population' is a product of the rise of modernity, closely linked with the formation of the administrative apparatus of the modern state.

'Population' became an issue for the state that needed to be taken care of, and by doing so the family became the central place of producing a healthy population. It is the basic or first institution of learning social norms. The notion of the

---

5   Poverenik za zaštitu ravnopravnosti [Commissioner for Protection of Equality], *Pritužba udruženja J. protiv grada Jagodine zbog diskriminacije u ostvarivanja prava na jednokratnu pomoć po osnovu osnovu rođenja i bračnog i porodičnog statusa* [Complaint of Association J. against the City of Jagodina for Discrimination in the One-Time Financial Aid Based on Place of Birth, Marital and Family Status], July 28, 2011, available at www.ravnopravnost.gov.rs/sr/višestruka-diskriminacija/pritužba-udruženja-j-protiv-grada-jagodine-zbog-diskriminacije-u-ostvarivanja-prava-na-jednokratnu-pomo, last accessed on June 4, 2013.

6   Foucault, *op. cit.*

7   *Ibid.*, 140.

8   Susan Greenhalgh and Edwin A. Winckler, *Governing China's Population: From Leninist to Neoliberal Biopolitics* (Stanford: Stanford University Press, 2005), 25.

family itself: what it is and how it should look like needed to become normalized, in the sense that the state had the power and legitimacy to prescribe what a normal family is. A possible framework for this prescription is population policies dealing with the issues of family and reproduction. The central assumption for such policies is the long-term stability of the "conjugal family as a closed physical, economic, and emotional unit within which children are planned, born, and reared."[9] What constitutes this stable "family" is not universal and fixed, however. On the contrary, what is considered to be the desirable family model is very much embedded in the socio-historical context and the analysis of population policies, such as the one examined here, can highlight this embeddedness. For this reason it is important to look at how policies are implemented in specific socio-cultural contexts and ask the question what type of subject do they produce. In this case, what family structure is seen as the norm and what is seen as the deviancy from this norm? Although this issue has been addressed on the national policy level, the local policy level can also provide interesting insight as its targeted population is smaller and thus allows for a more specific policy making process than the broader national ones.

Population Politics at the Local Level:
A Case Study of Jagodina, Serbia

Jagodina is a municipality in Serbia that has 71,195 inhabitants[10] and lies 136 km south of the capital Belgrade. This municipality has an ethnic majority of Serbs, and around 50.70 percent of the population lives in the city itself, while the rest live in the surrounding rural areas.[11] The last national census, in 2011, on the whole showed that Serbia has is experiencing a demographic drop, while Jagodina was one of the few municipalities that experienced demographic growth.[12] One possible explanation for the population increase in Jagodina, at least the official explanation of the current government of the municipality, is its focus on pronatalist policies. For example, as of February 1, 2009 pregnant women of this municipality receive financial aid for six months of their pregnancy and for a year post child birth.[13] Aside from these policies that directly target newborn babies and children, in 2011, Jagodina implemented a new policy aimed at married

9   Cynthia B. Lloyd, Family and Gender Issues for Population Policies, in Laurie Ann Mazur (ed.), *Beyond the Numbers: A Reader on Population, Consumption, and the Environment* (Washington, DC: Island Press, 1994), 242–256.
10 Grad Jagodina, O gradu—Stanovnistvo [The City of Jagodina, About the City—Population], available at www.jagodina.org.rs/o-gradu/stanovnistvo/, last accessed on June 4, 2013.
11 *Ibid.*
12 Statistical Office of the Republic of Serbia, *Popis 2011* [Census 2011]; available at popis2011.stat.rs/, last accessed on June 4, 2013.
13 Grad Jagodina, Vesti [The City of Jagodina, news]; available at www.jagodina.org.rs/vesti/, last accessed on June 4, 2013.

couples. As a form of public promotion of this policy, the mayor of Jagodina, Dragan Marković, nicknamed Palma, organized special "match making events" for unmarried citizens. One such event was a free holiday (paid by the municipality) to Greece for seven hundred potential couples, one of whom had to be over thirty-eight years old and had to be born or living in Jagodina. Apparently, the organizers managed to gather seven hundred potential Jagodinan bachelors but only seventy bachelorettes.[14] Given that there were more unwed men than women, the municipality offered the possibility for women from other cities to also come along for the holiday trip (forty-six cities from Serbia and Republic of Srpska in Bosnia and Herzegovina). Six hundred and thirty women joined in, agreeing to get married and move to Jagodina.[15] The goal, as the mayor stated, was to have seven hundred new marriages upon returning from the holiday.

> The best thing would be if the master of ceremonies could be there the moment they step out of the bus. So they do not change their minds. We will do everything that is in our power to create this "chemistry" between these singles. Sea, sun, the beach, music . . . if they still do not have butterflies in their stomachs after that, I do not know when they ever will! Even if only one marriage is made that will be our success and if we get a baby out of it our happiness is even greater![16]

This match-making event was a seen a promotion of the policy adopted in late December 2010 to provide a one-time financial aid for married couples. This decision entailed that upon marriage the couple would receive 3,000 euros (35,000 dinars). It was put in effect as of January 1, 2011. Yet this one-time financial aid did not come without some strings attached. According to Article 2 of the decision, this had to be the first marriage for both spouses.[17] At least one of them had to be over the age of thirty-eight and at least one of them had to be born or living in the municipality of Jagodina for over ten years prior to the date the decision was put into effect. Another major condition was that neither of the spouses were to have children prior to this marriage and that they were not prior to this living in a common-law marriage. Also the couple had to sign a document stating that they would stay married for at least five years and that during that time they would both be living in the same address. Most important of all, during this time frame at least one child must be born. If the couple could not conceive naturally the municipality would offer financial assistance for IVF treatments. According to Article 4 of the same decision, there shall be a check-up on the existence of the marriage and its status by municipality officials.

---

14 B92, *Palma finansira, ljudi ženite se* [Palma Is Paying, Get Married, People], *B92*, June 6, 2011; available at www.b92.net/biz/vesti/srbija.php?yyyy=2011&mm=06&dd=04&nav_id=516701, last accessed on June 4, 2013.

15 *Ibid.*

16 *Ibid.*

17 Poverenik za zaštitu ravnopravnosti, *op. cit.*

Due to the intense media campaign against this decision and the remarks made by the Serbian Commissioner for Protection Equality, the Assembly has replaced this decision with a new policy that provides all babies born in the municipality from June 1 until December 31, 2012 with a one-time financial aid of 1,200 euros (14,000 dinars).[18] Even though the policy is no longer in effect it is important to take a closer look at what kind of families this policy wanted to produce.

Jagodina's Policy from a Foucauldian Perspective

This decision of the municipality of Jagodina can be read as an expression of biopower in the sense that it tries to control and intervene in every aspect of an individual's life and life choices. It targets a very limited and specific type of citizen—unmarried, older Jagodinians. It is plausible to state that this particular part of the population was perceived as deviating from the desired social norm, which is that all the municipalities' citizens who are of marriageable age should be married and should have children. It is possible to infer that the policy was created in order to resolve the problem of this deviant population and produce out of them 'proper' and desired citizens.

Discussions with the citizens of Jagodina suggest that they expressed a general approval of the Mayor's and the assembly's social policies. That they felt that it was a good step. This type of faith in the good intentions of the government and the understanding that it is the role of public officials to solve social welfare issues of the citizens can be seen as a belonging to previous Yugoslavian socialist times when most people expected the state to provide them with a stable job and good opportunities to raise a family. The role of the mayor in deciding or 'helping' single Jagodinians was not seen as problematic.

Yet, legislations and municipal decision do not happen in a social vacuum. Policies are created within specific socio-political context and to be openly accepted and treated as universal they have to adhere and be compatible with socio cultural values and norms of the society as a whole. Serbian society, as Marina Blagojević points out, due to the war and the sanctions of the 1990s has become "re-patriachalized."[19] Due to the political and economic crisis it was women who were the first to lose their jobs and return exclusively to domestic work putting women in an even more marginalized position. Blagojević shows that even after the democratic revolution of 2000 and the declared commitment of the politicians towards gender equality this commitment remains on paper only.[20] Thus the underlining premise is that Serbian society is still very *patrifo-*

---

18 *Ibid.*
19 Marina Blagojevic, *Položaj žena u zemljama Balkana: komparativni pregled* [The Position of Women in the Balkan Countries: Comparative Review] (Beograd: Gender Centar Vlade RS, 2002), 31–61.
20 *Ibid.*

cal—in that it is both *patrilineal* (the family name is passed down on the male side only) and *patrilocal* (women when married leave their household and relocate to their husbands families and tend to be considered solely as part of that new family).

The embedded gender aspect behind such a limit is also that, if the goal is to have children out of this marriage than the age of thirty eight is seen as highly problematic because most women become less fertile at age thirty and the chances of conceiving a child drop. This means that implicitly the beneficiary of this policy is male and this is confirmed by the fact that only seventy women of the municipality participated in the vacation, while male participation was seven hundred. From this it is plausible to conclude that within this context a greater threat to social stability is if men remain single, do not get married and do not procreate. This socio-cultural context allows for a better understanding of the policies condition that at least one of the potential spouses has to be over thirty-eight and why the majority of Jagodinan holiday and party event attendees were older men. It is unmarried older men who are seen as a deviation from the patrifocal social norm.

Thus, the goal was to find wives for the over thirty eight year old male citizens of the municipality and as the Article 2, which stipulated that only one of the had to be born or living in Jagodina they could go about finding eligible women from any other part of Serbia, or in the Republic of Srpska in Bosnia and Herzegovina. A second problematic issue of the decision, with regards to gender, is that Article 2 states that the couple has to be married for five years. This decision is problematic because it is blind to the possibilities and dangers of potentials domestic violence, which sadly is not a rare case in Serbia.[21] Legally coercing the couple to stay married for at least five years or they would have to pay the money back puts some of these women, who have moved from their hometowns to a new environment, in vulnerable positions.

In this particular policy what is interesting is that it does not target children directly but tries to provide the desired preconditions for the birth of new citizens. Its main focus is traditional, heterosexual marriage. The desired child in accordance with this policy is a child born into a heterosexual marriage. This can, also, be read through the fact that couples who had children out of wedlock were excluded from financial aid as it too deviated from the social norm. This means that there is only one specific form of family structure that is seen as desirable for the municipality and all other forms of family relations are perceived as deviant and to be corrected.

In order to highlight this socio-political ideology behind this desired family model even further it is necessary to draw attention to the political position and statements of the mayor in regards to homosexual relationships in Serbia

---

21 Osservatorio Balcani e Caucaso, *Domestic Violence in Serbia: The Law Is Not Enough*, May 19, 2011; available at www.balcanicaucaso.org/eng/Regions-and-countries/Serbia/Domestic-violence-in-Serbia-the-law-is-not-enough-94265, last accessed on June 4, 2013.

as these sexual identities and relations are seen as the most problematic form of sexual deviancy. Mayor Marković is firmly against homosexuality and the rights of homosexuals. On numerous occasions he has spoken against the organizations of Pride events in the country. One of these cases is when a day after the Pride Parade was cancelled in Belgrade, in 2012, he organized a "wedding" to which all the members of the assembly were invited to join directly after a meeting. The striking thing about this event was the fact that the marriage was between two giraffes. Several years before Marković invested municipal money in the construction of a local zoo in the city of Jagodina and the first animal that he bought for this zoo was a male giraffe named Jovanche. As was the case with the human citizens of Jagodina, the male giraffe's future wife was from another city, the city zoo in Belgrade. By drawing a parallel between the giraffe and the citizens of Jagodina the major wanted to emphasize his view that heterosexual marriage is not just a social institution but a 'natural fact'.

> It is a pleasure to see how much they love each other; we here in Jagodina are not only fighting against the low birth rates amongst people but amongst animals as well. Especially amongst exotic types such as giraffes, we expect that in two years' time we will have four giraffes in our Zoo. This might not be the time to talk about animal marriages when we are fighting for the better life of *every man* in Serbia, but I think it is important to send a message that a male and a female should get married not two males. (Emphasis added by the author.)[22]

The heteronormative, patrifocal family structure is the desired norm for family life in Jagodina not only for human but for animal residence as well. This type of event sends a clear symbolic message that the only acceptable structure for raising and having children is traditional marriage. It also sends a clear message that the 'exotic' type of citizen in Jagodina, the older man, has to be controlled in order to prevent his already existing deviancy to turn into homosexuality, which is perceived as the most threatening form of sexual deviancy from the prescribed social norm.

Conclusion

To conclude, this decision of the municipality of Jagodina is a form of population policy that as its ultimate goal has influencing demographic change in the municipality. What is important to note is that this type of policy is not interested in demographic growth as such but it is asserting cultural preferences as to whom and in what social institution should procreate. Even though the Commissioner

---

22 Blic, Palma "venčao" žirafe i poslao poruku gejevima [Palma 'Weds' Giraffes and Sends a Message to Gays], *Blic*, October 9, 2012; available at www.blic.rs/Vesti/Srbija/346879/Pama-vencao-zirafe-i-poslao-poruku-gejevima, last accessed on June 4, 2013.

for Protection of Equality described the decision as discriminatory it failed to comprehend the other intersecting levels of discrimination based on gender and sexual orientation that were implied by this policy. The fact that the targeting beneficiaries of the policy would be mostly older single men signals both the cultural preference for patrifocal families and for preventing potential sexual deviancy of this already deviant social group. Marriage is perceived solely as between men and women. Presuming thus not only that gender itself is a fixed, biological and individual trait but also directly excluding any other forms of sexual orientations that deviate from this norm.

Through studying a specific population policy at the local level and paying close attention to the political rhetoric and socio-cultural context of the policy I have shown the mechanisms though which individuals as citizens are created, classified, and shaped. As Wright and Shore explained this process of subjectification stretches "from the cradle to the grave."[23] I would add that the regulation, classification, and disciplining begin even before the cradle, as municipal policy in the Jagodina case targets the pre-conception phases of social life. A person born in Jagodina is taken care of by the municipality before birth through social care and financial aid to the pregnant women; after birth until adulthood via financial benefits, cheaper kindergartens, and paid excursions; and during adulthood in the form of providing match-making services for single men and women if they agree to become traditionally married spouses. Thus, the municipality of Jagodina makes great investments into the biovalue of the welfare of its citizens—as long as they comply with the prescribed and desired norm of social behavior.

---

23 Wright and Shore, *op. cit.*, 7.

UNFULFILLED PROMISES: COMMERCIAL SURROGACY AND REPRODUCTIVE TRAVEL IN INDIA

Attila Seprődi

"A vital industry," as India's Supreme Court has termed it, India's commercial surrogacy sector relies on cheap home-labor, international clientele, specialized medical infrastructure and a business friendly legislative climate.[1] The business was estimated to worth 445 million dollars in 2008, with a potential to expand to several billions, making India the second largest surrogacy market after the United States.[2] The country's emergence as a top destination spot for transnational fertility travel in recent years is partly the result of concentrated efforts from the part of the Indian government to promote medical tourism, and it is in line with a general expansion of health tourist markets in Asia.[3] Cross-border

---

1 Mina Chang, Womb for Rent: India's Commercial Surrogacy, *Harvard International Review*, Spring 2009, 31(1): 11–12; Usha Rengachary Smerdon, Crossing Bodies, Crossing Borders: International Surrogacy between the United States and India, *Cumberland Law Review*, 2008, 39(1): 15–85; and SAMA—Resource Group for Women and Health, The Myth of Regulation: A Critique of the 2008 Draft ART (Regulation) Bill and Rules, *Medico Friend Circle Bulletin*, No. 335–336, June–September 2009, 8–13.

2 SAMA—Resource Group for Women and Health, *Constructing Conceptions. The Mapping of Assisted Reproductive Technologies in India* (New Delhi: SAMA, 2010); Ruby L. Lee, New Trends in Global Outsourcing of Commercial Surrogacy: A Call for Regulation, *Hastings Women's Law Journal*, Summer 2009, 20(2): 275–300.

3 On the expansion of health tourism, see Andrea Whittaker, Pleasure and Pain: Medical Travel in Asia, *Global Public Health*, July 2008, 3(3): 271–290 and Milica Z. Bookman and Karla R. Bookman, *Medical Tourism in Developing Countries* (New York: Palgrave MacMillan, 2007). Pushpa Bhargava estimated in 2003 that there could be around 300 clinics offering ART treatments in India; see Bhargava, Ethical Issues in Modern Biological Technologies, *Reproductive Biomedicine Online*, July 2003, 7(3): 276–285. Estimates of scope may be wildly different. SAMA, a resource group for women's health mentions in a more recent study that 116 clinics are listed in the National ART registry in India, emphasizing that while the real number cannot be assessed, it is certainly much higher, and in general the ART industry is growing. See SAMA, *Constructing Conceptions, op. cit.*, 155–157.

surrogacy arrangements and the phenomenon of reproductive tourism increasingly attract the attention of scholars, and Indian surrogacy figures centrally
in this scholarship. However there seems to be no consensus over how such
practices should be best assessed and interpreted.[4]

Many of its critics argue that commercial surrogacy represents a form of
women's exploitation.[5] Approaching international commercial surrogacy, my
paper starts from the standpoint that indeed, this may be the case. However
exploitation is but one side of the coin. "Being poor is worse than being exploited," goes the argument of some commentators.[6] Those who oppose commercial surrogacy "are advocating legislation for women in an ideal world,
whereas women in the real world need these opportunities and should be
able to take advantage of them," is the opinion of another.[7] Finally there are
voices that urge us to rather "concentrate on improving the conditions under
which surrogates work and changing the background conditions (in particular, the unequal distribution of power and wealth) which generate exploitative
relationships."[8]

The main argument of this paper is that surrogacy has the subversive potential of creating alternative forms of social and human relatedness, and that
this potential is underplayed by incorporating surrogacy into the market. More
specifically I will argue that the marketization of surrogacy in India goes hand
in hand with its 'normalizing' on the discursive level in a way that clearly fa-
vors the interests of clinics and intended parents. Similar points were already
made in the few ethnographic studies available on surrogacy, particularly in
Charis Thompson's account of the normalizing strategies of naturalization and

---

4   On reproductive travel in general, see Eric Blyth and Abigail Farrand, Reproductive Tourism:
    A Price Worth Paying for Reproductive Autonomy? *Critical Social Policy*, February 2005, 25(1):
    91–114; Deech, Ruth, Reproductive Tourism in Europe: Infertility and Human Rights, *Global
    Governance*, October–December 2003, 9(4): 425–432; Guido Pennings, Reproductive Tourism
    as Moral Pluralism in Motion, *Journal of Medical Ethics*, December 2002, 28(6): 337–341; Guido
    Pennings, Legal Harmonization and Reproductive Tourism in Europe, *Reproductive Health
    Matters*, May 2005, 13(25): 120–128; Richard F. Storrow, Quests for Conception: Fertility Tourists,
    Globalization and Feminist Legal Theory, *Hastings Law Journal*, December 2005, 57(2): 295–330;
    and Marcia C. Inhorn and Pasquale Patrizio, Rethinking Reproductive "Tourism" as Reproductive
    "Exile," *Fertility and Sterility*, September 2009, 92(3): 903–906. On the particular case of Indian
    surrogacy see Smerdon, *op. cit.*; Lee, *op. cit.*; Amrita Pande, Commercial Surrogacy in India:
    Manufacturing A Perfect Mother-Worker, *Signs*, Summer 2010, 35(4):969–992; and Kalindi Vora,
    Indian Transnational Surrogacy and the Disaggregation of Mothering Work. *Anthropology News*,
    February 2009, 50(2): 9–12.
5   Robyn Rowland, *Living Laboratories. Women and Reproductive Technologies* (Bloomington: Indiana
    University Press, 1992); Janice G. Raymond, *Women as Wombs. Reproductive Technologies and the
    Battle over Women's Freedom* (San Francisco: HarperSanFrancisco, 1993); and Elizabeth S. Anderson,
    Is Women's Labor a Commodity? *Philosophy and Public Affairs*, Winter 1990, 19(1): 71–92.
6   Rassaby, quoted in Rowland, *op. cit.*, 169.
7   Martha A. Field, *Surrogate Motherhood. The Legal and Human Issue* (Cambridge, Massachusetts:
    Harvard University Press, 1990).
8   Stephen Wilkinson, The Exploitation Argument Against Commercial Surrogacy, *Bioethics*, April
    2003, 17(2): 169–187.

socialization that occur in fertility clinics, and Helena Ragoné's description of the wish to attain traditional ends with unconventional means in surrogacy and the efforts to place it "inside tradition."[9]

The Promises and Dangers of Surrogacy

For a non-reductionist, general theoretical frame in which to place new reproductive technologies and their various social, cultural, economic implications, Marx's analysis of technology and social change could serve as a suggestive starting point.[10] Although *Biocapital, Volume 1* still has to be written,[11] I argue, following Thompson, that we need to anchor our approach to new reproductive technologies strongly into the capitalist mode of production of which they represent a part.[12] This would go well beyond acknowledging the intimate relationship between technology (and the natural sciences, producing machines, tools, technical innovations) and the capitalist enterprise. According to Marx, technology is also expressive, in the sense that it discloses forms of human relatedness, modes of dealing with nature, the process of production, the reproduction of daily life, social relations, and mental concepts.[13] As Harvey argues, the impetus of social change can appear in any of these relatively autonomous and interacting domains, and attention has to be directed towards the forces which are holding it down or which give it certain directionality.[14]

From a different starting point, Marilyn Strathern arrives to very similar ideas.[15] In Strathern's view facts of life considered to be natural are becoming

---

9   See Charis Thompson, *Making Parents. The Ontological Choreography of Reproductive Technologies* (Cambridge, MA: Massachusetts Institute of Technology, 2005); and Helena Ragoné, Chasing the Blood Tie: Surrogate Mothers, Adoptive Mothers and Fathers, *American Ethnologist*, May 1996, 23(2): 352–365.

10 My understanding of Marx's ideas about the relation of technology and social change is primarily based on Chapter 15 in Karl Marx, *Capital. A Critique of Political Economy* (Harmondsworth, Middlesex: Penguin Books, 1982), 492–636, and follows the interpretation given by David Harvey, see especially *The Limits to Capital* (Oxford: Basil Blackwell, 1982), 98–136 and *Justice, Nature and the Geography of Difference* (Cambridge, MA: Blackwell Publishers, 1996), 105–109.

11 Donna J. Haraway, *When Species Meet* (Minneapolis: University of Minnesota Press, 2008), 66.

12 Thompson, *op. cit.*, 247.

13 See, for example, "Technology reveals the active relation of man to nature, the direct process of the production of his life, and thereby it also lays bare the process of the production of the social relations of his life and of the mental conceptions that flow from those relations." Marx, *op. cit.*, 493:

14 Harvey argues that "... the presumption from a dialectical process based and historical materialist view of the world is that it is not change *per* se that has to be explained, but the forces that hold down change and/or which give it a certain directionality. There is no single moment within the social process devoid of the capacity of transformative activity." Harvey, *Justice . . . , op. cit.*, 105.

15 Marilyn Strathern, *Reproducing the Future: Essays on Anthropology, Kinship and the New Reproductive Technologies* (Manchester: Manchester University Press 1992); and Marilyn Strathern, *The Relation: Issues in Complexity and Scale* (Cambridge: Prickly Pear Press, 1995).

to an increasing degree a matter of choice under the influence of new reproductive technologies. Her case is made in a witty analysis of the decision in
the *Johnson vs. Calvert* surrogacy case, where the criteria for judging who is
the 'real' mother—since biology was not of much help—became a sort of
intellectual copyright.[16] According to Strathern, in this new context of choice
both persons and relations are assisted, in the sense that they have to be,
(and they are) conceived.[17] The idea has far-reaching implications, since the
ways how persons and relations are conceived in un-natural contexts matters a lot. In *Johnson vs. Calvert* for example the ruling linked a woman and
a child through a line of argumentation typically used in assessing property rights. In the end, Strathern seems to be more hopeful than pessimistic
about the possibly open forms of relatedness created out of knowledge,
rather than prescribed by a patriarchally constructed nature. However she
also points to some of the dangers of enterprising up kinship, tendencies of
framing the persons and relations created by new reproductive technologies
in terms of consumer choice.[18] Looking at commercial surrogacy in India
these concerns appear as not without foundation. Lack of state regulations
contributed substantially to the expansion of the Indian surrogacy market,
leaving its participants on their own in negotiating positions and conditions
of trade.[19] This situation empowers clinics and intended parents to interpret
and impose conditions according to their interest. Not only the interests of
surrogate mothers are misrecognized, but the promises of surrogacy are also
denied in the process.

The Unfulfilled Promise of Surrogacy in India

The ethnographic material of my research consists in narratives publicly available in the form of internet diaries of people who were involved in commercial
surrogacy arrangements with Indian clinics. Two arguments are brought for the
legitimacy of this research strategy. First, internet is used extensively as a resource
in surrogacy market, as a means of orientation, information gathering and com-

---

16 *Johnson vs. Calvert*, Supreme Court of California, 5 Cal.4th 84, 851 P.2d 776, judgment of March
    20, 1993. The reasoning of the court stated that "the mental concept of the child is a controlling
    factor of its creation, and the originators of that concept merit full credit as *conceivers*," quoted in
    Strathern, *The Relation . . .* , *op. cit.*, 7.
17 Strathern, *Reproducing . . .* , *op. cit.*
18 *Ibid.*, 31–43.
19 A guideline was issued by the Indian government (see Government of India, *National Guidelines
    for Accreditation, Supervision and Regulation of ART Clinics in India* New Delhi: Indian Council of
    Medical Research, available at icmr.nic.in/art/art_clinics.htm, last accessed on May 28, 2013),
    but clinics are not legally bound to follow its recommendations. A draft Assisted Reproductive
    Technology Regulation Bill was initiated in 2008 (for an overview and critique see SAMA, *The
    Myth of Regulation, op. cit.*, 8–13), revised in 2010, and waiting to be passed since then.

munication between the parties.[20] Second, besides being informative, these accounts offer crucial insights on the practical and ethical difficulties encountered by intended parents and on their strategies to handle them. Normalizing efforts are essential in this context, and they can be grasped through looking at the discursive framing of events, meanings, relations that occur during the process.

Surveying a number of ten blogs shows that for the intended parents struggling with infertility surrogacy appears as a means to a desperately wanted end. The costs and risks involved in the procedure in the United States made this option for a long time beyond their reach. As an apparent paradox, the opening up of the surrogacy market in India made surrogacy a more affordable and safer solution.[21] There are two major risks for intended parents engaging in surrogacy. On the one hand unsuccessful pregnancies may transform in growing expenditures, on the other there is a potential of birth mothers claiming the child. Several highly publicized cases in the United States show that parental claims are not easily handled by the courts and surrogacy contracts are not always enforceable.[22] The particularities of the Indian surrogacy market make these potential claims highly improbable.[23]

Having a child in India is portrayed in the blogs as an adventure, a mission or a journey, which begins with selecting a clinic to work with and ends with picking up the baby. These tropes imply a closed temporal frame and a great spatial distance, which help intended parents to detach themselves from the unwanted commitments and consequences potentially coming with surrogacy. In a letter for the future child one mother expresses the need of detachment openly:

There were some surrogates that I spoke with (in Canada), but they wanted too much involvement in our child's life after the birth. I kinda

---

20 On the role of the internet see Derek Morgan, Enigma Variations: Surrogacy, Rights and Procreative Tourism, in Rachel Cook, Shelley D. Sclater and Felicity Kaganas (eds.), *Surrogate Moterhood: International Perspectives* (Oxford and Portland, OR: Hart Publishing 2003), 75–92. Typically, an arrangement between a US citizen and an Indian surrogate, mediated by an agency and a clinic, requires two trips, one for delivering the eggs, the other for picking up the baby, and this can be reduced to one, if frozen eggs are shipped, not carried. In this context the reliability of information available on internet becomes crucial, and blogs about personal experiences to some extent function as a form of consumer control over the market.

21 Reporting the same or even higher success rates, the overall projected costs of the procedure in India are approximately the half of the costs in the United States.

22 Janet L. Dolgin, *Defining the Family. Law, Technology and Reproduction in an Uneasy Age* (New York: New York University Press, 1997).

23 The main pro and counter arguments for surrogacy in India are well summarized by Mike and Mike, a homosexual couple undergoing a surrogacy arrangement with two surrogates and egg-donation at Rotunda, on their blog: the total cost of 55,000 dollars (compared to 160,000 dollars in the United States), the surrogate's "pure" monetary motivations, the legal environment favoring intended parents, or the travel experience. The only counter argument appears to be the distance and the culture-shock. See Mike and Mike, Million Rupee Babies . . . *Spawn of Mike And Mike*, August 2008; available at spawnofmikeandmike.blogspot.com/2008/08/million-rupee-babies. html, last accessed on March 27, 2013; see also Terry and Steve, Mumbai for a Jiffy—Literally 72 Hours, But Who's Counting? *Christmas Eve Boys: In Pursuit of Paternity*, May 2009; available at christmaseveboys.blogspot.com/2009/05/mumbai-or-bust.html, last accessed on March 27, 2013.

wanted severed ties. Not that I am heartless, but you are our child, and I would always think of this woman as an angel, but preferred an angel from afar.[24]

Closure and detachment are emphasized also by the following quote: "It is/ was a commercial arrangement and both parties fulfilled their obligations."[25] This sentence also captures the essence of the major normalizing strategy revealed by these accounts, namely a discursive framing which reduces surrogacy relations to mere commercial arrangements. The claim is as old as commercial surrogacy itself. If accepted as legitimate, it would enforce the position of intended parents in two fundamental ways: by ruling out any non-economic implication from the part of the surrogate on the one hand and creating a form of contractually enforceable accountability on the other. However even under a permissive legislative context, intended parents are not empowered to the extent they are in India. The heart of the matter is concisely formulated by another couple, referring to the situation in the United States:

> The contracts are also risky and there have been instances of surrogates asserting parental rights. We have also had friends who experienced nightmares with unsophisticated surrogates, who ate poorly, smoked, drank or worse.[26]

As for in India: ". . . it is somewhat unregulated at present—there are guidelines in place but no real oversight to ensure compliance."[27] It is more than telling that this allusion to unregulatedness appears in a positive context, as being in the benefit of the intended parents. It implies that regulating surrogacy would alter a situation in which they are empowered in the first place.[28] Moreover, perceiving surrogacy as an enterprise which becomes not safer but riskier when regulated entails an ambiguous approach to law. It is truly remarkable from this point of view the reaction of a blogger on an article which suggests that intended parents who enter in surrogacy arrangements abroad skirt the laws of their countries:

> So? Of course we do. If commercial surrogacy were legal in Australia I would be doing it here. Your point is? Yes, we are. And the problem is? We

---

24 Baby Dreams, Canadian Surrogacy Pioneers . . . From India with Love, *Baby Dreams . . . From India with Love!* May 2009; available at babydreamsfromindiawithlove.blogspot.com/2009/05/surrogacy-pioneers.html, last accessed on March 27, 2013.
25 Peter, To Meet the Surrogate? *Peter's Surrogacy Blog*, November 2009; available at peterssurrogacyblog.blogspot.com/2009/11/to-meet-surrogate.html, last accessed on March 27, 2013.
26 Terry and Steve, Mumbai for a Jiffy, *op. cit.*
27 *Ibid.*
28 More experienced travelers will disagree on this, as I will show later. Loose regulations empower intended parents in their relation with the surrogates but make them vulnerable in their relation with clinics.

wouldn't need to evade laws if the laws were reasonable in our countries of origin.[29]

One thing is sure: guidelines in India are 'reasonable' to the extent that they do not even have to be ensured. It is more than probable that clinics also play an active role in the empowerment of intended parents at the expense of surrogate mothers. The following quote is suggestive for the means through which potential claims for the baby from the part of the birth-mother are underplayed: "She signed a contract, so she has no legal claim to the baby. Also, the baby will be turned over to us immediately after the birth."[30]

The other form of empowerment, implicit in the framing of surrogacy as a 'purely' economic relationship lies in subjecting the surrogate to forms of accountability characteristic to market-relations. While fulfilling 'her part of the obligation' the body of the birth-mother is subjected to a great degree of medical control from the part of the clinic and a partial control from the part of intended parents. Surrogates are encouraged to live in temporary housing provided by the clinics, where they can be under surveillance. Furthermore their rights over their body (whether to terminate or not the pregnancy for example) are seriously limited by the arrangement. One of the reasons of high success rates achieved by Indian clinics is that they may implant more embryos then generally recommended, dramatically increasing the risk of multiple pregnancies.[31] While the practice assures higher success rates, the risks it implies and the corollary fetal reduction make it ethically disputed. In line with their interest, intended parents try to put pressure on medical staff to implant as much embryos as possible. The

---

29 Amani, Back to the Serious Stuff: Educating the Masses. *Amani and Bob's Indian Surrogacy*, November 2008; available at amaniandbobsurrogacy.blogspot.com/2008/11/back-to-serious-stuff-educating-masses.html, last accessed on March 27, 2013.

30 Million Rupee Baby, How We Announced Our Pregnancy, *Million Rupee Baby*, October 2008; available at millionrupeebaby.blogspot.com/2008/10/how-we-announced-our-pregnancy.html, last accessed on March 27, 2013.

31 The *Guidelines for ART Clinics in India* imposes the implantation of no more than three embryos per cycle; see Chapter 3.2.7 in Government of India, *National Guidelines for Accreditation, Supervision and Regulation of ART Clinics in India* (New Delhi: Indian Council of Medical Research); available at icmr.nic.in/art/art_clinics.htm, last accessed on May 27, 2013. With a telling ambiguity the site of Rotunda Clinic states: Presently, all IVF clinics are supposed to work under these *Guidelines* which should be considered "legal" (quotation marks in original), see Rotunda, The Rotunda Gestational Surrogacy/Gestational Carrier ART Program, *I Wanna Get Pregnant*; available at www.iwannagetpregnant.com/legislation.shtml, last accessed on March 27, 2013. As for actual implantation practices: Brian reports five embryos, while Mike and Mike four, see Brian, The Waiting Game, *Switzertwins Weblog*, April 29, 2008; available at switzertwins.wordpress.com/2008/04/29/the-waiting-game/, last accessed on March 27, 2013; Mike, and Mike, A Serious Note . . . And a Nervous Laugh, *Spawn of Mike And Mike*, August 2008; available at spawnofmikeandmike.blogspot.com/2008/08/serious-noteand-nervous-laugh.html, last accessed on March 27, 2013. Among the "medical issues" related to multiple births, Mike and Mike enlists "premature birth, low birth weight and associated medical problems." More risks and the intricate connection between hormonal superovulation protocols, medical reproductive theory and practice and the superovulatory drug market are explored by See Thompson, *op. cit.*, 96–99.

only instance of expressed ethical concerns I found shows the full ambiguity of the situation. The objection is raised by a professed Christian intended parent, who takes abortion as a matter of conscience. Apparently this ethical awareness did not impede her in trying to convince the medical staff to permit the potential gestation of quadruplets.

I spent a lot of it [discussion with her husband, *Author's note*] feeling sick, just wishing that we could transfer four embryos like Dr. Yash wants us to, but get them to agree that they won't perform a selective reduction. The only thing I knew was that I would never be able to live with myself if I killed my child. And that is what I would be doing if we did what the doctors want and more than two embryos implanted.[32]

In any case, decisions over these "medical issues" are preserved for the clinics and intended parents. Considering that the issue of control over one's own body for now became a corner-stone of Western liberal values, Mike's comment appears as a bitter patriarchal farce: "I have always supported a woman's right to choose but I never really thought that such a difficult decision would be mine to take."[33]

Whatever the practical advantages of establishing surrogacy as a purely commercial arrangement, it is hard to deny that essentially it is not recognized as such. The blogs show clearly the great emotional load involved in the practice, as intended parents try to cope with intricate questions posed by themselves and by others. Some of these concerns are matching those formulated generally in the literature on surrogacy: exploitation, commoditization, degradation, selfishness, social inequality, male-domination, just to quote a few from a blog-entry.[34] Building up legitimacy for this practice proceeds through elaborating a

---

32 Jo Carry, Posting Potpourri, *Procreated in India*, November 2008; available at procreatedinindia. blogspot.com/2008/11/posting-potpourri.html, last accessed on March 27, 2013.

33 Mike and Mike, Million Rupee Babies . . . , *op. cit.*

34 See Amani, We Have a Surrogate. *Amani and Bob's Indian Surrogacy*, September 2008; available at amaniandbobsurrogacy.blogspot.com/2008/09/we-have-surrogate.html, last accessed on March 27, 2013. For a very suggestive early dystopic vision on the future of commercial surrogacy see Gena Corea, *The Mother Machine: Reproductive Technologies from Artificial Insemination to Artificial Wombs* (New York: Harper and Collins, 1986), 214–215. It must be noted however that this emotional tension is far from being disinterested, partly is caused by the insecurity of the investment. Many of the intended parents realize at a certain point that there is a darker side of the largely unregulated business of surrogacy. This point usually arrives when clinics come up with an extended bill, or other conflicts of interests appear. Moral considerations tend to attenuate at this point, and the celebratory tone of writing becomes darker. Consider the following quote as illustrative: "never think any service provider with this journey is not making a good buck out of it, no matter how sweet and lovely they may appear, they are in it for the money," Amani, Options, So Few—And Very Very Pissed Off with Life Right Now . . . *Amani and Bob's Indian Surrogacy*, February 2008; available at amaniandbobsurrogacy.blogspot.com/2009/02/options-so-few-and-very-very-pissed-off.html, last accessed on March 27, 2013. Among the "realities" enlisted under the title of "Third World Countries and Surrogacy" we do not find any moralizing on exploitation, see Crystal, Third World Countries and Surrogacy, *Crystal's Blog*, August 2009; available at crystal-crystaltravis.blogspot.com/2009/08/third-world-countries-and-surrogacy.html, last accessed on March 27, 2013.

normalizing narrative centered on the figure of the surrogate mother. In the last part of my analysis I propose to take a closer look on this speech-figure.

The narrative figure of the surrogate mother as it appears in the blogs is essentially an ambivalent construction along the lines of culture, class and gender. These dimensions are linked together in an intricate manner. There is an element of distancing coming from a perceived cultural difference, experienced as a culture-shock. Indian culture is seen as beautiful and charming but struck by unimaginable poverty, which defines the character and actions of its people. "India is raw and its people are rich in character," as one commentator notes.[35] "Rawness" comes from the "heartbreaking" and "heart-wrenching" hardships they endure with "impressive work ethic" and "impressive soul." They do "whatever work needs to be done" in order to survive or to get out somehow from the poverty trap. Apparently this cultural trait makes the exclusive financial interest of surrogate mothers plausible and unproblematic.[36] There is very little actual connection between intended parents and surrogate mothers, usually resuming to the emotional moment of "meeting the surrogate." Most of the blogs report very little willingness in entering into more sustained relations than small gift giving, tearful expressions of gratitude and some self-reassuring questions. This restraint however does not discourage intended parents to articulate bold assumptions which go as far as to define the process as one of empowerment.

> It is very demeaning to Indian women to suggest they cannot make up their own minds about whether they wish to be surrogates. Their bodies, their choice. Isn't this what the feminist movement has been fighting for decades?[37]

Surrogate mother fees are equivalent to 10–15 years of average salary, and are seen as a chance for them and their children to secure a better future.[38] The obvious point obscured here is that high fees permitted by the high profit rate also function as a powerful incentive that may result in various social and familiar

---

35 The following quotes are from Brian, Break for Commentary. *Switzertwins Weblog*, April 21, 2008; available at switzertwins.wordpress.com/2008/04/21/break-for-commentary/, last accessed on March 27, 2013; and Brian, The Waiting Game, *op. cit.*

36 The arguments employed here bear resemblance with those put forward by some early defenders of commercial surrogacy. The assumptions are that lower-class women are less tied emotionally to their children and they are more willing to give them up in order to overcome their financial needs, see Thompson, *op. cit.*, 66. Clinics are reinforcing this comforting view, as the following account shows: "I remember sitting down with Dr. Hitesh Patel, asking him if he knew how the donor's or the surrogates felt about surrogacy. He said that most of the people do not think that much about things, they live for today, and have to figure out how they will get money to survive. Most are not even able to envision getting seven thousand dollars," see Crystal, A New Journey! *Crystal's Blog*, June 2009; available at crystal-crystaltravis.blogspot.com/2009/06/new-journey.html, last accessed on March 27, 2013.

37 Amani, Conception Day, *Amani and Bob's Indian Surrogacy*, February 2009; available at amaniandbobsurrogacy.blogspot.com/2009/02/conception-day.html, last accessed on March 27, 2013.

38 Vora, *op. cit.*, 9–12.

pressures on women. The existence of these pressures is confirmed by several bloggers in their account on how the family of the surrogate tried to extort them for more money. However instead of acknowledging the obvious implications of these embarrassing situations, intended parents understand them as resulting from the Indian cultural character, which driven by poverty, is accustomed to cadging and hard bargain.[39]

> Remember—Indians grow up in a culture with more bargaining and negotiation (and less fixed prices) than westerners are used to. In India, even overseas Indians who visit Mumbai get over-charged for taxi rides. And more similar to the Chinese culture than the American culture, a signed contract is more like the start of the negotiating process rather than the end of the negotiating process.[40]

While there is a chance to be "over-charged" by despairingly inventive locals, surrogacy in India is generally understood by intended parents in terms of mutual benefit. At the end, they benefit in a child, much-wanted and longed for, and that is truly priceless. As for the other part:

> At least I am comforted by the fact that any of us travelling to India for surrogacy are making a huge difference in the lives of our surrogates, and also contributing to the livelihoods of our doctors, lawyers, our personal drivers, and everyone who is employed in the tourism game in India, from the waiters to the cab drivers, rickshaw drivers, shop keepers . . . the list goes on.[41]

Conclusive Remarks

In the theoretical part of my article I argued for a multidimensional approach that focuses on the interfaces where technology, nature, the labor process, reproduction of daily life, social relations and mental concepts meet each other. A large body of literature documents the potential of new reproductive technologies to catalyze the reorganization of these domains. Discussing international commercial surrogacy in India this paper showed that the discursive framing of the process by intended parents and clinics, coming from a clearly empowered

---

39 Power dynamics within the family are often overlooked when discussing surrogate motivations, see Robyn Rowland, *op. cit.*, 164. They are disregarded in the Indian case through explaining "attempts of extortion" in terms of some cultural inclination towards bargaining. Accounts of bargaining situations abound in the blogs, their customary moral being that of "watch out for your purse." For some of these, see Mike and Mike, Million Rupee Babies . . . , *op. cit.* For a case of "attempted extortion," see Peter, To Meet the Surrogate? *op. cit.*

40 Peter, To Meet the Surrogate? *op. cit.*

41 Amani, Photos: Day One—India, *Amani and Bob's Indian Surrogacy*, December 2008; available at amaniandbobsurrogacy.blogspot.com/2008/12/photos-day-one-india_21.html, last accessed on March 27, 2013.

position, 'normalizes' surrogacy in a way that is rather familiar and has nothing revolutionary in it. Through framing surrogacy as an adventure and as a purely commercial arrangement as well as through an arbitrary interpretation of the motivations of the surrogate, intended parents are able to detach themselves from undesired forms of relatedness, deny the rights and claims related to the child from the part of birth mothers, legitimate ethically questionable control over the birth mother's body and overlook the deeply unequal power relations inherent in the surrogacy arrangement.

RENT-A-WOMB SERVICE: AN OVERVIEW OF COMMERCIAL SURROGACY IN INDIA

Debjyoti Ghosh

Introduction

Women have historically had a very paradoxical position in the Indian subcontinent. To be worshipped in the form of many powerful goddesses, while at the same time being burnt at their dead husbands' pyre, is a situation that has often defined the fight and the plight of women in India. Throughout India's colonial and post-colonial history, time and again, women have had to bear the brunt of the patriarchal norms, which started improving only near the end of British rule in India.[1] Although the Constitution of India, adopted in 1947, provides for equal opportunity between women and men, as well as universal adult suffrage[2], in real terms gender equality is yet to translate as a nation-wide experience. While there has been a surge of female representation in the corporate sector as well as the political sector, with new reservations for women's seats in the Indian Parliament, similar shifts are seldom seen at the grass-root levels. While rights-oriented mind-sets are not just existent in the homes of the literate, sadly, there is a lack of empowerment which would allow the exercising of the rights. Overall, in Indian society, women are subjugated and made to do the bidding of the men.

---

1 Status of Women in India Report of International Labour Organisation published in 1996; available at www.ilo.org/public/english/region/asro/bangkok/library/download/pub96-01/chapter2.pdf, last accessed on June 4, 2013.
2 Part III, Fundamental Rights, The Constitution of India, adopted in New Delhi on November 26, 1949, and came into effect on January 26, 1950; available at indiacode.nic.in/coiweb/coifiles/part.htm, last accessed on June 4, 2013.

Till date, India has a large number of female infanticide and feticide[3] along with families selling their daughters into sex work.

At the same time, when family fortunes dwindle, it is up to the same woman who has generally been kept away from socializing with the rest of society to provide for the family—whether it is through the unorganized sector of domestic labor, sex work or becoming a surrogate mother. Surrogacy in India is not so much about women choosing to give their wombs to parents who are unable to deliver a child on their own, but mostly about a socially oppressed woman (possibly from the lower financial strata, as well as a low caste), who needs to utilize her body in order to make ends meet. In our contemporary times, with medical tourism becoming a much-touted industry in India, women have once again been objectified into the conduit for making money—by renting out their wombs.

This paper looks into the actual scenario, beyond the rosy picture of the parents holding their child delivered by an unknown surrogate. I analyze the mind-sets which have led to the growth of the commercial surrogacy industry in India, and how the biopolitical inactions (in order to keep the industry going) is undermining or threatening the human rights of the surrogate mothers. I shall bring together a substantiated argument about the positive and negative aspects regarding surrogacy in India, by examining the agents and biopolitical processes involved, while also looking at the medical rules and guidelines as well as jurisprudence around it. In this endeavor, my aim is to evidence that the rights of the surrogate mothers is the most important issue at stake, rather than the fact that surrogacy has become a branch of a highly commercially viable branch of medical tourism.

Surrogacy Industry in India: Facts and Regulations

Medical tourism in India has been growing steadily over the last two decades.[4] Costs are estimated to be a tenth of what one could expect in an European country[5], which makes it an attractive destination with world-class facilities (albeit within a bubble), which are mushrooming all over the country at a fast pace due to the lack in regulatory factors. Of course, this situation creates an issue, as there is no guarantee of the quality standards of private clinics unless they have

---

3   Sharda University Blog, Female Infanticide: The National Shame of India, posted on May 18, 2012; available at www.sharda.ac.in/blog/female-infanticide-the-national-shame-of-india/, last accessed on June 4, 2013.

4   Jasleen Kaur Batra, Medical Tourism in India: A Boost to the Economy, *Modern Medicare*, March 19, 2012; available at modernmedicare.co.in/articles/medical-tourism-in-india-a-boost-to-the-economy/, last accessed on June 4, 2013.

5   Stephanie M. Lee, Commercial Surrogacy Grows in India, *The San Francisco Gate*, October 20, 2012; available at www.sfgate.com/health/article/Commercial-surrogacy-grows-in-India-3968312.php, last accessed on June 4, 2013.

received the right certifications from the government, which happens slower than the number of clinics coming up. Notwithstanding the administrative impasse, the medical tourism industry in India generates revenue of over two billion US dollars annually.[6]

In this context, the commercial practice of surrogacy emerges as a surprise within medical tourism. Commercial surrogacy was made legal in India only in 2002 by the Supreme Court of India, through the case of *Baby Manji* (elaborated below), but without any further legislation to regulate its operation. As of now, the Law Commission of India has sent its observations to the Indian Parliament, which is currently considering what is generally known as the 'Surrogacy Bill'.[7] As common arguments go, surrogacy is the perfect revenue generator for a developing country where there are many women who would be glad to "rent"[8] out their wombs for money which they desperately need. Moreover, the cost of such womb-renting is far cheaper in India, as compared to developed countries where the cost might go up to over a hundred and fifty thousand US dollars.[9] Another incentive is the fact there are still European countries where surrogacy is still illegal, which is also the case of some states in the United States.[10]

In 2003, Doctor Nayna Patel[11] put an obscure place like Anand in the state of Gujarat on the world map by doing what was considered to be ground-breaking. She and her clinic successfully assisted in the impregnation of a woman through *in vitro* fertilization where the surrogate was carrying the children of her own daughter, who at the time was living in the United Kingdom. As of 2012, Dr. Patel's clinic had forty-five surrogate mothers who are at various points of time in their pregnancy terms, all bearing children for childless couples living outside India. However, when her clinic was opened, it was an exception. Today,

---

6   Priya Shetty, India's Unregulated Surrogacy Industry, *The Lancet*, November 10, 2012, 380(9854): 1633–1634; available at download.thelancet.com/pdfs/journals/lancet/PIIS0140673612619333.pdf, last accessed on June 4, 2013.

7   The Draft Bill of 2010 on Assisted Reproductive Technologies (Regulation) has been tabled at the Indian Parliament but not yet promulgated as an Act (hereinafter referred to in footnotes as the ART Bill). Th official text is available through the Indian Council of Medical Research website at icmr.nic.in/guide/ART Regulation Draft Bill1.pdf, last accessed on June 4, 2013. Section 2(h) of the Bill defines couples as those whose sexual relationship is recognized in India, which apparently excludes gay couples. However, since it suggests a sexual relationship and not a legal relationship, it does not absolutely exclude homosexual couples once the Section 377 of the Indian Penal Code, prohibiting sodomy and other non-procreative sexual acts gets read down. The case is currently *sub judice* at the Supreme Court of India.

8   Helen Roberts and Frances Hardy, Our 'Rent a Womb' Child from an Indian Baby Farm: British Couple Paying £20,000 for a Desperately Poor Single Mother to Have Their Child, *The Daily Mail*, August 31, 2012.

9   Priya Shetty, *op. cit.*, 1634.

10 *Ibid.*

11 Dr. Patel runs the Akansha Infertility Clinic in Gujarat, and appeared on the Oprah Winfrey Show, which set the ground for further clients for surrogate mothers from abroad. For more information on Dr. Patel and her clinic, please go to www.ivfcharotar.com/meet_dr_patel.php, last accessed on May 4, 2013. Also, her clinic has been documented in detail through the video documentary, *The Google Baby* (2009, directed by Zippi Brand Frank).

it is just one of the many clinics catering to the needs and wants of prospective parents across the world which want gestational surrogacy—where only the womb is employed and has nothing to do with the genetic material of the bearer of the child. One such clinic has over two hundred and fifty surrogates, who are kept in a dormitory-like facility and taken care of by the clinic that got them the contracts.[12]

Recognizing the movement away from the general global altruistic agenda surrounding surrogacy and the gift of a child that the bearing mother is supposed to give (such as in the United Kingdom where only basic health costs are covered for the child-bearer[13]), the Indian Council for Medical Research decided to create guidelines around surrogacy. In 2005, the Indian Council for Medical Research put down the regulations for assisted reproductive technologies[14], which provide for health issues more than legal (read parental custody and immigration) issues.

Although there is no law regarding the status of the surrogate mother or the child yet[15], cases involving surrogacy have cropped up on surrogacy, but mostly regarding the citizenship of the new-born children. For instance, in *Baby Manji Yamada v. Union of India*[16], the case was about a surrogate child conceived in Anand, Gujarat, and her citizenship. The egg was from an anonymous donor, and the surrogate mother was a Mrs. Mehta. The parents to be of Baby Manji, Mr. and Mrs. Yamada, divorced a few days before the full pregnancy term, and when they went to India to collect the child, many legal issues cropped up because of the recent divorce, and the mother to be no longer had any claim over the child. The child was deemed stateless, and after long legal battles in Japan, the home country of the Yamadas, provided a passport on humanitarian grounds stating that once paternity was established, full citizenship would be granted. What was really surprising, however, was a non-governmental organization suing the surrogate service clinic on the grounds of child-trafficking, alleging that it was a money-making racket in the name of surrogacy.[17]

---

12   Amrita Pande, Transnational Commercial Surrogacy in India: Gifts for Global Sisters?, *Reproductive Biomedicine Online*, November 2011, 23(5): 618–625; available as e-publication since July 23, 2011 at www.ncbi.nlm.nih.gov/pubmed/21958916, last accessed on June 4, 2013. While on the face of it, the surrogates are getting much more money than they ever could, as well as healthcare, shelter and food, it is an exploitative situation where the clinics make much more money than the surrogates.

13   Priya Shetty, *op. cit.*, 1634.

14   For the official guidelines on surrogacy, see Indian Council of Medical Research, *National Guidelines on Accreditation, Supervision, and Regulation of ART Clinics in India* (New Delhi: Ministry of Health and Family Welfare, Indian Council of Medical Research, and National Academy of Medical Sciences, 2005); available at icmr.nic.in/art/Chapter_3.pdf, last accessed on May 1, 2013.

15   As mentioned earlier on, the bill is still pending with the Law and Health Ministries as I write this.

16   See the judgment in the case *Baby Manji Yamada v. Union of India and Anr*; Supreme Court of India, 2008 I.N.S.C. 1656, writ petition (C) No. 369 of 2008, judgment of September 29, 2008; available at www.indiansurrogacylaw.com/blog/2009/03/baby-manji-yamada-vs-union-of-india-uoi-and-anr/, last accessed on May 4, 2013.

17   While the court did not expand on the standing of the NGO, it dismissed the intervention alleging it to be *mala fide*.

In the *Jan Balaz v. Anand Municipality* case[18], yet another case from the same place in Gujarat, the Gujarat High Court declared that the rights of the newborns (born of the eggs of an Indian donor, with Balaz's sperm) was of ultimate importance, and the rights of the other people involved here were entirely secondary—although admitting that emotional and legal kinship with the biological parents and the surrogate were important. Yet again it was a case of citizenship, where Balaz's home country, Germany, was refusing to give citizenship (due to non-recognition of surrogacy agreements) policy and India had withdrawn citizenship due to the genetic father of the children taking them away to Germany. However, things got resolved in 2010, but it became a one-off, and not a rule. Germany did not set anything more than a persuasive precedent for similar cases in the future.

But these cases have pushed the Supreme Court of India to recognize the need for prompt legislation on surrogacy, especially when it came to the citizenship of the child: a situation in which the new-born might end up rendered without a home, without parents, and without any support. The counterpoint, however, is that at the same time, the surrogate mother is neglected, and her rights are overlooked entirely, due to the main focus being on the new-born. For instance, in the above instances, while the Gujarat High Court had the chance to proclaim the rights of the surrogate mother, it did not venture into that territory. Thus, in these cases, the surrogate mother just remains a "vessel"[19] to carry a child to full term—an inanimate object, a body, who is the least of anyone's concern. In a way, the surrogate mother is turned into a "homo sacer"[20]—she is useful but without any rights, bound to the system not because she wants to be in it, but because she is coerced by circumstances.

The current legislative scenario, as mentioned earlier, is the Assisted Reproductive Technologies (Regulation) Bill of 2010, lying in front of the Parliament, much changed in nature since its original inception. The Bill proposes setting up womb banks to make the link between private clinics and surrogates weak. These organizations may be both private and government-run, but both would require to be accredited to the state medical boards. It also suggests that prospective parents would require appointing a local guardian for the surrogate mother.[21] The Bill also stipulates an age criteria limiting the age of a surrogate mother to

---

18 See the judgment in the case *Jan Balaz v. Anand Municipality*, High Court of Gujarat at Ahmedabad, Letters Patent Appeal No. 2151 of 2009 with Special Civil Application No. 3020 of 2009, judgment of November 11, 2009; available online at www.indiansurrogacylaw.com/blog/2009/11/gujarat-high-court-rules-on-surrogacy-case/, last accessed on June 4, 2013.

19 Helen Roberts and Frances Hardy, *op. cit.*

20 See generally Giorgio Agamben, *Homo Sacer: Sovereign Power and Bare Life* (Stanford: Stanford University Press, 1998). Agamben speaks of the Ancient Roman concept of 'homo sacer' and how it applies in the modern state.

21 This is to make sure that the health of the surrogate mother and her rights do not suffer—however, the feasibility of this is highly questionable, when the surrogate mother is more than willing to sacrifice her rights to get money which would aid her family.

35 years, while limiting that she should have no more than five children in her lifetime, which would include her own children.[22] While this is meant to prevent commercial exploitation from all sides, there is difficulty in enforcement, especially because many of the women who agree to be surrogates are from rural areas, where they are often kept away from educational institutions as well as personal information about themselves.[23]

Reality Bites

Indian women who generally submit themselves to becoming commercial surrogates mostly come from economically marginalized backgrounds. Over and above that, during the pregnancy, they are generally taken care of by the clinic so that they produce a healthy child. Also, instead of them craving for the child as their own once it is born, their apprehension that the biological parents will not take the child is higher. In fact, many of these women pretend to be away on work, and have a child in secret. These women earn around five to seven thousand dollars per baby[24], which, given the poor economic conditions in which they are embedded, makes for a good pay. In this context, the practice of commercial surrogacy is not looked on as exploitation by the clinics that are carrying out the services. For them, this is a "mutually beneficial"[25] scenario, where couples desperately seeking children meet women desperately seeking money and both their needs are met.

However, while all this might seem like a rosy future for the surrogate mothers on the financial front, fertility experts fear that surrogates are being planted with more than the allowed number of embryos in India, with one clinic reporting over five or six embryos per surrogate. This increases health risks for the surrogates due to immune mismatch, which can lead to various complications for these women's general health in the future.[26] For instance, in 2010, a seventeen-year old girl, Sushma Pandey, died due to issues related to egg harvesting which were conducted by a fertility clinic in Mumbai—which she had been doing since almost the age of fifteen. Two years down the line, the Mumbai High Court reprimanded the Mumbai police for not prosecuting the clinic which had disobeyed the rules and regulations of the Indian Council for Medical Research on Assisted Reproductive Technologies.[27] This was one of the first instances in Indian jurisprudence where the surrogate was treated

---

22 ART Bill, *op. cit.*, 26.
23 It is not uncommon for rural Indian to signify the year of their birth by some big event that might have happened in their region or village, such as a flood or famine.
24 Priya Shetty, *op. cit.*, 1633–1634.
25 *Ibid.*
26 *Ibid.*
27 Mayura Janwalkar, 17-Yr-Old Egg Donor Dead, HC Questions Fertility Center's Role, *The Indian Express,* July 12, 2012.

as a human being. Unfortunately, the cost of this legal recognition was one such woman's life.

More recently, in 2012, Premila Vaghela, a 30-year old woman, also lost her life to the surrogacy industry. According to reports, she was at the fertility clinic when she started suffering from convulsions, and passed out. The doctors, realizing that she was near full-term, decided to carry out a caesarean section from which came a relatively healthy baby boy, and then sent her to another hospital. However, by the time she reached the location, she was already dead—and this happened under absolute contractual obligation. Most surrogacy contracts in India are under the Indian Contract Act, 1872, and one important clause inserted in the contract is that surrogate mothers will be put on life-support till the end of the pregnancy term in case such situations occur. Under these conditions, the clinic's responsibility ended with Premila 'delivering' the child.[28]

In general, there is no health follow-up stipulated for the surrogate mother post-delivery of the child to the client parents, unless the parents of the child want to take on the responsibility due to breastfeeding purposes. The clinics' responsibilities end with delivery. However, carrying out C-sections to deliver children at the convenience of the biological parents is generally assigned by the contract. Thus, a procedure which is bodily invasive, with sometimes irreversible consequences, is being carried out regularly with absolute nonchalance, and entirely unregulated. This can have a devastating—and as we have seen, even deadly—impact on the lives and bodies of hundreds of women who are giving out their wombs. In fact, for many of these women their body is possibly their only possession—which has been appropriated, commodified, and commercialized through India's engagement with the uneven networks of global capitalism. In this context, there is a striking resemblance between organ selling and womb-renting. However, while the former is considered to be socially and legally problematic, the latter has massive economic considerations for the medical tourism industry, thus not being problematized legally. The question that arises here is, at what cost?

Rhetoric Rising from the Womb

Motherhood is made sacramental in many cultures, especially in South Asian. When women who come from suburban or rural homes are convinced to let out their womb for another woman to be a mother, irrespective of the financial conditions involved, a kinship is felt with the biological mother—a bond of sisterhood. Thus, unintentionally, the women serving as the carriers are portrayed as self-less by doing an unimaginable favor for someone.[29] At the same time, the surrogate is aware of the financial disparity between her and the intended

---

28 Kishwar Desai, India's Surrogate Mothers Are Risking their Lives: They Urgently Need Protection, *The Guardian*, June 5, 2012.
29 Amrita Pande, *op. cit.*, 621.

mother. Perhaps this disparity is felt to be neutralized when the action is equaled with sacrifice and selflessness, thus in a way making the surrogate mother more powerful as a character.

At the other end of the relation, the intended mother also looks on the money being given as altruistic, although, as per general norms, payment for a service cannot be considered altruism. For the first-world mothers to be, it is often assumed that their money is going for a 'good cause', where the lives of the women who are womb-letting will change with the money received. Here, motherhood itself is articulated with more general tropes of Western pity for the suffering of the developing world. Even in cases where client parents prefer not having any ties with the surrogate—it makes it easier to treat the surrogate merely like a carrier rather than as a human being[30]—the idea of the money going for a good cause exists.

The doctors also feel that they are doing this for a good cause—creating financial independence where there is none, considering the economic background of most of the surrogates. For instance, Dr. Patel feels that she helps set the women up on their feet and as long as they are not being coerced into the practice by their husbands, they have agency and are in control of their decisions.[31] In reality, rural Indian women are often under the control of a patriarchal set up where they are subject to abuse and extortion even within their families. Situations have arisen where they have become the main bread-earners of their families, and have undertaken surrogate motherhood in order to provide for various expenses.[32] One instance came to light where a woman, above the age limit provided by medical guidelines, underwent the treatment, in order to provide for her daughter's wedding dowry (an outlawed practice, but nevertheless a social reality).[33]

In this context, the main reason behind surrogacy is obvious—systemic poverty. Yet, at the same time, one cannot help but wonder whether taking on surrogacy is a strategy through which impoverished women are able to take an active role in their lives, in an extension of the right to personal autonomy. Some critics have argued that being a surrogate is a sign of women's rights being exercised and enhanced, whereas others against it quip that it creates greater subjection of women. In this perspective, taking away the power to be surrogate mothers could be interpreted as not having faith in the capability of women for self-determination.[34]

---

30 Helen Roberts and Frances Hardy, *op. cit.*
31 Abigail Haworth, Womb for Rent: Surrogate Mothers in India, *Marie Claire Magazine*, July 29, 2007; available at www.webmd.com/infertility-and-reproduction/features/womb-rent-surrogate-mothers-india, last accessed on May 4, 2013.
32 The identity-formation of Indian surrogates as victims of circumstances has been elaborated by Emma Baumhofer, Commodifying the Female Body: Outsourcing Surrogacy in a Global Market, *Thinking Gender Papers* (Los Angeles: UCLA Center for the Study of Women, 2012).
33 Lata Mishra, An Apartment Just for Surrogate Moms, *Mumbai Mirror*, May 29, 2012.
34 Stanford University, Surrogate Motherhood in India: Understanding and Evaluating the effects of Gestational Surrogacy on Women's Health and Rights, *Women's Courage Group*, 2008 available at www.stanford.edu/group/womenscourage/Surrogacy/index.html, last accessed on May 4, 2013.

Those who speak against surrogacy often compare it with sex work or prostitution—after all, it is the body which is being rented out. There is little doubt that surrogacy contracts are all but virtuous. As we saw in the case of Premila Vaghela, surrogacy contracts might assume "dehumanizing and alienating" form, "since they deny the legitimacy of the surrogate's perspective on her pregnancy."[35] The issue that arises (and is purposely overlooked) is the bonding that a mother and child are supposed to form—in the case of a surrogate mother, the bonding is avoided as far as possible, despite weaning and feeding the child in the early days.

Without entering the lives of the women who are offering their wombs for gestation surrogacy, it is difficult to say why they are doing it—whether it is an expression of agency or empowerment or an act of coercion either by the family or by circumstances. Nevertheless, the fact that there is entrenched social inequality between the clients and the service providers can give rise to speculation about the inherent inequality of the relationship being drawn. In fact, the unevenness between the two ends of surrogacy can be seen as an expression of economic coercion, even though the service providers might have entered the contract of surrogacy willfully.

The client-mothers who hire surrogate wombs are also exercising their agency in becoming a parent of their own biological child (in most cases) where they are unable to conceive themselves. This exercising of self-determination, albeit coming from an educated woman, possibly from the upwardly mobile middle class, as well as from the Global North, creates a new rhetoric which moves away from the traditional role of women as child-bearers.[36] However, this improvement happens more for the client than the service provider, because the later is trapped in a particular cultural context which allows the paternalistic society to take away women's autonomy in multiple ways. It is extremely difficult to be absolutely clear regarding what drives an impoverished Indian woman to rent out her womb— overall abject poverty, altruism, the wish to rise in status as a breadwinner for the family, or pure subjugation to the family. The fact that nine months of childbearing ensures four square meals a day at least for nine months, as well as way more money than the annual income of a surrogate's entire family raises questions about the economic and social impact of the process in these women's lives.

Conclusion

Margaret Atwood's *The Handmaid's Tale*[37] is a futuristic novel about a theocratic Republic of Gilead, where women have no agency, and the Handmaids are taken on to conceive children for a rapidly declining population. The tale continues to

---

35 Raghav Sharma, An International, Moral and Legal Perspective: The Call for Legalization of Surrogacy in India, July 2, 2007; manuscript document available through ssrn.com/abstract=997923, last accessed on May 4, 2013.
36 Rosemarie Tong, Anne Donchin, and Susan Dodds, *Linking Visions: Feminist Bioethics, Human Rights, and the Developing World* (Lanham: Rowman & Littlefield, 2004).
37 Margaret Atwood, *The Handmaid's Tale* (New York: Anchor, 1998).

show a different exercising of female agency, whether it was the Commander's wife or the Handmaid, making use of their body as their resistance and locus of agency. The Indian situation with surrogate mothers can be likened to this tale. In situations where there is nothing, the body is being used to gain something and as a strategy of empowerment. However, while this might be financially beneficial for the surrogate mother, emotionally beneficial for the client parents, and overall beneficial for the Indian medical tourism industry, there are certain steps which have to be necessarily taken by the Government of India, the first of all of them being to regularize surrogacy and pass the intended Bill.

Then, keeping the socio-cultural context in mind—the intermingling of caste, class, education, and socio-religious affiliations—the environment around the surrogate mothers must improve from the current dormitory-like situations offered by most clinics, particularly considering the financial gains the clinics make out of the process. Secondly, the Government has to step up primary education, so that surrogate mothers are in a better position to engage with practices of surrogacy, particularly regarding the implications (and dangers) involved to their own health and bodies. Otherwise, the whole process will continue to be ambiguous insofar as whether it is exploitative or empowering. Thirdly, India needs to decide whether it wants to build an image of Aldous Huxley's baby farms with mass incubators in a totalitarian regime in his book *Brave New World*[38], or to make it seem ethically viable and in compliance with human rights.

Contractual obligations in these cases should not be allowed to include such acts which might willfully endanger the surrogate's life, as we saw in the case of Premila. A thoughtful act could have saved the life of a woman, who, after all, was going to make someone else a mother. Other issues like the ones which came up in the aforementioned cases (citizenship of new-borns) can be more easily regulated instead of leaving the children as stateless individuals.

India seems to be heading in the right direction with the upcoming Bill and the medical regulations already in place, but time is precious. The Bill has been in gestation long enough, and that definitely does not require a surrogate to bring it to full term. Perhaps it will be the first in a long line of thought which will emancipate the surrogacy rhetoric from the overall "victimization or empowerment" paradigm. While the Bill will not solve many issues, considering the fact that it is not dealing with (although it might seem like it) inanimate objects or externalized services, it will nonetheless establish a platform to work from and look into newer stances instead of letting surrogacy be a wing of the medical industry for the most part unregulated. As Feminist authors, particularly writing from the Third World, have found out, it is impossible to represent the experiences of another woman in its totality, forget about a full group of women performing a particular role, while coming from different socio-economic backgrounds.[39] Yet, it is important to give voice from an objective standpoint just to make sure that justice is done.

---

38 Aldous Huxley, *Brave New World* (London: Chatto & Windus, 1932).
39 See, generally, Gayatri Chakrabarti Spivak, *In Other Worlds: Essays in Cultural Politics* (New York: Routledge, 1988).

(RE)CONCEIVING KINSHIP: THE REPRODUCTIVE STRATEGIES OF GAY PARENTS IN ISRAEL

April Hovav

Many states employ strategies to increase or decrease the birthrate of their populations, but each does so differently, based on cultural and political priorities. There is a resounding consensus among scholars that Israel, as both a state and a society, is extremely pronatalist.[1] Scholars have identified numerous causes of Israeli pronatalism including the biblical injunction to "be fruitful and multiply"; pressure to repopulate after the death of six-million Jews in the Holocaust; militarism and the perceived need to bear soldiers to protect the nation; as well as the Israeli-Palestinian conflict and the on-going demographic struggle that accompanies it.[2] An oft mentioned example of this intense pronatalism is state support for assisted reproduction technologies (ARTs). The national health insurance covers unlimited use of in-vitro fertilization, artificial insemination, and egg donation for women regardless of sexual orientation or marital status, however surrogacy is limited to heterosexual couples. The restrictions on surrogacy have been subject to heated debate recently. With an eye towards these

---

1   Susan Martha Kahn, *Reproducing Jews: A Cultural Account of Assisted Conception in Israel* (Durham: Duke University Press, 2000); Jacqueline Portugese, *Fertility Policy in Israel: The Politics of Religion, Gender, and Nation* (Westport and London: Praeger Publishers, 1998); Ellen Waldman, Cultural Priorities Revealed: The Development and Regulation of Assisted Reproduction in the United States and Israel, *Health Matrix*, Winter 2006, 16(1): 65–106; and Nira Yuval-Davis, The Jewish Collectivity and National Reproduction in Israel, in Khamsin Collective (eds.) *Women in the Middle East* (London: Zed Books, 1987), 60–93.
2   Nitza Berkovitch, Motherhood as a National Mission: The Construction of Womanhood in the Legal Discourse in Israel, *Women's Studies International Forum*, September–December 1997, 20(5–6): 605–619; Rhoda Kanaaneh, *Birthing the Nation: Strategies of Palestinian Women in Israel* (Berkeley: University of California Press, 2002); and Tom Segev, *The Seventh Million: The Israelis and the Holocaust* (New York: Hill and Wang, 1993).

debates and discussions more broadly about the prevalence of both gay parenthood and ARTs in Israel I ask, how do gay parents in Israel negotiate pathways
to parenthood?

Like in many pronatalist states, there is not only a push to reproduce national
subjects, but specifically to reproduce certain national subjects. In Israel, pronatalist policies are explicitly concerned with increasing the *Jewish* population and
Judaism is determined through biological parenthood. The legal and cultural
adherence to biogenetics as the marker of lineage is at the base of defining who
is Jewish and is central to Israeli configurations of kinship. Both state policies
and societal norms operate on the assumption of a biogenetic Jewish identity,
thus ranking biological kinship above social kinship.[3]

Many scholars have discussed the repercussions of Israeli pronatalism
on women.[4] But writings on the impact of pronatalism on gay and lesbian
Israelis are mostly anecdotal.[5] The relationship between pronatalism and
the LGBT community in Israel has not been subject to the kind of scholarly
interrogation that pronatalism and gender have received. What has been
written on this matter indicates that neither lesbians nor gay men in Jewish-
Israeli society are exempt from the social pressure to reproduce. Given the
strict regulations on surrogacy and the small pool of children available for
adoption, the options for gay men are limited within Israel. Thus an increasing number of gay Israeli men employ surrogates in India and the United
States.[6] While scholars agree that gay parenthood is socially accepted in most
of Jewish-Israeli society, they do not discuss the impact of the privileging
of biological over social forms of kinship on gay parents. Likewise, the literature does not address how the imperative to (biologically) reproduce is
experienced and negotiated by gay couples, who cannot jointly contribute
gametes to a single child.

---

3   Daphna Birenbaum-Carmeli, Genetic Relatedness and Family Formation in Israel: Lay Perceptions
    in the Light of State Policy, *New Genetics and Society*, 2010, 29(1): 73–85; Carmel Shalev, *Halakha* and
    Patriarchal Motherhood: An Anatomy of the New Israeli Surrogacy Law, *Israel Law Review*, January
    1998, 32(1): 51–80; and Elly Teman, The Last Post of the Nuclear Family: A Cultural Critique of
    Israeli Surrogacy Policy, in Daphna Birenbaum-Carmeli and Yoram S. Carmeli (eds.), *Kin, Gene,
    Community: Reproductive Technologies among Jewish Israelis* (New York and Oxford: Berghahn, 2010),
    107–126.
4   Barbara Swirski and Marilyn Safir, eds., *Calling the Equality Bluff: Women in Israel* (New York:
    Pergamon Press, 1991); Berkovitch, *op. cit.*; and Susan Sered, *What Makes Women Sick: Maternity,
    Modesty, and Militarism in Israeli Society* (Hanover: Brandeis University Press, 2000).
5   Moshe Shokeid, Closeted Cosmopolitans: Israeli Gays between Centre and Periphery, *Global
    Networks*, July 2003, 3(3): 387–399.
6   Ron Friedman, J'lem Man Struggles to Bring Twin Sons Home from India, *The Jerusalem Post*, May
    10, 2010; available at www.jpost.com/International/Article.aspx?id=175147, last accessed on June
    2, 2013; Zvika Kreiger, Forget Marriage Equality; Israeli Gays Want Surrogacy Rights, *The Atlantic*,
    April 4, 2013; available at www.theatlantic.com/international/archive/2013/04/forget-marriage-
    equality-israeli-gays-want-surrogacy-rights/274639/, last accessed on June 2, 2013.

Finding Parents' Voices

This chapter is based on ethnographic and interview data collected in Israel in 2011. I found informants through friends and family and by posting a call for participants on Facebook groups for gay parents. The people I interviewed have a diverse range of family formations. Amongst the participants are lesbian couples who used artificial insemination to have children, gay couples who adopted or used surrogacy to have children, as well as gay men in co-parenting partnerships with heterosexual women. While the configurations of their families vary greatly amongst the participants, what they share is a status as outsiders from the heteronormative model of family and of reproduction. I interviewed three self-identified lesbians and eight self-identified gay men. Most of the participants are already parents, but some were in the process of surrogacy at the time of the interview.

There was some variation amongst the participants in terms of profession, birth place, and approach to religion but most have some post-secondary education and live in one the major metropolitan areas of Israel. About half of the participants had immigrated to Israel from other countries. Ages ranged from 35 to 50. When asked about religion, most participants described themselves as *hiloni'im* (secular).[7] Interviews varied in length from 45 minutes to two hours. Interviews with immigrants from the US and Canada were conducted in English, while the remainder were conducted in Hebrew.[8]

The information I gathered from interviews was supplemented by more informal ethnographic data. While in Israel, I followed news reports related to gay parenthood, spoke with locals I encountered about the subject, and attended an event for "rainbow families." I also met with Irit Rosenblum, an outspoken advocate of family rights. As director of New Family, she has represented gay parents in a number of court cases.

There are several limitations to my research. The men and women I interviewed are not a representative sample and my study is not intended reflect the experiences of all gay parents in Israel. While I did not exclusively seek Jewish participants, all the informants I spoke with identified as Jewish and thus the scope of this study is limited to gay parenthood amongst Jewish Israelis. My position as a researcher may have influenced the way the interviewees answered questions. Almost every respondent asked about my academic background and research interests. Knowing that my research would be read outside of Israel, interviewees may have tried to portray Israeli society in a certain light to outsiders. Likewise, interviewees were probably aware of feminist critiques of surrogacy and egg donation as exploitative and thus may have spoken more cautiously and warmly about surrogates and donors to demonstrate awareness of the ethical concerns and stave off critique. However, I am not concerned in this paper with uncovering the reasons that gay

---

7   *Hiloni'im* usually identify as Jewish and attend holiday gatherings, but do not follow Jewish law closely.
8   All translations are my own. All names are pseudonyms.

parents chose different pathways to parenthood, but rather in understanding their strategies for legitimizing their reproductive decisions, which include the narratives they present about themselves and their families.

Social Acceptance of Gay Parenthood

In a comparative study of US and Israeli ART policies, Ellen Waldman concludes that "Israeli enthusiasm for child-bearing cuts across all categories of family structure. Legal and financial support for single and gay-headed families is robust."[9] This statement was echoed in both my formal and informal discussions with Jewish Israelis. For example, during our interview, Daniel interrupted me, pointed to my voice recorder, and said "the most important thing I want you to know for your research is that Israelis love children . . ." Daniel, like many others, took pride in the fact that Israel is a family-oriented country and wanted that to be emphasized in my study of gay parents. Aaron, who at the time was awaiting the birth of his child via surrogacy, also noted Israeli enthusiasm for children, but more critically. He explained that "you're not fully part of Israeli society until you have children . . . not everyone wants to have children, but there isn't much of a choice." While he expressed an uneasiness with the necessity of parenthood for integration into Israeli society, he also maintained that this attitude enabled greater acceptance for gay parents.

In his book on the gay and lesbian communities in Israel, Lee Walzer argues that "having children as a gay man or lesbian in Israel often grants greater legitimacy in the eyes of family, friends, and the wider society."[10] This observation was echoed by nearly all of the men and women I interviewed. Some interviewees were shocked by the amount of positive attention they received upon the birth of their children. For example, Naomi, a lesbian mother and well-known figure in Jerusalem's LGBT community, stated that she was surprised by the way her mostly religious co-workers responded to her pregnancy:

> Most of the other teachers are orthodox . . . The teachers were very happy for me. They were very excited for me. Even the teachers that are more homophobic were very happy and excited. I saw that really in Israel, if you have children, you're accepted . . . doesn't matter what, you've been accepted.

---

9   Waldman, *op. cit.*, 105. Some argue that the Israeli government engages in pinkwashing: strategically using the gay rights movement to raise its international profile, promote gay tourism, divert attention from the Israeli-Palestinian conflict, and mark itself as "Western." While the government's motivation for enabling certain gay rights is beyond the scope of this thesis, it is important to note that community acceptance for gay parenting is tied to importance of *Jewish* reproduction, whether or not this of importance to the parents themselves. For more on this perspective see Jaspir Puar, Israel's Gay Propaganda War, *The Guardian*, July 1, 2010.
10 Lee Walzer, *Between Sodom and Eden: A Gay Journey Through Today's Israel* (New York: Columbia University Press, 2000), 192.

Pregnancy and parenthood not only gave Naomi an additional topic of conversation with her co-workers, it appeared to ease tensions with some of her co-workers who had previously expressed discomfort with her sexuality. According to Naomi, the joy surrounding the birth of a child outweighed the homophobic attitudes of her co-workers. David, who lives in a fairly religious neighborhood of Jerusalem, told me about being treated to a warm welcome when he returned from India with his twins: "There are a lot of religious people here, but when I came back with the twins, people were waiting for me with balloons and flowers. Everyone was very happy for me."

Both Naomi and David specifically mentioned the positive reactions of ob-servant Jews to the birth of their children. These stories are couched in a deep secular/religious divide within Jewish-Israeli society. In describing his neighbors as supportive despite their religious beliefs, David implies that the elation over children overrides religious edicts against homosexuality. Naomi, meanwhile, explicitly describes her coworkers as homophobic. But she reports that their bigotry was tempered by the news of her pregnancy. Both Naomi and David described a sense of increased community acceptance ushered in by the arrival of their children.

Many interviewees noticed increased acceptance by their parents of both their sexuality and their relationship with their partner after children were added to the family unit. As David explained "at first they were a bit hesitant about our decision . . . but once the twins were born, they have really brought the fam-ily together." Amongst the men and women I interviewed, even those who did not notice a change in their parents' acceptance of their sexuality, were still overwhelmed by their parents' joy at the addition of a new grandchild. Naomi explained that while her relationship with her parents remained strained after the birth of her son, "Oren they really love. They have a connection with him that bypasses us." The relationship between Oren and his grandparents speaks to the importance attached to parenthood as a form of (biological) family continuation.

Misrecognition

While Jewish-Israeli society is generally accepting of gay parenthood, these families still face obstacles, in terms of both legal and social recognition. The ob-stacles gay parents in Israel face are often due to the privileging of genetic over social parenthood in Israel society and the Israeli legal system. One way in which the Israeli government reinforces the biogenetic model of kinship is through the birth certificates of children born to same-sex couples. When a child is born to a heterosexual couple, the husband is assumed to be the biological father, and registered on birth certificates as such, unless otherwise notified or paternity is contested. In the case of same-sex couples, only one parent is recognized as the real parent and registered as such, even when the same-sex couple is legally recognized as married. Thus the biological parent's partner must adopt his or her own child. This process can take anywhere from 16 months to three years, leaving everyone in a precarious position. For example, a lesbian prison guard who died in the 2011 Carmel fires in Israel was survived by three children, but the youngest one has not been legally recognized as her daughter because the adoption process had not been finalized.[11] The mother's tragic death has been compounded by the government's refusal to recognize their familial bond, an issue which her partner is now fighting in court.

The dichotomy between biological and social parenthood leads to misrecognition or non-recognition, which according to Charles Taylor, "can be a form of oppression, imprisoning someone in a false distorted, and reduced mode of being."[12] The misrecognition of familial relationships can be seen most clearly in the struggles of non-biological parents in same-sex partnerships to be regarded as equal parents. Their perspectives as parents are marginalized and their relationship to their child is distorted by misrecognition.

The men and women I interviewed expressed their frustrations with the constant misrecognition of their families. For example, Naomi expressed non-recognition as the primary difficulty she faces as a lesbian mother:

In my opinion, the most widespread difficulty on a day to day basis, is that we are exposed to the outside world that never understands us as a couple of parents with a child. The guess is always that we are sisters, or friends, and that he is the child of one of us.

While Naomi reports that most people seem accepting of her family, she believes that they have trouble looking beyond genetics and the heterosexist family model to recognize her and her partner as equal parents of their child. Many people insist on finding out which one of them gave birth to Oren and thus who the 'real' mother is. As Naomi explained:

When Oren was already born, people asked which one of us is the mother. So we answer: both of us are the mothers. So they ask but who gave birth to him . . . Shira felt very uncomfortable with these questions. She said that I answered as I should but then they would only speak to me. And she feels outside of the conversation.

Shira's exclusion is "expressed in the dearth of established, much less positive, terms for the role of the 'co-mother' often represented as the proverbial 'lack', she is the 'nonbiological mother', the 'nonbirth mother', the 'other mother'."[13] These

---

11 Aviel Maganzi, Dead Guard Raised Three Children, Only Two Orphans, *Y-Net News*, May 22, 2011; available at www.ynet.co.il/articles/0,7340,L-4072254,00.html, last accessed on June 2, 2011.
12 Charles Taylor, *Multiculturalism and "The Politics of Recognition": An Essay* (Princeton: Princeton University Press, 1992), 25.
13 Corrine Hayden, Gender, Genetics, and Generation: Reformulating Biology in Lesbian Kinship, *Cultural Anthropology*, February 1995, 10(1): 41–63, at 49.

English terms are similar to those used in Hebrew.[14] The lack of appropriate language with which to convey Shira's position *vis-à-vis* her child reflects the lack of recognition that these forms of kinship have in society. Shira and Naomi's experiences also demonstrate an incessant need to identify and categorize familial relations according to a biological model. Naomi told me that because Shira and Oren have a stronger physical resemblance, Shira is often assumed to be his birth mother. When this assumption is made, questions and praise are addressed to her, while Naomi is ignored. With obvious angst, Naomi explained: "Never [are we understood] if we don't talk about our relationship and our joint parenthood. The only option we have is to expose ourselves. If not, they don't see us."

Same-sex couples are more accepted once they have children, but their relationship to their children and the organization of their families is often difficult for others to understand and accept. Aaron noted that whose sperm was used "is often the first question asked." He explained the frustration that this question causes him: "that really bothers me, because we are going to be equal parents even though my sperm was used."

Normative definitions of parenthood haunt same-sex parents. The parents I interviewed were upset by how often an egg-donor or a sperm-donor was referred to as the child's mother or father. When discussing my research with friends and family, I heard the terms interchanged many times. Unlike heterosexual couples who are assumed to be joint parents, parenthood for same-sex couples is assumed to be uneven. Their relationship to their children is mediated and misconstrued through the categorization of biological versus non-biological parenthood. Joint parenthood, Naomi argues, must be explained to contradict these assumptions and render both parents visible as parents.

I witnessed this process of misrecognition first hand in a conversation between one of the interviewees, David, whose twins were born to a surrogate, and Rebecca an elderly, heterosexual woman:

Rebecca: "Is the mother also light?" [15]

David: "It is not the mother, it is the donor. They don't have a mother. But yes, the egg donor is light, like me."

While Rebecca was aware of the entire surrogacy process and expressed full support of gay parenthood, she referred to the egg donor as the children's mother, demonstrating the difficulty that even open-minded Israelis have in understanding, recognizing, and naming forms of kinship that do not coincide with biogenetic definitions of kinship.

Similarly Jonathan, who along with his husband, adopted three African-American children in the United States before immigrating to Israel, described

---

14 Michal Tamir and Dalia Cahana-Amitay, 'The Hebrew Language Has Not Created a Title for Me': A Legal and Sociolinguistic Analysis of New-Type Families, *Journal of Gender, Social Policy, and the Law*, 2009, 17(3): 545–600.

15 Light in this context meant light skin, hair, and eye color.

the typical questions asked about his children: "We get asked if they are related." To which he generally responds, "Of course they are related, they're siblings. You should ask if they are biologically related." Although all three children were adopted in infancy and were raised as siblings, Jonathan regularly fields questions about their biogenetic connection. In replying that "of course they are related" Jonathan distinguishes social kinship from biological kinship, and argues that siblinghood can be defined through social modes of kinship. According to the men and women I interviewed, the obstacles facing gay parents in Israel are not primarily couched in assumptions about sexuality and parenthood but rather an adherence to biogenetic kinship that disadvantages same-sex couples.

Strategies for Legitimacy

A number of the men and women I interviewed challenged the privilege afforded to biogenetic parenthood through discursive and legal means. By downplaying the importance of biology, these families are destabilizing the normative paradigm of kinship in Jewish-Israeli society.

Natan, who has two children born via surrogacy, runs a company that facilitates surrogacy abroad. Through his business, Natan has become well-known amongst gay parents as an expert on transnational surrogacy and the legal impediments presented by the Israeli government. During our discussion Natan explained his issue with the requirement that children born to a surrogate abroad undergo a paternity test before being issued a birth certificate and Israeli citizenship:

> We both donated the sperm . . . whatever stuck, stuck . . . we didn't know until the birth and it didn't interest us to know. In the end the state forced us to check . . . if they hadn't forced us to we would not have checked, it doesn't interest us, it's not relevant. With the second child, we didn't agree to check. We filed a lawsuit against the state. We are requesting that they recognize both of us as the parents, regardless of the genetic connection, because it's simply irrelevant.

Natan insisted that the biological basis of parenthood is unimportant to him and his partner. However, they understand the weight it carries in society and thus, "We don't tell the families who is related [genetically] to whom." Understanding the cultural importance attached to biogenetic parenthood, Natan and his partner, used a technique of mixing their sperm before it was used to create embryos in an attempt not to know or define which of them the biogenetic parent is. While they are well aware of the fact that each resulting child would only be biologically related to one of them, this technique could allow them to keep that knowledge from themselves, their children, and society in general. Their attempt to circumvent the system of biogenetic parenthood was disrupted by the government. But while Natan and his partner now know which one of them contributed genetic material to their child, they refuse to tell anyone including their children and their parents because they do not want their parenthood defined accordingly. Natan and his partner are thus challenging the privilege assigned to biogenetic kinship in determining parentage and defining families.

Other respondents made similar statements contesting the biogenetic paradigm of kinship. Naomi told me that she and her partner tried to use different sperm donors for their two children, particularly in order to not give weight to the genetic connection between their children as "biology is not important to us." Their plans changed, however, when they were told that getting a new sperm donor would require waiting for several months and if they agreed to use the same donor sperm, they could begin the process immediately. For Natan and Naomi negating the importance of biology is a strategy for challenging normative conceptions of family and legitimizing the parentage of both partners.

The interviewees were consistent in de-emphasizing biological kinship when discussing adoption. Knowing that all but one of the parents I interviewed had used ARTs to have children, I was surprised to find that many had considered, and even would have preferred, to adopt children. Several scholars have noted a tremendous gap between government support for ARTs and the lack of support for adoption in Israel which is coupled with a pervasive attitude that adoption should be considered a last resort.[16] This was not the case for most of the men and women I interviewed. In fact, all the couples that employed a surrogate had tried adoption first, but were unsuccessful. I spoke with Aaron at length about the options he considered before turning to surrogacy. He explained that first he and his partner had looked into adoption, calling a number of adoption agencies, but it "was a very frustrating experience." After months of not having their messages returned, Aaron told me that despite gay adoption being legal in Israel, "we learned from other people as well that is was an avenue that wasn't going to lead us anywhere."[17] David who already has twins through surrogacy now wants to adopt a child. He explained that while he had wanted to adopt originally, he knew that it was unlikely that he would get a child through adoption. Now that he already two children, he is willing to take on the challenges of a system that discriminates against him.

Many of the men I interviewed expressed that the lack of options available to them as openly gay men was a determining factor in their decision to pursue

---

16 Dapha Birenbaum-Carmeli, The Politics of 'the Natural Family' in Israel: State Policy and Kinship Ideologies, *Social Science & Medicine*, October 2009, 69(7): 1018–1102; Susan Martha Kahn, *Reproducing Jews: A Cultural Account of Assisted Conception in Israel* (Durham: Duke University Press, 2000); and Carmel Shalev and Sigal Gooldin, The Uses and Misuses of In Vitro Fertilization: Some Sociological and Ethical Considerations, *Nashim: Journal of Jewish Women's Studies and Gender Issues*, Fall 2006, 12: 151–176.

17 Gay men and women are legally permitted to adopt children in Israel. However, the waiting list for children within Israel is about five years and many of the interviewees sensed that there is undocumented discrimination against same-sex couples in this process. Countries on the sending side of international adoption (i.e., China, Russia, or Ethiopia) tend to ban adoption by same-sex couples.

surrogacy. As Aaron explained, having wanted children for years and having spent the last few looking into every possibility, "we've realized that this is our last option." When asked about the decision to work with a surrogate David answered in a similar manner: "we didn't have much of a choice, it's not like we have a lot of options." So while at first glance it may seem that gay men are turning towards surrogacy because of a desire for biological kinship, for those I interviewed this was not the case. With the number of obstacles they faced, surrogacy is one of the few options remaining for those who can afford it.

Although in all but one case, the interviewees' children were biologically related to one of the parents, they unilaterally placed social parenthood over biogenetic parenthood. None felt strongly about whether gamete donors should be anonymous or not. Likewise, none of them considered the selection of a gamete donor to be a particular important or noteworthy part of the process. For example, when I asked David about selecting an egg donor, he responded, "our goal was to bring a healthy child to the world — the details were not as important to us." Naomi made a similar remark, stating that "people always ask about the process and the details, but that's not what is important." While some aspects of the selection were normalized ("of course we wanted someone healthy, who looks more or less like us"), they all agreed that "in the end, once the child is born, you realize that these decisions are really trivial." Defining the selection of gametes as inconsequential "details" can be understood as a strategy for combating the misrecognition of their families that stems from biogenetic definitions of parenthood.

Same-sex couples cannot hide the fact that their children were either adopted or created through ARTs and the help of donor gametes. But, from what the interviewees told me, they do not want to hide these facts. While on one hand, they argue that the technicalities are unimportant, especially once the child is born, on the other hand, they embrace their child's conception and birth stories as evidence of their deep desire to have children despite the complexity of the process. Every person I interviewed told me that they had no qualms about explaining to their children how they were born, and also planned to be forthcoming with every aspect from the start. The respondents said that they were open with their children about the existence of gamete donors and surrogates from the start. I asked each interviewee about what they planned to tell their children. They all seemed surprised by the question and answered much like Amit, who has just begun the surrogacy process, did: "I'll tell them the truth. What else would I tell them?"

When I asked Natan how he plans to tell his children about their birth he explained,

> We've told them from age zero . . . dad and dad wanted children very much, to have a child we needed a woman to help us. There is one woman in the United States who agreed to help us. She gave us some material, we mixed it with dad's material and then we put it into the belly of another woman who took care of you for nine months.

As his children are young, "the story is very simple at this point, because that's what they understand." He also told me that his daughter knows how to tell the story herself, and does so regularly. When giving advice to clients, Natan advocates a similar strategy, "I recommend that they tell the story from the beginning. That they look at the egg donor and surrogate in a very positive light, but not to use the word mother . . . and to always focus on what the children have, not what they don't have."

Natan keeps in touch with the woman who donated her eggs for both of his children. He sends her pictures of the children on a regular basis and even hosted her in Israel for a week. When I asked about his relationship with the egg donor, he proudly showed me pictures of her sitting with his children. In contrast with heterosexual couples, many of whom try to hide the fact that external gametes were used, gay couples do not have this option, and thus, perhaps, relate to gamete donation differently.[18]

In our discussions, the interviewees neither trivialized the contributions of gamete donors and surrogates nor equated parental status with biology. The men and women in this study challenge the normative narrative of reproduction by emphasizing social over genetic parenthood without trivializing or dehumanizing donors and surrogates. In choosing a surrogate, David expressed a desire to establish some form of relationship with the woman who would gestate and give birth to his children, "There were some that were anonymous, we didn't want that. We met her, we met her husband, we met her family . . . we're still in touch now."

These gay and lesbian parents did not affirm the normative emphasis put on biogenetic kinship, not to trivialize the contributions of the donors, but to emphasize the view that biology does not determine kinship for them. The one interviewee who adopted children (prior to immigrating to Israel) expressed a similar position regarding the birth parents of his children. He explained, "We talk very openly about their adoption situation." Jonathan told me that he and his partner share all the information they have and feel in no way threatened by their children's curiosity about their birth parents. For Israelis adopting children within the country, open adoption is not an option. In Israel the birth parents, like sperm and egg donors, are required to be anonymous. Thus, had Jonathan adopted children in Israel, he would not have been able to access information about his children's birth parents. The regulation of anonymity in cases of adoption and gamete donation can be seen as an attempt to preserve the nuclear, biological family model.

While the Israeli regulation, "symbolically erases the genitors in cases of sperm and egg donation"[19] through anonymity, the gay couples I interviewed saw no reason to hide their use of third-party genitors and did not feel that their existence

---

18 Daphna Birenbaum-Carmeli and Yoram S. Carmeli. Ritualizing the 'Natural Family': Secrecy in Israeli Donor Insemination, *Science as Culture*, 2000, 9(3): 301–325; and Yael Hashiloni-Dolev, Between Mothers, Fetuses, and Society: Reproductive Genetics in the Israeli Jewish Context, *Nashim: A Journal of Jewish Women's Studies and Gender Issues*, Fall 2006, 12: 129–150.

19 Teman, The Last Post . . ., *op. cit.*, 117.

threatened their relationship to their children. Through these regulations, the government tries to ensure that even in cases of unorthodox kinship configurations, the guise of a 'natural' genetic kinship is undisturbed. By contrast, the gay and lesbian parents that I interviewed, who cannot disguise their families as 'natural' biological families, chose not to hide the processes through which they created their families nor to emphasize their biological parenthood, even when presumably the biological relation between one parent and the child would strengthen their claim to parenthood within a society that esteems biogenetic kinship. Because gay men using surrogacy work outside the Israeli system they can expose the ambiguities of parenthood in a way that is not allowed in Israel, for example by inviting egg donors into their lives and insisting on equal parenthood regardless of biological ties.

De-Naturalizing the Family

The gay parents I spoke with went against the dominant discourse in Jewish-Israeli society by contesting the biogenetic definition of parenthood. In doing so, these men and women present a radical challenge to the status quo. Through their struggles with misrecognition and the strategic reconfiguration of kinship away from a biological model, these men and women are deconstructing naturalized assumptions about the meaning of kinship, and by extension citizenship. Their reproductive strategies are quintessentially political and, at the same time, they are deeply political.

Numerous studies of assisted reproductive technologies (ARTs) in Israel have concluded that while traditional understandings of kinship are challenged by the use of reproductive technologies, policy makers, practitioners, and consumers engage in a complex choreography that ultimately reinforces the traditional biogenetic nuclear family model.[20] These studies, however, did not explore the use of ARTs by gay parents, who may understand and discuss kinship in a different manner. The men and women I interviewed tended not to emphasize traditional concepts of kinship such as biology and genetics. Considering the importance of blood lines to the Israeli understanding of kinship and to the Jewish collective identity, this departure is far more radical than their sexual identity. The extreme pronatalism in Israel enables gay parenthood to be a socially salient option, but nonetheless tensions exist between gay parents, the government, and mainstream society. The main arena of tension is the biogenetic construction of kinship and its destabilization by gay couples. While gay couples who use reproductive technologies to have children constitute a small portion of the population in Israel, their redefinition of parenthood exposes the cultural embeddedness of traditional assumptions about kinship, and thus has the potential to deconstruct and challenge normative paradigms.

---

20 Birenbaum-Carmeli and Carmeli, eds., *op. cit.*; Elly Teman, *Birthing a Mother: The Surrogate Body and the Pregnant Self* (Berkeley: University of California Press, 2010).

PRE-IMPLANTATION GENETIC DIAGNOSIS IN GERMANY

Anna Borbála Bodolai

This paper investigates the new regulation of pre-implantation genetic diagnosis in Germany and explores the ethical concerns that have developed around this technique. Pre-implantation genetic diagnosis (PGD) refers to the genetic examination of *in-vitro* fertilized (IVF) embryos before their transfer into the uterus focusing on characteristics that may result in a serious genetically inherited disease.[1] Originally, the technique of pre-implantation genetic diagnosis was developed for therapeutic use to free couples, who are at an increased risk of having a child with a genetic disorder, from the potential burden of giving birth to a child suffering from a serious genetic disease or terminating the pregnancy.

The technology has undergone a significant development since the 1990s and current applications of PGD also have the potential to screen for genetic conditions that are unrelated to medical necessity. Pre-implantation genetic screening (PGS) is considered as an 'advanced' form of PGD, which is used to test *in vitro* embryos for multiple genetic characteristics, and not only those marking a generically inherited disease.[2]

The regulation of PGD or PGS would require a complex approach in every country, since it touches upon such sensitive issues as creating, testing and selecting embryos, and the application of the technique involves not only legal and medical questions but also ethical concerns. The question whether to choose a more 'pragmatic' or 'normative' approach in relation to the regulation of PGD varies from country to country, and it also depends on the culturally specific moral traditions and ethical principles that the given state perpetuates.

---

1 Bundesärztekammer, Memorandum zur Präimplantationsdiagnostik [Federal Medical Association, Memorandum on Pre-Implantation Genetic Diagnosis], Berlin, February 25, 2011; available at www.bundesaerztekammer.de/page.asp?his=0.5.1160.9051, last accessed on June 10, 2013.
2 Jamie King, Predicting Probability: Regulating the Future of Preimplantation Genetic Screening, *Yale Journal of Health Policy Law and Ethics*, Summer 2008, 8(2): 283–358, at 290.

After a period of legal uncertainty regarding the German regulation on the application of PGD, the Bundestag (the lower house of the federal parliament) voted for a "restricted use" of PGD, and amended the 1990 Embryo Protection Act.[3] After long debates, both the Bundestag and the Bundesrat (the upper house of the federal parliament) voted on the Government Decree regulating the Act's implementation, which will become applicable from 2014.[4]

However, controversies emerged already after the adoption of the new Act[5], and most of the technique's opponents predicted that a Pandora's box was about to open by allowing the use of this technology, even in a restricted form. Applying a 'slippery slope argument', according to which even a restricted legalization of PGD constitutes a first step towards a 'liberal use' of the technology, they claimed that in the end embryos would be screened for genetic characteristics that have nothing to do with genetically transmittable diseases.[6] People fearing the technology also anticipate that PGD would be used by parents to 'create children' according their wishes.[7] Moreover, pre-implantation genetic diagnosis is used also in human embryo research, but this aspect of the technology is not going to be discussed in the following analysis.

In this chapter, I suggest that even though the wording of the amended act allows for certain subjective interpretations of the scope of PGD, this is very likely not going to lead to the lack of transparency in the application of PGD. The reason for this is that, first, there is a balancing between the interests of scientists, individual patients, and the society in general in the German system: different organizations are responsible for decision-making and review, for implementation and application, and for interpretation. And second, ethical reviews have started to play a very important role in Germany, thus, besides medical scientists and professionals, ethics committees, inquiry commissions, and ethics councils have started to participate in the debate on how to regulate PGD. This suggests that ethical principles in general play a strong role in the German society, which could provide for safeguards against an easy extension in the scope of PGD's application.

---

3   *Ibid.*

4   Verordnung zur Regelung der Präimplantationsdiagnostik (Präimplantationsdiagnostikverordnung, PIDV) [Government Decree on the Regulation of Pre-Implantation Genetic Diagnosis]; available at www.bundesgesundheitsministerium.de/fileadmin/dateien/Downloads/Gesetze_und_Verordnungen/ Laufende_Verfahren/P/PID/Verordnung-Regelung-PID_130218.pdf, last accessed on June 10, 2013.

5   Frank Czerner, Die Kodifizierung der Präimplantationsdiagnostik (PID) in 3§ ESchG im Ensemble pränataldiagnostischer und schwangershaftsbezogener Untersuchungen des Fötus [Regulation of Pre-Implantation Genetic Diagnosis (PGD) in Section 3 of the German Embryo Protection Act together with the Pre-Natal Diagnosis- and Pregnancy-Related Testing of the Embryo], *Medizinrecht*, December 2011, 29(12): 783–789.

6   See, for example, Jonathan Glover, *Choosing Children. Genes, Disability and Design* (Oxford: Oxford University Press, 2006), 39; and D. S. King, Pre-Implantation Genetic Diagnosis and the 'New' Eugenics, *Journal of Medical Ethics*, April 1999, 25(2): 176–182.

7   Uta Zielger, *Präimplantationsdiagnostik in England und Deutschland* [Pre-Implantation Genetic Diagnosis in England and Germany] (Frankfurt am Main: Campus Verlag, 2004), 77; and David Galton, *Eugenics. The Future of Human Life in the 21st Century* (London: Abacus, 2002), 105–117.

Global and European Perspectives in the Regulation of Pre-Implantation Genetic Diagnosis

In general, it must be emphasized that it is very difficult to argue against the medical applications of PGD.[8] Forcing a woman to get pregnant for a third or a fourth time after she went through stillbirths or abortion at a later stage of her pregnancy could easily violate women's reproductive rights and at the same time underlines PGD's legitimacy. Claiming in these situations that women should not get pregnant at all seems again nonsense.

This is also what a recent judgment by the European Court of Human Rights (ECtHR) emphasized. Although the European Convention of Human Rights (ECHR) is less specific in terms of bioethical norms, in the case of *Rosetta Costa and Walter Pavan v. Italy*[9], an Italian couple, who were both carriers of cystic fibrosis, decided to challenge the Italian regulation, according to which PGD was forbidden.[10] The couple had already aborted the birth of a child who would suffer from cystic fibrosis. Accordingly, they asserted in front of the ECtHR that the prohibition of PGD by the Italian Law no. 40 of 2004 "infringes their private and family life."[11]

In its judgment the European Court agreed with the "strict interpretation of the Italian law on assisted human reproduction," but also underlined that Article 8 of the Convention (right to privacy) entails "a broad concept, which encompasses also the right to respect for the decisions both to have and not to have a child . . . the right to respect for the decision to become genetic parents."[12] The Court also referred to the case *S.H. v. Austria*, in which it was concluded that the "right of a couple to conceive a child and to make use of artificial reproductive technologies for that purpose is also protected by Article 8 as such a choice is an expression

---

8   According to the opinion of the German Research Institute 'Leopoldina', "pre-implantation genetic diagnosis (PGD) is a diagnostic procedure that enables parents who are at an increased risk of having of a child with a serious hereditary disease, to give life to a child, who is not affected by the disease"; available at www.leopoldina.org/en/publications/detailview/?publication[public ation]=298, last accessed on June 10, 2013. However, the issue of "savior siblings" is much debated. See for example Robert Sparrow and David Cram, Saviour Embryos? Pre-Implantation Genetic Diagnosis as a Therapeutic Technology, *Reproductive BioMedicine Online*, May2010, 20(5): 667–674.

9   *Costa and Pavan v. Italy*. ECtHR, application no. 54270/10, judgment of August 28, 2012.

10 According to this Italian law, married couples "may have access to assisted reproductive technologies exclusively in order to bypass infertility or sterility," see Simone Penasa, European Court of Human Rights Declared Incoherent and Disproportionate the Italian Ban on Preimplantation Genetic Diagnosis, *Bioethics International*, September 15, 2012; available at www. bioethicsinternational.org/blog/2012/09/15/european-court-of-human-rights-declared-incoherent-and-disproportionate-italian-ban-of-preimplantation-genetic-diagnosis-pdg/, last accessed on June 10, 2013.

11 Grégor Puppnick, European Court of Human Rights Hears Italian Bioethics Case, *Lifenews*, September 14, 2011; available at www.lifenews.com/2011/09/14/european-court-of-human-rights-hears-italian-bioethics-case/, last accessed on June 10, 2013

12 Penasa, *op. cit.*; see also the cases *Evans v. the United Kingdom*, ECtHR, application no. 6339/05, judgment of March 7, 2006; *A, B and C v. Ireland*, ECtHR, application no. 25579/05, judgment of December 16, 2010; and *Dickson v. the United Kingdom*, ECtHR, Application no. 44362/04, judgment of December 4, 2007.

of private and family life."[13] In its judgment, the Court extended the content of protection provided by Article 8 of the Convention "to include also the desire to procreate a child that not suffers from genetically transmissible diseases."[14]

Nevertheless, it remains difficult to determine how to define "serious genetically transmittable diseases" or a "healthy offspring" and whether parents' perception about the seriousness of the disability and what services are available in the society should be taken into account when making decision about these questions.[15]

Globally, there is no uniform regulation for pre-implantation genetic diagnosis. In the USA, for example, the regulation of this technique varies from state to state.[16] Even within Europe, it is difficult to say that there is a common approach in the regulation of PGD. European Council and European Union Directives and Covenants say relatively little about the rules of applying PGD.[17] Within Europe and in the neighborhood of Germany, different examples can be found for the regulation of PGD. For example, in Belgium, Denmark, the United Kingdom, France, Netherlands, Sweden, Norway, and Spain pre-implantation genetic diagnosis is possible within a certain statutory framework. Italy, Austria and Switzerland are examples for countries prohibiting PGD. In Portugal, Luxembourg, and Ireland there are no clear provisions about the application of PGD.[18]

---

13 Simone Penasa, *op. cit.*, see also *S.H. and Others v. Austria*. ECtHR, application no. 5781/00, judgment of November 3, 2011.

14 Simone Penasa, *op. cit.*

15 Chong-Wen Wang, Ethical, Legal and Social Implications of Prenatal and Pre-implantation Genetic Testing for Cancer Susceptibility, *Reproductive BioMedicine Online*, September 19, 2009, 19(Supplement 2): 23–33; Julia Diekämper, *Reproduziertes Leben: Biomacht in Zeiten der Präimplantationsdiagnostik* [Reproduced Life: Biopolitics in Times of Pre-Implantation Genetic Diagnosis] (Bielefeld: Transcript Verlag, 2011).

16 Michael Gortakowski, A Parent's Choice v. Governmental Regulations: A Bioethical Analysis in an Era of Pre-Implantation Genetic Diagnosis, *Buffalo Public Interest Law Journal*, 2011, 29: 85–109.

17 The Oviedo Convention (Convention for the Protection of Human Rights and Dignity of the Human Being with Regard to the Application of Biology and Medicine: Convention on Human Rights and Biomedicine, adopted in Oviedo, on April 4, 1997; available at conventions.coe.int/Treaty/en/Treaties/Html/164.htm) does not rule on PGD explicitly, nor does it prohibit. As paragraph 83 of the Explanatory Report to the Convention reads, "Article 12 as such does not imply any limitation of the right to carry out diagnostic interventions at the embryonic stage to find out whether an embryo carries hereditary traits that will lead to serious diseases in the future child"; Explanatory Report to the Convention on Human Rights and Biomedicine, publication authorized on December 17, 1996; available at conventions.coe.int/Treaty/En/reports/Html/164.htm, last accessed on June 10, 2013.

18 For an overview, see the Max Planck Institute's chart, titled Max-Planck-Datenbank zu den rechtligen Regelungen zur Fortpflanzungsmedizin in europäischen Ländern [Databank on the Regulation of Reproductive Medicine in European countries]; available at hwww.mpicc.de/meddb/show_all.php, last accessed on June 10, 2013; as well as Dirk Lanzerath, Präimplantationsdiagnostik: Zentrale Fakten und Argumente, *Analysen und Argumente Nr. 85*, November 2010 (Berlin: Konrad Adenauer Stiftung, 2010), available at www.kas.de/wf/doc/kas_21194-544-1-30.pdf, last accessed on June 10, 2013.

The Regulatory Framework in Germany

Despite of the fact that in Germany the technique had already been practiced by a couple of clinics, PGD was thought for long to be prohibited based on the 1990 Embryo Protection Act.[19] The reason for this was that the Act—before its amendment in 2011—did not specifically cover PGD. Nevertheless, according to the previous Act, firstly, the destruction of embryos was forbidden and secondly, according to Section 2(1) of the Act, "[a]nyone who disposes of, or hands over or acquires or uses for a purpose not serving its preservation, a human embryo produced outside the body, or removed from a woman before the completion of implantation in the uterus, will be punished with imprisonment up to three years or a fine."[20]

Finally, on July 6 2010, the German Federal Court of Justice (Bundesgerichtshof) ruled in its decision that the ban of the 1990 Embryo Protection Act on pre-implantation genetic diagnosis cannot be upheld for the current forms of PGD, which are based upon medical scientific advances introduced since this legislation came into effect.[21] Applying PGD on no longer "totipotent cells"[22] is not against the law.[23] The court also argued that when the gynecologist conducted the PGD examination, it was with the primary aim to establish pregnancy, even in case of a negative result.[24]

When the Bundestag approved the amended Act, it imposed strict conditions on PGD's application. In the first place, the Act gave a definition to PGD, according to which PGD is the "genetic examination of the in-vitro fertilized embryo's cells before their implantation in the uterus." It seems likely, and may be controversial to say that the amended Act—even with the possibility for applying PGD—results a stricter and a more straightforward situation than the one before the Federal Court's judgment. The reason for this is that following the amendment; the Act now explicitly (compared to the previous stage where this was only implied) bans PGD's application and allows for its implementation only in exceptional cases, where certain conditions of the pregnancy are present. Basically, the application of PGD is punishable under criminal act with imprisonment up to one year.

Doctors are allowed to conduct the screening only in cases when a "genetic or chromosomal characteristic is diagnosed at both or one of the parents that

---

19 Gesetz zum Schutz von Embryonen (Embryonenschutzgesetz, ESchG), *op. cit.*
20 *Ibid.*
21 Leopoldina Working Group, Pre-Implantation Genetic Diagnosis: The Effects of Limited Approval in Germany, Ad-Hoc Statement (Halle: Deutsche Akademie der Naturforscher Leopoldina, 2011); available at www.leopoldina.org/uploads/tx_leopublication/stellungnahme_PID_2011_final_a4ansicht_EN_02.pdf, last accessed on June 10, 2013.
22 Hilde Van de Velde, Lessons from Human Embryo, *Reproductive BioMedicine Online*, May 2010, 20(Supplement 1): S5–S6.
23 Germany Allows for Controversial PID, *ScienceGuide*, July 26, 2011; available at www.scienceguide.nl/201107/germany-allows-for-controversial-pid.aspx, last accessed on June 10, 2013; see also www.drze.de/in-focus/preimplantation-genetic-diagnosis/legal-aspects, last accessed on June 10, 2013.
24 Decision of the German Federal High Court of Justice for violation of the ESchG, para. 30.

will with strong likelihood lead to the impairment of the embryo, fetus or the future child, which could result in stillbirth or death in the first year."[25] The German MPs finally rejected the idea of defining a list of diseases in which cases PGD would be automatically allowed, because the German Parliament did not want to stigmatize certain diseases. At the same time, the possibility to use PGD for sex selection is, according to Section 3 of the amended Act, forbidden.

On the one hand, it may be argued that even though there is an explicit ban on the application, the wording of the law on PGD's exceptional use allows for certain subjectivity, which results in uncertainty and could easily lead to more permissive interpretation on the long run. Not to mention the issue whether the criminal liability is deterrent enough and how far it is going to be enforced strictly.

However, on the other hand, it seems likely that there are other elements in the regulation that might counter-balance this subjectivity. From the regulation and, more specifically, from the Executive Order adopted on February 1, 2013 it follows that different (and from each other independent) organizations will be responsible for the different segments of the regulation, which strengthens legal certainty and could set limits to further extensions of the scope of applying PGD.[26]

Firstly, there will be a separate body for the interpretation and application of the law.[27] According to the executive order, "as a result of Article 1(3a)(3)(2) of the amended Act," independent and interdisciplinary ethics committees will be responsible for checking whether the criteria defined in Article (3a)(3)(2) of the amended Act are present in a specific case. Only when an ethics committee is convinced that these criteria are present, will give its approval of the treatment.[28]

The ethics committees will be solely responsible for licensing PGD on a "case-by-case basis."[29] The ethics committees will scrutinize not only that the relevant, primarily medical criteria are fulfilled, but they will consider also psychological, social and ethical aspects.[30] Additionally, according to the Executive Order

---

25 "Bei den Eltern oder bei einem Elternteil eine genetische oder chromosomale Disposition diagnostiziert ist, die [...] mit hoher Wahrschinlichkeit eine Schädigung des Embryos, Fötus oder Kindes zur Folge hat, die zur Tod-oder Fehlgeburt oder zum To dim ersten Lebensjahr führen kann." Article 1(3a)(2)(3) of the amended Act, Gesetz zum Schutz von Embryonen, *op. cit.*; and Der Spiegel, Controversial Genetic Tests: German Parliament Allows Some Genetic Screening, *Spiegel Online*, July 7, 2011; available at www.spiegel.de/international/germany/controversial-genetic-tests-german-parliament-allows-some-embryo-screening-a-773054.html, last accessed on June 10, 2013.

26 Verordnung zur Regelung der Präimplantationsdiagnostik, *op. cit.*

27 The establishment of the ethics committees is set out in Article 3a(3)(2) of the amended German Embryo Protection Act, see Gesetz zum Schutz von Embryonen, *op. cit.*

28 Verordnung zur Regelung der Präimplantationsdiagnostik, Article 4.

29 *Ibid.*, Article 5(1).

30 Bundesministerium für Gesundheit, Kabinett macht endgültig den Weg für Regelungen zur Präimplantationsdiagnostik frei, *Bundesministerium für Gesundheit Pressemitteilung*, February 19, 2013 [Cabinet Finally Agrees to the Regulation of Pre-implantation Genetic Diagnosis, Press Release on February 19, 2013]; available at www.bmg.bund.de/ministerium/presse/pressemitteilungen/2013-01/weg-frei-fuer-pid-regelungen.html, last accessed on June 10, 2013.

regarding the amended Act, the members of the ethics committees should be composed of members from different interdisciplinary fields. Two further important criteria are the following: they should, first, have the "required professional expertise" and, second, they should not be at the same time related to any of the PGD-licensed centers. These criteria, again, strengthen the independency of the ethics committees.[31]

Secondly, according to the regulation, PGD can be implemented only at fertility centers that are licensed by an ethics committee and only in cases when the ethics committee explicitly allows it. This also means that unlike in the United Kingdom, for example, where there is a general Code of Practice to guide these decisions, the individual PGD application requests in Germany will be decided on a case-by-case basis, which automatically leads to a stricter surveillance of the technology. However, since there will be many ethics committees[32], not just one, differences between interpreting these individual cases might arise.[33] Nevertheless, these issues are not strongly connected to the general design of the regulation.

Thirdly, in terms of reviewing general policies about PGD's application, the ethics committees' possibilities will remain potentially very limited. It follows from the Act and the Executive Order that individuals may challenge the ethics committees' decisions only at courts and only in relation whether they properly applied the law. As these committees will not take part in ethical and legal research, reviewing policies on the application of PGD will not belong to the responsibilities of these institutions.

This also means that a change in the interpretation of the law itself will not be easy and cannot be carried out by the ethics committees or the clinics themselves—this role is assigned to the courts. It also follows that in Germany a change in the practice of applying PGD will be possible only by a review and amending laws, which, in turn, can be carried out only by the parliament.

In summary, this results in a more balanced regulation in Germany as three different institutions (the courts, the licensed centers, and the ethics committees) are responsible for the different segments of the regulation: decision-making/review, implementation and interpretation/application. This also helps developing a more balanced negotiation of interests between the researchers, patients, and the wider society in the application of PGD.

---

31 Verordnung zur Regelung der Präimplantationsdiagnostik, *op. cit.*, Section 4.
32 *Ibid.*, Section 4(1).
33 For further information, see Marlis Hübner and Wiebke Pühler, Die neuen Regelungen zu Präimplantationsdiagnostik—wesentliche Fragen bleiben offen. [The New Regulation of Pre-Implantation Genetic Diagnosis—Important Questions Remain Open], *Medizinrecht*, December 2011, 29(12): 789–796.

The Role of Ethical Arguments in the German Society

In the second part of this essay I explore if there are specific ethical traditions in German society that might calm down those who predict a snake in the grass regarding the amended regulation allowing a "restricted use of PGD" in specific cases.

In Germany, ethical debates about the regulation of PGD and IVF date back to the 1980s. Already in May 1984, a working party called "In Vitro Fertilization, Genome Analysis and Gene Therapy" was set up by the Federal Ministry of Justice under the direction of the former president of the Federal Constitutional Court, Ernst Benda. The Benda Commission's main goal was in particular to handle legal and ethical questions stemming from new reproductive technologies and to make "large numbers of suggestions for possible legal measures in its final report."[34]

Since that time, a number of institutions have been involved in the debate on the regulation of artificial insemination and later also on the amendment of the German Embryo Protection Act. These debates also included ethical, medical and legal concerns. Since the 1990s many experts have argued that it was actually the lack of clarity in the 1990 Act that served as an indirect permission for applying PGD; however, this argumentation was finally refused.[35] The fact that most of the experts refused a change in the practice with a simple change in the text's interpretation[36] shows that there was a general refusal in the public to allow an unclear situation to regulate PGD, which could have actually led to unpredictable changes in its application.[37]

Besides voices that explicitly urged the drawing of clear boundaries in the regulation,[38] advocates of PGD in Germany have sometimes also mentioned the aspect of reproductive autonomy. As already indicated, human rights and especially *women's reproductive rights* could serve as strong counter-arguments against the ethical concerns refusing the application of PGD. However, it seems that these opinions were less debated in Germany: human rights arguments on women's reproductive rights regarding PGD became an important focus of the debate only after the new ruling by the Federal Court of Justice—this is also what the evolution of the German Ethics Council's argumentation, presented later, underlines.

The debate was further complicated when pre-implantation genetic diagnosis was compared to prenatal diagnosis (PND). Difficulties of interpretation arise from the fact that PND allows for the late termination of pregnancy in case it turns out that the unborn child has a genetically inherited disorder. Even

---

34 Ulla Wessels, Genetic Engineering and Ethics in Germany, in Anthony Dyson and John Harris (eds.), *Ethics and Biotechnology* (London: Routledge, 1994), 230–258.
35 Uta Zielger, *op. cit.*
36 *Ibid.*
37 *Ibid.*, 124.
38 *Ibid.*, 112.

though PND, under certain conditions, has been allowed in Germany for a long time, PGD, where embryos are merely a few days old, has been prohibited. Birnbacher, for example, makes the following comments in relation to this question:[39]

As for the similarities, both methods [PGD and PND] involve the selective destruction of human life for the sake of the reproductive freedom of parents, i.e. the freedom to have a choice concerning the children they want to bring up . . . On the other hand, the normatively relevant differences between the two methods suggest that PGD should be regarded at less, and not as more, problematic than PND.

Much before the amendment adopted in 2011, there had been a widespread consent among professionals that PGD, which had so much potential and could also bring fear, needed both a very straightforward regulation and a very strict control. The debate at the same time continued around PGD with parliamentary and governmental commissions and working groups, professional organizations, research centers and the German Ethics Council.

The fact that the German Ethics Council (Deutscher Ethikrat) was established in 2001 (as National Ethics Council or Nationaler Ethikrat) highlights that in the German society there was a need to establish an institutionalized framework for discussing ethical considerations at the national level. Besides the German Ethics Council, Parliamentary Inquiry Commissions have also been involved in this system.

Parliamentary Inquiry Commissions in Germany are set up by the Bundestag (the German lower house of Parliament) and function as advisory bodies for legislators; however, their decisions are not binding on the parliament itself.[40] The Inquiry Commission for Law and Ethics in Modern Medicine was, for example, set up in March 2000 by the Bundestag. Its 26 members included 13 members of the Parliament and other professionals.[41] The previous Commission for Opportunities and Risks of Gene Technology in 1987 was the first in the series of these special parliamentary bodies.[42]

Since their foundation, national ethics bodies have already published two official opinions on PGD. The Inquiry Commission for Law and Ethics in Modern

---

39 Dieter Birnbacher, Prenatal Diagnosis Yes, Preimplantation Genetic Diagnosis No: A Contradictory Stance? *Reproductive BioMedicine Online*, 2007 (on web: October 4, 2006), 14(Supplement 1): 109–113, at 110.

40 Article 44 of the Basic Law for the Federal Republic of Germany, revised version published in the *Federal Law Gazette* Part III, classification number 100-1, as last amended by the Act of 21 July 2010 (*Federal Law Gazette* I p. 944); available at www.gesetze-im-internet.de/englisch_gg/englisch_gg.html, last accessed on June 10, 2013.

41 Schlussbericht der Enquete-Kommission "Recht und Ethik der modernen Medizin," Deutscher Bundestag—14. Wahlperiode, Bundestagsdrucksache 14/9020 [Final Report of the "Law and Ethics in the Modern Medicine" Parliamentary Inquiry Commission of the 14th Bundestag], May 14, 2002; available at dip21.bundestag.de/dip21/btd/14/090/1409020.pdf, last accessed on June 10, 2013.

42 Ulla Wessels, *op. cit.*, 231.

Medicine was the first in 2003, and the German Ethics Council was the second in 2011, after the Federal Court of Justice made its decision. In 2003, two members of the parliamentary commission voted explicitly for the allowance of PGD, 16 voted for an explicit prohibition, and three members were of the opinion that PGD should be allowed restrictively.[43] In its argumentation against allowing PGD, the commission emphasized, among others, that there are alternatives to PGD in the testing for health risks before insemination, and highlighted the risks of *in-vitro* fertilization for women.[44] Furthermore, in relation to questions of reproductive autonomy, the Inquiry Commission argued that even if the couple's desire to have a genetically healthy child has to be taken seriously, their intention cannot be justified conclusively as a right on their own. [45]

The minority, three members of the commission, voted for a "restricted permission of PGD" for couples, who are at increased risk of transferring a serious genetically inhibited disease. However, at that time, their argumentation accepted the supremacy of Article 1 of the German Basic Law, namely that the inviolability of human dignity shall prevail, and found that a destruction of an embryo, even in this early phase, would violate this basic right. This is why it was suggested in this report that PGD should be prohibited across the board, and allowed only in exceptional cases. As the Inquiry Commission phrased it:

An arbitrary selection is a violation of a basic right in the Basic Law, namely a violation, on all accounts, against an earlier form of the right to life, and may be even against human dignity.[46]

In 2011, the majority of the German Ethics Council followed the view of the Inquiry Commission's minority in 2003, and voted for a restricted permission of PGD.[47] This time they held their opinion ethically justified because PGD, first, enables to avoid the termination of pregnancy at a later stage, which would be more dangerous to the health of the woman and, second, allows reproductive autonomy to couples living with a risk of passing over a genetically inherited disease to the child.[48]

This time the Council could no longer avoid discussing human rights arguments, when it formed the following opinion. "For many people, having biological children and in this way passing on life is part of a fulfilled life. It is also their constitutionally protected right."[49] The Council strengthened these

---

43 Schlussbericht, *op. cit.*
44 *Ibid.*, 96.
45 *Ibid.*
46 *Ibid.*, 108.
47 Deutscher Ethikrat, *Präimplantationsdiagnostik: Stellungnahme* [Official Opinion of the German Ethics Council on Pre-Implantation Genetic Diagnosis] (Berlin: Deutscher Ethikrat, 2011); available at www.ethikrat.org/dateien/pdf/stellungnahme-praeimplantationsdiagnostik.pdf, last accessed on June 10, 2013.
48 *Ibid.*, 77–84.
49 *Ibid.*, 73.

arguments when it stated that "PGD does not encroach upon the embryo's right to life in a fundamentally different way than a termination of pregnancy" and also that allowing the application of GPD for "a couple [at serious risk] does not constitute discrimination against persons with disabilities."[50]

Sizing up the scope of applying PGD was also important in the debate: before May 2001, only 693 babies were born with this technique worldwide. Even though PGD is still relatively rare, the University Clinic in Brussels alone, for example, "performs about 600 PGD cycles every year," which suggests that PGD is now considered as a "safe technology."[51] In addition, in 2011, eleven European countries allowed PGD under certain conditions. The report of the Council emphasizes that "[a] number of states replaced implicit by explicit provisions after the year 2000."[52] In summary, the German Ethics Council had no other rational solution after the ruling of the Federal Court, but to allow the application of PGD under very strict conditions. The question of this paper was only if they succeeded in doing this.

As for the concept of 'dignity' in the German Basic Law, it seems likely that solely based on this Article, the complete refusal of PGD cannot be established. This is what Latsiou also emphasizes in her book.[53] Latsiou investigates the relevance of Article 1 in relation to PGD by segmenting the process itself into three different activities. She comes to the conclusion in relation to the phases of 'artificial insemination', 'cell examination' and 'non-implantation of the damaged embryos' that Article 1 has hardly any relevance whether the application of PGD itself is confronted with basic constitutional principles. On the opposite, it seems likely that a call to obligatorily implant an 'affected embryo' would provide for an interference with the couples' right to self-determination and women's right to physical integrity (Article 2 of the Basic Law).

Conclusion

This paper investigated, in its first part, the new German regulatory framework on the application of pre-implantation genetic diagnosis. One of the main arguments of the opponents of the new regulation was that even a "restricted permission" could lead to unpredictable changes in the technology's use in the future. It is likely that an absolute and definite answer cannot be given to this question. However, by examining the new law's construction, the extent to

---

50 *Ibid.*, 79.
51 James Gallagher, Pre-Implantation Genetic Diagnosis for IVF Is 'Safe', *BBC News*, July 3, 2012; available at www.bbc.co.uk/news/health-18676894, last accessed on June 10, 2013.
52 Deutscher Ethikrat, *op. cit.*, 67.
53 Charikleia Z. Latsiou, *Präimplantationsdiagnostik: Rechtsvergleichung und bioethische Fragestellungen* [Pre-Implantation Genetic Diagnosis: Comparison of Law and Bioethical Questions] (Berlin: Duncker und Humblot, 2008), 104.

which the new law leads to legal certainty and hinders unpredictable changes in PGD's application, may be assessed.

Regarding pre-implantation genetic diagnosis, the amended Act is actually more straightforward and strict than the previous one was: it is because that, first, PGD now finally has a textual basis in the amended Act and, second, a separation in the functions regarding PGD's application and regulation is guaranteed by the amended Act. This also means that the stakeholders' (patients, doctors, society) different interests are well balanced in the system.

The purpose of the second part of this chapter was to analyze the German society's general approach to such ethically sensitive issues as PGD. The analysis' result serves firstly to see how far ethical concerns have played an important role in the German evolution of PGD's application. Ethical arguments' strength and frequency in the society and among decision-makers may be indicative of the society's capability for limiting access to PGD's novel treatment methods.

In sum, by the time of the German Ethics Council published its opinion on PGD in 2011, two things became obvious. First, before any change in regulation takes place, it is now unavoidable that ethical concerns are discussed with the relevant ethics bodies—and this highlights the embeddedness of these institutions in German society. Second, even such a respected institution as the German Ethics Council is, has to take into consideration the recent technological advances and changes in techniques when forming its opinion. As technology advances there will always be novel therapeutical methods and practices available. In addition, such sensitive issues as IVF and PGD will always have ethical consequences for the society. It has become a delicate task to balance between responsiveness to the technological advances, on one hand, and loyalty to ethical principles, on the other. This chapter has shown that Germany has managed to accomplish this.

The German regulation on the application of pre-implantation genetic diagnosis has remained 'conservative' and somewhat 'normative'. It seems that decision-makers and scientists in Germany were quite reluctant to introduce this new method for a long time, up to a certain point when they had no other logical solution than to allow it to some extent. Even when it was finally decided to permit the application of PGD in certain cases, the regulation was complemented with various checks and balances instruments. However, it needs to be emphasized, with special reference to the German case, that even if a country tries to resist the introduction of some new technology, once the spreading of that technology reaches a critical level, even the more conservative state legislations have to see that the introduction of this technology can only be delayed.

STEM CELL RESEARCH: MAGIC TOOL FOR SOLVING HEALTH PROBLEMS IN RUSSIA?

Yuliya Pleshakova

Stem cell research evokes curiosity in both popular and scientific discussions all over the world. The significance of the subject has been highlighted by the 2012 Nobel Prize in Physiology or Medicine given to Sir John B. Gurdon and Shinya Yamanaka.[1] Their outstanding discovery has made it possible to view mature cells in the body as perfectly able to turn into pluripotent stem cells. For scientific community it means that no longer are highly contentious embryonic stem cells the sole depository for essentially limitless research and application capacities in this domain. This ground-breaking contribution brings closer a bright and hopeful future for many of those afflicted with diabetes, cardiovascular diseases, Alzheimer's, blindness, cancer and auto-immune diseases due to already acquired knowledge of cells' abilities to cure from them completely. Not only does stem cell therapy promise the restoration of health, but also the solution to such pressing social problems as aging and health care. Not surprisingly, many countries have been following stem cell investigation and cooperating in making its use a reality for a wide medical practice. Russia, however, was seriously lagging behind in stem cell exploration until relatively recently. This is remarkable as the term itself, 'stem cell', was proposed by the Russian histologist Alexander Maksimov at the Congress of Hematologic Society in Berlin in 1908.[2] Some argue that existing corruption and legislation's underdevelopment in this field have been prevent-

---

1   The Nobel Committee for Physiology and Medicine, The Nobel Prize in Physiology or Medicine 2012, (Stockholm: Karolinska Insitutet, 2012); available at www.nobelprize.org/nobel_prizes/medicine/laureates/2012/popular-medicineprize2012.pdf, last accessed on May 17, 2013.
2   Igor E. Konstantinov, In Search of Alexander A. Maximow: The Man Behind the Unitarian Theory of Hematopoiesis, *Perspectives in Biology and Medicine*, Winter 2000, 43(2): 269–276.

ing any sound consideration of the subject. Medical harm potentially inflicted on ordinary people by such biotechnologies is said to outweigh its incredible healing powers and significantly block its effective implementation. At the same time, it becomes evident that irrespective of the controversy surrounding clinical stem cell use, increasing number of scientists are now persevering in research and regard these cells' potential as "truly magic."[3] In this chapter I aim to emphasize the scale of ethical and practical concerns confronting actual stem cell therapy in Russia. Moreover, I would like to identify motives for the present-day heightened investment into this new biomedical technology and evaluate opportunities that stem cell research affords to relieve the demographic crisis that have developed in the Russian Federation since the collapse of the Soviet Union.

To advance original research in stem cell insights and its effective application, both intellectual and financial resources are being accumulated. The opening of the long-awaited Institute of Science and Technology in Skolkovo in 2011 aims to stimulate innovation and advance cooperation among the most prominent researchers, businesses and investors in the field of IT, energy, aerospace, biomedical science and nuclear technology. One of the missions which captures scientific preoccupation of the Institute specifically delves into examination of stem cell fundamental knowledge. Agenda has been decided by an international consortium of scientific establishments organized by the UMCG Institute for Healthy Ageing and the University of Groningen, the Hubrecht Institute of the Royal Netherlands Academy of Arts and Sciences (KNAW) and the University Medical Center in Utrecht, and the Massachusetts Institute of Technology. These top institutions in the field of stem cell research simultaneously channel substantial funding into the venture.[4] Furthermore, Russian government has directed 675 million dollars on a variety of projects in Skolkovo and 50 million dollars directly into stem cell projects.[5] Thirteen world-wide renowned experts will engage in the activities of the new stem cell research institute including several Russian scientists from top institutions in bioengineering and cytology in the country. It is envisioned that Russia will soon be represented in the list of 200 leading universities of the world.[6] Besides the scholars' and government's

---

3   Tom Parfitt, Russian Scientists Voice Concern over "Stem-Cell Cosmetics," *The Lancet*, 365, 9466: 1219–1220, April 2, 2005; available at www.thelancet.com/journals/lancet/article/PIIS0140-6736(05)74795-4/fulltext, last accessed on May 17, 2013.

4   The University Medical Center Groningen (UMCG), Dutch Scientists to Open Institute for Stem Cell Research in Russia, *UMCG Press Release*, October 2, 2012; available at www.umcg.nl/EN/corporate/News/Pages/DutchscientiststoopeninstituteforstemcellresearchinRussia.aspx, last accessed on May 17, 2013.

5   Olga Sobolevskaya, V Skolkovo sozdadut tsentr izucheniya stvolovykh kletok [Center to Study Stem Cells Will Be Established in Skolkovo], *The Voice of Russia Radio*, October 5, 2012; available at rus.ruvr.ru/2012_10_05/V-Skolkovo-sozdadut-centr-izuchenija-stvolovih-kletok/, last accessed on May 17, 2013.

6   Yevgeniy Kadyshev, Gollandskiye i rossiyskiye universitety sozdayut nauchno-issledovatel'skiy tsentr [Dutch and Russian Universities Create Scientific Research Center], *TG Daily*, April 13, 2013; available at tgdaily.ru/?p=1669, last accessed on May 17, 2013.

concentration on this domain, aluminum magnate Oleg Deripaska, who is third on the Forbes rich list of wealthy Russians with an estimated fortune of more than 8 billion dollars, already invested more than 40,000 dollars in the Institute of Physical and Chemical Biology at Moscow State University in 2005. In 2009 he launched an IPO of the Human Stem Cell Institute (HSCI) founded in 2003 with the forecast of the Russian stem cell storage market value of 94 million dollars in 2013. Consequently, it is evident that advancement of stem cell research mobilizes the greatest minds and arrests the largest sums in the country.[7]

Research Objectives In Relation to Demographic Crisis

The crucial need to promote stem cell research in Russia can be understood once the main research objectives are juxtaposed with the health care statistics and demographic data. According to international and local experts, demographic situation in Russia qualifies as "nothing short of a humanitarian catastrophe."[8] Since the collapse of the Soviet Union, the population had declined 0.5 percent per year due to decreasing birth and increasing death numbers until 2009 when the population of Russia started to increase again.[9] The 2012 census recorded 143,300,000 inhabitants which figure was still lower than the one in 1991 by 5 million.[10]

Eberstadt reports that, on average, the death rate across Russia is fifty percent higher than in the former Soviet countries that joined the European Union. The leading causes of death remain health conditions associated with cardiovascular diseases, 56 percent of fatalities in 2010, and cancer, 14.3 percent.[11] The incidence of death from cardiovascular diseases (CVDs) is 40 percent more than in Finland, which ranks first in Europe by quantity of death from heart attacks. Furthermore, a distinctive feature of cardiovascular disease mortality in Russia is that most deaths occur in working age groups. Cancer, another huge claimer of lives in Russia, 300,000 people per annum, is said to inflict 2.5 million Rus-

7   Polya Lesova, Russian Stem Cell Firm Hopes to Raise $5.5 million in IPO, *MarketWatch*, October 7, 2009; available at www.marketwatch.com/story/stem-cell-firm-launches-first-russian-ipo-2009-10-07, last accessed on May 17, 2013.

8   Nicholas Eberstadt, Russia's Peacetime Demographic Crisis: Dimensions, Causes, Implications, NBR Project Report, May 2010 (Seattle, WA: The National Bureau of Asian Research, 2010); available at www.nbr.org/publications/specialreport/pdf/preview/Russia_demography_preview. pdf, last accessed on May 17, 2013.

9   Federal State Statistics Service, Russia in Figures 2012, Population (as of January 1 of the Corresponding Year); available at www.gks.ru/bgd/regl/b12_12/IssWWW.exe/stg/d01/05-01.htm, last accessed on May 17, 2013.

10 Federal Service of State Statistics, Chislennost' naseleniya na 1 yanvarya [Population Size as of January 1]; available at www.gks.ru/bgd/regl/B09_16/IssWWW.exe/Stg/01-03.htm, last accessed on May 17, 2013.

11 *Ibid.*

sians.[12] Top oncologists in the country enunciate "cancer epidemic" (according to 2008 newspaper's article in the *St. Petersburg Times*).[13]

Similarly, diabetes mellitus, according to the WHO, spreads as a pandemic in all developed nations.[14] As of January, 2008, nearly 2,834 million patients were diagnosed with diabetes mellitus in Russia combining 282,501 patients with type 1 diabetes and 2,551,115 patients with type 2 diabetes.[15] The true number of patients with diabetes in this country is said to reach 3 to 4 times more than the officially registered; in other words, approximately 8 million people or 5.5 percent of Russia's total population may experience the symptoms without realizing it. What makes the numbers highly relevant is that like CVD, diabetes mellitus also affects the working age population: a nationwide health survey revealed that diabetes mellitus was newly diagnosed in 7.1 percent of the 6.7 million people aged between 35 and 55 who work in the social services sector.[16] This situation is dramatic for Russia because, if diabetes is not diagnosed timely, the condition resists treatment and leads in short time to severe vascular complications. Without reacting urgently with preventative and therapeutic measures, Nicholas Eberstadt infers, the poor situation in healthcare will bear an imminent critical influence on the country's demographic profile and political and economic viability.[17]

Combating health issues in Russia with the help of stem cells is a valid proposition based on established research on these cells' curative potential. Researchers assert that the therapeutic regulation of the immune system will make it possible to overcome morbidity and mortality due to deficiency in adaptive immunity or malignancies untreatable by chemotherapy or surgery. Stem cells will treat autoimmune and inflammatory chronic diseases and also restore the adaptive forces of the body in a relatively little time period.[18] With stem cell injections, diabetes will not go into a chronic stage or develop side-effects. Moreover, the application of stem cells promises full recovery from such severe diseases as a multiple sclerosis, AIDS, children's cerebral paralysis and many

---

12 Igor S. Petruhkin and Elena Yu. Lunina, Cardiovascular Disease Risk Factors and Mortality in Russia: Challenges and Barriers, *Public Health Reviews*, 2011, 33(2): 436–449.

13 Galina Stolyarova, Experts: Russia Hit by Cancer Epidemic, *The St. Petersburg Times*, 1345, February, 5, 2008; available at www.sptimesrussia.com/index.php?action_id=2&story_id=24903, last accessed on May 17, 2013.

14 World Health Organization, *World Health Statistics 2012* (Geneva: WHO, 2012); available at www.who.int/gho/publications/world_health_statistics/EN_WHS2012_Full.pdf, last accessed on May 17, 2013.

15 International Forum "Unite to Change Diabetes", Diabetes in Russia: Problems and Solutions, 2011, 4–6; available at www.novonordisk.com/images/about_us/changing-diabetes/PDF/Leadership forum pdfs/Briefing Books/Russia II.pdf, last accessed on May 17, 2013.

16 *Ibid.*, 4.

17 Eberstadt, *op. cit.*

18 Alejandro Madrigal, Immunological Properties of Cord Blood; Current Topics in Gene and Cell Technologies, Annual International Symposium, Moscow, April 15, 2011; *Proceedings of the 2011 Symposium*, 19–21; available at www.celltech.ru/uploads/files/11-28.pdf, last accessed on May 17, 2013.

others, including rescuing lives of patients with burn damages to 60 or even 90 percent of the skin surface.[19]

It is clear then why the latest project of the Institute of Science and Technology on stem cells will simultaneously deal with the following aspects of research.[20] It will commence with stem cell therapy for cardio-vascular diseases and diabetes; incorporate stem cell treatment for traumatic skin injuries and cancer; and cover neurodegenerative diseases like Alzheimer's and Parkinson's. The potential of stem cells to heal and restore the diseased person from such a wide range of illnesses without a question makes cellular technologies revolutionary and per-haps compared only to the discovery of antibiotics or vaccination. Specifically for Russia, to deal with the drastic decline in the country's human resources, this new biotechnology may prove equally if not more important in the long run as the speculated advancement of the nuclear power on the world market.

Increasing Population Longevity

By its curing capacities, stem cells make it possible to prolong life generously and make the person active and full of energy longer. Looking up the definition of stem cells, they are called "the progenitor cells" which possess "the undif-ferentiated power ability" to become any cell.[21] They are known to be tissue generators and maintainers in the process of coordinated and programmed divisions. Researchers state that stem cells' functional properties comprise "self-renewal capacity" and "multi-lineage differentiation" which promote the body's capability to renew and mend its tissues internally and independently.[22] Regenerative domain is at the forefront of this stem cell quality and involves the „process of replacing or regenerating human cells, tissues or organs to re-store or establish normal function."[23] Such approach stimulates the body's own repair mechanisms to heal previously irreparable tissues or organs and has the potential to solve the problem of the shortage of organs available for donation compared to the number of patients that require life-saving organ transplanta-tion. Some organs and tissues can already be created and are effectively used in laboratory treatment of people as part of regenerative medicine. Examples of

---

19 Junying Yu and James A. Thomson, Embryonic Stem Cells, in *Regenerative Medicine* (Bethesda, MD: National Institutes of Health, U.S. Department of Health and Human Services, 2006–2011), 1–12; available at stemcells.nih.gov/staticresources/info/scireport/PDFs/Regenerative_Medicine_2006.pdf, last accessed on May 17, 2013.

20 UMCG, *op. cit.*

21 *Webster's New World Medical Dictionary*, 3rd Edition, Wiley Publishing, Inc., May 2008.

22 National Institutes of Health, Stem Cell Basics: Introduction, *Stem Cell Information*, Bethesda, MD: National Institutes of Health, U.S. Department of Health and Human Services, April 28, 2002; available at stemcells.nih.gov/info/basics/pages/basics1.aspx, last accessed on May 17, 2013.

23 Stem Cell, Cord Blood and Regenerative Medicine, *Disabled World News*, (n.d.); available at www.disabled-world.com/news/research/stemcells/#ixzz2E4hLRXpY, last accessed on May 17, 2013.

this most actively pursued biomedical technology in Russia include chondral tissue for repairing a knee joint, a bladder, an urethra, mitral valves, trachea, cornea and skin.[24] If growing skin is a simpler task for present-day scientists, vessels, bladder, uterus, heart and kidneys are the most complex but deemed feasible with further research.

Moreover, injections of stem cells invigorate the body and can slower the biological process in ways that no vitamins, diets or sport can. Vladimir Skulachev, the institute director and a full member of the Russian Academy of Sciences, talks about ageing extensively and exclaims that "any programme can be turned off."[25] During therapy, cells are not spent all at once, but are redistributed and kept as reserves in all the body and fabrics. While stem cells in an organism are abundant, the body is said to remain practically healthy. Naturally, with the passing of time, their number decreases and the organism becomes inevitably infirm. However, considering the longevity of stem cells, the person receiving injections may indeed live remarkably long and healthy. There are reports of an Englishman named F. Karne who lived 207 years and Shirali Muslimov from the Soviet Union who died at the age of 169.[26] Stem cells can theoretically make it a reality for everyone.

New Medicine, a stem cell clinic in Russia has recently claimed that anyone could easily shed ten to twenty years and regain lost health without any effort. It praises that cellular treatment can resupply lost stem cells for the last 15–20 years if the patient reached his/her biological 40s and result in the patient looking and feeling at his/her 25 and 30.[27] The entire procedure takes about 1 or 2 hours which speaks of incredible time efficiency of the treatment. Whether such claims are trustworthy is a different question which I will address further in the chapter, but researchers admit stem cells' rejuvenating power.

In Russia this sounds particularly relevant as, in comparison with 1950 when the USSR claimed a higher level of life expectancy than the United States, it has since lost its position in terms of both mortality and life expectancy. In 2004 Mikhail Zurabov, the Minister of Health and Social Development, noted that at the end of the 20th century, Russia "entered into the period of depopulation."[28]

---

24 Larisa Aksenova, Osobennosti natsional'noy regeneratsii [Specificities of National Regeneration], *Nauka i Zhizn'* [Science and Life], 2012; available at www.nkj.ru/articles/110/20384, last accessed on May 17, 2013.

25 Aaron Saenz, Did A Russian Scientist Really 'Cure Aging' or Is It Just a Fluke? *Singularity Hub,* September 21, 2010; available at singularityhub.com/2010/09/21/did-a-russian-scientist-really-cure-aging-or-is-it-just-a-fluke-video/, last accessed on May 17, 2013.

26 Vil Timerbulatov, Meditsina XXI Veka: Stvolovyye kletki—vozmozhnosti ogromny [Medicine of XXI Century: Stem Cells—Enormous Opportunities], *Vechernyaya Ufa,* March 22, 2013; available at vechufa. ru/medicine/1426-stvolovye-kletki-vozmozhnosti-ogromny.html, last accessed on May 17, 2013.

27 Klinika Stvolovykh Kletok 'Noveyshaya Meditsina' [Stem Cell Clinic 'New Medicine'], *Zhizn' bez starosti* [Life without Aging]; available at www.stvolkletki.ru/articles/2.html, last accessed on May 17, 2013.

28 Komersant, Russian Men Live 19 Years Less than Men in Developed Countries. *Kommersant,* December 1, 2004; available at www.kommersant.com/p-3446/r_500/Russian_Men_Live_19_Years_Less_than_Men_in_Developed_Countries/, last accessed on May 17, 2013.

Life expectancy topped at about 70 years in 1986 but from the 1990s it started to decrease steadily in Russia while increasing in the rest of the world. It has recently begun to take a rise but the disparity between the life expectancy of women and men is substantial, almost 13 years.[29] Drawing on this, stem cell research is finding dedicated and hopeful supporters in Russia. Experts demonstrate that, on the micro level, stem cells are able to create and take shape of any organ, tissue; help the body fight the most debilitating diseases; promote recuperation fast, and with lasting results. On the macro level, it can be surmised that stem cells possess powers that may produce a complete makeover of people's lives, improve health care and alleviate demographic concerns.

Ethical Dilemmas

While stem cell therapy promises a transformation of life and a sustainable way of living, there are serious ethical, medical and legal dilemmas which impede its progress and utilization in a routine practice for everyone. Two most debated ethical issues looks at whether embryos or pre-embryos have a right to life and analyze the potential for human cloning as viability. The ethical acuteness of the former concentrates on the moral and social status of pre-embryos in conducting experiments.[30] Given that the human embryo at conception is a "fully integrated, genetically unique self-directed human life that can only develop into a more mature member of the species *Homo sapiens* and no other," this unique human life possesses dignity which must be protected under the bioethical principle of 'nonmaleficence' or 'do no harm'.[31] The use of embryos in research or for therapeutic purposes is therefore unethical, it makes embryonic life of lesser value than life after birth, and leads to the death of one human being as a sacrifice for another. Proponents of embryonic research respond that the social and financial expenses are so high for many diseases that these ethical convictions are not sufficient reasons for banning stem cell research and therapy alltogether. Yet others fear that creating and destroying embryos to produce a potential medical product constitutes a form of commodification of human life which may result in nurturing embryos into their later phase of development—all because of their enhanced therapeutic qualities.

---

29 Earth Policy Institute, Life Expectancy for Russia, 1950–2010; available at www.quandl.com/EPI-Earth-Policy-Institute/2-Life-Expectancy-for-Russia-1950-2010, last accessed on May 17, 2013; see also the chart at en.wikipedia.org/wiki/File:Russian_male_and_female_life_expectancy.PNG, last accessed on May 17, 2013.
30 Kristina Hug, Therapeutic Perspectives of Human Embryonic Stem Cell Research versus the Moral Status of a Human Embryo—Does One Have to Be Compromised for the Other? *Medicina (Kaunas)*, February 2006; 42(2):107–114.
31 Bennett Gaymon, Lebacqz Karen and Peters Ted, Stem Cell Ethics: A Theological Brief (Seattle, WA: Counterbalance Foundation, 2005); available at http://www.counterbalance.org/stem-brf/index-frame.html, last accessed on May 17, 2013.

Another set of ethical problems are related to the abuse of a woman's capacity to produce eggs as part of stem cell research or 'therapeutic cloning' purposes. Women, especially low-income and disadvantaged women, are bound to become exploited as 'donors' of eggs. They will supply eggs for stem cell research and with hyper ovulation—which is necessary to obtain eggs in sufficient quantities—their own good health may be threatened and sacrificed for the recovery of others. In the case of 'therapeutic cloning' this means that a new embryo is created deliberately, with the sole intent to destroy it once its material is utilized. Here the ethical dilemma is deemed more serious and the ethical debate will confront the controversial issues of not simply destructing embryos but also creating them for research purposes.

This ethical question creates divisions between religious authorities as well. While the Roman Catholic, Orthodox, and conservative Protestant Churches view the moral status of the human embryo from conception and forbid embryo research, Judaism and Islam do not entitle full human status to the early embryo until 40 days and advocate research as it helps others. Vatican Catholics articulate their stance in the 1987 encyclical *Donum Vitae* which ties together "ensoulment, dignity, moral protection, and genetic novelty" by referring to the unique genetic code, which once established ought to be protected from the scientists' harm. Although the Russian Orthodox Church also does not agree with embryonic stem cell research, in 2011 there was an increase of financing for adult stem cells. Religious authorities hope that greater interest to use those will prompt reduction in use of embryonic stem cells.[32] Overall, destroying human embryos remains unsolved and extremely sensitive topic in Russia and internationally.

Sources of Stem Cells

Without doubt, considering the possible and acceptable sources of stem cells would require thorough deliberation. The possible sources may be umbilical cord blood, bone marrow, skin, aborted fetuses, surplus embryos remaining after artificial fertilization, and products of 'therapeutic cloning', that is artificial creation of human embryos for their use as biomedical and genetic raw material. The latter two are so far viewed as unacceptable in Russia on the grounds that compared to aborted fetuses that are already dead and counted as natural loss, the other sources are living organisms that are meant to develop under the right conditions and artificially creating to kill is plain murder.

Aborted fetuses, however, are not regarded as acceptable source of stem cells either, but for other reasons. With regard to this type of source, Larissa Zhi-

---

32 Dmitriy Rebrov, Tserkov' dovol'na novym zakonoproyektom o stvolovykh kletkakh [Church Is Content with the New Bill on Stem Cell Research], *Zhurnal o pravoslavnoy zhizni Neskuchnyy Sad* [Neskuchnyy Sad: Journal of Orthodox Life], April 26, 2012; available at www.nsad.ru/articles/cerkov-dovolna-novym-zakonoproektom-o-stvolovyh-kletkah, last accessed on May 17, 2013.

ganova, senior lecturer at North American universities and biology professor at the Lomonosov State University, discusses the scenario of treating diabetes with the use of the stem cells of aborted fetuses in the United States.[33] According to statistics, for one operation it is required to arrange eight aborted embryos in the age of 14 to 20 weeks. She calculated that if there are 1.5 million persons in the United States suffering from diabetes, then it would be necessary to find 12 million aborted fetuses. However, only around 120,000 embryos a year are aborted in the US and if this source is distributed on additional patients, suffering from other diseases in the area of stem cell clinical application like Parkinson's and Alzheimer's, multiple sclerosis, spinal cord damages, heart attacks, birth defects of heart, immunodeficiencies, leukaemias, tumours, congenital illnesses of blood, hepatitis, cirrhosis, burns, wounds, and molecular and muscular dystrophy, then even more aborted fetuses would be required. If similar calculations are done in Russia, then with eight aborted embryos for a single patient and 3 million people who are already sick with diabetes (and this is only the official figure, the actual number is said to be three times higher), 24 million aborted fetuses would be necessary to treat all diabetics in Russia. Considering that the official data on the number of abortions is 1 million, it would require a sharp increase in abortions, 23 million to be exact.

The situation of such discrepancy between supply and demand will certainly generate commercialization of capacities of the woman to be a source of ova and sale by mother of the embryos, all according to the laws of the market economy. Taking into account that in Russia there has been an ardent campaign against abortion due to the very slowly recovering growth in population, as well as due to the low birthrate and high mortality, just the prospect of increasing the number of abortions in this range is horrifying. In fact, in 2003 the government of the Russian Federation started to reduce the list of accepted conditions for artificial interruption of pregnancy, and in 2012 there remains only one item—the pregnancy which has come as a result of a crime committed according to Article 131 on Rape in the Criminal Code of the Russian Federation.[34] The share of abortions out of all pregnancies in 2007 was an estimated 45.8 percent and in 2009 it went down to 40.2 percent.[35] As far as the proposed script of using aborted fetuses is concerned, this source of stem cells becomes highly controversial.

Unofficially and implicitly, the decision to abort is stimulated by the prices set for aborted fetuses. One of the articles in *The Guardian* reports that Ukrainian women as well as impoverished women from Russia are paid 100 pounds per

---

33 Larissa P. Zhiganova, Bioetika v Rossii [Bioethics in Russia], *Slovo* [Word, An Educational Portal], n.d.; available at www.portal-slovo.ru/art/36427.php, last accessed on May 17, 2013.
34 Chapter 18. Crimes Against Sexual Inviolability and Sexual Freedom of the Person. The Criminal Code of The Russian Federation, adopted by the State Duma on May 24, 1996; available at www.russian-criminal-code.com/PartII/SectionVII/Chapter18.html, last accessed on May 17, 2013.
35 Viktoriya Sakevich, Novyye ogranicheniya prava na abort v Rossii [New Restriction on Abortion Rights in Russia], *Demoscope Weekly*, 499–500, February 20, 2012; Available at demoscope.ru/weekly/2012/0499/reprod02.php, last accessed on May 17, 2013.

fetus.[36] These fetuses are then cryogenically frozen and sold to beauty clinics for as much as 5,000 to 10,000 pounds. The demand for "youth injections" is high and remunerated well. It is difficult tell apart the legal use for research and the illegal use for cosmetics and it is because there exist corrupt agreements between respected doctors and academics. Sergei Shorobogatko, a former Kiev policeman who is investigating the trade, said abortion clinics in the poor eastern regions of Ukraine are selling fetuses and charge more for illegal abortive fetuses (older than 12 weeks) as their curative potential is deemed greater. The most recent scandal alarmed Russian society in July 2012. Several local and international newspapers headlined the discovery of 248 human fetuses, aged 12 to 16 weeks near the town Nevyansk in the Urals. It was proposed that the fetuses were from at least four different institutions and could have likely been used in pharmacological and cosmetics research. Elena Mizulina, the head of the State Duma committee on Family, Women and Children, attributed this to the fact that fetuses at this later stage of development are especially valuable and effective for acquiring stem cells.[37] She added that despite the higher costs "the demand for such 'material' is huge." Her claim is supported by the gynecologist Yuliana Abaeva, who shared with the Russian News Service that those fetuses could be unused abortive material which allows cell therapy, so "extremely popular in cosmetics today." No official investigation has followed this claim, but the news unavoidably instigated a lot of anxiety regarding acquisition of stem cells.

Cord blood stem cells and adult stem cells from a bone marrow or skin of the person cause less tension. In the case of cord blood, the blood is drawn from the umbilical cord and the placenta after the baby is born. While it was discarded before as medical waste, nowadays cord blood stem cells can be frozen and ethical problems practically do not arise once the informed agreement of parents is achieved. The first cryobanks of umbilical cord blood stem cells were established in America in the 1990s and today there are more than 200 banks worldwide. Gemabank in Russia is a high-tech medical institution which runs the largest number of cord blood stem cells for private use in the country and the CIS countries. It runs the laboratories for stem cells research and estimates that 17,000 families keep the stem cells of their child's cord blood with them.[38] Children whose cord blood stem cells undergo cryoconservation methods can potentially benefit from new therapies as soon as enough experimental data are accumulated and they become available. Cord blood becomes logistically and

36 Tom Parfitt, Beauty Salons Fuel Trade in Aborted Babies, The Observer, *The Guardian*, April 17, 2005; available at www.guardian.co.uk/world/2005/apr/17/ukraine.russia, last accessed on May 17, 2013.
37 Russia Today, Medical Mystery over Discarded Fetuses: Stem-Cell Research or Illegal Abortions? *Russia Today*, July 24, 2012; available at rt.com/news/russia-embryos-abortions-955/, last accessed on May 17, 2013.
38 Gemabank, Vydeleniye i khraneniye stvolovykh kletok [Extraction and Storage of Stem Cells], Gemabank: Bank stvolovykh kletok [Gemabank: Stem Cell Bank], 2013; available at www. gemabank.ru, last accessed on May 17, 2013.

clinically advantageous over other sources of stem cells for additional reasons. Not only does it offer access to the therapy with prompt availability, but also allows higher frequency of less representative tissue types as it happens with bone marrow registries.[39] Scientists prefer it for the lower incidence of transmitting infection by latent viruses and for the lack of donor attrition, not to mention the lack of risk to the donor. Finally, stem cells are abundant in cord blood and serve as limitless material for research and testing.

Debates among Professionals and Stakeholders on the Use of Stem Cell Therapy

Apart from theoretical and ethical concerns, the highly unsettling issue is associated with the use of the stem cell therapy in the hands of unqualified and uncertified specialists. By investigating newspaper articles, it becomes obvious that with the buzz in the media about miraculous interventions through stem cell research and the absence of concrete regulations and monitoring from the officials, the cases of fraud and financial gain over people's misfortunes are inevitable. According to some estimates, the 'grey' and 'black' market of 'stem cell therapy' in Russia comprises no less than 2 billion dollars which speaks of a huge demand for tissue and cell therapy.[40] The reason for people accosting private clinics or illegal services is especially dire conditions of state's medical treatment. Scientific progress takes place in Russian reality where lack of control and order pervade even routine medical inspections with ultrasound technology. It is said that while the newest equipment can be delivered in state's clinics, there may be no qualified specialists or no money to pay these new specialists who will deliver the services.

Under such circumstances, clinics and beauty salons prosper and may pass unquestioned in terms of legitimacy and veracity of their claims. To illustrate, according to an article published in *Seattle Times*, a resident of the city of Perm in the Ural Mountains responded to the advertisements of one Moscow clinic to seek remedy for multiple sclerosis with embryonic stem cell treatment and paid twenty-thousand dollars.[41] Despite the failure of these injections, she received additional treatment at a beauty clinic by the injection of adult stem cells. Long story short, she remained in a wheelchair (although she can now stand up for short periods) and was basically robbed of her savings and hope. The article emphasizes that despite the lack of trustworthiness connected with some forms of stem cell therapy, many ordinary people and especially celebrities rush to try

---

39 Madrigal, *op. cit.*
40 Aksenova, *op. cit.*
41 Maria Danilova, Russians Ignore Risks, Seek Stem-Cell Therapy, *The Seattle Times*, March 14, 2005; available at seattletimes.com/html/nationworld/2002206894_russstem14.html, last accessed on May 17, 2013.

it to enhance their looks and have little reservations about future risks. Women resort to it to erase wrinkles and get rid of cellulite (the price ranging from $2,850); men may use it to cope with impotence. Pharmaceutical magnate and former presidential candidate Vladimir Bryntsalov, who in his 50s is one of Russia's billionaires, declared in public that he had paid 2,000 per session of stem cell therapy in a private clinic to erase the wrinkles on the face and childhood scars on the body, and that they have miraculously disappeared.[42] Nonetheless, as Andrei Yuriyev who works as a deputy head of the Federal Health Care Inspection Service asserted, the law permits extraction and storage of stem cells only. Because enforcement is negligent, the Ministry of Health admits, most of the 41 clinics that advertise stem-cell treatments in Moscow and offer illegal services continue to operate. Experts warn that their services can be either a complete fraud or a highly dangerous practice if stem cells are indeed used. Possible short-term and long-term side effects may appear.[43] Dr Stephen Minger of King's College, London speculates that clinics may use fetal-tissue extract or even animal stem cells instead of embryonic stem-cells because of the lack of skills and expensive equipment that they cannot afford to acquire.[44]

With respect to international commercial practices, the situation is portrayed similarly. Stephen Barrett, co-founder of the National Council Against Health Fraud, investigates stem cell services offered by the Embryonic Tissues Center in the Ukraine, Stem Cell of America in Mexico, the Brain Therapeutics Medical Clinic in Mission Viejo, California, the Vita Nova Clinic in Barbados, and the Beijing Xishan Institute for Neurogeneration and Functional Recovery in China and renders it extremely doubtful that any present-day commercial stem-cell clinic can provide legitimate service and follow up on its promises.[45] He justifies his skepticism by pointing out to the lack of credible outcome data, simplicity of methods, and the unavailability of data on adverse effects in the long-term. Vladimir Smirnov, a professor and director of the Institute of Experimental Cardiology, explains some of the successful stories on stem cell treatment in the media by indicating that it is the introduction of "foreign material into the body which causes immune-stimulation" and creates initial positive effect.[46] He cautions that such illusion of cure is not lasting and may disappear after a month or 6 weeks without adhering to correct regime of treat-

---

42 Parfitt, Russian scientists . . . , *op. cit.*
43 A. A. Starchenko *et al.*, Quality Management of Medical Aid and Validity of Risk at Use of Cellular Technologies in System of Obligatory Medical Insurance; Current Topics in Gene and Cell Technologies: Annual International Symposium, Moscow, September 27, 2010; *Proceedings of the 2010 Symposium*, 49–51; available at http://www.celltech.ru/uploads/files/13-56.pdf, last accessed on May 17, 2013.
44 Maria Danilova, *op. cit.*
45 Stephen Barrett, The Shady Side of Embryonic Stem Cell Therapy, *Quackwatch*, September 14, 2012; available at www.quackwatch.org/06ResearchProjects/stemcell.html, last accessed on May 17, 2013.
46 Parfitt, Russian Scientists . . . , *op. cit.*

ment. Simultaneously, side effects may follow, such as malignant teratomas or accidental infections from unchecked viruses in the embryo material. While no licenses are given for the use of stem cells in treatment and such practices are penalized, Dr. Alexander Teplyashin, head of Beauty Plaza, says he has tried adult stem cells from patients' or donors' fat and bone marrow to treat diabetes, vision disorders and other diseases because if it gives a person a chance to recover sooner than they are obliged to attempt. He adds that "We are taking advantage of the loopholes in the law . . . what is not forbidden is allowed." Thus, with vaguely defined regulations and uncertainty surrounding the long-term impact of stem cell therapy, dozens of clinics continue working unchecked within and outside Russia.

Legislative Faults

In light of the worldwide media's interest and tabloid coverage of recent scientific achievements, plenitude of advertisements on availability of stem cell treatment in the clinics, and intense research in the laboratories of numerous countries, the international legislative platform for scientific research with stem cells aims to prevent and resolve issues pertaining to their extraction and use. The Universal Declaration on the Human Genome and Human Rights of UNESCO is the most cited legal document in this field.[47] Article 12 of the Declaration states that "freedom of research, necessary for the progress of knowledge, is part of freedom of thought. The applications of research shall seek to offer relief from suffering and improve the health of individuals and humankind as a whole."[48] These principles are in line with Article 41 of the Constitution of the Russian Federation that provides the right to health protection and free medical service to all citizens. Article 21 of the Constitution states that "no one may be subject to medical, scientific and other experiments without voluntary consent."[49] This means in practice that the person who participates in research or who is exposed to di-agnostic and therapeutic intervention is required to sign a voluntary informed consent. Mandatory availability of consultations for examinees is designed to inform and explain; doctors or researchers ought to refrain from imposing or advising a choice to make in case of the patient's hesitation. Furthermore, confidentiality of the test results and the medical history of the patients are also to be maintained. However, the lack in sufficient normative base in Russia does

---

47   United Nations Educational, Scientific, and Cultural Organization, The Universal Declaration on the Human Genome and Human Rights, adopted in Paris, November 11, 1997; official text available at portal.unesco.org/en/ev.php-URL_ID=13177&URL_DO=DO_TOPIC&URL_SECTION=201.html, last accessed on May 17, 2013.
48   Ibid.
49   Chapter 2: Rights and Freedoms of Man and Citizen, The Constitution of the Russian Federation; available at www.constitution.ru/en/10003000-03.htm, last accessed on May 17, 2013.

little to prevent unauthorized access to the private and extremely meaningful information on the individual.[50]

Russian scientists have been warning that the absence of comprehensive legal regulation in the field of stem cell technologies and their application has adverse effects for both research and therapeutical practice.[51] For example, the law ought to prevent 'charlatans' and 'commercial speculators' from applying patented substances in the field of cosmetics irresponsibly. Law should not only limit irresponsible and fraudulent applications, but also create a number of control bodies for the examination and certification of innovative production. Moreover, Andrey Vasiliyev, associate director in science of Biology Institute by N.K.Koltsova, explains that new methods cannot be introduced and used beyond laboratory experiments when there is absence of legislations. Yuriy Sukhanov, president of the association "Union of Experts on Biomedical Cellular Technologies and Regenerative Medicine," adds that any medical product must pass full testing and biomedical cellular technologies must obtain a passport confirming their biosecurity and efficiency.[52] Once again the legislative base for this purpose does not exist at this moment. In response to state's meeting legislative demands for application of cellular technologies, scientists are ready to refuse the use of human embryos. It is important because, while in Russia there is currently a temporary five years' moratorium on reproductive cloning, no legislative restrictions take place on working with embryonic stem cells with the objective of 'therapeutic cloning'.

Rights of the early embryos can be protected only by means of bioethics which breeds hostility to stem cell research in its entirety. To attend to numerous criticisms, on April 26, 2012 in the State Duma there was a meeting organized in order to amend the legislative regulation of biomedical cell technologies.[53] Leading experts in the field from academic, scientific and clinical centers as well as representatives of the public appeared to discuss the issue of stem cell research and the bill to be offered to legislators to regulate this branch of medicine. Dmitry Pershin acted on behalf of the Russian Church and the committee on biomedical ethics of the All-Russia orthodox youth society. He expressed satisfaction with the fact that the project makes distinction between embryonic stem cells and intervention done without embryonic origins. However, not all experts agreed to eschew from embryonic material and felt content with the bill statements. They responded that no method at this stage should be denied if it can be used in the interests of the patient. So even then, this version of the bill does not put an end to disputes between Church, representatives of a secular science and Christian doctors and without sufficient reconciliation advancement in stem cell research is complicated.

---

50 Genebank, Zakonodatel'stvo [Legislation]; available at genebank.ru/articles.php?cat_id=6, last accessed on May 17, 2013.
51 Parfitt, Russian Scientists . . . , *op. cit.*
52 Aksenova, *op. cit.*
53 Rebrov, *op. cit.*

Conclusion

To conclude, the pursuit of stem cell research is a timely and relevant investment in Russian science. Cell therapy promises to eradicate some of the pressing and severe health problems in the country, thus it could alleviate, to a significant degree, the demographic concerns associated with high mortality. Of course, cell therapy can be understood not only as a secret demographic weapon, but also as a magic tool to cure the ills and imperfections of individuals. Affluent and well-positioned members of the society have already spent fortunes on stem cell therapy, with mixed results.[54] Furthermore, lack of validated information extends the already wide gap between scientists and the lay society, which leaves the truly effective methods obscure and reproduces the ignorance of the general public.

Though stem cells present bountiful new opportunities, their extraction and isolation also raise challenging ethical concerns which, in turn, require that the acceptable applications of stem cell therapy are clearly regulated. Alexei Ivanov, deputy director of the Research Institute of Molecular Medicine at Moscow's Sechenov Medical Academy, acknowledges this by saying that "there is still so much we don't know about [the stem cells] and the effects they have on the body," therefore it is necessary to "get all unregulated practice under control."[55] Nevertheless, he adds that under no circumstances it should detract scientists from researching the potential of stem cells. Thanks to the emerging collaboration of research teams and the diversification of financial resources worldwide, there is now a 'road map' in Russia for the further development of stem cell research and the biomedical application of its results. Consequently, there is much confidence in the success of stem cell research.[56] If there are ethical and scientific standards in place and legal regulations make the practice of stem cell research and therapy transparent and safe, then the magic of stem cells can indeed be turned into reality for the citizens of the Russian Federation.

---

54 Parfitt, Russian scientists . . . , *op. cit.*
55 *Ibid.*
56 Aksenova, *op. cit.*

BIBLIOGRAPHY

Books, Book Chapters, Journal Articles

Abrejo, Farina Gul, Babar Tasneem Shaikh and Narjis Rizvi (2009) And They Kill Me, Only Because I Am a Girl' ... A Review of Sex-Selective Abortions in South Asia, *The European Journal of Contraception and Reproductive Health Care*, February 2009, 14(1): 10–16.

Agamben, Giorgio (1998) *Homo Sacer: Sovereign Power and Bare Life*. Stanford: Stanford University Press.

Agamben, Giorgio (2005) *State of Exception*. Chicago: The University of Chicago Press.

Aksenova, Larisa (2012) Osobennosti natsional'noy regeneratsii [Specificities of National Regeneration]. *Nauka i Zhizn'* [Science and Life]. Available at www.nkj.ru/articles/110/20384.

Anderson, Elizabeth S. (1990) Is Women's Labor a Commodity? *Philosophy and Public Affairs*, Winter 1990, 19(1): 71–92.

Andreasen, Robin O. (1998) A New Perspective on the Race Debate. *British Journal for the Philosophy of Science*, June 1998, 49(2): 199–225.

Arat, Zehra F. (1994) Turkish Women at the Republican Reconstruction of Tradition. In Gocek Fatma Muge and Balaghi Shiva (eds.), *Constructing Gender in the Middle East*. New York: Columbia University Press, 57–78.

Atwood, Margaret (1998) *The Handmaid's Tale*. New York: Anchor.

Azoulay, Katya G. (2006) Reflections on Race and the Biologization of Difference. *Patterns of Prejudice*, November 2004, 40(4–5): 353–379.

Balen, Frank van and Marcia C. Inhorn (2003) Son Preference, Sex Selection, and the 'New' New Reproductive Technologies. *International Journal of Health Services*, 33(2): 235–252.

Barany, Zoltan (1998) Ethnic Mobilization and the State: The Roma in Eastern Europe. *Ethnic and Racial Studies*, March 1998, 21(2): 308–327.

Batra, Jasleen Kaur (2012) Medical Tourism in India: A Boost to the Economy. *Modern Medicare*, March 19, 2012. Available at modernmedicare.co.in/articles/medical-tourism-in-india-a-boost-to-the-economy/.

Baumhofer, Emma (2012) Commodifying the Female Body: Outsourcing Surrogacy in a Global Market, *Thinking Gender Papers*. Los Angeles: UCLA Center for the Study of Women.

Bayertz, Kurt (1984) The Concept of Moral Consensus: Philosophical Reflections. In Kurt Bayertz (ed.), *The Concept of Moral Consensus: The Case of Technological Interventions in Human Reproduction*. Dordrecht: Kluwer Academic Publishers, 41–58.

Bekker, Marrie H. J. (1996) Reconstructing Hymens or Constructing Sexual Inequality? Service Provision to Islamic Young Women Coping with the Demand to Be a Virgin. *Journal of Community and Applied Social Psychology*, December 1996, 6(5): 329–334.

Bennett, Sara, David Gotsadze, David Gzirishvili, and Kent Ranson (2005) Health Care-Seeking Behavior and Out-of-Pocket Payments in Tbilisi, Georgia. *Health Policy and Planning*, 20(4): 232–242.

Béres, Judit (2003) A magyarországi népesség genetikai rokonsága [Genetic Ancestry of the Hungarian Population]. In Egon Hídvégi (ed.), *A Genom* [The Genome]. Budapest: Széphalom Könyvműhely, 171–186.

Berkovitch, Nitza (1997) Motherhood as a National Mission: The Construction of Womanhood in the Legal Discourse in Israel. *Women's Studies International Forum*, 20(5–6): 605–619.

Bharadwaj, Prashant and Leah K. Lakdawala (2013) Discrimination Begins in the Womb: Evidence of Sex-Selective Prenatal Investments. *The Journal of Human Resources*, Winter 2013, 48(1): 71–113. Available as manuscript at mitsloan.mit.edu/neudc/papers/paper_146.pdf

Bhargava, Pushpa (2003) Ethical Issues in Modern Biological Technologies. *Reproductive Biomedicine Online*, July 2003, 7(3): 276–285.

Birenbaum-Carmeli, Daphna (2009) Contested Surrogacy and the Gender Order in Israel. In Daphna Birenbaum-Carmeli and Marcia C. Inhorn (eds.), *Assisting Reproduction, Testing Genes: Global Encounters with the New Biotechnologies*. New York and Oxford: Berghahn.

Birenbaum-Carmeli, Daphna (2009) The Politics of 'the Natural Family' in Israel: State Policy and Kinship Ideologies. *Social Science & Medicine*, 69(7): 1018–1102.

Birenbaum-Carmeli, Daphna (2010) Genetic Relatedness and Family Formation in Israel: Lay Perceptions in the Light of State Policy. *New Genetics and Society*, 29(1): 73–85.

Birenbaum-Carmeli, Daphna, and Yoram S. Carmeli (2000) Ritualizing the 'Natural Family': Secrecy in Israeli Donor Insemination. *Science as Culture*, 9(3): 301–325.

Birenbaum-Carmeli, Daphna, and Yoram S. Carmeli, eds. (2010) *Kin, Gene, Community: Reproductive Technologies among Jewish Israelis*. New York and Oxford: Berghahn Books.

Birnbacher, Dieter (2007) Prenatal Diagnosis Yes, Preimplantation Genetic Diagnosis No: A Contradictory Stance? *Reproductive BioMedicine Online*, on web: October 4, 2006, 14(Supplement 1): 109–113.

Blagojevic, Marina, ed. (2002) *Položaj žena u zemljama Balkana: komparativni pregled* [The Position of Women in the Balkan Countries: Comparative Review]. Beograd: Gender Centar Vlade RS, 31–61.

Blyth, Eric and Abigail Farrand (2005) Reproductive Tourism: A Price Worth Paying for Reproductive Autonomy? *Critical Social Policy*, February 2005, 25(1): 91–114.

Bodman, Herbert L. and Tohidi Nayreh, eds. (1998) *Women in Muslim Societies: Diversity within Unity*. London: Lyenne Rienner Publishers.

Bodnar, Adam (2008) Case-Law Concerning the Lack of Availability of Services for Terminating Pregnancy. In Wanda Nowicka (ed.), *Reproductive Rights in Poland: The Effects of the Anti-Abortion Law. Report: March 2008*. Warsaw: Federation for Women and Family Planning, 45–64. Available at www.federa. org.pl/dokumenty_pdf/english/report Federa_eng_NET.PDF.

Bookman, Milica Z. and Karla R. Bookman (2007) *Medical Tourism in Developing Countries*. New York: Palgrave MacMillan.

Brodwin, Paul E. ed. (2000) *Biotechnology and Culture: Bodies, Anxieties, Ethics*. Bloomington and Indianapolis: Indiana University Press.

Brown, Sarah Graham. (2001) Women's Activism in the Middle East. In Joseph Suad and Susan Slyomovics (eds.), *Women and Power in the Middle East*. Philadelphia: University of Pennsylvania Press, 23–33.

Burchell, Graham, Colin Gordon and Peter Miller, eds. (1991) *The Foucault Effect: Studies in Governmentality, with Two Lectures by and an Interview with Michel Foucault*. Chicago: University of Chicago Press.

Cavalli-Sforza, Luigi Luca (2000) *Genes, Peoples, and Languages*. London: The Penguin Press.

Chang, Mina (2009) Womb for Rent. India's Commercial Surrogacy. *Harvard International Review*, Spring 2009, 31(1): 11–12.

Chong, Erica, Tamar Tsereteli, Susanna Vardanyan, Gayane Avagyan, and Beverly Winikoff (2009) Knowledge, Attitudes, and Practice of Abortion among Women and Doctors in Armenia. *The European Journal of Contraception and Reproductive Health Care*, October 2009; 14(5): 340–348.

Cockburn, Cynthia (2004) The Continuum of Violence: A Gender Perspective on War and Peace. In Wenona Giles and Heather Hyndman (eds.), *Sites of Violence: Gender and Conflict Zones*. Berkeley: University of California Press, 24–44.

Cohen, Jean (2006) Procreative Tourism and Reproductive Freedom. *Reproductive BioMedicine Online*, 13 (1): 145–146.

Corea, Gena (1986) *The Mother Machine: Reproductive Technologies from Artificial Insemination to Artificial Wombs*. New York: Harper and Collins.

Cowan, Ruth Schwarz (2008) *Heredity and Hope: The Case for Genetic Screening*. Cambridge, MA: Harvard University Press.

Cutaş, Daniela (2007) Postmenopausal Motherhood: Immoral, Illegal? A Case Study. *Bioethics*, October 2007, 21(8): 458–463.

Cutaş, Daniela (2008) On a Romanian Attempt to Legislate on Medically Assisted Human Reproduction. *Bioethics*, January 2008, 22(1): 56–63.

Czeizel, Endre (2003 [1990]) *A magyarság genetikája* [Genetics of the Hungarian Population]. Budapest: Galenus Kiadó.

Czeizel, Endre and Pál Magyar (1974) *A születendő gyermek védelmében* [For the Protection of the Prospective Child]. Budapest: Medicina Könyvkiadó.

Czerner, Frank (2011) Die Kodifizierung der Präimplantationsdiagnostik (PID) in 3§ ESchG im Ensemble pränataldiagnostischer und schwangershaftsbezogener Untersuchungen des Fötus [Regulation of Pre-Implantation Genetic Diagnosis (PGD) in Section 3 of the German Embryo Protection Act together with the Pre-Natal Diagnosis- and Pregnancy-Related Testing of the Embryo]. *Medizinrecht,* December 2011, 29(12): 783–789.

Czerwińska, Anna (2009) Poland: 20 Years–20 Changes. In Justyna Włodarczyk (ed.), *Gender Issues 2009: Gender Equality Discourse in Time of Transformation, 1989–2009.* Warsaw: the Heinrich Böll Foundation Regional Office, 37–61. Available at www.pl.boell.org/downloads/gender_issues_2009_www.pdf.

Deech, Ruth (2003) Reproductive Tourism in Europe: Infertility and Human Rights. *Global Governance,* October–December 2004, 9(4): 425–432.

Demény, Enikő (forthcoming) Networks of Reproduction in the Globalized World. In Róisín Ryan-Flood and Jenny Gunnarsson Payne (eds.), *Transnationalizing Reproduction: Gamete and Embryo Donation in a Globalized World* (Chapter presented at the European Science Foundation Workshop, Essex, September 12, 2012.).

Demeny, Paul (2003) *Population Policy: A Concise Summary.* New York: Buch.

Dick-Read, Grantly (1942) *Revelation of Childbirth: The Principles and Practice of Natural Childbirth.* London: Heinemann.

Diekämper, Julia (2011), *Reproduziertes Leben: Biomacht in Zeiten der Präimplantationsdiagnostik* [Reproduced Life: Biopolitics in Times of Pre-Implantation Genetic Diagnosis]. Bielefeld: Transcript Verlag.

Dolgin, Janet L. (1997) *Defining the Family. Law, Technology and Reproduction in an Uneasy Age.* New York: New York University Press.

Dolian, Gayane, Frank Lüdicke, Naira Katchatrian, Aldo Campana, and Alfredo Morabia (1998) Contraception and Induced Abortion in Armenia: A Critical Need for Family Planning Programs in Eastern Europe. *American Journal of Public Health,* May 1998, 88(5): 803–805.

Domaradzka, Anna (2008) *Report of the Expert Research with Gynaecologists and Midwives.* In Wanda Nowicka (ed.), *Reproductive Rights in Poland: the Effects of the Anti-abortion Law. Report: March 2008.* Warsaw: Federation for Women and Family Planning, 65–79. Available at www.federa.org.pl/dokumenty_pdf/english/report Federa_eng_NET.PDF.

Dourglishvili, Nino (1997) *Social Change and the Georgian Family.* Tbilisi: United Nations Development Programme.

D'Souza, Irene (2012) Where Have the Girls Gone? Gender-Selection Technology Has Skewed the Number of Girls Born in Some Countries, *Herizons,* Fall 2012, 26(2): 30–33. Available at www.herizons.ca/node/528.

Duster, Troy (2006) The Molecular Reinscription of Race: Unanticipated Issues in Biotechnology and Forensic Science. *Patterns of Prejudice*, November 2006, 40(4–5): 427–441.

Duthé, Géraldine France Meslé, Jacques Vallin, Irina Badurashvili, and Karine Kuyumjyan (2012) High Sex Ratios at Birth in the Caucasus: Modern Technology to Satisfy Old Desires, *Population and Development Review*, September 2012, 38(3): 487–501.

El Saadawi, Nawal (1977) *The Hidden Face of Eve*. London and New York: Zed Books.

El Saadawi, Nawal (1997) *The Nawal El Saadawi Reader*. London and New York: Zed Books.

El-Gilany, Abdel-Hacly and Ibrahim Shady (2007) Determinants and Causes of Son Preference among Women Delivering in Mansoura, Egypt. *Eastern Mediterranean Health Journal*, January 2007, 13(1):119–128.

Eltahawy, Mona (2012) Why Do They Hate Us? *Foreign Policy*, May–June 2012. Available at www.foreignpolicy.com/articles/2012/04/23/why_do_they_hate_us.

Engelhardt, Hugo Tristam (1991) *Bioethics and Secular Humanism: The Search for a Common Morality*. Philadelphia: Trinity Publisher International.

Federation for Women and Family Planning, ed. (2005) *Contemporary Women's Hell. Polish Women's Stories*. Warsaw: Federation for Women and Family Planning. Available at www.federa.org.pl/dokumenty_pdf/english/pieklo_ang.pdf.

Ferraretti, Anna Pia, Guido Pennings, Luca Gianaroli, Francesca Natali, and M. Cristina Magli (2010) Cross-Border Reproductive Care: A Phenomenon Expressing the Controversial Aspects of Reproductive Technologies. *Reproductive BioMedicine Online*, 20: 261–266.

Fiatal, Szilvia and Róza Ádány, (2009) A népegészségügyi szempontból jelentős betegségekre hajlamosító genetikai mutációk a magyar populációban [Genetic Mutations in the Hungarian Population That Cause Susceptibility in Significant Diseases from a Public Health Perspective]. *Népegészségügy*, 87(3): 185–194.

Field, Martha A. (1990) *Surrogate Motherhood. The Legal and Human Issue*. Cambridge, MA: Harvard University Press.

Foucault, Michel (1990) *The History of Sexuality, Volume I: An Introduction*. New York: Vintage Books.

Foucault, Michel (2003) *"Society Must Be Defended": Lectures at the Collège de France, 1975–1976*, Mauro Berani and Alessandro Fontana (eds.), translated by David Macey. New York: Picador.

Fuchs, Michael (2005) *National Ethics Councils: Their Backgrounds, Functions and Modes of Operation Compared*. Berlin: Nationaler Ethikrat.

Fuszara, Małgorzata (1991) Legal Regulation of Abortion in Poland. *Signs: Journal of Women in Culture and Society*, 17(1): 117–128.

Gagoshashvili, Mariam (2006) Law and Tradition: Women's Reproductive Decisions in Urban and Rural Georgia: Case Studies of Tbilisi and Svaneti. MA thesis. Budapest: Central European University.

Gagoshashvili, Mariam (2008) Shaping Women's Reproductive Decisions: The Case of Georgia. *Gender & Development*, 16(2): 273–285.

Galton, David (2002) *Eugenics. The Future of Human Life in the 21st Century*. London: Abacus.

Gannett, Lisa (2004) The Biological Reification of Race. *British Journal for the Philosophy of Science*, June 2004, 55(2): 323–345.

Gaymon, Bennett, Lebacqz Karen and Peters Ted (2005) Stem Cell Ethics: A Theological Brief. Seattle, WA: Counterbalance Foundation. Available at www.counterbalance.org/stem-brf/index-frame.html.

Glasgow, Joshua (2003) On the New Biology of Race. *Journal of Philosophy*, September 2003, 100(9): 456–474.

Glover, Johnatan (2006) *Choosing Children: Genes, Disability and Design*. Oxford: Oxford University Press.

Gluck, Sherna (1996) What Is So Special About Women? Women's Oral History. In David K. Dunaway and Willa K. Baum (eds.), *Oral History: an Interdisciplinary Anthology*. Lanham MD: Altamira Press, 215–230.

Gortakowski, Michael (2011) A Parent's Choice v. Governmental Regulations: A Bioethical Analysis in an Era of Pre-Implantation Genetic Diagnosis. *Buffalo Public Interest Law Journal*, 29: 85–109.

Government of India (2005) *National Guidelines for Accreditation, Supervision and Regulation of ART Clinics in India*. New Delhi: Indian Council of Medical Research.

Graves, Joseph L. and Michael R. Rose, (2006) Against Racial Medicine. *Patterns of Prejudice*, November 2006, 40(4–5): 481–493.

Greenhalgh, Susan, and Edwin A. Winckler (2005) *Governing China's Population: From Leninist to Neoliberal Biopolitics*. Stanford: Stanford University Press, 2005.

Guțan, Sabin (2011) *Reproducerea Umană Asistată Medical și Filiația* [Medically Assisted Human Reproduction and Lineage]. București: Humangiu.

Gyűrűs, Péter, János Molnár, Béla Melegh, Gábor Tóth, Éva Morava, György Kosztolányi, and Károly Méhes (1999) Trinucleotide Repeat Polymorphism at Five Disease Loci in Mixed Hungarian Population. *American Journal of Medical Genetics*, November 1999, 87(3): 245–250.

Habermas, Jürgen (2003) *The Future of Human Nature*. Cambridge: Polity Press.

Hanigsberg, Julia E. (1994) Homologizing Pregnancy and Motherhood: A Consideration of Abortion. *Michigan Law Review*, 94(2): 371–393.

Haraway, Donna J. (2008) *When Species Meet*. Minneapolis: University of Minnesota Press.

Harvey, David (1982) *The Limits to Capital*. Oxford: Basil Blackwell.

Harvey, David (1996) *Justice, Nature and the Geography of Difference*. Cambridge, MA: Blackwell Publishers.

Hashiloni-Dolev, Yael (2006) Between Mothers, Fetuses, and Society: Reproductive Genetics in the Israeli Jewish Context. *Nashim: A Journal of Jewish Women's Studies and Gender Issues*, 12: 129–150.

Hayden, Corrine (1995) Gender, Genetics, and Generation: Reformulating Biology in Lesbian Kinship. *Cultural Anthropology*, 10(1): 41–63.

Heinen, Jacqueline and Anna Matuchniak-Krasuska (1992) *L'avortement en Pologne: la Croix et la Banniere* [Abortion in Poland: the Cross and the Banner]. Paris: l'Harmattan.

Hudgins, Tony and Raja Rao (2004) *Republic of Georgia, Contraceptive Availability Assessment: Final Report*. Boston: JSI Research and Training Institute Inc.

Hübner, Marlis and Wiebke Pühler (2011) Die neuen Regelungen zu Präimplantationsdiagnostik — wesentliche Fragen bleiben offen. [The New Regulation of Pre-Implantation Genetic Diagnosis — Important Questions Remain Open]. *Medizinrecht*, December 2011, 29(12): 789–796.

Hug, Kristina (2006) Therapeutic Perspectives of Human Embryonic Stem Cell Research versus the Moral Status of a Human Embryo — Does One Have to Be Compromised for the Other? *Medicina (Kaunas)*, February 2006; 42(2):107–114.

Human Rights Watch (2010) *A State of Isolation: Access to Abortion for Women in Ireland*. New York: Human Rights Watch. Available at www.hrw.org/sites/default/files/reports/ireland0110webwcover.pdf.

Huxley, Aldous (1932) *Brave New World*. London: Chatto and Windus.

Inhorn, Marcia C. (2003) Global Infertility and the Globalization of New Reproductive Technologies: Illustrations from Egypt. *Social Science and Medicine*, May 2003, 56(9): 1837–1851.

Inhorn, Marcia C. (2003) *Local Babies, Global Science: Gender, Religion and In Vitro Fertilization in Egypt*. New York and London: Routledge.

Inhorn, Marcia C. (2006) Making Muslim Babies: IVF and Gamete Donation in Sunni versus Shi'a Islam. *Culture, Medicine and Psychiatry*, December 2006, 30(4): 427–450.

Inhorn, Marcia C. and Pasquale Patrizio (2009) Rethinking Reproductive "Tourism" as Reproductive "Exile." *Fertility and Sterility*, September 2009, 92(3): 903–906.

Inhorn, Marcia C., Pasquale Patrizio and Gamar I. Serour (2010) Third-Party Reproductive Assistance around the Mediterranean: Comparing Sunni Egypt, Catholic Italy and Multisectarian Lebanon. *Reproductive BioMedicine Online*, December 2010, 21(7), 848–853. Available at www.rbmojournal.com/article/S1472-6483(10)00622-X/fulltext.

Irish Family Planning Association (2012) Psychological, Physical, and Financial Costs of Abortion. Dublin: IFPA. Available at www.ifpa.ie/node/506.

Jankowska, Hanna (1991) Abortion, Church and Politics in Poland. *Feminist Review*, 39: 174–181.

Jankowska, Hanna (1993) The Reproductive Rights Campaign in Poland. *Women's Study International Forum*, 16(3): 291–296.

Joób, Sándor (2012) Közelít az abortusztabletta Magyarországra [The Abortion Pill Approaches Hungary], *Index.hu*, April 23, 2012. Available at index.hu/belfold/2012/04/23/abortusztabletta_nincs_es_megis_van/.

Kahn, Susan Martha (2000) *Reproducing Jews: A Cultural Account of Assisted Conception in Israel.* Durham: Duke University Press.

Kakuk, Péter (2009) Cloning and Research Misconduct: The Woo-Suk Hwang Case. In Judit Sándor (ed.) *Perfect Copy? Law and Ethics of Reproductive Medicine.* Budapest: CELAB, 35–52.

Kanaaneh, Rhoda (2002) *Birthing the Nation: Strategies of Palestinian Women in Israel.* Berkeley: University of California Press.

Kandiyoti, Deniz (1988) Bargaining with Patriarchy. *Gender and Society,* 2(3): 278–287.

Kassim, Hussein (2004) 'Race', Genetics and Human Difference. In Justine Burley and John Harris (eds.), *A Companion to Genethics.* Oxford: Blackwell, 302–316.

Keddie, Nikky R. and Beth Baron, eds. (1991) *Women in Middle Eastern History.* New Haven and London: Yale University Press.

Kekelia, Mikhako, ed. (1988) *Qartuli chveulebiti samartali* [Georgian Customary Law]. Tbilisi: Metsniereba.

King, D. S. (1999) Pre-Implantation Genetic Diagnosis and the 'New' Eugenics. *Journal of Medical Ethics,* April 1999, 25(2): 176–182.

King, Jamie (2008) Predicting Probability: Regulating the Future of Preimplantation Genetic Screening. *Yale Journal of Health Policy Law and Ethics,* Summer 2008, 8(2): 283–358

Kleinman, Arthur and Joan Kleinman (1991) Suffering and Its Professional Transformation: Toward an Ethnography of Interpersonal Experience. *Culture, Medicine and Psychiatry,* 15(3): 275–301.

Kligman, Gail (1998) *The Politics of Duplicity: Controlling Reproduction in Ceausescu's Romania.* Berkeley: University of California Press.

Kligman, Gail (2000) *Politicle duplicității: Controlul reproducerii în România lui Ceașescu* [The Politics of Duplicity: Controlling Reproduction in Ceaușescu's Romania]. București: Humanitas.

Knoppers, Bartha M. and Sonia LeBris (1991) Recent Advances in Medically Assisted Conception: Legal, Ethical, and Social Issues. *American Journal of Law and Medicine,* Winter 1991, 17(4): 329–361.

Konstantinov, Igor E. (2000) In Search of Alexander A. Maximow: The Man Behind the Unitarian Theory of Hematopoiesis, *Perspectives in Biology and Medicine,* Winter 2000, 43(2): 269–276.

Kósa, Karolina and Róza Ádány (2007) Studying Vulnerable Populations: Lessons from the Roma Minority. *Epidemiology,* May 2007, 18(3): 290–299.

Kósa, Zsigmond, György Széles, László Kardos, Karolina Kósa, Renáta Németh, Sándor Országh, Gabriella Fésüs, Martin McKee, Róza Ádány, and Zoltán Vokó (2007) A Comparative Health Survey of the Inhabitants of Roma Settlements in Hungary. *American Journal of Public Health,* May 2007, 97(5): 853–859.

Kulczycki, Andrzej (1995) Abortion Policy in Postcommunist Europe: The Conflict in Poland. *Population and Development Review,* 21(3): 471–505.

Kulczycki, Andrzej (1999) *The Abortion Debate in the World Arena.* New York: Routledge.

Lanzerath, Dirk (2010) Präimplantationsdiagnostik: Zentrale Fakten und Argumente, *Analysen und Argumente Nr. 85*, November 2010. Berlin: Konrad Adenauer Stiftung. Available at www.kas.de/wf/doc/kas_21194-544-1-30.pdf.

Larijani, Bagher and Farzaneh Zahedi (2007) Ethical and Religious Aspects of Gamete and Embryo Donation and Legislation in Iran. *Journal of Religion and Health*, September 2007, 46(3): 399–408.

Lasco, Chanté (2002) Virginity Testing in Turkey: A Violation of Women's Human Rights. Washington, DC: American University Center for Human Rights and Humanitarian Law. *Human Rights Brief*, Spring 2002, 9(3): 10–13. Available at www.wcl.american.edu/hrbrief/09/3lasco.pdf.

Latsiou, Charikleia Z. (2008) *Präimplantationsdiagnostik: Rechtsvergleichung und bioethische Fragestellungen* [Pre-Implantation Genetic Diagnosis: Legal Comparison and Bioethical Questions]. Berlin: Duncker und Humblot.

Lee, Ruby L. (2009) New Trends in Global Outsourcing of Commercial Surrogacy: A Call for Regulation. *Hastings Women's Law Journal*, Summer 2009, 20(2): 275–300.

Lemke, Thomas (2011) *Biopolitics: An Advanced Introduction*. New York: New York University Press.

Lloyd, Cynthia B. (1994) Family and Gender Issues for Population Policies. In Laurie Ann Mazur (ed.), *Beyond the Numbers: A Reader on Population, Consumption, and the Environment*. Washington, DC: Island Press, 242–256.

Lundin, Susanne (2012) "I Want a Baby; Don't Stop Me from Being a Mother": an Ethnographic Study on Fertility Tourism and Egg Trade. *Cultural Politics*, July 2012, 8(2): 327–343.

Madrigal, Alejandro (2011) Immunological Properties of Cord Blood. Current Topics in Gene and Cell Technologies: Annual International Symposium, Moscow, April 15, 2011. *Proceedings of the 2011 Symposium*, 19–21. Available at www.celltech.ru/uploads/files/11–28.pdf.

Martin, Emily (1987) *The Woman in the Body A Cultural Analysis of Reproduction*. Boston: Beacon Press.

Marx, Karl (1982) *Capital. A Critique of Political Economy*. Harmondsworth, Middlesex: Penguin Books.

Mason, Jennifer (2002) *Qualitative Researching*, 2nd Edition. London: Sage.

Matorras, Roberto (2005) Reproductive Exile versus Reproductive Tourism (letter). *Human Reproduction*, December 2005, 20(12): 3571.

Matossian, Mary Allerton Kilbourne (1962) *The Impact of Soviet Policies in Armenia*. Leiden: E. J. Brill.

Mazur, D. Peter (1981) Contraception and Abortion in Poland. *Family Planning Perspectives*, 13(4): 195–198.

Melegh, Béla, Judit Bene, Gábor Mogyorósy, Viktória Havasi, Katalin Komlósi, László Pajor, Éva Oláh, Gyula Kispál, Balázs Sümegi, and Károly Méhes (2004) Phenotypic Manifestations of the OCTN2 V295X Mutation: Sudden Infant Death and Carnitine-Responsive Cardiomyopathy in Roma Families. *American Journal of Medical Genetics*, December 2004, 131A(2): 121–126.

Merabishvili, Jamlet (1988) sergi makalatia da qartuli chveulebiti samartali [Sergi Makalatia and Georgian Customary Law]. In Mikhako Kekelia (ed.), *Qartuli chveulebiti samartali* [Georgian Customary Law]. Tbilisi: Metsniereba, 120–143.

Miller, Ruth A. (2007) Women and the Political Norm. In *The Limits of Bodily Integrity: Abortion, Adultery, and Rape Legislation in Comparative Perspective.* Aldershot, Hampshire, England; Burlington, VT: Ashgate, 149–174.

Mishtal, Joanna Z. (2009) Matters of "Conscience": The Politics of Reproductive Healthcare in Poland. *Medical Anthropology Quarterly,* 23(2): 161–183.

Mokni, Jamel (2010) *Hymen National.* Directed by Jamel Mokni. Tunisia: Centre de l'Audiovisuel à Bruxelles (CBA), Centre National Cinématographique Tunisien.

Molnár, Ágnes, Róza Ádány, Béla Ádám, Gabriel Gulis, and Karolina Kósa (2010) Health Impact Assessment and Evaluation of a Roma Housing Project in Hungary. *Health Place,* November 2010, 16(6): 1240–1247.

Morgan, Derek (2003) Enigma Variations: Surrogacy, Rights and Procreative Tourism. In Rachel Cook, Shelley D. Sclater and Felicity Kaganas (eds.), *Surrogate Moterhood: International Perspectives.* Oxford and Portland, OR: Hart Publishing, 75–92.

Musallam, Basim (1990) The Human Embryo in Arabic Scientific and Religious Thought. In Gordon Reginald Dunstan (ed.), *The Human Embryo: Aristotle and the Arabic and European Traditions.* Exeter, Devon: University of Exeter Press.

Nahman, Michal (2008) Nodes of Desire. Romanian Egg Sellers, 'Dignity' and Feminist Alliances in Transnational Ova Exchanges. *European Journal of Women Studies,* May 2008, 15(2): 65–82.

Nahman, Michal (2011) 'Reverse Traffic': Intersecting Inequalities in Human Egg 'Donation'. *Reproductive Biomedicine Online,* November 2011, 23(5): 626–623.

Nash, Catherine (2004) Genetic Kinship. *Cultural Studies,* January 2004, 18(1): 1–33.

National Institute for Statistics of Romania (2011) *Statistical Yearbook 2011.*

National Institutes of Health (2011) Regenerative Medicine. In *Stem Cell Information.* Bethesda, MD: National Institutes of Health, U.S. Department of Health and Human Services. Available at stemcells.nih.gov/info/scireport/Pages/2006report.aspx.

Nowicka, Wanda (1993) Two Steps Back: Poland's New Abortion Law. *Planned Parenthood in Europe,* 22(2):18–20.

Nowicka, Wanda (2001) Struggles For and Against Legal Abortion in Poland. In Barbara Klugman and Debbie Budlender (eds.), *Advocating for Abortion Access: Eleven Countries Studies.* Johannesburg: Witwatersrand University Press, 223–249. Available at *www.federa.org.pl/dokumenty_pdf/english/Advocating-abortionAccess.pdf.*

Nowicka, Wanda (2008) The Anti-abortion Act in Poland–the Legal and Actual State. In Wanda Nowicka (ed.), *Reproductive Rights in Poland: The Effects of the Anti-Abortion Law. Report: March 2008.* Warsaw: Federation for Women and Family Planning, 17–44. Available at www.federa.org.pl/dokumenty_pdf/english/report Federa_eng_NET.PDF.

Oakley, Ann (1984) *The Captured Womb: A History of the Medical Care of Pregnant Women*. Oxford: Basil Blackwell.

Okólski, Marek (1983) Abortion and Contraception in Poland. *Studies in Family Planning*, 14(11): 263–274.

Pande, Amrita (2010) Commercial Surrogacy in India: Manufacturing A Perfect Mother-Worker. *Signs: Journal of Women in Culture and Society*, Summer 2010, 35(4):969–992.

Pande, Amrita (2011) Transnational Commercial Surrogacy in India: Gifts for Global Sisters? *Reproductive Biomedicine Online*, November 2011, 23(5): 618–625. Available as e-publication since July 23, 2011 at www.ncbi.nlm.nih.gov/pubmed/21958916.

Parfitt, Tom (2005) Russian Scientists Voice Concern over "Stem-Cell Cosmetics." *The Lancet*, 365(9466): 1219–1220, April 2, 2005; available at www.thelancet.com/journals/lancet/article/PIIS0140-6736(05)74795-4/fulltext.

Pateman, Carole (1988) *The Sexual Contract*. Stanford, CA: Stanford University Press.

Patent Association (2011) Jogi szabályozás [Legal Regulations]. *Abortusz.info*. Available at abortusz.info/info/jogi-szabalyozas.

Pennings, Guido (2002) Reproductive Tourism as Moral Pluralism in Motion. *Journal of Medical Ethics*, December 2002, 28(6): 337–341.

Pennings, Guido (2005) Legal Harmonization and Reproductive Tourism in Europe. *Reproductive Health Matters*, May 2005, 13(25): 120–128.

Petruhkin, Igor S. and Elena Yu. Lunina (2011) Cardiovascular Disease Risk Factors and Mortality in Russia: Challenges and Barriers. *Public Health Reviews*, 2011, 33(2): 436–449.

Pongrácz, Tiborné and Edit S. Molnár (1992) Terhességmegszakítások a statisztikai adatok és a közvélemény tükrében [Abortions as Reflected by Statistical Data and in Public Opinion]. In Andorka Rudolf, Kolosi Tamás, and Vukovich György (eds.), *Társadalmi riport 1992* [Social Report 1992]. Budapest: TÁRKI, 289–317.

Portugese, Jacqueline (1998) *Fertility Policy in Israel: The Politics of Religion, Gender, and Nation*. Westport, CT and London: Praeger.

Radenković, Sandra Karel Turza, Zoran Todorović, and Vida Jeremić (2012) Insitucionalizacija Bioetike u Srbiji. *Socijalna ekologija, Zagreb*, 21(3): 311–328.

Ragoné, Helena (1996) Chasing the Blood Tie: Surrogate Mothers, Adoptive Mothers and Fathers. *American Ethnologist*, May 1996, 23(2): 352–365.

Raskó, István (2010) *Honfoglaló Génjeink* [Our Conquistador Genes]. Budapest: Medicina.

Raskó, István and Tibor Kalmár (2003) Emberi populáció genetika: Különbségek emberek között, politika nélkül [Human Population Genetics: Differences between Humans without Politics]. In Egon Hídvégi (ed.), *A Genom* [The Genome]. Budapest: Széphalom Könyvműhely, 105–112.

Raymond, Janice G. (1993) *Women as Wombs. Reproductive Technologies and the Battle over Women's Freedom*. San Francisco: HarperSanFrancisco.

Remennick, Larissa L. (1993) The Patterns of Birth Control. In Igor Kon and James Riordan (eds.), *Sex and Russian Society*. London: Pluto Press, 45–63.

Risch, Neil, Esteban Burchard, Elad Ziv, and Hua Tang (2008) Categorization of Humans in Biomedical Research: Genes, Race, and Disease. In Evelynn M. Hammonds and Rebecca M. Herzig (eds.), *The Nature of Difference: Sciences of Race in the United States from Jefferson to Genomics*. Cambridge, MA: MIT Press, 325–345.

Rizk, Botros R. M. B., Sherman J. Silber, Gamal I. Serour, and Michel Abou Abdallah (2008) Religious Perspectives of Ethical Issues in Infertility and ART. In Botros R. M. B. Rizk, Juan A. Garcia-Velasco, Hassan N. Sallam, and Antonis Makrigiannakis (eds.), *Infertility and Assisted Reproduction*. Cambridge: Cambridge University Press, 728–746.

Robertson, John A. (2003) Extending Preimplantation Genetic Diagnosis: Ethical Issues in New Uses of Preimplantation Genetic Diagnosis. *Human Reproduction*, March 2003, 18(3): 465–471.

Rogers, Wendy Anne, Heather Draper, Angela Jean Ballantyne (2007) Is Sex-Selective Abortion Morally Justified and Should It Be Prohibited? *Bioethics*, November 2007, 21(9): 520–524.

Rose, Nikolas (2007) Race in the Age of Genomic Medicine. In Nikolas Rose, *The Politics of Life Itself*. Princeton and Oxford: Princeton University Press, 155–186.

Rose, Nikolas (2007) *The Politics of Life Itself*. Princeton: Princeton University Press.

Rowland, Robyn (1992) *Living Laboratories. Women and Reproductive Technologies*. Bloomington: Indiana University Press.

Sabedashvili, Tamar (2007) *Gender and Democratization: The Case of Georgia, 1991–2006*. Tbilisi: Heinrich Boell Foundation.

SAMA (2009) The Myth of Regulation: A Critique of the 2008 Draft ART (Regulation) Bill and Rules. *Medico Friend Circle Bulletin*, No. 335–336, June–September 2009: 8–13.

SAMA (2010) *Constructing Conceptions. The Mapping of Assisted Reproductive Technologies in India*. New Delhi: SAMA—Resource Group for Women and Health.

Sándor, Judit and Márton Varju (2013) The Multiplicity of Norms: The Bioethics and Law of Stem Cell Patents. In Andrew Webster (ed.), *The Global Dynamics of Regenerative Medicine: A Social Science Critique*. New York: Palgrave Macmillan, 169–194.

Sándor, Judit, ed. (2003) *Society and Genetic Information. Codes and Laws in the Genetic Era*. Budapest and New York: Central European University Press.

Sándor, Judit, ed. (2009) *Perfect Copy? Law and Ethics of Reproductive Medicine*. Budapest: Center for Ethics and Law in Biomedicine.

Schenker, Joseph G. (2002) Gender Selection: Cultural and Religious Perspectives. *Journal of Assisted Reproduction and Genetics*, September 2002, 19(9): 400–410.

Schumann, Marion (2011) From Social Care to Planning Childbirth. In Kathrin Braun (ed.), *Between Self-Determination and Social Technology*. Bielefeld: Transcript Verlag.

Segev, Tom (1993) *The Seventh Million: The Israelis and the Holocaust*. New York: Hill and Wang.

Serbanescu, Florina, *et al.* (2005) *Reproductive Health Survey Georgia, 2005: Final Report*. Atlanta: United Nations Population Fund.

Sered, Susan (2000) *What Makes Women Sick: Maternity, Modesty, and Militarism in Israeli Society*. Hanover: Brandeis University Press.

Serour, Gamal I. (2005) Religious Perspectives of Ethical Issues in ART. *Middle East Fertility Society Journal*, 10(3): 185–190.

Serour, Gamal I. (2008) Islamic Perspectives in Human Reproduction. *Reproductive BioMedicine Online*, May 2008, 17(3):34–38. Available at www.rbmonline.com/Article/3378.

Shalev, Carmel (1998) *Halakha* and Patriarchal Motherhood: An Anatomy of the New Israeli Surrogacy Law. *Israel Law Review*, 32(1): 51–80.

Shalev, Carmel and Sigal Gooldin (2006) The Uses and Misuses of In Vitro Fertilization: Some Sociological and Ethical Considerations. *Nashim: Journal of Jewish Women's Studies and Gender Issues*, 12: 151–176.

Sharda University Blog, Female Infanticide: The National Shame of India, posted on May 18, 2012. Available at www.sharda.ac.in/blog/female-infanticide-the-national-shame-of-india/.

Sharma, Raghav (2007) *An International, Moral and Legal Perspective: The Call for Legalization of Surrogacy in India*. Manuscript available through ssrn.com/abstract=997923.

Shetty, Priya (2012) India's Unregulated Surrogacy Industry. *The Lancet*, November 10, 2012, 380(9854): 1633–1634. Available at download.thelancet.com/pdfs/journals/lancet/PIIS0140673612619333.pdf.

Shokeid, Moshe (2003) Closeted Cosmopolitans: Israeli Gays between Centre and Periphery. *Global Networks*, July 2003, 3(3): 387–399.

Sipeky, Csilla, Veronika Csöngei, Luca Járomi, Enikő Sáfrány, Anita Maász, István Takács, Judit Béres, Lajos Fodor, Melinda Szabó, and Béla Melegh (2011) Genetic Variability and Haplotype Profile of MDR1 (ABCB1) in Roma and Hungarian Population Samples with a Review of the Literature. *Drug Metabolism and Pharmacokinetics*, April 2011, 26(2): 206–215.

Smerdon, Usha Rengachary (2008) Crossing Bodies, Crossing Borders: International Surrogacy between the United States and India. *Cumberland Law Review*, 2008–2009, 39(1): 15–85.

Sparrow, Robert and David Cram (2010) Saviour Embryos? Pre-Implantation Genetic Diagnosis as a Therapeutic Technology. *Reproductive BioMedicine Online*, May2010, 20(5): 667–674.

Spivak, Gayatri Chakrabarti (1998) *In Other Worlds: Essays in Cultural Politics*. London: Routledge.

Stanford Women's Courage Group (2008) Surrogate Motherhood in India: Understanding and Evaluating the effects of Gestational Surrogacy on Women's Health and Rights. *Women's Courage Group,* 2012. Available at www.stanford.edu/group/womenscourage/Surrogacy/index.html.

Starchenko, A. A. *et al.* (2010) Quality Management of Medical Aid and Validity of Risk at Use of Cellular Technologies in System of Obligatory Medical Insurance. Current Topics in Gene and Cell Technologies: Annual International Symposium. Moscow, September 27, 2010. *Proceedings of the 2010 Symposium,* 49–51. Available at www.celltech.ru/uploads/files/13-56.pdf.

Statistical Office of the Republic of Serbia (2011) *Popis 2011* [Census 2011]. Available at popis2011.stat.rs.

Stern, Alexandra Minna (2005) *Eugenic Nation: Faults and Frontiers of Better Breeding in Modern America.* Berkeley: University of California Press.

Storrow, Richard F. (2006) Quests for Conception: Fertility Tourists, Globalization and Feminist Legal Theory. *Hastings Law Journal,* December 2005, 57(2): 295–330.

Strathern, Marilyn (1992) *Reproducing the Future: Essays on Anthropology, Kinship and the New Reproductive Technologies.* Manchester: Manchester University Press.

Strathern, Marilyn (1995) *The Relation: Issues in Complexity and Scale.* Cambridge: Prickly Pear Press.

Suad Joseph (2001) Women and Politics in the Middle East. In Joseph Suad and Susan Slyomovics (eds.), *Women and Power in the Middle East.* Philadelphia: University of Pennsylvania Press, 34–40.

Swirski, Barbara, and Marilyn Safir, eds. (1991) *Calling the Equality Bluff: Women in Israel.* New York: Pergamon Press.

Tamir, Michal and Dalia Cahana-Amitay (2009) 'The Hebrew Language Has Not Created a Title for Me': A Legal and Sociolinguistic Analysis of New-Type Families. *Journal of Gender, Social Policy, and the Law,* 17(3): 545–600.

Taylor, Charles (1992) *Multiculturalism and "The Politics of Recognition": An Essay.* Princeton: Princeton University Press.

Teman, Elly (2010) *Birthing a Mother: The Surrogate Body and the Pregnant Self.* Berkeley: University of California Press.

Teman, Elly (2010) The Last Post of the Nuclear Family: A Cultural Critique of Israeli Surrogacy Policy. In Daphna Birenbaum-Carmeli and Yoram S. Carmeli (eds.), *Kin, Gene, Community: Reproductive Technologies among Jewish Israelis.* New York: Berghahn Books, 107–126.

Thompson, Charis (2005) *Making Parents. The Ontological Choreography of Reproductive Technologies.* Cambridge, MA: Massachusetts Institute of Technology.

Titkow, Anna (1999) Poland. In Henry P. David and Joanna Skilogianis (eds.), *From Abortion to Contraception. A Resource to Public Policy and Reproductive Behavior in Central and Eastern Europe from 1917 to the Present.* Westport, CT: Greenwood Press, 165–190.

Tong, Rosemarie, Anne Donchin, and Susan Dodds (2004) *Linking Visions: Feminist Bioethics, Human Rights, and the Developing World*. Lanham: Rowman and Littlefield.

Tsintsadze, Khatuna (2007) Legal Aspects of Church–State Relations in Post-Revolutionary Georgia. *Brigham Young University Law Review*, 2007(3): 751–774.

Tuttle, Leslie (2010) *Conceiving the Old Regime, Pronatalism and the Politics of Reproduction in Early Modern France*. Oxford: Oxford University Press.

United Nations Educational, Scientific, and Cultural Organization (2000) *The Universal Declaration on the Human Genome and Human Rights. From Theory to Practice*. Paris: UNESCO. Available at unesdoc.unesco.org/images/0012/001229/122990eo.pdf.

United Nations Educational, Scientific, and Cultural Organization (2011) *Ethics and Law in Biomedicine and Genetics: An Overview of National Regulations in the Arab States*. Cairo: UNESCO Cairo Office.

Unnithan-Kumar, Maya (2010) Female Selective Abortion—Beyond 'Culture': Family Making and Gender Inequality in a Globalizing India. *Culture, Health & Sexuality*, 2010, 12(2): 153–166.

Van de Velde, Hilde (2010) Lessons from Human Embryo. *Reproductive BioMedicine Online*, May 2010, 20(Supplement 1): S5–S6.

Vlădescu, Cristian, Gabriela Scântee and Victor Olsavszky (2008) Romania: Health System Review. *WHO Health Systems in Transition*, 10(3):1–181.

Voell, Stéphane (2012) Local Legal Conceptions in Svan Villages in the Lowlands. *Caucasus Analytical Digest*, No. 42: 2–4.

Vokó, Zoltán, Péter Csépe, Renáta Németh, Karolina Kósa, Zsigmond Kósa, György Széles, and Róza Ádány (2009) Does Socioeconomic Status Fully Mediate the Effect of Ethnicity on the Health of the Roma People in Hungary? *Journal of Epidemiology and Public Health*, June 2009, 63(6): 455–460.

Vora, Kalindi (2009) Indian Transnational Surrogacy and the Disaggregation of Mothering Work. *Anthropology News*, February 2009, 50(2): 9–12.

Wald, Priscilla (2006) Blood and Stories: How Genomics is Changing Race, Medicine and Human History. *Patterns of Prejudice*, November 2006, 40(4–5): 303–333.

Waldby, Catherine (2002) Stem Cells, Tissue Cultures, and the Production of Biovalue. *Health*, 6(3): 305–323.

Waldman, Ellen (2006) Cultural Priorities Revealed: The Development and Regulation of Assisted Reproduction in the United States and Israel. *Health Matrix*, 16: 65–106.

Walzer, Lee (2000) *Between Sodom and Eden: A Gay Journey through Today's Israel*. New York: Columbia University Press.

Wang, Chong-Wen (2009) Ethical, Legal and Social Implications of Prenatal and Pre-Implantation Genetic Testing for Cancer Susceptibility. *Reproductive BioMedicine Online*, September 19, 2009, 19(Supplement 2): 23–33.

Ware, Norma C. and Arthur Kleinman (1992) Culture and Somatic Experience: The Social Course of Illness in Neurasthenia and Chronic Fatigue Syndrome. *Psychosomatic Medicine*, September 1, 1992, 54(5): 546–560.

Wellman, Carl (1984) Moral Consensus and the Law. In Kurt Bayertz (ed.), *The Concept of Moral Consensus: The Case of Technological Interventions in Human Reproduction*. Dordrecht: Kluwer Academic Publishers, 109–122.

Wessels, Ulla (1994) Genetic Engineering and Ethics in Germany. In Anthony Dyson and John Harris (eds.), *Ethics and Biotechnology*. London: Routledge, 230–258.

Westoff, Charles F. (2005) Recent Trends in Abortion and Contraception in Twelve Countries. *DHS Analytical Studies No. 8*, February 2005. Available at pdf.usaid.gov/pdf_docs/pnadb984.pdf.

Whittaker, Andrea (2008) Pleasure and Pain: Medical Travel in Asia. *Global Public Health*, July 2008, 3(3): 271–290.

Wilkinson, Stephen (2003) The Exploitation Argument against Commercial Surrogacy. *Bioethics*, April 2003, 17(2): 169–187.

Wolchik, Sharon L. (2000) Reproductive Policies in Czech and Slovak Republics. In Susan Gal and Gail Kligman (eds.), *Reproducing Gender: Politics, Publics and Everyday Life after Socialism*. Princeton NJ: Princeton University Press, 58–91.

Wright, Susan, and Chris Shore (1997) *Anthropology of Policy. Critical Pespectives on Governance and Power*. New York and London: Routlegde.

Yu, Junying and James A. Thomson (2006) Embryonic Stem Cells. In *Regenerative Medicine*. Bethesda, MD: National Institutes of Health, 1–12. Available at stemcells.nih.gov/staticresources/info/scireport/PDFs/Regenerative_Medicine_2006.pdf.

Yuval-Davis, Nira (1987) The Jewish Collectivity and National Reproduction in Israel. In Khasmin Collective (eds.), *Women in the Middle East*. London: Zed Books, 60–93.

Yuval-Davis, Nira (1997) *Gender & Nation*. London: Sage.

Zhiganova, Larissa P. (n.d.) Bioetika v Rossii [Bioethics in Russia]. *Slovo* [Word, An Educational Portal]. Available at www.portal-slovo.ru/art/36427.

Zielger, Uta (2004) *Präimplantationsdiagnostik in England und Deutschland* [Pre-Implantation Genetic Diagnosis in England and Germany]. Frankfurt am Main: Campus Verlag.

Policy Documents and Reports

Adhikari, Mushahida (2010) *Submissions to the Ministry of Justice and Constitutional Development on Suggested Law Reforms in Respect of Virginity Testing*. Cape Town: Women's Legal Center. Available at www.wlce.co.za/morph_assets/themelets/explorer/health/Submissions on virginity testing.pdf.

Ali Gomaa (2013) What Is the Ruling on Gender Selection for Medical Intervention? *Ali Gomaa, Grand Mufti of Egypt*. Available at www.ali-gomaa.com/?page=fatwas&fatwa_details=478.

Bundesärztekammer (2011) Memorandum zur Präimplantationsdiagnostik [Federal Medical Association, Memorandum on Pre-Implantation Genetic Diagnosis], Berlin, February 25, 2011. Available at www.bundesaerztekammer.de/page.asp?his=0.5.1160.9051.

Bundestag (2002) Schlussbericht der Enquete-Kommission "Recht und Ethik der modernen Medizin," Deutscher Bundestag—14. Wahlperiode, Bundestagsdrucksache 14/9020 [Final Report of the "Law and Ethics in the Modern Medicine" Parliamentary Inquiry Commission of the 14th Bundestag], May 14, 2002. Available at dip21.bundestag.de/dip21/btd/14/090/1409020.pdf.

Chancellery of the Sejm, The Bureau of Research and Expertise (1996) *Raport Nr 90. Wyniki sondaży opinii publicznej o prawnej dopuszczalności przerywania ciąży w latach 1989–1993* [Report No.90. The Results of Public Opinion Polls on Legal Admissibility of Pregnancy Termination Conducted in 1989–1993]. Warsaw: The Bureau of Research and Expertise. Available at biurose.sejm.gov.pl/teksty_pdf_96/r-90.pdf.

Council of Ministers of the Republic of Poland (2012) *Sprawozdanie Rady Ministrów z wykonania oraz o skutkach stosowania w roku 2011 ustawy z dnia 3 stycznia 1993 r. o planowaniu rodziny, ochronie płodu ludzkiego i warunkach dopuszczalności przerywania ciąży* [Report of the Council of Ministers on the Realization and Effects of the Act January 7, 1993 on Family Planning, Protection of the Human Fetus and Conditions Permitting Pregnancy Termination in 2011]. Warsaw: the Council of Ministers. Available at www.mz.gov.pl/wwwfiles/ma_struktura/docs/sprawozdzust_matdziec_20121123.pdf.

Deutscher Ethikrat (2011) *Präimplantationsdiagnostik: Stellungnahme* [Official Opinion of the German Ethics Council on Pre-Implantation Genetic Diagnosis]. Berlin: Deutscher Ethikrat. Available at www.ethikrat.org/dateien/pdf/stellungnahme-praeimplantationsdiagnostik.pdf.

Eberstadt, Nicholas (2010) Russia's Peacetime Demographic Crisis: Dimensions, Causes, Implications, NBR Project Report, May 2010. Seattle, WA: The National Bureau of Asian Research. Available at www.nbr.org/publications/specialreport/pdf/preview/Russia_demography_preview.pdf.

European Court of Human Rights (2012) *Research Report: Bioethics and the Case-Law of the Court*. Available at www.coe.int/t/dg3/healthbioethic/texts_and_documents/Bioethics_and_caselaw_Court_EN.pdf.

European Society for Human Reproduction (2008) *Comparative Analysis of Medically Assisted Reproduction in the EU: Regulation and Technologies*. Final Report. Available at ec.europa.eu/health/blood_tissues_organs/docs/study_eshre_en.pdf.

Geneva Foundation for Medical Education and Research (2012) *Reproductive Health for All: Armenia*. Versoix: GFMER. Available at www.gfmer.ch/Endo/Reprod_health/Reprod_Health_Eastern_Europe/armenia/Armenia_Martirosyan.html

Government of India (2005) *National Guidelines for Accreditation, Supervision and Regulation of ART Clinics in India*. New Delhi: Indian Council of Medical Research.

Helliwell, John F. Richard Layard, and Jeffrey D. Sachs, eds. (2012) *The World Happiness Report*. New York: The Earth Institute, Columbia University. Available at www.earth.columbia.edu/sitefiles/file/Sachs Writing/2012/World Happiness Report.pdf.

Indian Council of Medical Research, *National Guidelines on Accreditation, Supervision, and Regulation of ART Clinics in India* (New Delhi: Ministry of Health and Family Welfare, Indian Council of Medical Research, and National Academy of Medical Sciences, 2005). Available at icmr.nic.in/art/Chapter_3.pdf.

International Forum "Unite to Change Diabetes" (2011) *Diabetes in Russia: Problems and Solutions*. Available at www.novonordisk.com/images/about_us/changing-diabetes/PDF/Leadership forum pdfs/Briefing Books/Russia II.pdf.

International Labor Organization (1996) *Status of Women in India*, Report. Bangkok: ILO Regional Office. Available at www.ilo.org/public/english/region/asro/bangkok/library/download/pub96-01/chapter2.pdf.

Leopoldina Working Group (2011) *Pre-Implantation Genetic Diagnosis: The Effects of Limited Approval in Germany, Ad-Hoc Statement*. Halle: Deutsche Akademie der Naturforscher Leopoldina. Available at www.leopoldina.org/uploads/tx_leopublication/stellungnahme_PID_2011_final_a4ansicht_EN_02.pdf

National Chamber of Physicians (1999) *Kodeks Etyki Lekarskiej* [The Code of Medical Ethics], adopted in Warsaw, December 14, 1991. Available at www.oil.org.pl/xml/nil/wladze/str_zl/zjazd2/uc?rok=1991.

National Statistical Service and Ministry of Health of the Republic of Armenia (2010) *Armenia: Demographic and Health Survey*, Preliminary Report, 2010. Available at www.armstat.am/file/article/dhs_pr_2010_eng.pdf

Parliamentary Assembly of the Council of Europe (2011) Draft Resolution on Pre-Natal Sex Selection. Strasbourg: PACE Committee on Equal Opportunities for Women and Men. A available at www.assembly.coe.int/CommitteeDocs/2011/ASEGAselectionprenataleE.pdf

Serbanescu, Florina, *et al.* (2005) *Reproductive Health Survey Georgia, 2005: Final Report*. Atlanta: United Nations Population Fund.

Steering Committee on Bioethics (2011) *Developments in the Field of Bioethics in Member States, Other States and International Organizations*. Strasbourg: Council of Europe. Available at www.coe.int/t/dg3/healthbioethic/Source/developments 2011.doc.

United Nations Educational, Scientific, and Cultural Organization (2011) *Ethics and Law in Biomedicine and Genetics: An Overview of National Regulations in the Arab States*. Cairo: UNESCO Cairo Office.

United Nations Human Rights Committee (2010) Consideration of Reports Submitted by States Parties Under Article 40 of the Covenant. Concluding Observations of the Human Rights Committee — Poland, adopted in Geneva. October 26, 2010. U.N. Doc. CCPR/C/POL/CO/6. Available at daccess-dds-ny.un.org/doc/UNDOC/GEN/G10/466/84/PDF/G1046684.pdf.

United Nations Population Fund Armenia Country Office (2011) Factsheet on Prevalence and Reasons of Sex Selective Abortions in Armenia, December 19, 2011. Available at unfpa.org/webdav/site/eeca/shared/documents/Sex Selective Abortions-brief_factsheet-Eng.pdf.

United Nations Population Fund Armenia Country Office (2012) *Prevalence and Reasons of Sex Selective Abortions in Armenia.* Yerevan: UNFPA. Available at unfpa.am/sites/default/files/Sex-selective_abortions_report_Eng.pdf.

Vlădescu, Cristian, Gabriela Scântee and Victor Olsavszky (2008) Romania: Health System Review. *WHO Health Systems in Transition*, 10(3):1–181.

World Health Organization (2011) *WHO Model List of Essential Medicines for Adults*, Seventeenth Edition, March 2011. Geneva: WHO. Available at whqlibdoc.who.int/hq/2011/a95053_eng.pdf.

World Health Organization (2012) *Safe Abortions: Technical and Policy Guidance for Health Systems*, Second edition. Geneva: WHO. Available at apps.who.int/iris/bitstream/10665/70914/1/9789241548434_eng.pdf.

World Health Organization (2012) *World Health Statistics 2012*. Geneva: WHO. Available at www.who.int/gho/publications/world_health_statistics/EN_WHS2012_Full.pdf.

Legal Norms

Council of Europe (1950) European Convention of Human Rights; signed in Rome on November 4, 1950 and entered in force on September 3, 1953. Full text available at www.echr.coe.int/Documents/Convention_ENG.pdf.

Council of Europe (1996) Explanatory Report to the Convention on Human Rights and Biomedicine, publication authorized on December 17, 1996. Available at conventions.coe.int/Treaty/En/reports/Html/164.htm.

Council of Europe (1997) Convention for the Protection of Human Rights and Dignity of the Human Being with regard to the Application of Biology and Medicine: Convention on Human Rights and Biomedicine; adopted in Oviedo on April 4, 1997 and entered in force on December 1, 1999. Available at conventions.coe.int/Treaty/en/Treaties/Html/164.htm.

European Parliament (2005) Resolution on the Trade of Human Egg Cells, adopted on March 10, 2005.

Ministry of Health and Family Welfare of the Union of India (2010) Draft Bill on Assisted Reproductive Technologies. Official text available at the Indian Council of Medical Research website, icmr.nic.in/guide/ART REGULATION Draft Bill1.pdf.

Ministry of Health and Social Welfare of the Republic of Poland (1997) Rozporządzenie Ministra Zdrowia i Opieki Społecznej z dnia 22 stycznia 1997 r. w sprawie kwalifikacji zawodowych lekarzy, uprawniających do dokonania przerwania ciąży oraz stwierdzania, że ciąża zagraża życiu lub zdrowiu kobiety lub wskazuje na duże prawdopodobieństwo ciężkiego i nieodwracalnego upośledzenia płodu albo nieuleczalnej choroby zagrażającej jego życiu [Regulation of the Minister of Health and Social Welfare of January 22, 1997, on Professional Qualifications of Physicians Authorized to Carry out Termination of Pregnancy, or Authorized to Certify that the Pregnancy Endangers the Women's Life or Health, or that it Indicates a High Probability of Severe and Irreversible Damage to the Fetus or Incurable Illness Threatening its Life]. *Dziennik Ustaw* [Journal of Laws], 1997, no. 9, item 49.

Ministry of Health and Social Welfare of the Republic of Poland (1990) Zarządzenie Ministra Zdrowia i Opieki Społecznej OZN nr 022/90 z dnia 16 stycznia 1990 r. [Instruction of the Ministry of Health and Social Welfare OZN no. 022/90, of January 16, 1990].

Ministry of Health and Social Welfare of the Republic of Poland (1990) Rozporządzenie Ministra Zdrowia i Opieki Społecznej z dnia 30 kwietnia 1990 r. w sprawie kwalifikacji zawodowych, jakie powinni posiadać lekarze dokonujący zabiegu przerwania ciąży oraz trybu wydawania orzeczeń o dopuszczalności dokonania takiego zabiegu [Regulation of the Minister of Health and Social Welfare of April 30, 1990, on Professional Qualifications of Physicians Authorized to Carry out Termination of Pregnancy and on the Procedure of Issuing Certificates on Admissibility of Pregnancy Termination]. *Dziennik Ustaw* [Journal of Laws], 1990, no. 29, item 178.

Ministry of Health of the Federal Republic of Germany (2013) Verordnung zur Regelung der Präimplantationsdiagnostik (Präimplantationsdiagnostikverordnung, PIDV), vom 21. Februar 2013 [Government Decree on the Regulation of Pre-Implantation Genetic Diagnosis, February 21, 2013]. Available at www.bundesgesundheitsministerium.de/fileadmin/dateien/Downloads/Gesetze_und_Verordnungen/Laufende_Verfahren/P/PID/Verordnung-Regelung-PID_130218.pdf.

Ministry of Health of the People's Republic of Poland (1956) Rozporządzenie Ministra Zdrowia z dnia 11 maja 1956 r. w sprawie przerywania ciąży [Regulation of the Minister of Health of May 11, 1956, on Pregnancy Termination]. *Dziennik Ustaw* [Journal of Laws], 1956, no. 13, item 68.

Ministry of Health of the People's Republic of Poland (1959) Rozporządzenie Ministra Zdrowia z dnia 19 grudnia 1959 r. w sprawie przerywania ciąży [Regulation of the Minister of Health of December 19, 1959, on Pregnancy Termination]. *Dziennik Ustaw* [Journal of Laws], 1960, no. 2, item 15.

Ministry of Health of the Republic of Poland (2012) Rozporządzenie Ministra Zdrowia z dnia 20 września 2012 r. w sprawie standardów postępowania medycznego przy udzielaniu świadczeń zdrowotnych z zakresu opieki okołoporodowej sprawowanej nad kobietą w okresie fizjologicznej ciąży, fizjologicznego porodu, połogu oraz opieki nad noworodkiem [Regulation of the Minister of Health of September 20, 2012, on Standard Operational Procedures in Medical Care over a Woman in Physiological Pregnancy and Physiological Labour, and Over a Newborn]. *Dziennik Ustaw* [Journal of Laws], 2012, item 1100.

Ministry of Health of the Republic of Poland (2012) Rozporządzenie Ministra Zdrowia z dnia 6 grudnia 2012 r. w sprawie świadczeń gwarantowanych z zakresu programów zdrowotnych [Regulation of the Minister of Health of December 6, 2012 on Healthcare Services Financed from Public Funds via Healthcare Programs]. *Dziennik Ustaw* [Journal of Laws], 2012, item 1422.

Ministry of Health of the Republic of Romania (2006) Normele metodologice de aplicare a Capitolului VI. a legii nr. 95 din 2006, publicat în Monitorul Oficial al României, Partea I, nr. 916 din 10 noiembrie 2006 [Ministerial Order No. 1.290 of 2006 on the Methodological Norms for the Application of Chapter VI. of Law No. 95 of 2006]. *Official Gazette*, Part I., No. 916 of November 10, 2006.

Ministry of Health of the Republic of Romania (2009) Ordin nr. 1.156 din 23 septembrie 2009 pentru abrogarea articolului 6 din Normele metodologice de aplicare a titlului VI "Efectuarea prelevării și transplantului de organe, țesuturi și celule de origine umană în scop therapeutic" din Legea nr. 95/2006 privind reforma în domeniul sănătății, aprobate prin Ordinul ministrului sănătății publice nr. 1.290/2006, Monitorul Oficial nr. 640 din 29 septembrie, 2009 [Ministerial Order No. 1.156]. *Official Gazette*, No. 640, September 29, 2009.

Ministry of Health of the Republic of Romania (2012) Lege privind reproducerea umană asistată medical cu terț donator [Draft Law on Third Party Medically Assisted Reproduction; by the Senate in 2012]. Available in at www.cdep.ro/proiecte/2012/000/60/3/se99.pdf.

Ministry of Health of the Republic of Romania and President of the National Health Insurance Agency (2010) Ministerial Order No. 1591/1110 of 2010 on Approving the Technical Norms for the Realization of National Health Programs for 2011 and 2012. *Official Gazette*, No. 53 and No. 53 bis of January 21, 2011, with later modifications and amendment.

Russian Federation (1993) The Constitution of the Russian Federation. Adopted by national referendum on December 12, 1993. Official text available at www.constitution.ru/en/10003000-03.htm

Russian Federation (1996) The Criminal Code of The Russian Federation. Adopted by the State Duma on May 24, 1996. Official text available at www.russian-criminal-code.com.

The Federal Republic of Germany (1949, 2010) Basic Law for the Federal Republic of Germany, revised version published in the *Federal Law Gazette* Part III, classification number 100-1, as last amended by the Act of 21 July 2010 (*Federal Law Gazette* I p. 944); available at www.gesetze-im-internet.de/englisch_gg/englisch_gg.html

The Federal Republic of Germany (1990, 2011) Gesetz zum Schutz von Embryonen (Embryonenschutzgesetz, ESchG) [Embryo Protection Act]. *Bundesgesetzblatt*, I S. 2746 (December 13, 1990), as amended in 2011, *Bundesgesetzblatt*, I S. 2228 (November 21, 2011), "Begrenzte Zulassung" [Restricted Use]. Available at www.gesetze-im-internet.de/eschg/BJNR027460990.html.

The People's Republic of Poland (1956) Ustawa z dnia 27 kwietnia 1956 r. o warunkach dopuszczalności przerywania ciąży [Act of April 27,1956, on Conditions Permitting Pregnancy Termination]. *Dziennik Ustaw* [Journal of Laws], 1956, no. 12, item 61.

The People's Republic of Poland (1956) Ustawa z dnia 5 grudnia 1996 r. o zawodzie lekarza [Act of December 5, 1996 on the Physician's Profession]. *Dziennik Ustaw* [Journal of Laws], 1997, no. 28, item 152.

The People's Republic of Romania (1986) Decret-Lege nr.1 din 26 decembrie 1989 privind abrogarea unor legi, decrete şi alte acte normative. *Monitorul Oficial*, nr. 4/27 decembrie 1989 [Decree No. 1 of December 26, 1989 repealing Decrees 770/1966 and 441/1985, as well as Articles 185–188 of the Penal Code on Abortion. *Official Gazette*, No. 4 of December 27, 1989].

The Republic of Armenia (2002) Act no. 474 of December 11, 2002 on Human Reproductive Health and Rights to Reproduction. Available in Armenian at www.parliament.am/legislation.php?sel=show&ID=1339&lang=arm.

The Republic of Georgia (1997) Act of December 10, 1997 on Health Care.

The Republic of Poland (1993) Ustawa z dnia 3 stycznia 1993 r. o planowaniu rodziny, ochronie płodu ludzkiego i warunkach dopuszczalności przerywania ciąży [Act of January 7, 1993 on Family Planning, Protection of the Human Fetus and Conditions Permitting Pregnancy Termination]. *Dziennik Ustaw* [Journal of Laws], 1993, no. 17, item 78 with later amendments.

The Republic of Poland (1995) Ustawa z dnia 30 marca 1995 r. o zmianie ustawy o planowaniu rodziny, ochronie płodu ludzkiego i warunkach dopuszczalności przerywania ciąży [Act of March 30, 1995, on Amending the Act on Family Planning, Protection of the Human Fetus and Conditions Permitting Pregnancy Termination]. *Dziennik Ustaw* [Journal of Laws], 1995, no. 66, item 334.

The Republic of Poland (1996) Ustawa z dnia 30 sierpnia 1996 r. o zmianie ustawy o planowaniu rodziny, ochronie płodu ludzkiego i warunkach dopuszczalności przerywania ciąży oraz o zmianie niektórych innych ustw [Act of August 30, 1996, on Amending the Act on Family Planning, Protection of the Human Fetus and Conditions Permitting Pregnancy Termination, and Amending Other Acts]. *Dziennik Ustaw* [Journal of Laws], 1996, no.139, item 646.

The Republic of Poland (2004) Ustawa z dnia z dnia 27 sierpnia 2004 r. o świadczeniach opieki zdrowotnej finansowanych ze środków publicznych [Act of August 27, 2004, on Healthcare Services Provided from Public Funds]. *Dziennik Ustaw* [Journal of Laws], 2004, no. 210, item 2135, with later amendments.

The Republic of Romania (2006) Legea nr. 95 din 14 aprilie 2006 privind reforma în domeniul sănătăţii, Capitolul VI, cu Anexele I-XIII, şi normele metodologice de aplicare a Capitolului VI, adoptat pe 14 aprilie 2006, publicat în Monitorul Oficial nr. 372 din 28 aprilie 2006 [Law No. 95 of 2006 on the Reform of the Health Care System, Chapter VI on the Procurement and Transplant of Human Organs, Tissues and Cells for Therapeutic purposes, with the Annexes I–XIII, and Methodological Norms of Application, adopted on April 14, 2006, entered into force on May 1, 2006, amended later]. *Official Gazette*, No. 372 of April 28, 2006.

The Republic of Romania (2011) Noul Cod Civil Republicat 2011. Legea 287/2009 privind Codul Civil [Law 287/2009 on the New Civil Code of Romania, in force as of October 1, 2011]. *Official Gazette*, Part I., No. 505 of July 15, 2011.

The Republic of Serbia (2005) Zakon o zdravstvenoj zaštiti [Act on Health Care]. *Službeni glasnik Republike Srbije*, broj 107/2005, 72/2009—dr. zakon, 88/2010, 99/2010, 57/2011 i 119/2012. Available at www.paragraf.rs/propisi/zakon_o_zdravstvenoj_zastiti.html.

The Republic of Serbia (2006) Ustav Republike Srbije [The Constitution of the Republic of Serbia]. *Službeni glasnik Republike Srbije*, broj 98/2006.

The Republic of Serbia (2009) Zakon o lečenju neplodnosti postupcima biomedicinski potpomognutog oplođenja [Act on the Treatment of Infertility by Biomedically Assisted Fertilization Procedures]. *Službeni glasnik Republike Srbije*, broj 72/2009. Available at www.zakon.co.rs/zakon-o-lecenju-neplodnosti-postupcima-biomedicinski-potpomognutog-oplodjenja.html.

The Union of India (1949) The Constitution of India, Part III, Fundamental Rights. Official text available at indiacode.nic.in/coiweb/coifiles/part.htm.

United Nations Educational, Scientific, and Cultural Organization (1997) The Universal Declaration on the Human Genome and Human Rights. Paris: UNESCO. Official text available at portal.unesco.org/en/ev.php-URL_ID=13177&URL_DO=DO_TOPIC&URL_SECTION=201.html.

Court Cases

European Court of Human Rights

Glass v. United Kingdom. ECtHR, application no. 61827/00, judgment of March 9, 2004.

Evans v. the United Kingdom. ECtHR, application no. 6339/05, judgment of March 7, 2006.

Dickson v. the United Kingdom. ECtHR, application no. 44362/04, judgment of December 4, 2007.

Tysiąc v. Poland. ECtHR, application no. 5410/03, judgment of March 21, 2007.

S.H. and Others v. Austria. ECtHR, application no. 5781/00, judgment of November 3, 2011.

Ternovszky v. Hungary. ECtHR, application no. 67545/09, judgment of December 14, 2010.

A, B and C v. Ireland. ECtHR, application no. 25579/05, judgment of December 16, 2010.

R.R. v. Poland. ECtHR, application no. 27617/04, judgment of May 26, 2011.

Costa and Pavan v. Italy. ECtHR, application no. 54270/10, judgment of August 28, 2012.

P and S v. Poland. ECtHR, application no. 57375/08, judgment of October 30, 2012.
Z v. Poland. ECtHR, application no. 46123/08, judgment of November 13, 2012.
Knecht v. Romania. ECtHR, application no. 10048/10, judgment of October 2, 2012, final judgment of February 11, 2013.

Court of Justice of the European Union

Oliver Brüstle v. Greenpeace e.V. ECJ, Case C–34/10, judgment of October 18, 2011.

Court Cases from Other Jurisdictions

Johnson vs. Calvert. Supreme Court of California, 5 Cal.4th 84, 851 P.2d 776, judgment of March 20, 1993.
Ruth Nahmani v. Daniel Nahmani and Others. CFH 2401/95, Civil Appeal 5587/93, Supreme Court judgment of March 30, 1995.
Baby Manji Yamada v. Union of India and Anr. Supreme Court of India, 2008 I.N.S.C. 1656 (India), writ petition (C) No. 369 of 2008, judgment of September 29, 2008.
Jan Balaz v. Anand Municipality. High Court of Gujarat at Ahmedabad, Letters Patent Appeal No. 2151 of 2009 with Special Civil Application No. 3020 of 2009, judgment of November 11, 2009.

Newspaper Articles and Online News

Amnesty International (2011) Egypt: Admission of Forced 'Virginity Tests' Must Lead to Justice. *Amnesty International*, May 31 2011. Available at www.amnesty.org/en/news-and-updates/egypt-admission-forced-virginity-tests-must-lead-justice-2011-05-31.
Amnesty International (2012) Egypt: A Year after 'Virginity Tests', Women Victims of Army Violence Still Seek Justice. *Amnesty International*, March 9, 2012. Available at www.amnesty.org/en/news/egypt-year-after-virginity-tests-women-victims-army-violence-still-seek-justice-2012-03-09.
ARKA (2012) Census: Number of Population Available in Armenia 2,781,771, Number of Registered Population 3,018,854. *ARKA News Agency*, October 31, 2012. Available at arka.am/en/news/society/census_number_of_popu-lation_available_in_armenia_2_781_771_number_of_registered_popula-tion_3_018_854/.
Awadalla, Ahmed (2011) Tunisian Film on Virginity Stirs Debate at Cairo Screening. *Egypt Independent*, June 9, 2011. Available at www.egyptindependent.com/news/tunisian-film-virginity-stirs-debate-cairo-screening.
B. I. M. (2012) Vita az élet feletti döntés jogáról [Debate on the Right to Decide over Life]. *Népszava Online*, May 23, 2012. Available at www.nepszava.hu/articles/article.php?id=553101.

B92 (2011) Palma finansira, ljudi ženite se [Palma is paying, get married people]. *B92*, June 6, 2011. Available at www.b92.net/biz/vesti/srbija. php?yyyy=2011&mm=06&dd=04&nav_id=516701.

Bakró Nagy, Ferenc and Péter Szabó (2012) A magyarok abortusszal teszik boldoggá a Sátánt [Hungarians Make the Satan Happy with Abortion]. *Index. hu Video*, May 23, 2012. Available at index.hu/video/2012/05/23/abortuszellenes_tuntetes/.

Barrett, Stephen (2012) The Shady Side of Embryonic Stem Cell Therapy. *Quackwatch*, September 14, 2012. Available at www.quackwatch.org/06ResearchProjects/stemcell.html.

Barsoumian, Nanore (2011) The Baby Doom: Selective Abortions in Armenia, *The Armenian Weekly*, November 23, 2011; available at www.armenianweekly. com/2011/11/23/the-baby-doom-selective-abortions-in-armenia/.

BBC (2012) Egypt's Sexual Harassment of Women 'Epidemic'. *BBC News*, September 3, 2012. Available at www.bbc.co.uk/news/world-middle-east-19440656.

Blackburn-Starza, Antony (2012) No Violation of Human Rights in Romanian Egg Storage Case, European Court Says. *BioNews*, No. 682, November 19, 2012. Available at www.bionews.org.uk/page_213876.asp.

Blic (2012) Palma "venčao" žirafe i poslao poruku gejevima [Palma "Marries" Giraffes and Sends a Message to Gays]. *Blic*, October 9, 2012. Available at www. blic.rs/Vesti/Srbija/346879/Pama-vencao-zirafe-i-poslao-poruku-gejevima.

Breyer, Hiltrud (2005) Egg Cells Trade Endangers the European Union as a Community of Values. *BioNews*, No. 310, June 6, 2005. Available at www. bionews.org.uk/page_37805.asp.

Bucsy, Levente (2012) Ez a tabletta nem lesz bevezetve Magyarországon [This Pill Will Not Be Introduced in Hungary]. *Magyar Nemzet Online,* May 23, 2012. Available at mno.hu/belfold/ez-a-tabletta-nem-lesz-bevezetve-magyarorszagon-1078255.

Bundesministerium für Gesundheit, Kabinett macht endgültig den Weg für Regelungen zur Präimplantationsdiagnostik frei. *Bundesministerium für Gesundheit Pressemitteilung*, February 19, 2013 [Cabinet Finally Agrees to the Regulation of Pre-implantation Genetic Diagnosis, Press Release on February 19, 2013]. Available at www.bmg.bund.de/ministerium/presse/pressemitteilungen/2013-01/weg-frei-fuer-pid-regelungen.html.

China Daily (2006) China: Drug Bid to Beat Child Ban. *China Daily*, February 14, 2006. Available at www.chinadaily.com.cn/english/doc/2006-02/14/content_520025.htm.

China Daily (2007) Over 1,900 Officials Breach Birth Policy in China. *China Daily*, July 8, 2007. Available at www.chinadaily.com.cn/china/2007-07/08/content_912620.htm.

Családháló.hu (2012) Hogy pusztítja el a magzatot az abortusztabletta? [How Does the Abortion Pill Destroy the Fetus?]. *Magyar Nemzet Online*, May 28, 2012. Available at mno.hu/csaladhalo/hogy-pusztitja-el-a-magzatot-az-abortusztabletta-1079204.

Csuhaj, Ildikó (2012) A KDNP megfúrta a tablettát? [Has KNDP Dodged the Pill?]. *NOL,* May 22, 2012. Available at nol.hu/lap/mo/20120522-a_kdnp_ megfurta_a_tablettat.

Danilova, Maria (2005) Russians Ignore Risks, Seek Stem-Cell Therapy. *The Seattle Times,* March 14, 2005. Available at seattletimes.com/html/nation-world/2002206894_russstem14.html

Danó, Anna (2012) Szócska Miklós nem tilthat, van tabletta [Miklós Szócska Cannot Ban the Pill]. *NOL,* May 23, 2012. Available at nol.hu/belfold/20120523-van_tabletta.

Demoscope (2010) O demograficheskoy situatsii v Rossii [On the Demographic Situation in Russia]. *Demoscope Weekly,* 431–432, August 23, 2010. Available at demoscope.ru/weekly/2010/0431/gazeta019.php.

Desai, Kishwar (2012) India's Surrogate Mothers Are Risking Their Lives: They Urgently Need Protection. *The Guardian,* June 5, 2012.

Dreissiger, Ágnes (2012) Abortuszszigorítást kényszerítene ki az Alaptörvény? [Could the Fundamental Law Lead to a Tightening of Abortion Regulation?]. *HVG.hu,* January 21, 2012; available at hvg.hu/itthon/20120119_alkotmany_abortusz.

Fadel, Leila (2011) Egyptian Court Bans Virginity Tests on Female Detainees. *The Washington Post,* December 27, 2011. Available at articles.washingtonpost.com/2011-12-27/world/35285121_1_virginity-tests-samira-ibrahim-tests-on-female-detainees.

Flock, Elizabeth (2012) Morocco Outraged Over Suicide of Amina Filali, Who Was Forced to Marry Her Rapist. *The Washington Post,* March 15, 2012. Available at www.washingtonpost.com/blogs/blogpost/post/morocco-outraged-over-suicide-of-amina-filali-who-was-forced-to-marry-her-rapist/2012/03/15/gIQApTq4DS_blog.html.

Friedman, Ron (2010) J'lem Man Struggles to Bring Twin Sons Home from India. *The Jerusalem Post,* May 10, 2010. Available at www.jpost.com/International/Article.aspx?id=175147.

Gallagher, James (2012) Pre-Implantation Genetic Diagnosis for IVF Is 'Safe'. *BBC News,* July 3, 2012. Available at www.bbc.co.uk/news/health-18676894.

Grad Jagodina (2012) O gradu—Stanovnistvo [The City of Jagodina, On the City—Its Population]. Available at www.jagodina.org.rs/o-gradu/stanovnistvo/.

Grad Jagodina (2012) Vesti [The City of Jagodina, News]. Available at www.jagodina.org.rs/vesti/.

Greif, James (2012) New Study Examines How Health Affects Happiness. *George Mason University News,* November 13, 2012. Available at newsdesk.gmu.edu/2012/11/new-study-examines-how-health-affects-happiness/.

Grigoryan, Marianna (2011) Armenia: Are Selective Abortions Behind Birth Ratio Imbalance? *EurasiaNet,* July 6, 2011. Available at www.eurasianet.org/node/63812.

Grigoryan, Marianna (2012) Armenian Women Turn to Ulcer Medication for Do-It-Yourself Abortions. *EurasiaNet,* October 30, 2012. Available at www.eurasianet.org/node/66124.

Haworth, Abigail (2007) Womb for Rent: Surrogate Mothers in India. WebMD Feature from *Marie Claire* Magazine, July 29, 2007. Available at www.webmd.com/ infertility-and-reproduction/features/womb-rent-surrogate-mothers-india.

Hirado.hu (2012) Nem lesz abortusztabletta Magyarországon [There Will Not Be an Abortion Pill in Hungary]. *Magyar Hírlap Online*, May 23, 2012. Available at www.magyarhirlap.hu/node/323585.

Hoffman, Matthew Cullinan (2011) Hungary Sponsors Bold Pro-Life Campaign with EU Money: Eurocrats Enraged. *LifeSiteNews.com*, June 15, 2011. Available at www.lifesitenews.com/news/hungary-sponsors-bold-pro-life-campaign-with-eu-money-eurocrats-enraged.

Index, A magzatvédők szerint az abortusztabletta a rejtőzködő fasizmus eszköze [According to the Pro-Life Advocates, the Abortion Pill Is a Means of Clandestine Fascism]. *Index*, May 23, 2012. Available at index.hu/belfold/2012/05/23/a_ magzatvedok_szerint_az_abortusztabletta_a_rejtozkodo_fasizmus_eszkoze/.

Janwalkar, Mayura (2012) 17-Yr-Old Egg Donor Dead, HC Questions Fertility Center's Role. *The Indian Express*, July 12, 2012.

Jobbágyi, Zsófia (2012) Napi százötven magzatot ölnek meg hazánkban [Hundred and Fifty Fetuses Are Killed Each Day in Our Country]. *Magyar Hírlap Online*, May 24, 2012. Available at www.magyarhirlap.hu/belfold/napi_szazotven_magzatot_olnek_meg_hazankban.html.

Kadyshev, Yevgeniy (2013) Gollandskiye i rossiyskiye universitety sozdayut nauchno-issledovatel'skiy tsentr [Dutch and Russian Universities Create Scientific Research Center]. *TG Daily*, April 13, 2013. Available at tgdaily.ru/?p=1669.

Kapronczay, Stefánia and Melinda Zsolt (2012) Alkotmányos támogatás az abortuszturizmusnak? [Constitutional Support for Abortion Tourism?]. *A TASZ jelenti Blog* [TASZ Reports], September 28, 2012. Available at ataszjelenti.blog. hu/2012/09/28/alkotmanyos_tamogatas_az_abortuszturizmusnak.

Kassab, Bisan and Mahmoud Rana (2012) The Widespread Plague of Sexual Harassment in Egypt. *Al-Akhbar*, September 20, 2012. Available at english. al-akhbar.com/node/12456.

Klinika Stvolovykh Kletok 'Noveyshaya Meditsina' [Stem Cell Clinic 'New Medicine'] (n.d.) *Zhizn' bez starosti* [Life without Aging]. Available at www. stvolkletki.ru/articles/2.html.

Komersant (2004) Russian Men Live 19 Years Less than Men in Developed Countries. *Kommersant*, December 1, 2004. Available at www.kommersant.com/p-3446/r_500/ Russian_Men_Live_19_Years_Less_than_Men_in_Developed_Countries/.

Kreiger, Zvika (2013) Forget Marriage Equality; Israeli Gays Want Surrogacy Rights. *The Atlantic*, April 4, 2013. www.theatlantic.com/international/archive/2013/04/forget-marriage-equality-israeli-gays-want-surrogacy-rights/274639/, last accessed on May 30, 2013.

LaFraniere, Sharon (2012) Mainland Chinese Flock to Hong Kong to Have Babies, *The New York Times*, February 22, 2012. Available at www.nytimes. com/2012/02/23/world/asia/mainland-chinese-flock-to-hong-kong-to-have-babies.html.

Lee, Stephanie M. (2012) Commercial Surrogacy Grows in India. *The San Francisco Gate*, October 20, 2012. Available at www.sfgate.com/health/article/Commercial-surrogacy-grows-in-India-3968312.php.

Lesova, Polya (2009) Russian Stem Cell Firm Hopes to Raise $5.5 million in IPO. *MarketWatch*, October 7, 2009. Available at www.marketwatch.com/story/stem-cell-firm-launches-first-russian-ipo-2009-10-07.

Lobzina, Alina (2012) Russia in the Middle of World Happiness Rankings. *The Moscow News*, April 5, 2012. Available at themoscownews.com/russia/20120405/189593174.html

Maganzi, Aviel (2011) Dead Guard Raised Three Children, Only Two Orphans. *Y-Net News*, May 22, 2011. Available at www.ynet.co.il/articles/0,7340,L-4072254,00.html.

Magyar Hírlap (2012) Nem tervez változást a Fidesz az abortusz szabályozásában [Fidesz Does Not Plan to Modify the Abortion Regulation]. *Magyarhirlap.hu*, September 27, 2012. Available at www.magyarhirlap.hu/egeszsegugy/nem-tervez-valtozast-a-fidesz-az-abortusz-szabalyozasaban.

Magyar Távirati Iroda (2012) "Nemzeti vészkorszak" Együtt tilakozott Semjén, Dúró és Novák ["Holocaust of the Nation": Semjén, Dúró, and Novák Protest Together]. *ATV.hu*, May 23, 2012. Available at atv.hu/cikk/20120523_politikusok_is_tiltakoztak_az_abortusztabletta_bevezetese_ellen.

Magyar Távirati Iroda (2012) Abortusztabletta: együtt tüntet a Novák család és Semjén [Abortion Pill: The Novák Family and Semjén Protest Together]. *HVG.hu*, May 23, 2012. Available at hvg.hu/itthon/20120523_abortusztabletta_tuntetes.

Magyar Távirati Iroda (2012) Az MSzP támogatja az abortusztablettát [The MSzP Supports the Abortion Pill]. *HVG.hu*, March 23, 2012. Available at hvg.hu/itthon/20120523_abortusztabletta_mszp.

Magyar Távirati Iroda (2012) Szócska: Hazánkban nem kerül forgalomba az abortusztabletta [Szócska: The Abortion Pill Will Not Be Marketed in Our Homeland]. *Fidesz.hu*, May 22, 2012. Available at www.fidesz.hu/index.php?Cikk=180909.

Magyar Távirati Iroda [Hungarian Cable Bureau] (2005) Még idén bevezethetik az abortusztablettát Magyarországon [The Abortion Pill Might Be Introduced in Hungary Already This Year]. *Velvet.hu*, June 7, 2005. Available at velvet.hu/onleany/abort0607/.

Mandić, B. (2011) Sve brojnije bebe 'sa leda' [More and More Babies 'from Ice']. *Vesti online*, Jun 24, 2011. Available at www.vesti-online.com/ Vesti/Srbija/146404/Sve-brojnije-bebe-sa-leda.

Matalin, Dóra (2012) Részvét nélkül [Without Compassion]. *NOL*, May 22, 2012. Available at nol.hu/belfold/20120522-reszvet_nelkul.

Mishra, Lata (2012) An Apartment Just for Surrogate Moms. *Mumbai Mirror*, May 29, 2012.

Muhari, Judit (2012) Férfiak hajtják el az abortusztablettát [It Is Men Who Drive Away the Abortion Pill]. *Népszava Online*, May 22, 2012. Available at www.nepszava.hu/articles/article.php?id=552689.

Népszabadság Online (2012) Engedélyezték Magyarországon is az abortusz tablettát [The Abortion Pill Has Been Licensed in Hungary, As Well]. *NOL,* May 19, 2012. Available at nol.hu/belfold/engedelyeztek_magyarorszagon_ is_az_abortusz_tablettat.

Népszabadság Online (2012) Vészharangot kongattak az abortusztabletta miatt [Ringing Alarm Bells Because of the Abortion Pill]. *NOL,* May 23, 2012. Available at nol.hu/belfold/veszharangot_kongattak_az_abortusztabletta_miatt.

Nobel Committee for Physiology and Medicine (2012) The Nobel Prize in Physiology or Medicine 2012. Stockholm: Karolinska Insitute. Available at www. nobelprize.org/nobel_prizes/medicine/laureates/2012/popular-medicine-prize2012.pdf

Nobel Media AB (2012) The 2012 Nobel Prize in Physiology or Medicine: Popular Information. *Nobelprize.org,* November 27, 2012. Available at www.nobel-prize.org/nobel_prizes/medicine/laureates/2012/popular.html.

Nyusztay, Máté (2012) Koszos lábú hangulatkeltők, szemét haszonlesők—így vitázott a "T." Ház [Dirty Footed Malcontents, Trashy Profiteers—Thus Clashed the "Honorable" House]. *NOL,* May 21, 2012. Available at nol.hu/ belfold/hangulatkeltesnek_koszos_a_laba_-_a_parlamentbol_jelentjuk.

Osservatorio Balcani e Caucaso (2011) Domestic Violence in Serbia: The Law Is Not Enough. *OBC News,* May 19, 2011. Available at www.balcanicaucaso. org/eng/Regions-and-countries/Serbia/Domestic-violence-in-Serbia-the-law-is-not-enough-94265.

Parfitt, Tom (2005) Beauty Salons Fuel Trade in Aborted Babies. *The Guardian,* April 17, 2005. Available at www.guardian.co.uk/world/2005/apr/17/ukraine. russia.

Patent Association Activists (2011) Variációk egy szándékra—Nyíltan a burkolt abortuszszigorításról [Variations of an Intention—Speaking Openly on a Hidden Tightening of Abortion Regulation]. *Abortusz.info,* July 13, 2011. Available at abortusz.info/hirek/hirek/variaciok-egy-szandekra-nyiltan-a-burkolt-abortuszszigoritasrol.

Penasa, Simone (2012) European Court of Human Rights Declared Incoherent and Disproportionate the Italian Ban on Preimplantation Genetic Diagnosis. *Bioethics International,* September 15, 2012. Available at www.bioethicsin-ternational.org/blog/2012/09/15/european-court-of-human-rights-declared-incoherent-and-disproportionate-italian-ban-of-preimplantation-genetic-diagnosis-pdg/.

Phillips, Melanie (2010) From the Archive: Airport Virginity Tests Banned by Rees. *The Guardian,* February 3, 2010. Available at www.guardian.co.uk/ uk/2010/feb/03/airport-virginity-tests-banned.

Puar, Jaspir (2010) Israel's Gay Propaganda War. *The Guardian,* July 1, 2010.

Puppinck, Grégor (2011) European Court of Human Rights Hears Italian Bioethics Case. *Lifenews,* September 14, 2011. Available at www.lifenews. com/2011/09/14/european-court-of-human-rights-hears-italian-bioethics-case/.

Rebrov, Dmitriy (2012) Tserkov' dovol'na novym zakonoproyektom o stvolovykh kletkakh [Church Is Content with the New Bill on Stem Cell Research]. *Zhurnal o pravoslavnoy zhizni Neskuchnyy Sad* [Neskuchnyy Sad: Journal of Orthodox Life], April 26, 2012. Available at www.nsad.ru/articles/cerkov-dovolna-novym-zakonoproektom-o-stvolovyh-kletkah.

Roberts, Helen and Frances Hardy (2012) Our 'Rent a Womb' Child from an Indian Baby Farm: British Couple Paying £20,000 for a Desperately Poor Single Mother to Have Their Child. *The Daily Mail*, August 31, 2012.

Russia Today (2012) Medical Mystery over Discarded Fetuses: Stem-Cell Research or Illegal Abortions? *Russia Today*, July 24, 2012. Available at rt.com/news/russia-embryos-abortions-955/.

Saenz, Aaron (2010) Did A Russian Scientist Really 'Cure Aging' or Is It Just a Fluke? *Singularity Hub*, September 21, 2010. Available at singularityhub.com/2010/09/21/did-a-russian-scientist-really-cure-aging-or-is-it-just-a-fluke-video/.

Sakevich, Viktoriya (2012) Novyye ogranicheniya prava na abort v Rossii [New Restriction on Abortion Rights in Russia]. *Demoscope Weekly*, 499–500, February 20, 2012. Available at demoscope.ru/weekly/2012/0499/reprod02.php

Schemm, Paul (2012) Amina Filali, Morocco Rape Victim, Commits Suicide after Forced Marriage To Rapist. *The Huffington Post*, March 14, 2012. Available at www.huffingtonpost.com/2012/03/14/amina-filali-morocco-rape_n_1345171.html.

Science Guide (2011) Germany Allows for Controversial PID. *ScienceGuide*, July 26, 2011. Available at www.scienceguide.nl/201107/germany-allows-for-controversial-pid.aspx.

Smith-Spark, Laura and Peter Taggart (2013), Husband Testifies His Wife Died after Abortion Was Denied in Ireland. *CNN*, April 8, 2013. Available at edition.cnn.com/2013/04/08/world/europe/ireland-abortion-controversy.

Sobolevskaya, Olga (2012) V Skolkovo sozdadut tsentr izucheniya stvolovykh kletok [Center to Study Stem Cells Will Be Established in Skolkovo]. *The Voice of Russia Radio*, October 5, 2012. Available at rus.ruvr.ru/2012_10_05/V-Skolkovo-sozdadut-centr-izuchenija-stvolovih-kletok/

Spiegel, der (2011) Controversial Genetic Tests: German Parliament Allows Some Genetic Screening. *Spiegel Online*, July 7, 2011. Available at www.spiegel.de/international/germany/controversial-genetic-tests-german-parliament-allows-some-embryo-screening-a-773054.html.

Stolyarova, Galina (2008) Experts: Russia Hit by Cancer Epidemic. *The St. Petersburg Times*, 1345, February, 5, 2008. Available at www.sptimesrussia.com/index.php?action_id=2&story_id=24903.

Szinapszis (2011) Lehet-e magánügy az abortusz? — Kutatás [Could Abortion Be a Private Matter? — Research Results]. *Webbeteg.hu*, March 22, 2011. Available at www.webbeteg.hu/cikkek/egeszseges/10647/lehet-e-maganugy-az-abortusz.

Szócska, Miklós (2012) Közlemény az abortusztabletta engedélyezéséről [Announcement on the licensing of the abortion pill]. *Kormányportál* [Government Portal], May 23, 2012. Available at www.kormany.hu/hu/emberi-eroforrasok-miniszteriuma/egeszsegugyert-felelos-allamtitkarsag/hirek/kozlemeny-az-abortusztabletta-engedelyezeserol.

Timerbulatov, Vil (2013) Meditsina XXI Veka: Stvolovyye kletki—vozmozhnosti ogromny [Medicine of XXI Century: Stem Cells—Enormous Opportunities]. *Vechernyaya Ufa*, March 22, 2013. Available at vechufa.ru/medicine/1426-stvolovye-kletki-vozmozhnosti-ogromny.html.

University Medical Center Groningen (2012) Dutch Scientists to Open Institute for Stem Cell Research in Russia. *UMCG Press Release*, October 2, 2012. Available at www.umcg.nl/EN/corporate/News/Pages/Dutchscientist-stoopeninstituteforstemcellresearchinRussia.aspx, last accessed on May 17, 2013.

Wunderli, László (W. L.) (2012) Tiltakoznak az abortusztabletta ellen [Demonstration against the Abortion Pill]. *Magyar Nemzet Online*, May 21, 2012. Available at mno.hu/magyar_nemzet_belfoldi_hirei/tiltakoznak-az-abortusztabletta-ellen-1077535.

ABOUT THE AUTHORS

Anna Borbála Bodolai has graduated at the Legal Studies Department of the Central European University, Budapest. She has been following the German public debate on the regulation of Pre-implantation Genetic Diagnosis (PGD) since 2010, when she worked at a Hungarian foreign-policy newspaper as a journalist. While studying at Central European University, she wrote her thesis on the comparison of regulating PGD in the United Kingdom and in Germany, and also had the opportunity to conduct research on the issue at the German Reference Centre for Ethics in the Life Sciences (DRZE) in Dresden.

Weronika Chańska, is a graduate of the Centre for Inter-Faculty Individual Studies in the Humanities, Warsaw University with a master's degree in philosophy and a graduate of the Helsinki Foundation School of Human Rights. She is an assistant professor at the Medical College of Jagiellonian University. Her research interests focus on the concept of quality of life and reproductive ethics. Currently she is involved in an international cooperation analyzing the ethical aspects of prenatal diagnosis and care for extremely premature infants. She is the author of *Nieszczęsny dar życia* [The Unfortunate Gift of Life] (Warsaw, 2009) and co-editor of *Bioethics for Medical Professionals*. She is a member of Bioethics Committee of the Polish Academy of Sciences and a member of executive board of the Polish Unit of the UNESCO Chair in Bioethics.

Enikő Demény is a Researcher at the Central European University, Center for Ethics and Law in Biomedicine (CELAB). She has a Ph.D. in Philosophy (2006). Previously she studied sociology, anthropology and gender studies. Between 1998 and 2009 she was a Visiting Lecturer at the Babes-Bolyai University, where she offered, among other courses an MA seminar on *Family, Identity and Gender in the Age of Genetics*. Her research interest include: the social, ethical, legal and policy impacts of new converging technologies; social science and bioethics, gender and science, feminist epistemology, the anthropology of international bioethics governance.

Mariam Gagoshashvili is a queer feminist based in Tbilisi, Georgia. She holds a BA in Social Psychology from the Tbilisi State University, Georgia and an MA in Gender Studies from the Central European University, Hungary. In 2007, after returning from Berlin where she spent a year studying at the European College of Liberal Arts, she started working at a local feminist grant-making organization, the Women's Fund in Georgia, where she presently works as a Program Coordinator. She is also a lecturer in the Gender Studies MA program at the Tbilisi State University, Georgia.

Debjyoti Ghosh is a human rights lawyer from India. He did his BA LLB at the Department of Law, University of Calcutta (India) and his LLM in human rights from Central European University, Budapest (Hungary). Currently, he is pursuing his SJD at Central European University where he is researching on the Right to Health for Transgender populations in India, Brazil, and South Africa. Professionally, he has been associated with various projects in India funded by the UNDP, DFID and, most recently, the Global Fund. His work has revolved around community strengthening, legal literacy, HIV support and public interest litigation, focusing on MSM, Transgender and Hijra populations.

Shushan Harutyunyan is a journalist and editor specialized in online media and women's representation. She holds a BA in Journalism at Yerevan State University and an MA in Gender Studies at the Central European University, Budapest. She is currently working as chief editor of the online version of Cosmopolitan Armenia and she has experience of working in news media for seven years including editing social and political daily newspaper and running a debate TV program. She is a recipient of the Na-Ne woman journalists' award given by the British Council and OSCE, and the youngest honored speaker at TEDx Yerevan 2011 under TED license. Her current academic interests include gender privacy issues in social networking sites.

April Hovav is a doctoral student in Sociology and Gender Studies at the University of Southern California. She earned a BA in Women's Studies from Barnard College in 2007 and an MA in Gender Studies from Central European University in 2011. Her current research is on transnational surrogacy.

Orio Ikebe studied and conducted research on glycosphingolipids in lung cancer cells at Gakushuin University and Tokyo University, then studied bioethics, medical anthropology, and medical and social sciences in Leuven University in Belgium. She joined UNESCO in 2000 at the Bioethics Section of the Social and Human Sciences Sector in Paris. Since 2007, she has been working at the Cairo Office of UNESCO as a focal point for UNESCO's projects on bioethics, as well as ethics of science and technologies in the Arab Region.

Slavica Karajičić has graduated from Public Administration. In 2011 she received a scholarship from European Commission as outstanding student and became an ErasmusMundus student of the European Master in Sustainable Regional Health System. In 2012, she was a junior fellow-researcher at the Center for Ethics and Law in Biomedicine (CELAB), Budapest, Hungary researching on the topic Perspectives of IVF/ICSI methods in Serbia and Hungary: Comparative Analysis. As a junior researcher, she joined Health Policy Institute in March 2013 and made research on Policy on Assisted Reproduction in the Slovak Republic.

Aleksandar Krstić is working as clinical embryologist at a private clinic for gynecology, and he is an ESHRE certified embryologist from 2011. Currently, he is a PhD student at the Department for Cell and Tissue Biology at the University of Belgrade, Serbia, working on the role of zinc in the maturation of oocytes. He is also collaborator on the project "Energy Efficient Synthesis and Investigation Surface Occurrences on Selected Oxide Materials" at the Faculty of Natural Sciences and Mathematics of the University of Banja Luka, Bosnia and Herzegovina.

Anna Mondekova is a graduate student of Gender Studies at the Central European University in Budapest, Hungary. She earned her first Master's degree in Communications from the University of Constantine the Philosopher in Slovakia where she focused on media representations of women and feminism. After graduating, Anna spent a year working and studying in Cairo with special interest in population issues and reproductive health. Currently, she works as a consultant at the Institute for Gender Equality in Slovakia where her main activities include identifying regional challenges in relation to gender equality and equal opportunities as well as designing awareness raising campaigns.

Ljiljana Pantović is a Serbian anthropologist and ethnologist. Her previous education (BA and MA) was at the University of Belgrade and is currently finishing a second masters in Gender Studies at the Central European University, Budapest. Her research interest is in political anthropology and anthropology of policies, with special emphasis on gender.

Ioana Petre is a doctoral candidate in Political Theory and Human Rights at the Central European University, Budapest. Her research interests range from ethics and bioethics to theories of justice and applied justice. The topic of her dissertation, "Genetic Justice and Future Generations," explores the way in which the distribution of genetic interventions among the present generation affects the interests and wellbeing of future generations.

Yuliya Pleshakova is a Master's student at the Department of Gender Studies of the Central European University, Budapest. Born and raised in Kazakhstan, in 2008 she graduated from La Roche College in Pittsburgh, USA, completing Honors Directed Research on female and male adult same-sex friendships and receiving a William James Award for the Highest Academic Achievement and Excellent Scholarship in the field of psychology. At present, she is researching men's family role attitudes in contemporary Kazakhstan in light of the alleged crisis or, as some researchers claim, a transformation from patriarchal toward more egalitarian form of the male role in the domestic sphere.

Gordana Radović Tripinović is currently a PhD student at the Department of Political Science, University of Belgrade, where she also works as a researcher at the Center for Ecological Policy and Sustainable Development (CEPOR). Her PhD thesis is on "Public services and sustainable development." She holds an MA from Public Administration and Local Government and has published articles on sustainable development and education.

Joanna Różyńska holds academic degrees in the fields of law, philosophy, sociology, and bioethics. She is an Assistant Professor at the University of Warsaw, Institute of Philosophy (ethics and bioethics), and at the Warsaw University of Physical Education (bioethics and medical law). Her research interests focus on procreative ethics and research ethics. She is an author of numerous scientific publications, including two books: *From Zygote to Person: Potentiality, Identity, and Abortion*, and [with M. Czarkowski] *Informed Consent for Medical Research: A Manual for Researchers*. She is a member and the Secretary of the Bioethics Committee of the Polish Academy of Sciences; member of the National Committee for Cooperation with the European Network of Research Integrity Offices; and the Head of the Polish Unit of the UNESCO Chair in Bioethics.

Judit Sándor is a professor at the Departments of Political Science, Legal Studies and Gender Studies of the Central European University, Budapest. She had a bar exam in Hungary and conducted legal practice at Simmons and Simmons in London. She had fellowships at McGill University (Montreal), Stanford University (Palo Alto), University of Chicago, and Maison de sciences de l'homme (Paris). In 1996 she received Ph.D. in law and political science. In 2004–2005 she served as the Chief of the Bioethics Section at the UNESCO. She published seven books in the field of human rights and biomedical law. Her works appeared in different languages, including Hungarian, English, French and Portuguese. Since September 2005 she is a founding director of the Center for Ethics and Law in Biomedicine (CELAB) at the Central European University.

Attila Seprődi is a PhD student at the Sociology and Social Anthropology Department of the Central European University, Budapest. He earned an MA from the same department, and a BA in sociology from the Babes-Bolyai University in Cluj, Romania. He is interested in science and technology studies, sociology and anthropology of gender, the state, reproduction and new reproductive technologies, post-socialism, his current research is on commercial surrogacy arrangements in the Ukraine.

Barna Szamosi is a doctoral candidate in Comparative Gender Studies at the Central European University, Budapest. He graduated from English language and literature (BA), philosophy (MA), and applied linguistics (MA) at the University of Miskolc, Hungary, as well as from gender studies (MA) at CEU. His research interests include: science studies, bioethics, genetics, and eugenics.

Sára Vitrai is an editor of *The Activist*, an annual publication of the Human Rights Initiative (HRSI) and was recently a volunteer manager of the Freedom for Birth Campaign in Hungary. She has graduated at the Critical Gender Studies MA program of the Central European University, Budapest. During her studies at CEU she was an intern at the Hungarian Civil Liberties Union (HCLU) and the Pro Familia Hungarian Scientific Society. Her research interests are related to the influence of the state on women's reproductive rights and its implications for public policy, from a biopolitical and a feminist perspective; studies of medical science; and eugenics.